Research and Development in Intelligent Systems XVII

D1343078

Springer

London
Berlin
Heidelberg
New York
Barcelona
Hong Kong
Milan
Paris
Singapore
Tokyo

Max Bramer, Alun Preece and Frans Coenen (Eds)

Research and Development in Intelligent Systems XVII

Proceedings of ES2000, the Twentieth SGES International Conference on Knowledge Based Systems and Applied Artificial Intelligence, Cambridge, December 2000

Springer

Max Bramer, BSc, PhD, CEng
Faculty of Technology, University of Portsmouth, Portsmouth, UK

Alun Preece, BSc, PhD
Department of Computer Science, University of Aberdeen, Aberdeen, UK

Frans Coenen, PhD
Department of Computer Science, University of Liverpool, Liverpool, UK

ISBN 1-85233-403-7 Springer-Verlag London Berlin Heidelberg

British Library Cataloguing in Publication Data
A catalog record for this book is available from the British Library.

Library of Congress Cataloging-in-Publication Data
A catalog record for this book is available from the Library of Congress.

Apart from any fair dealing for the purposes of research or private study, or criticism or review, as permitted under the Copyright, Designs and Patents Act 1988, this publication may only be reproduced, stored or transmitted, in any form or by any means, with the prior permission in writing of the publishers, or in the case of reprographic reproduction in accordance with the terms of licences issued by the Copyright Licensing Agency. Enquiries concerning reproduction outside those terms should be sent to the publishers.

© Springer-Verlag London Limited 2001
Printed in Great Britain

The use of registered names, trademarks etc. in this publication does not imply, even in the absence of a specific statement, that such names are exempt from the relevant laws and regulations and therefore free for general use.

The publisher makes no representation, express or implied, with regard to the accuracy of the information contained in this book and cannot accept any legal responsibility or liability for any errors or omissions that may be made.

Typesetting: Camera ready by contributors
Printed and bound at the Athenæum Press Ltd., Gateshead, Tyne and Wear
34/3830-543210 Printed on acid-free paper SPIN 10786381

TECHNICAL PROGRAMME CHAIRMAN'S INTRODUCTION

M.A. Bramer
University of Portsmouth, UK

This volume comprises the refereed technical papers presented at ES2000, the Twentieth SGES International Conference on Knowledge Based Systems and Applied Artificial Intelligence, held in Cambridge in December 2000, together with an invited keynote paper by Professor Austin Tate. The conference was organised by SGES, the British Computer Society Specialist Group on Knowledge Based Systems and Applied Artificial Intelligence.

The papers in this volume present new and innovative developments in the field, divided into sections on learning, case-based reasoning, knowledge representation, knowledge engineering, and belief acquisition and planning.

The refereed papers begin with a paper entitled 'A Resource Limited Artificial Immune System for Data Analysis', which describes a machine learning algorithm inspired by the natural immune system. This paper was judged to be the best refereed technical paper submitted to the conference.

The considerable growth in interest in machine learning in recent years is well reflected in the content of the next three sections, which comprise four papers on case-based reasoning and nine papers on other areas of machine learning.

The remaining papers are devoted to knowledge engineering, knowledge representation, belief acquisition and planning, and include papers on such important emerging topics as knowledge reuse and representing the content of complex multimedia documents on the web.

This is the seventeenth volume in the *Research and Development* series. The Application Stream papers are published as a companion volume under the title *Applications and Innovations in Intelligent Systems VIII*.

On behalf of the conference organising committee I should like to thank all those who contributed to the organisation of this year's technical programme, in particular the programme committee members, the referees and our administrators Linsay Turbert and Maria Doran.

Max Bramer
Technical Programme Chairman, ES2000

ACKNOWLEDGEMENTS

ES2000 CONFERENCE COMMITTEE

Dr Frans Coenen, University of Liverpool *(Conference Chairman)*
Dr Robert Milne, Intelligent Applications Ltd *(Deputy Conference Chairman, Finance and Publicity)*
Richard Ellis, Stratum Management Ltd *(Deputy Conference Chairman, Exhibition)*
Dr. Adrian Hopgood, Open University *(Tutorial Organiser)*
Ann Macintosh, Napier University *(Application Programme Chair)*
Mike Moulton, University of Portsmouth *(Deputy Application Programme Chair)*
Professor Max Bramer, University of Portsmouth *(Technical Programme Chair)*
Dr. Alun Preece, University of Aberdeen *(Deputy Technical Programme Chair)*

TECHNICAL PROGRAMME COMMITTEE

Prof. Max Bramer, University of Portsmouth *(Chair)*
Dr. Alun Preece, University of Aberdeen *(Vice-Chair)*
Dr. Frans Coenen, University of Liverpool
Mr. John Kingston, University of Edinburgh
Dr. Rob Milne, Intelligent Applications Ltd.

TECHNICAL PROGRAMME REFEREES

Samir Aknine (University of Paris Dauphine)
Rosy Barruffi (University of Bologna)
Andrew Basden (University of Salford)
Max Bramer (University of Portsmouth)
Frans Coenen (University of Liverpool)
Stephane Coulondre (University of Montpellier)
Susan Craw (Robert Gordon University, Aberdeen)
Bruno Cremilleux (University of Caen)
Jeremy Ellman (University of Sunderland)
David Camacho Fernandez (University Carlos III, Madrid)
Hermann Kaindl (Siemens Austria, Vienna)
John Kingston (University of Edinburgh)
Peter Lane (University of Nottingham)
Brian Lees (University of Paisley)
Hui Liu (Birkbeck College, London)
Peter Lucas (University of Aberdeen)
Ann Macintosh (Napier University)
Robert Milne (Intelligent Applications Ltd, Scotland)
Alun Preece (University of Aberdeen)
Kai Ming Ting (Deaking University, Australia)
Ian Watson (University of Auckland, New Zealand)

CONTENTS

TECHNICAL KEYNOTE ADDRESS

Intelligible AI Planning
A. Tate 3

BEST TECHNICAL PAPER

A Resource Limited Artificial Immune System for Data Analysis
J. Timmis and M. Neal 19

SESSION 1: LEARNING I

Experiences with a Weighted Decision Tree Learner
J. Cleary, L. Trigg, G. Holmes and M. Hall 35

A Case Study of Strategic Induction: the Roman Numerals Data Set
D. McSherry 48

Selecting Optimal Split-Functions for Large Datasets
K. Stoffel and L. Raileanu 62

Learning with C4.5 in a Situation Calculus Domain
K. Karimi, and H.J. Hamilton 73

SESSION 2: CASE BASED REASONING

Incremental Footprint-Based Retrieval
B. Smyth and E. McKenna 89

Macro and Micro Applications of Case-Based Reasoning to Feature-Based
Product Selection
G. Saward and T. O'Dell 102

Formal Concept Analysis as a Support Technique for *CBR*
B. Díaz-Agudo and P. A. González-Calero 115

2D vs 3D Visualisation Techniques for Case-Based Reasoning
B. Smyth, M. Mullins and E. McKenna 129

SESSION 3: LEARNING II

An Instance-Based Approach to Pattern Association Learning with Application to the English Past Tense Verb Domain
R. Hickey and R. Martin 145

Rule Generation Based on Rough Set Theory for Text Classification
Y. Bi, T. Anderson and S. McClean 157

Grouping Multivariate Time Series Variables: Applications to Chemical Process and Visual Field Data
A. Tucker, S. Swift, N. Martin, and X. Liu 171

Genetic Algorithm Behaviour in the Task of Finding the Multi-Maximum Domain
A. Takahashi, A. Borisov 185

A Modified Perceptron Algorithm for Computer-Assisted Diagnosis
A. Albrecht, M. Loomes, K. Steinhöfel, M. Taupitz 199

SESSION 4: KNOWLEDGE REPRESENTATION

Uniform Representation of Content and Structure for Structured Document Retrieval
M. Lalmas 215

Implementing Metadata on the Web: a Conceptual, NKRL-Based Approach
G.P. Zarri 229

Design and Development of a Decision Support System to Support Discretion in Refugee Law
T. Meikle and J. Yearwood 243

Orthofaces for Face Recognition
B. Li and V. P. Siang 257

SESSION 5: KNOWLEDGE ENGINEERING

Supporting Knowledge-Driven Processes in a Multiagent Process Management System
J. Debenham 273

The Y Link Oriented Technique for Reuse in KBS
K. Messaadia, M. Oussalah 287

Modelling Agents and Communication using Common KADS
J. Kingston 301

Designing for Scalability in a Knowledge Fusion System
A. Preece, K. Hui, A. Gray and P. Marti 320

SESSION 6: BELIEF ACQUISITION AND PLANNING

Acquiring Information from Books
A. Diller 337

Container Stowage Pre-Planning: Using Search to Generate Solutions.
A Case Study
I.D. Wilson, P.A. Roach and J.A. Ware 349

A Correct Algorithm for Efficient Planning with Preprocessed Domain Axioms
M. Gragnani 363

Multi-Layered PSMs for Planning
F. Teruel-Alberich, M. Romero-Castro and A. Rodríguez-Rodríguez 375

Author Index 389

TECHNICAL KEYNOTE ADDRESS

Intelligible AI Planning - Generating Plans Represented as a Set of Constraints

Austin Tate

Artificial Intelligence Applications Institute

University of Edinburgh, UK

Abstract

[1]Realistic planning systems must allow users and computer systems to co-operate and work together using a "mixed initiative" style. Black box or fully automated solutions are not acceptable in many situations. Studies of expert human problem solvers in stressful or critical situations show that they share many of the problem solving methods employed by hirearchical planning methods studied in Artificial Intelligence. But powerful solvers and constraint reasoners can also be of great help in tparts of the planning process. A new more intelligible approach to using AI planning is needed which can use the best "open" styles of planning based on shared plan representations and hierarchical task networks (HTN) and which still allow the use of powerful constraint representations and solvers.

I-Plan is a design for a new planning system based on these principles. It is part of the I-X suite of intelligent tools. I-Plan is modular and can be extended via plug-ins of various types. It is intended to be a "lightweight" planning system which can be embedded in other applications. In its simplest form it can provide a small personal planning aid that can be deployed in portable devices and other user-orientated systems to add planning facilities into them. In its more developed forms it will approach the power of generative AI planners such as O-Plan. It provides a framework for including powerful constraint solvers in a framework that is intelligible to the users.

I-Plan is grounded in the <I-N-OVA>[2] (*Issues – Nodes – Orderings / Variables / Auxiliary*) constraints model used to represent plans and processes. <I-N-OVA> is intended to support a number of different uses:

- for automatic and mixed-initiative generation and manipulation of plans and to act as an ontology to underpin such use;
- as a common basis for human and system communication about plans;
- as a target for principled and reliable acquisition of plans, process models and process product information;
- to support formal reasoning about plans.

The I-Plan design and the <I-N-OVA> ontology provide an extensible framework for adding detailed constraint representations and reasoners into planners. These can be based on powerful automated methods. But this can be done in a context which provides overall human intelligibility.

---

[1]This paper is partly based on a technical note to the AAAI-2000 Workshop on Representational Issues for Real-World Planning Systems, AAAI-2000 (Tate, 2000).

[2]<I-N-OVA> is pronounced as in "Innovate".

1 Introduction

Planning is about much more than solving specifically stated problems as efficiently as possible. It is also about modelling domains in which planning takes place, understanding the roles of the various human and system agents involved in the planning process and in the domain in which plans are executed, and it is about communicating tasks, plans, intentions and effects between those agents. Realistic planning systems must allow users and computer systems to cooperate and work together using a "mixed initiative" style. Black box or fully automated solutions are not acceptable in many situations. Studies of expert human problem solvers in stressful or critical situations (Klein, 1998) show that they share many of the problem solving methods employed by some of the methods studied in AI planning to address these issues.

This paper argues that a Hierarchical Task Network (HTN) least commitment planning approach - as used for many years in practical planning systems such as NOAH (Sacerdoti, 1975), Nonlin (Tate, 1977), SIPE (Wilkins, 1988) and O-Plan (Currie and Tate, 1991) - provides an intelligible framework for mixed-initiative multi-agent human/system planning environments. When joined with a strong underlying constraint-based ontology of plans it can provide a framework in which powerful problem solvers based on search and constraint reasoning methods can be employed and still retain human intelligibility of the overall planning process and the plan products that are created.

I-Plan is a design for a new "lightweight" planning system based on these principles. It is part of the I-X[3] suite of intelligent tools and is being designed to be embedded in other applications. I-Plan is modular and can be extended via plug-ins of various types. In its simplest form it can provide a small planning aid that can be deployed in portable devices and other user-orientated systems to add planning facilities into them. In its more developed forms it will approach the power of major generative AI planners such as O-Plan (Tate et. al, 1994; Tate et. al., 2000).

2 I-X

Work in Intelligent Planning and Activity Management at the University of Edinburgh[4] has led to a number of planning systems and approaches that are re-used on a number of projects. New work will drawn on this work, generalise it, and significantly extend the application of the core concepts and assets, leading to new re-usable components, and create opportunities for applications and further research.

This new programme is called I-X and the core components are a shared model representation called <I-N-CA> and a systems integration architecture. A variety of re-usable components and systems will be built on the new architecture and these will be collectively referred to as I-Technology and I-Tools.

---

[3]I-X is the successor project to O-Plan - see http://www.aiai.ed.ac.uk/project/ix/.

[4]See http://www.aiai.ed.ac.uk/project/plan/.

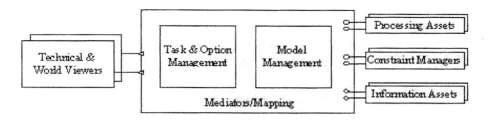

Figure 1: I-X Components

I-X provides a systems integration architecture. Its design is based on the O-Plan agent architecture. I-X incorporates components and interface specifications which account for simplifications, abstractions and clarifications in the O-Plan work. I-X provides an issue-handling workflow style of architecture, with reasoning and functional capabilities provided as plug-ins. Also via plug-ins it allows for sophisticated management and use of the internal model representations to reflect the application domain of the system being built in I-X. I-X agents may be recursively or fractally composed, and may interwork with other processing cells or architectures. This is a systems integration approach now being advocated by a number of groups concerned with large scale, long-lived, evolving and diverse systems integration issues.

The I-X approach has 5 aspects:

1. Systems Integration - A broad vision of an open architecture for the creation of intelligent systems for the synthesis of a result or "product" which is based on a "two cycle" approach which uses plug-in components to "handle issues" and to "manage and respect the domain model".

2. Representation - a core notion of the representation of a process or plan as a set of nodes making up the components of the process or plan model, along with constraints on the relationship between those nodes and a set of outstanding issues. This representation is termed <I-N-CA> - Issues, Nodes, Critical Constraints and Auxiliary Constraints.

3. Reasoning - the provision of reusable reasoning capabilities.

4. Viewers and User Interfaces - to understand user roles in performing activities and to provide generic modules which present the state of the process they are engaged in, their relationships to others and the status of the artifacts/products they are working with.

5. Applications - work in various application sectors which will seek to create generic approaches (I-Tools) for the various types of task in which users may engage. One important application is I-Plan for planning tasks.

We propose to bring together a number of threads of previous research and development, and use state-of-the-art understanding of the conceptual basis for flexible, incremental, mixed-initiative planning and activity management systems. We will incorporate these into an open, flexible, lightweight and embeddable system. This will be written in Java for portability and to maximise reuse potential. The core of the system will be an agenda-based issue handling system based on workflow principles. It will be specialised to any particular task by incorporating suitable issue-handling capabilities which could be supplied by human or system components. It will be designed to allow for very significant extension via an open capability plug-in interface and via an interface to allow for the use of constraint management methods, feasibility estimators, simulators, etc. The system will be able to inter-work with other workflow and cooperative working support systems, and will not make assumptions about the internal architecture of those other systems.

The components of the I-X systems integration architecture are shown diagrammatically in figure 1 and are as follows:

- Task and Option Management – The capability to support user tasks via appropriate use of the processing and information assets and to assist the user in managing options being used within the model.

- Model Management – coordination of the capabilities/assets to represent, store, retrieve, merge, translate, compare, correct, analyse, synthesise and modify models.

- Issue Handlers – Functional components (distinguished into those which can add to the model (synthesis) and those which analyse the model (to add information only).

- Constraint Managers – Components which assist in the maintenance of the consistency of the model.

- Information Assets – Information storage and retrieval components.

- Viewers – User interface, visualisation and presentation viewers for the model - sometimes differentiated into technical model views (charts, structure diagrams, etc.) and world model views (simulations, animations, etc.)

- Mediators – Intermediaries or converters between the features of the model and the interfaces of active components of the framework (such as viewers, processing assets, constraint managers and information assets).

A number of different types of "sockets" are available within the framework to reflect the protocols or interfaces into which the various components can fit. The necessity for specific sockets and the types of components vary across projects to some extent, but the separation into viewers, processing assets, constraint managers and information assets has been found to be useful in a number of AIAI projects. This also puts the I-X work on a convergent path with other Model/Viewer/Controller styles of systems framework.

3 <I-N-OVA> and <I-N-CA>

I-Plan is grounded in the <I-N-OVA> *Issues – Nodes – Auxiliary)* constraints model which is used to represent plans and processes. The more general <I-N-CA> *(Issues – Nodes – Critical/Auxiliary)* constraints model can be used for wider applications in design, configuration and other tasks which can be characterised as the synthesis and maintenance of an artifact or product.

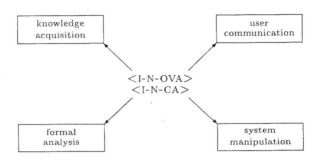

Figure 2: <I-N-OVA> and <I-N-CA> Support Various Requirements

As shown in figure 2, the <I-N-OVA> and <I-N-CA> constraint models are intended to support a number of different uses:

- for automatic and mixed-initiative generation and manipulation of plans and other synthesised artifacts and to act as an ontology to underpin such use;

- as a common basis for human and system communication about plans and other synthesised artifacts;

- as a target for principled and reliable acquisition of plans, process models and process product information;

- to support formal reasoning about plans and other synthesised artifacts.

These cover both formal and practical requirements and encompass the requirements for use by both human and computer-based planning and design systems.

The <I-N-OVA> *(Issues – Nodes – Orderings / Variables / Auxiliary)* Model is a means to represent plans and activity as a set of constraints. By having a clear description of the different components within a plan, the model allows for plans to be manipulated and used separately from the environments in which they are generated. The underlying thesis is that plans can be represented by a set of constraints on the behaviours possible in the domain being modelled and that plan communication can take place through the interchange of such constraint information.

<I-N-OVA>, when first designed (Tate, 1996), was intended to act as a bridge to improve dialogue between a number of communities working on formal planning theories, practical planning systems and systems engineering process management methodologies. It was intended to support new work then emerging on automatic manipulation of plans, human communication about plans, principled and reliable acquisition of plan information, and formal reasoning about plans. It has since been utilised as the basis for a number of research efforts, practical applications and emerging international standards for plan and process representations. For some of the history and relationships between earlier work in AI on plan representations, work from the process and design communities and the standards bodies, and the part that <I-N-OVA> played in this see Tate (1998).

In Tate (1996), the <I-N-OVA> model is used to characterise the plan representation used within O-Plan and is related to the plan refinement planning method used in O-Plan. The <I-N-OVA> work is related to emerging formal analyses of plans and planning. This synergy of practical and formal approaches can stretch the formal methods to cover realistic plan representations as needed for real problem solving, and can improve the analysis that is possible for practical planning systems.

We have generalised the <I-N-OVA> approach to design and configuration tasks with I, N, CA components - where C represents the "critical constraints" in any particular domain - much as certain O and V constraints do in a planning domain. We believe the approach is valid in design and synthesis tasks more generally - we consider planning to be a limited type of design activity. <I-N-CA> is used as an underlying ontology for the I-X project.

The <I-N-OVA> and <I-N-CA> work is intended to utilise a synergy of practical and formal approaches which are stretching the formal methods to cover realistic representations, as needed for real problem solving, and can improve the analysis that is possible for practical planning systems.

4 <I-N-OVA> - Representing Plans as a Set of Constraints on Behaviour

A plan is represented as a set of constraints which together limit the behaviour that is desired when the plan is executed. The set of constraints are of three principal types with a number of sub-types reflecting practical experience in a number of planning systems.

The node constraints (these are often of the form "include activity") in the <I-N-OVA> model set the space within which a plan may be further constrained. The I (issues) and OVA constraints restrict the plans within that space which are valid.

Planning is the taking of planning decisions (I) which select the activities to perform (N) which creates, modifies or uses the plan objects or products (V)

```
Plan Constraints
    I   - Issues (Implied Constraints)
    N   - Node Constraints (on Activities)
    OVA - Detailed Constraints
        O - Ordering Constraints
        V - Variable Constraints
        A - Auxiliary Constraints
            - Authority Constraints
            - Condition Constraints
            - Resource Constraints
            - Spatial Constraints
            - Miscellaneous Constraints
```

Figure 3: <I-N-OVA> Constraint Model of Activity

at the correct time (O) within the authority, resources and other constraints specified (A). The node constraints in the <I-N-OVA> model set the space within which a plan may be further constrained. The I (issues) and OVA constraints restrict the plans within that space which are valid. The Issues are the items on which selection of Plan Modification Operators is made in agenda based planners.

Others have recognised the special nature of the inclusion of activities into a plan compared to all the other constraints that may be described. Khamb-hampati and Srivastava (1996) differentiate Plan Modification operators into "progressive refinements" which can introduce new actions into the plan, and "non-progressive refinements" which just partitions the search space with existing sets of actions in the plan. They call the former genuine planning refinement operators, and think of the latter as providing the scheduling component.

If we consider the process of planning as a large constraint satisfaction task, we may try to model this as a Constraint Satisfaction Problem (CSP) represented by a set of variables to which we have to give a consistent assignment of values. In this case we can note that the addition of new nodes ("include activity" constraints in <I-N-OVA>) is the only constraint which can add variables dynamically to the CSP. The Issue (I) constraints may be separated into two kinds: those which may (directly or indirectly) add nodes to the plan and those which cannot. The I constraints which can lead to the inclusion of new nodes are of a different nature in the planning process to those which cannot.

Some ordering (temporal) and variable constraints are distinguished from all other constraints since these act as "critical" constraints, usually being involved in describing the others – such as in a resource constraint which will often refer to plan objects/variables and to relationships between time points or intervals.

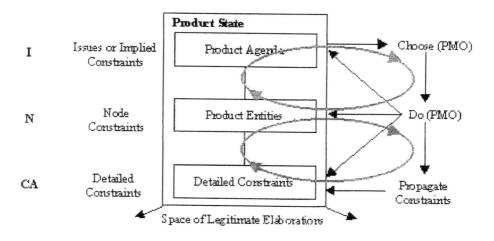

Figure 4: I-X and I-Plan Abstract Architecture: Two Cycles of Processing - Handle Issues, Respect Constraints. PMO=Product Modification Operator

5 I-Plan Abstract Design

The I-Plan design is based on two cycles of processing. The first addresses one or more "issues" from a task agenda, and the second ensures that constraints in the domain in which processing takes place is respected. So the processing cycles can be characterised as "handle issues, respect constraints". The emerging partial plan or schedule is analysed to produce a further list of issues or agenda entries. A choice of the issues to address is used to drive a workflow-style processing cycle of choosing 'Plan Modification Operators" and then executing them to modify the emerging plan state. Figure 4 shows this graphically for the more general case of designing or synthesising any product - where the issue handlers are labelled "PMO" - which then stands for the "Product Modification Operator".

This approach is taken in systems like O-Plan, OPIS (Smith, 1994), DIPART (Pollack, 1994), TOSCA (Beck, 1994), etc. The approach fits well with the concept of treating plans as a set of constraints which can be refined as planning progresses. Some such systems can also act in a non-monotonic fashion by relaxing constraints in certain ways.

Having the implied constraints or "agenda" as a formal part of the plan provides an ability to separate the plan that is being generated or manipulated from the planning system and process itself and this is used as a core part of the I-Plan design.

Mixed Initiative Planning approaches, for example in O-Plan (Tate, 1994), improve the coordination of planning with user interaction by employing a clearer shared model of the plan as a set of constraints at various levels that can be jointly and explicitly discussed between and manipulated by user or system in a cooperative fashion. I-Plan will adopt this approach.

6 Summary

The overall architecture of I-Plan has been described along with the <I-N-OVA> Constraint Model of Activity and the more general <I-N-CA> Constraint Model for Synthesised Artifacts. These are designed to draw on strengths from a number of different communities: the AI planning community with both its theoretical and practical system building interests; the issue-based design community, those interested in formal ontologies for processes and products; the standards community; those concerned with new opportunities in task achieving agents on the world wide web; etc.

<I-N-OVA> is intended to act as a bridge to improve dialogue between the communities working in these areas and potentially to support work on automatic manipulation of plans, human communication about plans, principled and reliable acquisition of plan information, and formal reasoning about plans. <I-N-CA> is designed as a more general underlying ontology which can be at the heart of a flexible and extensible systems integration architecture involving human and system agents.

The I-Plan planner and <I-N-OVA> ontology together provide an extensible framework for adding detailed constraint representations and reasoners which themselves can be based on powerful automated methods. But this can be done in a context which provides human intelligibility of the overall planning process[5].

Acknowledgements

The O-Plan and I-X projects are sponsored by the Defense Advanced Research Projects Agency (DARPA) and Air Force Research Laboratory Command and Control Directorate under grant number F30602-99-1-0024 ad the UK Defence Evaluation Research Agency (DERA). The U.S. Government, DERA and the University of Edinburgh are authorised to reproduce and distribute reprints for their purposes notwithstanding any copyright annotation hereon. The views and conclusions contained herein are those of the authors and should not be interpreted as necessarily representing official policies or endorsements, either express or implied, of DARPA, the Air Force Research Laboratory, the U.S. Government, DERA or the University of Edinburgh.

---

[5]The similarity of the AI planning techniques which can be employed within this framework to those observed in expert human problem solving in crisis situations (Klein, 1998) is described in the appendix.

References

Beck, H. (1993) TOSCA: A Novel Approach to the Management of Job-shop Scheduling Constraints, Realising CIM's Industrial Potential: Proceedings of the Ninth CIM-Europe Annual Conference, pages 138-149, (eds. Kooij, C., MacConaill, P.A., and Bastos, J.).

Currie, K.W. and Tate, A. (1991) O-Plan: the Open Planning Architecture, *Artificial Intelligence* 52(1), Autumn 1991, North-Holland.

Khambhampati, S. and Srivastava, B. (1996) Unifying Classical Planning Approaches, Arizona State University ASU CSE TR 96-006, July 1996.

Klein, G. (1998) Sources of Power - How People Make Decisions, MIT Press, 1998.

Pollack, M. (1994) DIPART Architecture, Technical Report, Department of Computer Science, University of Pittsburgh, PA 15213, USA.

Polyak, S. and Tate, A. (2000) A Common Process Ontology for Process-Centred Organisations, Knowledge Based Systems. Earlier version published as University of Edinburgh Department of Artificial Intelligence Research paper 930, 1998.

Sacerdoti, E. (1977) A structure for plans and behaviours. Artificial Intelligence series, publ. North Holland.

Smith, S. (1994) OPIS: A Methodology and Architecture for Reactive Scheduling, in Intelligent Scheduling, (eds; Zweben, M. and Fox, M.S.), Morgan Kaufmann, Palo Alto, CA., USA,

Tate, A. (1994) Mixed Initiative Planning in O-Plan2, Proceedings of the ARPA/Rome Laboratory Planning Initiative Workshop, (ed. Burstein, M.), Tucson, Arizona, USA, Morgan Kaufmann, Palo Alto.

Tate, A. (ed.) (1996a) Advanced Planning Technology - Technological Achievements of the ARPA/Rome Laboratory Planning Initiative (ARPI), AAAI Press.

Tate, A. (1996b) Representing Plans as a Set of Constraints – the <I-N-OVA> Model, Proceedings of the Third International Conference on Artificial Intelligence Planning Systems (AIPS-96), pp. 221-228, (Drabble, B., ed.) Edinburgh, Scotland, AAAI Press.

Tate, A. (1998) Roots of SPAR - Shared Planning and Activity Representation, Knowledge Engineering Review, Vol. 13, No. 1, March 1998. See also http://www.aiai.ed.ac.uk/project/spar/

Tate, A. (2000) <I-N-OVA> and <I-N-CA> - Representing Plans and other Synthesized Artifacts as a Set of Constraints, AAAI-2000 Workshop on Representational Issues for Real-World Planning Systems, at the National Conference of the American Association of Artificial Intelligence (AAAI-2000), Austin, Texas, USA, August 2000.

Tate, A., Drabble, B. and Kirby, R. (1994) O-Plan2: an Open Architecture for

Command, Planning and Control, in Intelligent Scheduling, (eds, Zweben, M. and Fox, M.S.), Morgan Kaufmann, Palo Alto, CA., USA.

Tate, A., Drabble, B. and Dalton, J. (1994) Reasoning with Constraints within O-Plan2, Proceedings of the ARPA/Rome Laboratory Planning Initiative Workshop, (ed. Burstein, M.), Tucson, Arizona, USA, Morgan Kaufmann, Palo Alto, CA, USA.

Tate, A., Levine, J., Jarvis, P. and Dalton, J. (2000) Using AI Planning techniques for Army Small Unit Operations, Poster Paper in the Proceedings of the Fifth International Conference on AI Planning and Scheduling Systems (AIPS-2000), Breckenridge, CO, USA, April 2000.

Wilkins, D. (1988) *Practical Planning*, Morgan Kaufmann, Palo Alto, 1988.

Appendix: Comparing the Intelligible Planning Approach to Studies of Expert Human Planners

This appendix describes some of the features of the O-Plan and I-Plan approaches and shows the similarity of these approaches with those observed in expert human problem solvers performing in stressful or unusual situations. These observations were made in studies over many years by Klein (1998) and he contrasts these with some automated "black box" AI and algorithmic techniques.

The following note was produced on the DARPA O-Plan Project for an US Army Small Unit Operations Application (Tate et. al., 2000) in June 1999 by Austin Tate

But I Don't Plan, I Just Know What to Do

There are different types of planning technology available from the AI community. This is not restricted to a simple kind of search from some known initial state to some final desired state seeking the best solution according to some predefined criteria. Gary Klein's book (Klein, 1998) on how people make decisions in situations such as military operations, fire fighting, or other life threatening environments provides a rich set of case studies to show that in relatively few situations were deliberative planning techniques in obvious use. People just seemed to be making the "right" choices - or a choice that worked which was all that was required. They attributed their rapid selection of a suitable course of action to training, experience, or even ESP! Where options were deliberated over and evaluated, the situation for those involved was novel or unusual to their previous experience.

Klein's studies show how people in stressful environments select a course of action and adapt it as circumstances alter. Many of the decisions made by the subjects relate to issues which AI planning researchers are addressing. However, they are far removed from the traditional search style of deliberative plan generation. So we need to establish for the outset that the techniques we are calling upon to address potential planning requirements also are much wider than these simple fully-automated search methods. We are seeking to use rich plan representations in a variety of ways. These are listed below, along with cross references to Klein's book, to show how we can address a variety of decision methods which he is advocating, and which are in use by real problem solvers and commanders . The hope is that the planning requirements we are identifying can be mapped to some of the AI concepts we are bringing to bear on practical planning problems.

- Overall management of the command, planning and control process steps to improve coordination.

- Expansion of a high level abstract plan into greater detail where necessary.

- High level "chunks" of procedural knowledge (Standard Operating Procedures, Best Practice Processes, Tactics Techniques and Procedures, etc.) at a human scale - typically 5-8 actions - can be manipulated within the system [Klein, p. 52 and p. 58].

- Ability to establish that a feasible plan exists, perhaps for a range of assumptions about the situation, while retaining a high level overview. [Klein, p.227, "Include only the detail necessary to establish a plan is possible - do not fall into the trap of choreographing each of their movements"].

- Analysis of potential interactions as plans are expanded or developed [Klein, p 53].

- Identification of problems, flaws and issues with the plan [Klein p. 63 and p. 71].

- Deliberative establishment of a space of alternative options perhaps based on different assumptions about the situation involved of especial use ahead of time, in training and rehearsal, and to those unfamiliar with the situation or utilising novel equipment [Klein p. 23].

- Monitoring of the execution of events as they are expected to happen within the plan, watching for deviations that indicate a necessity to re-plan (often ahead of this becoming a serious problem) [Klein p. 32-33].

- AI planning techniques represent the dynamic state of the world at points in the plan and can be used for "mental simulation" of the execution of the plan [Klein, p. 45].

- Pruning of choices according to given requirements or constraints [Klein, p. 94 "singular strategy"].

- Situation dependent option filtering (sometime reducing the choices normally open to one "obvious" one [Klein p.17-18].

- Satisficing search to find the first suitable plan that meets the essential criteria [Klein p. 20].

- Anytime algorithms which seek to improve on the best previous solution if time permits.

- Heuristic evaluation and prioritisation of multiple possible choices within the constraint search space [Klein, p. 94].

- Repair of plans while respecting plan structure and intentions.

- Uniform use of a common plan representation with embedded rationale to improve plan quality, shared understanding, etc. [Klein, p. 275 7 types of information in a plan].

Gary Klein was asked to comment upon this review of AI techniques as compared to his observations of natural problem solving and decision making in humans. He observed the following in this edited Personal Communication to Austin Tate on 24-Jun-1999 (quoted with permission):

1. I felt a strong kinship with what you are attempting. The effort to use satisficing criteria, the use of anytime algorithms to permit continual improvement, the shift from abstract to detailed plan when necessary, the analysis of interactions in a plan, the identification of flaws in a plan, the monitoring of execution, the use of mental simulation, the representation of a singular strategy, heuristic evaluation, plan repair, and so forth are all consistent with what I think needs to be done.

2. My primary concern is how you are going to do these things.... The discipline of AI can provide constraints that will help you understand any of these strategies in richer detail. But those constraints may also prevent you from harnessing these sources of power.

3. Your slogan "Search and you're dead" seems right. Unconstrained search is a mark of intellectual cowardice. And it is also not a useful strategy.

Edited version of Personal Communication from Austin Tate to Gary Klein on 25-Jun-1999:

I want to clarify my use of the slogan "Search and you're dead" over the last 20 years. This is the headline, but I then clarify what I mean as "(Unconstrained) search and you're dead".

I have found this to be a useful slogan to express my general approach, and it makes for good knock about fun on panels at conferences. The idea should be to richly describe the constraints known using whatever knowledge is available about the problem, and then to seek solutions in that constrained space. We seek to use knowledge of the domain to constrain the use of blind search or "black box" automated methods in ways which are intelligent and intelligible (to humans).

In reality all planning systems we build have sophisticated search and constraint management components, and it is an aim of our research to be able to utilise the best available in an appropriate context. Search can be a useful tactic in situations where you are underconstrained and stuck. AI has made enormous advances in constraint management using search and other methods over the last 5 years - so much so that some of its proponents argue that we do not need to bother with domain expertise or being knowledge-based about many of the problems we are addressing. It's this latter overenthusiasm for one approach which I seek to counter. Even very powerful search can be made more useful if put into a sensible knowledge-based context. This is, of course, more relevant when humans are involved in the decisions as then a more naturalistic style of mutually progressing towards a solution become a key to successful use of the technology.

BEST TECHNICAL PAPER

A Resource Limited Artificial Immune System for Data Analysis

Jon Timmis

Computing Laboratory, University of Kent at Canterbury
Canterbury, Kent. UK. CT2 7NF.
J.Timmis@ukc.ac.uk
www.cs.ukc.ac.uk/people/staff/jt6

Mark Neal

Department of Computer Science, University of Wales
Aberystwyth, Ceredigion, Wales, U.K.
mjn@aber.ac.uk

Abstract

This paper presents a resource limited artificial immune system for data analysis. The work presented here builds upon previous work on artificial immune systems for data analysis. A population control mechanism, inspired by the natural immune system, has been introduced to control population growth and allow termination of the learning algorithm. The new algorithm is presented, along with the immunological metaphors used as inspiration. Results are presented for Fisher Iris data set, where very successful results are obtained in identifying clusters within the data set. It is argued that this new resource based mechanism is a large step forward in making artificial immune systems a viable contender for effective unsupervised machine learning and allows for not just a one shot learning mechanism, but a continual learning model to be developed.

1 Introduction

The human immune system is a complex natural defense mechanism. It has the ability to learn about foreign substances (pathogens) that enter the body and to respond to them by producing antibodies that attack the antigens associated with the pathogen. Ultimately this removes the infection from the body. The human immune system has provided inspiration in the fields of computer science and other interdisciplinary problems[10, 7]. A detailed survey of this work can be found in [4]. Previous work in the field of Artificial Immune Systems (AIS) applied to the areas of machine learning has been shown to have great potential [3], [8] and [12]. This work took inspiration from the natural immune system, primarily the Immune Network Theory[9] and other immunological ideas[5], [1] and applied them to the field of unsupervised machine learning. This work was then taken a stage further [14], improving significantly on the performance and effectiveness and presented as a tool for effective data analysis. Indeed, the system developed was shown to compare favorably with other data analysis techniques[15].

The work presented here addresses problems that have been identified by extensive testing of the AIS presented in [14]. A new formulation for an AIS capable of unsupervised learning is given. This resource limited artificial immune system (RLAIS) has the ability to limit the size of networks, making them easy to interpret and allowing for termination conditions to be set. It also provides the possibility for continual learning.

This work is a significant improvement on the original work and goes a long way to making the RLAIS a real alternative to other unsupervised learning techniques.

This paper gives a brief overview of relevant immunology, previous work done and problems identified. The paper then goes on to describe the new RLAIS and discusses the impact of the results obtained. Conclusions are then drawn with directions given for future research.

2   Background

A simplified view of the human immune system is that it is made up of B Cells and T Cells. Upon encountering an antigen B Cells are stimulated by a number of sources and with the help of T Cells undergo cloning and somatic hyper-mutation. The antigens are then attacked by killer T Cells and removed from the system. The immune system maintains a memory of the infection so that if ever exposed to the same antigen a quicker response can be elicited against the infection. Several theories as to how immune memory works have been proposed. The Immune Network Theory, first proposed by Jerne[9] and reviewed by Perelson[13], proposes that a network dynamically maintains the immune memory using feedback mechanisms. Thus if something has been learnt, it can be "forgotten" unless it is reinforced by other parts of the network. With the B Cell clones undergoing mutation the immune system can defend itself not only against previously known antigens, but also slight variations of such antigens. It is this behavior on which the AIS capitalises. A diverse network representative of the data set is constructed by means of cloning, mutation and immune memory.

Work in [14] builds on the foundations laid in [8], [12]. To summarize work in [14] the AIS is initialized as a network of B Cell objects (T Cells are currently ignored). Links between cells are created if they are below the Network Affinity Threshold (NAT) which is the average distance between each item in the data set. The initial network is a cross section of the data set to be learnt, the remainder makes up the antigen data set. Each member of this set is matched against each B Cell in the network, with the similarity being calculated on Euclidean distance. B Cells are stimulated by this matching process and by connected B Cells in the network. The stimulation level of a B Cell determines the survival of the B Cell, as the weakest 5% of the population are removed at each iteration. The stimulation level also indicates if the B Cell should be cloned and the number of clones that are produced for that B Cell. Clones undergo a stochastic process of mutation in order to create a diverse network that can represent the antigen that caused the cloning as well as slight variations. There exist a number of parameters to the algorithm, network affinity scalar, mutation rate and training iterations, that can be used to alter algorithm performance.

This process results in a diverse network of B cell objects that reflects the main patterns in the data. The user can interact with this network to discover more subtle relationships. Figure 1(a) shows an example visualisation[16] of the results obtained from the AIS on the well known Fisher Iris data[6]. The Iris data set is a well known and well used benchmark data set in the machine learning community. The data consists of three varieties of Iris, Setosa, Virginica and Versicolor. There are 150 instances of plants that make up the three classes. The data consists of four numerical attributes which are used in the learning process. These variables are measurements of sepal and petal lengths and widths. Two of the groups, Versicolor and Virginica are known not to be linearly separable.

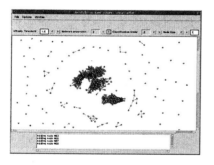 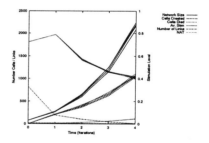

(a) Showing the Iris data set. Two separate clusters are clearly seen, with the larger one being made of up two further sub-clusters

(b) Showing exponential growth of the network. This produces networks so large, they are hard to interpret and produce little useful information

Figure 1: Performance of the original AIS

In order to assess the performance and behavior of the system, the resulting networks were visualised (figure 1(a)) and a variety of AIS properties were recorded and plotted against the number of iterations. This was done for Iris data with the results given in figure 1(b). Here, the algorithm was checked for consistency: each of the runs appears on the plot. Figure 1(a) shows two separate clusters, with the larger cluster showing two possible sub-clusters. This is indicative of the Iris data, with the separate cluster being the Setosa class and the remaining two classes making up the two sub-clusters of the other larger cluster; therefore the AIS has identified the clusters that are known to exist. The user is free to perform exploratory analysis on the network to attempt to understand why certain areas are connected and relationships exist. Figure 1(b) shows an exponential like growth in the size of the network, which is reflected in the number of cells created after each iteration. Additionally, the average stimulation level of the B cells in the network follows a pattern of quick increase followed by a steady decline. A number of initial observations were clear: the size of the network undergoes exponential population explosion; the NAT eventually becomes so low that only very similar, if not identical clones can ever be connected; the number of B cells removed from the system lags behind the number created to such an extent that the population control mechanism is not effective; the network grows so large that it becomes difficult to compute each iteration with respect to time and the resultant networks are so large, they are difficult to interpret, and are too big to be a sensible representation of the data. In some cases, a resultant network can reach over 1000 B cells to represent 150 training items. Experiments were also performed on a simple simulated two dimensional data set, which whist two clusters were identify, also exhibited the same population explosion behavior. Additionally, a problem rises as the amount of times that the antigen set should be presented is unknown. What would be desirable is an algorithm that would terminate once a good pattern has been found. Therefore, from these results it was clear that the AIS had to be improved to tackle these problem areas. This led to the research and results described in the following sections.

3 The Resource Limited Artificial Immune System

The Resource Limited Artificial Immune System (RLAIS) exhibits behavior such that once a strong pattern has been identified the network does not deteriorate or lose the pattern. It is proposed that the RLAIS can be used not only for clustering as one shot learning, but also presenting the possibility for the system to perform continual learning.

This paper introduces the concept of an Artificial Recognition Ball (ARB). An ARB is a representation of a number of identical B cells; individual B cells are no longer explicitly represented in the new system. The RLAIS is allowed to contain a pre-defined number of B cells, which the ARBs' must compete for based on their stimulation level. The higher the stimulation level, the more B cells an ARB can claim and, vice versa. If an ARB loses all B cells, then it is considered not to be representative of the data being learnt and is removed from the network. This competition for the allocation of B cells stabilises the structure of the network. This stabilising effect can be described as the identification of a strong pattern by the RLAIS and no matter how many time the training data is presented to the RLAIS, that representation will not change. Additionally, the NAT is no longer recalculated at the end of each training iteration, but is kept constant throughout the learning process.

The remainder of this paper describes the immunological metaphors that are used as inspiration for the enhancements to the algorithm and explains how they have been implemented. Initial results and observations are presented that show the ability of the RLAIS to find stable patterns in the data set being learnt.

3.1 Immunological Metaphor

In keeping with the metaphor employed by the researchers, inspiration was sought from the natural immune system. This section outlines those ideas gleaned from the natural immune system which were adapted to form useful solutions for the problems identified with the previous algorithm.

3.1.1 Population Control

Within the immune system, there is a finite number of B cells that can be produced, (otherwise, we would be nothing but B cells!) Clearly, an exponential growth in the number of B cells is unsustainable, and we therefore conclude that there are limited resources available within the immune system to create and sustain B cells. This limitation on resources leads, in effect, to a competition between B cells for survival; the strongest (most stimulated) being the ones that survive. An exponential growth in the number of B cells was shown to occur within the AIS (section 2) which could clearly not be sustained. Therefore, it is not unreasonable to use the idea of limiting the number of resources within the AIS, thereby forcing the B cells to compete for resources and hence survival. This is discussed in more detail in section 3.2.1

3.1.2 Immune System Metadynamics

The natural immune system affords a rapid proliferation of B cells in response to antigen presentation, while maintaining a diverse repertoire of B cells [18]. After infection from the antigen, B cells proliferate at a very high rate. Work in [19], suggests that, over time, a stable core immune network emerges that is representative of the antigens causing the immune response.

It was previously stated that very large numbers of B cells are produced in response to an antigen. Some of these B cells undergo somatic hypermutation, others do not. B cells which are a good match for the antigen are retained by the immune system by incorporation into the immune network, to act as immunological memory. The remaining B cells are eventually removed from the system. There is constant perturbation in the number of B cells and other immune system variables, such as antibody concentration after introduction of antigens. However, a core network of B cells is maintained by the immune network which is representative of the antigens to which it has been exposed. This behavior is called immune system *metadynamics*. It is therefore reasonable to utilise this idea of achieving a stable representation of the data being learnt

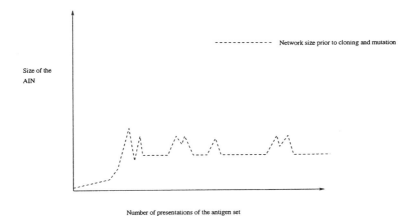

Figure 2: Expected behavior of the network. During presentation of the antigen set there are many perturbations in the number of B cells in the network. However, there should also be periods of stability on the number of B cells prior to a new period of mutation and clonal selection.

using the network. The network would subsequently undergo large perturbations in the size due to the stochastic nature of mutation operations, but a core network size and content should remain.

There are also likely to be variations in other variables in the network, such as number of links between B cells, the average stimulation levels and the number of B cells being removed. Despite all these, however, there should be periods of stability within the network. Figure 2 presents a simple diagram of the kind of behavior that would be expected. As can be seen, there are indeed perturbations in the network size, but a stable network size is also observed.

3.1.3   Recognition Ball

The idea of antibody repertoire completeness has been postulated by [2] and summarised by [13]. Repertoire completeness is the ability of the immune system to be able to recognise all antigens. It has been difficult for immunologists to demonstrate that the immune system actually does have a complete repertoire, but Perelsons' theory suggests that there exists a finite number of antibodies which may be said to be representative of an infinite number of antigens, based on the notion of shape space[13]. Figure 3 shows a diagrammatic representation of the notion of shape space: there is a certain volume V in the immune system that contains many paratopes (represented by the dark circles) and epitopes (represented by x). For each antibody (and thus paratope) there is a small surrounding region in shape space called a *recognition ball*, denoted by V_e. Within this *recognition ball* an antibody can recognise all epitopes, i.e. epitopes will share an affinity with the antibody paratope.

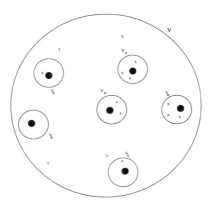

Figure 3: Showing the concept of shape space and completeness of the repertoire within the immune system.

As can be seen in the figure, there are a number of recognition balls that have many epitopes ($\mathbf{X}$) and a single paratope. Therefore a single B-cell can said to be representative of a number of epitopes, and therefore antigens. The strength of the bond between an antibody and an antigen may vary within the volume V_e but the B-cell will be stimulated by the interaction. It is this idea which leads the authors to believe the immune system has a complete ability to recognise all antigens; they argue that as each antibody is able to recognise all epitopes within a recognition ball, a finite number of antibodies can recognise an infinite number of epitopes. This will occur because an infinite number of epitopes could be placed within the volume V_e.

Employing this idea as a metaphor, it is reasonable to introduce a concept of the Artificial Recognition Ball (ARB). Each ARB within the network can be representative of a number of a number of identical B cells. Therefore, the need to explicitly represent identical B cells in the RLAIS is removed and the introduction of a recognition ball metaphor may be introduced to the RLAIS.

3.2   Implementing a Resource Limited Artificial Immune System

The Resource Limited Artificial Immune System (RLAIS) consists of a set of Artificial Recognition Balls (ARBs) and links between them, indicating similarity. ARBs compete for the ability to represent a number of B cells within the RLAIS, based on stimulation of the ARB. The number of B cells is limited at the start of the learning cycle. As in the AIS, cloning and mutation mechanisms are used to create a diverse representation of the training data.

Training data are continually presented to the network. The algorithm can either be terminated by a special termination condition once the network has stabilised, or it can go on learning indefinitely. It is conceivable that previously unseen data, could be presented to the network to continue the learning process. The new data would be incorporated into the network, and provided that original data was also being used for training, the original clusters in the data would remain, and new clusters could emerge.

Visualisation of the networks produced by the RLAIS is performed in the same manner as for the AIS[16].

3.2.1 The ARB Object and Stimulation Level Calculation

Each ARB contains a single piece of n-dimensional data and represents a number of identical B cells. B cells are no longer explicitly represented in the network. The RLAIS is limited to a maximum number of B cells that can be shared amongst the ARBs' defined as mb. An ARB undergoes stimulation calculations, using the following formula :

$$sl = \sum_{x=0}^{a}(1 - pd_x) + \sum_{x=0}^{n}(1 - dis_x) - \sum_{x=0}^{n}(dis_x) \qquad (1)$$

where a is the number of antigens the ARB has been exposed to, pd_x is defined as the distance between the ARB and the xth antigen in the normalized data space such that $0 \le pd \le 1$ and dis_x the distance of the xth neighbor from the B cell. ARBs' undergo cloning during the learning cycle at a rate using the following formula :

$$e_x = k \cdot (sl_x) \qquad (2)$$

where k is a constant value used to limit the number of clones produced and sl_x is the stimulation level of an ARB x. These clones then undergo stochastic mutation in an attempt to create a diverse representation of the data being learnt. Mutated clones are then incorporated into the network, if their affinity to other ARBs in the network is below the NAT. Non-mutated clones are not incorporated, as the need for identical clones has been removed from the RLAIS.

3.2.2 Reallocation of B cells to an ARB

After each presentation of the training data, B cells are allocated to each ARB according to (equation 3). At this point in the learning process the stimulation level of every ARB in the RLAIS is recalculated (equation 1). Then each ARB claims a number of B cells dependent on its stimulation level regardless of how many B cells are available, as defined by the following formula :

$$R_i = k \cdot (sl_i^2) \qquad (3)$$

where sl_i is the stimulation level of an ARB and k is a constant value used to limit the number B cells claimed by the ARB. Figure 4 shows the way in which B cells are allocated to ARBs. The higher the stimulation, the more B cells an ARB will claim. This has the effect that some ARBs claim only very few B cells and stand the risk of being removed from the network. If the number of

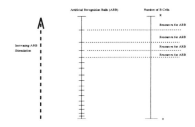

Figure 4: Showing the relationship between the ARBs and number of B cells allocated

B cells allocated is greater than the maximum number of B cells allowed, then the number of B cells that make up the difference must be removed.

In order to remove these the weakest (less stimulated) ARBs' are identified first. B cells are removed from the allocation of the ARB and if the ARBs' B cell count falls to zero then that ARB is removed from the network. This process is repeated on the next weakest ARB until there is no difference between the amount of B cells allocated and the maximum amount allowed. The constant reallocation of B cells to only the strongest ARBs allows for the development of competition between ARBs. Therefore, when mutated clones are produced, if they are a good match for the training data and surrounding ARBs then they will survive in the network, otherwise, they will eventually be removed.

3.3   Results Obtained

The results presented in this section are those based on the Iris data set. However, it should be noted that experiments were also conducted on a simulated data set, that yielded equally as good results but are not presented in this paper, but can be found in [17].

Figure 5 shows two graphs that plot the growth of the network over time, prior to cloning and mutation. These show a stabilising behavior with respect to the network size. Network size is monitored prior to cloning to attempt to identify the core network structure. This stabilisation of the network size also provides a possible termination condition for the algorithm.

Figure 5(a) shows the size of the network over six hundred iterations of the training set. The network repeatedly stabilises at various iterations of the training set Figure 5(b) shows the first twenty iterations of the training set. Clearly, there are periods when the size of the network is stable. These periods of stability are followed by perturbations where the RLAIS is generating a diverse set of ARBs to find other possible patterns in the data. These dis-

28

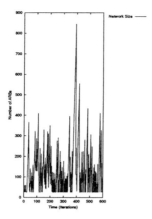

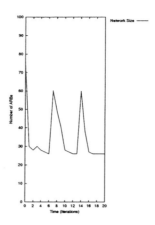

(a) With the Iris data a perturbation in network size is observed. However, there are periods of stable size of the network

(b) Showing the first twenty iterations of the training set.

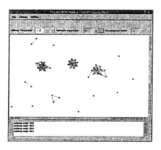

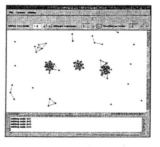

(c) After twelve iterations of the training data. Three distinct clusters are clearly visible

(d) After thirteen iterations of the training data. The pattern is three clusters is still present

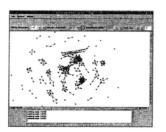

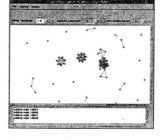

(e) After three hundred iterations. The network is large with a bridge between the Versicolor and Virginica data.

(f) After three hundred and fourteen iterations. The stable pattern of three distinct clusters has reappeared.

Figure 5: Virginica class left most cluster, Setosa in the middle and Versicolor in the right most cluster

turbances sometimes last for long periods of time, but always, the size of the network returns to the base line size.

In order to confirm this observation, networks were visualised to show that once a strong pattern has been found in the data, that pattern does not degrade over time (figure 5). Figure 5(c) shows the network after 12 iterations of the training data, the second consecutive iteration where the size of the base network is the same. Here, three distinct clusters are visible, with each one of the clusters being a representation of each of the three classes of data. This can be confirmed by the presentation of an unseen data item, where the RLAIS links the unseen item to the network. This pattern of three distinct classes continues for the next iteration (figure 5(d)).

Inspection of networks created later on in training, go to further back up the claim that a stable pattern emerge. Figure 5(e) shows a network at 300 iterations of the training data. It can be clearly seen that a large cluster has been formed on the left. This is an amalgamation of the Virginica and Versicolor data. A bridge between the two classes has been created and the network is also highly populated with ARBs. It is hard to glean any useful information from this network. Figure 5(f) shows the network after 314 iterations of the data. As can be seen the network has reverted back to a very similar state as shown in figures 5(c) and 5(d), where the majority of new clones have been removed from the network and the core pattern remains. A detailed investigation of figure 5(a) shows that at 314 iterations of the data representation, the size and structure of the network is very similar to that at 12 iterations. It should also be noted that the networks produced by the RLAIS are much easier to interpret than those produced by the AIS. When figure 1(a) is compared with figure 5(c), for example, the complexity of the networks has been significantly reduced, yet it is suggested that more information is available to the user as the RLAIS identified three distinct patterns, and exploring the networks an easier process.

The RLAIS is to some degree, mimicking the metadynamical behavior observed in the natural immune system. Patterns emerge from the RLAIS due to the fact that well stimulated ARBs, hence good matches for the antigen set, clone more rapidly. Mutated clones are then integrated into the network and, if they are a good match for the antigen set, will themselves become stimulated. These in turn, reinforce similar ARBs contained in the network, allowing for the regions of similarity, clusters or categories to emerge. Eventually, a strong pattern, i.e. many well stimulated ARBs, will claim all the resources; a core network will emerge. It is at this point that stabilisation occurs. The networks during the stable period each may be slightly different, but they yield the same information.

In order to tune the algorithm the RLAIS has three parameters. The NAT scalar is used to affect connectivity within the network, the lower the NAT scalar, the more stringent the network. The mutation rate can be used to affect diversity within the network. Therefore, if the data set is very dense in Euclidean space, a higher mutation rate may be employed to extract the useful patterns. Finally, the number of resources affects the overall size of the network. the more resources allocated to the RLAIS, the larger the resulting networks. As a rule of thumb, it has so far been found that twice the number of resources are required than antigen data items. A more detailed analysis of the algorithm can be found in [17].

3.4 Related Work

It is noted that the RLAIS shares some similarities with more traditional cluster analysis techniques and Self-Organising Feature Maps [11]. All techniques attempt, to some degree to find clusters, patterns etc within large amounts of data. There are significant differences, however, between each of these methods. To summarise, cluster analysis proves a useful first look at the data with results usually represented as a dendrogram. These are hard to interpret when data sets are large. Additionally, these techniques simply create a map of the input space, rather than a diverse representation of the data space. Similarly, SOFMs produce a topological map of the input data, but are more useful for visualisation than dendrograms and tend to concentrate on maintaining neighborhood relationships. Again, standard SOFMs do not have the emergent behavior that is exhibited by the RLAIS. The RLAIS differers not only in the mechanisms employed to achieve the results, but the RLAIS produces a diverse network of the data space. The RLAIS allows for the possibility of more subtle patterns to emerge from the antigen set, than may be achieved by the other techniques. Additionally, it is proposed that the RLAIS can be employed as a continual learning model, where new data can be presented to the network without the need to retrain. This is under research at the present time. A more detailed account of similarities and differences between the AIS and other methods can be found in [15].

4 Conclusions

This paper has introduced a resource limited Artificial Immune System (RLAIS). Deficiencies in previous work on AIS were identified and solutions provided.
The RLAIS introduces the concept of an Artificial Recognition Ball that is representative of a number of B cells. The ARBs compete for a limited allocation of B cells, based on stimulation level, and if an ARB no longer claims any B cells, it is removed from the network. This is an effective population control mechanism. This counteracts the exponential growth in the network size, as was prevalent in the original AIS.
The RLAIS captures the patterns in the data being learnt, by clustering similar ARBs together. Once a strong pattern has been learnt, it will be continually supported in the RLAIS, no matter how many times the training data is presented. In addition it has been proposed that the RLAIS can be used for continual learning. Previously unseen data could be presented to the RLAIS to allow new patterns to be learnt, without adversely affecting the patterns

already learnt. This has been identified as an avenue for future research.

The size of networks produced by the RLAIS is now suitably restricted allowing effective visualisation while maintaining an accurate and diverse representation of the data being learnt. A significant improvement is achieved for the visualisation of the networks evolved, due to the drop in network complexity, making the networks more useful for the exploratory process. The RLAIS builds up a network that allows for the discovery of subtle relationships between clusters and data items within the data being learnt. Additionally, the RLAIS can be used to present unseen data items to the evolved network and is thus useful for data exploration and categorisation.

5 Future Work

This work has identified many areas of possible research, some initial projects are currently being pursued. The first is the application of the RLAIS to data mining large collections of documents. This includes applying the RLAIS to large databases of documents, or in the first instance Web sites so that meaningful clusters can be discovered between documents. This is a much more complex domain than the RLAIS has been applied to and, if successful, will take the RLAIS another step forward in being a viable contender for effective unsupervised learning and data analysis. Secondly, the augmentation of the visualisation aspect of the work is being researched. This will included the creation of more analysis techniques to allow for greater understanding of cluster and inter-cluster relationships and automatic cluster identification.

References

[1] Bersini, H., Varela, F.J. *Hints for Adaptive Problem Solving Gleaned from Immune Networks*. Parallel Problem Solving from Nature. 1st Workshop PPSW 1, Dortmund, FRG, October 1990.

[2] Coutinho, A. *The self-non self discrimination and the nature and acquisition of the antibody repertoire*. **Annal of Immunology** (Inst. Past.) 131D. 1980

[3] Cooke, D.E and Hunt, J.E. *Recognising promoter sequences using an Artificial Immune System*. Proc. of Intelligent Systems in Molecular Biology 1995. AAAI Press.

[4] Dasgupta, D. *An Overview of Artificial Immune Systems and Their Applications*. **Artificial Immune Systems and their Applications**. Ed. Dipankar Dasgupta Pub. Springer-Verlag. ISBN 3-540- 64390-7. pp. 3-21 (1998)

[5] Farmer, J.D., Packard, N.H. *The Immune System, Adaptation and Machine Learning*. **Physica** 22D, pp. 187-204. 1986

[6] Fisher,R.A. (1936) *The use of multiple measurements in taxonomic problems.* **Annual Eugenics**, 7, Part II, 179-188

[7] Hart, E., Ross, P. and Nelson, J. *Producing Robust Schedules via an Artificial Immune System.* Proc. of IEEE International Conference on Evolutionary Computing, 1998.

[8] Hunt, J., Timmis, J., Neal, M. and King, C. *Jisys : The development of an Artificial Immune System for Real World Applications.* **Artificial Immune Systems and their Applications**. Ed. Dipankar Dasgupta. Pub Springer-Verlag. ISBN 3 540 64390 7 pp. 157-184. (1998)

[9] Jerne, N.K. (1974) *Towards a Network Theory of the Immune System.* **Annals of Immunology**. (Inst Pasteur) **125C**: 373-389

[10] Kephart, J.O. *A biologically inspired immune system for computers.* Artificial Life IV. Proc. of 4th Int. workshop on the Synthesis and Simulation of Living Systems, pp. 130-139. MIT Press eds. R.A.Brooks and P. Maes. (1994)

[11] Kohonen, T. *Self-Organising Maps.* 2nd Edition. Pub. Springer-Verlag. (1997)

[12] Neal, M., Hunt, J. and Timmis, J. *Augmenting an Artificial Immune Network.* Proceedings of the IEEE International Conference on Systems, Man and Cybernetics. San Diego. U.S.A. pp 3821-3826. (1998)

[13] Perelson, A. (1989). *Immune Network Theory.* **Immunological Review**, 110, 1989, pp 5-36

[14] Timmis, J., Neal, M. and Hunt, J. *An Artificial Immune System for Data Analysis.* **Biosystems**. Vol:55(1/3):143-150, 2000.

[15] Timmis, J., Neal, M. and Hunt, J. *Data Analysis with Artificial Immune Systems, Cluster Analysis and Kohonen Networks : Some Comparisons.* Proc. of Int. Conf. Systems and Man and Cybernetics, pages 922-927, Tokyo, Japan., 1999. IEEE.

[16] Timmis, J. *Visualising Artificial Immune Networks.* Technical report UWA-DCS-00-034. Department of Computer Science, University of Wales, Aberystwyth, 2000.

[17] Timmis, J. *Artificial Immune Systems : A novel data analysis technique inspired by the immune network theory.* Ph.D Thesis. University of Wales, Aberystwyth. 2000.

[18] Tizzard, I. *The Response of B Cells to Antigen* **Immunology : An Introduction. 2nd Edition**. pp. 199-223. Saunders College Publishing (1998)

[19] Varela, F and Coutinho, A. *Cognitive Networks: Immune, Neural and otherwise.* **Theoretical Immunology**, Vol:2, pp. 359-371. (1988)

SESSION 1

LEARNING I

Experiences with a weighted decision tree learner

John G. Cleary

Leonard E. Trigg

Geoffrey Holmes

Mark Hall

Department of Computer Science, University of Waikato

Hamilton, New Zealand

Abstract

Machine learning algorithms for inferring decision trees typically choose a single "best" tree to describe the training data. Recent research has shown that classification performance can be significantly improved by voting predictions of multiple, independently produced decision trees. This paper describes an algorithm, OB1, that produces a weighted sum over many possible models. Model weights are determined by the prior probability of the model, as well as the performance of the model during training. We describe an implementation of OB1 that includes *all* possible decision trees as well as naive Bayesian models within a single option tree. Constructing all possible decision trees is very expensive, growing exponentially in the number of attributes. However it is possible to use the internal structure of the option tree to avoid recomputing values. In addition, the current implementation allows the option tree to be depth bounded.

OB1 is compared with a number of other decision tree and instance based learning algorithms using a selection of data sets from the UCI repository and a maximum option tree depth of three attributes. Both information gain and percentage correct are used for the comparison. For the information gain measure OB1 performs significantly better than the other algorithms. When using percentage correct OB1 is significantly better than all the algorithms except naive Bayes and boosted C5.0[1], which perform slightly worse than OB1.

1   Introduction

The standard approach for inferring decision trees from training data is to choose a single "best" tree to describe the training data [11]. Following Occam's Razor, the best tree is usually defined as the simplest tree fitting the data. This is usually expressed as the Maximum Likelihood Principle and more generally as the Minimum Description Length (MDL) principle [3]. These tree-based systems have performed well on a variety of real-world tasks, and have the advantage that decision trees are relatively easy to understand. This approach has some problems however; in particular, what is the basis for choosing only

---

[1]C5.0 is the successor of C4.5 [11]. Although a commercial product, a test version is available from http://www.rulequest.com.

the simplest tree? Also, it is easy to overfit and choose a tree that is large and complex but which predicts less well than simpler trees on new data.

An alternative approach is rooted in the philosophy of Epicurus [10], who believed *all* hypotheses fitting the data should be retained. Along these lines recent research has shown that classification performance can be significantly improved by voting predictions of multiple decision trees [12]. A similar approach weights different trees and forms a weighted sum of their predictions. For example, Buntine [4] forms option trees which combine some subset of the possible trees by weighted averaging at internal nodes of the tree. A more dramatic approach is the Context Tree Weighting (CTW) models [14] used in text compression. CTW sums over all possible models, weighted according to the probability of all the preceding data. Volf [13] has applied the CTW approach to machine learning to derive MDL decision trees.

It might seem that summing over *all* possible models would be very expensive. However, it is possible to use the internal structure of the models to avoid recomputing values repeatedly. The result is a collapse in both the space and time required to construct and use the data.

This paper describes an algorithm called OB1 which has an Epicurean foundation. We show how the set of all decision trees can be represented compactly and efficiently. Some experiments are then described which compare OB1 against a number of other machine learning techniques. It is shown that depth bounded OB1 can perform significantly worse than a naive Bayesian [8] learner. This then motivates the inclusion of naive Bayesian models into OB1. Comparisons are then made between the OB1 system and a range of learning algorithms on a number of datasets taken from the UCI repository. The comparison is evaluated using both an information gain measure and classification accuracy of the schemes. The paper concludes with a summary of what has been achieved and of future developments in the implementation of OB1.

2 Constructing OB1 Option Trees

Supervised machine learning is concerned with the problem of predicting a set of data given instances of the data. Given some set of data values $D = \{v_1, \ldots, v_N\}$ and for each value a set of corresponding instances $\{x_1, \ldots, x_N\}$. Each instance x is a vector $\langle a_1, \ldots, a_m \rangle$ where the a_i are the individual attribute values for the instance. The problem then is to predict the next data value v given some attributes x and a set of prior data D. Prediction can be done two ways. One is to make a categorical prediction by selecting one of the possible values for v. The other is to produce a probability distribution over the possible values of v, this is written $P(v|D)$, the conditional probability of v given D. In what follows it is simpler to use the probability $P(D)$ that is, the probability of the entire set of data occurring. This can be interchanged with the conditional probability using the relation

$$P(v|D) = \frac{P(D \cup \{v\})}{P(D)} \tag{1}$$

In this paper we will restrict ourselves to the case where there are a finite number of discrete attributes and data values. In particular we do not consider the case of real values. The fundamental idea of Epicurean learning is that $P(D)$ can be computed by considering many different possible hypotheses. The fundamental relationship that is used to compute $P(D)$ is :

$$P(D) = \sum_{h \in H} P(D|h)P(h) \tag{2}$$

$P(D|h)$ is the probability of the data given the hypothesis h. H is the set of all possible hypotheses that we are considering. $P(h)$ is the prior likelihood of the hypothesis. $-\log_2(P(h))$ can be considered the complexity of the hypothesis—that is, the number of bits necessary to specify it.

Given a set of possible hypotheses we want to associate a recursive AND-OR tree structure with them. Each node I will have associated with it a set of hypotheses, H_I, a subset of the data, D_I, a prior $P_I(h)$ over H_I, and a probability estimate

$$P_I(D_I) = \sum_{h \in H_I} P_I(D_I|h)P_I(h)$$

The importance of the tree structure is that $P_I(D_I)$ can be expressed recursively in terms of its value on the child nodes. There are three types of nodes in the tree: AND, OR and LEAF nodes.

At an AND node I the data D_I is split according to the values of one of the attributes (this corresponds to an interior node in a standard decision tree). So for some attribute which can take on the values $a_1, \ldots, a_l$ there will be l children $I_1, \ldots, I_l$. Thus D_{I_i} is all the values in D_I whose corresponding attribute has the value a_i. The set of hypotheses H_I is all decision trees whose top level test is on the selected attribute. The set of hypotheses H_{I_i} is the same for each child, that is, the set of all decision trees that never test the selected attribute (again). Each hypothesis h in H_I splits into sub-hypotheses $h_1, \ldots, h_l$, that is h is composed of disjoint parts which apply to the disjoint data sets D_{I_i}. This implies that $P(D_I|h) = \prod_i P(D_{I_i}|h_i)$. Similarly the priors can be computed as $P_I(h) = \prod_i P_{I_i}(h_i)$. Any sub-hypothesis in the children can be combined with other sub-hypotheses in the other children to form a complete hypothesis. So, at least in the case where we are summing over all possible hypotheses, H_I is the cross product of the hypotheses in the children. Given all these relationships the overall probability of the data can be re-expressed as:

$$P_I(D_I) = \prod_i P_{I_i}(D_{I_i}) \tag{3}$$

An OR node I segregates the set of hypotheses by the first attribute tested in the hypothesis. So an OR node will have one child, I_i, for each attribute and possibly some leaf nodes. For each non-LEAF child I_i the set of hypotheses H_{I_i} will be all hypotheses in H_I with an initial test on the corresponding attribute. Each LEAF child will generate a probability using the statistics from all the values in D_I. (Some options for doing this are explained below). An OR-node corresponds to an option node in the work of Buntine [4]. The data set for each of the children is unchanged from the parent, that is, D_I. The priors for the children remain unchanged except for the assumption that all priors sum to 1. This requires that the priors at each child be renormalized by the term $S_{I_i} \equiv \sum_{h \in H_{I_i}} P_I(h)$. The new priors are then $P_{I_i}(h) = P_I(h)/S_{I_i}$. Note that $\sum_{h \in H_I} P_I(h) = 1$ implies $\sum_i S_{I_i} = 1$.

The probability of the data at I can be re-expressed as the weighted sum:

$$P_I(D) = \sum_i S_{I_i} P_{I_i}(D) \tag{4}$$

AND-nodes form their composite probability by taking the product of the probabilities from their children and the OR-nodes by taking a weighted sum of their children.

The LEAF nodes should use the statistics of the all the data in D and return from this an estimate of $P(D)$. One of the simplest such estimators is the Laplace estimator. This assumes that there are an infinite number of hypotheses each corresponding to a different probability between 0 and 1 for the next symbol. In the case where the values in D are binary, one of a or b, and c_a and c_b are the number times a and b respectively has occurred in D then using the integral form of Eqn.2

$$P(D) = \int_0^1 p^{c_a}(1-p)^{c_b} dp = \frac{c_a! c_b!}{(c_a + c_b + 1)!}$$

In the general form of this equation

$$P(D) = \frac{\prod_v c_v!}{(c + n - 1)!} \tag{5}$$

where v ranges over all possible data values, $c = \sum_v c_v$ and n is the number of different data values.

Given an AND-OR tree the most common use is to compute a conditional probability using Eqn.1 A simple recursive function can do this, using the following relationships. At an AND-node I

$$P_I(v|D_I) = \frac{\prod_i P_{I_i}((D \cup \{v\})_{I_i})}{\prod_i P_{I_i}(D_{I_i})}$$

However, $(D \cup \{v\})_{I_i}$ will be equal to D_{I_i} except for the one case where the attribute associated with v is equal to a_i. That is, most of the terms in the product above cancel giving

$$P_I(v|D_I) = P_{I_i}(v|D_{I_i})$$

At an OR-node I

$$P_I(v|D_I) = \frac{\sum_i S_{I_i} P_{I_i}(D_I \cup \{v\})}{\sum_i S_{I_i} P_{I_i}(D_I)} \quad \text{from Eqn.4}$$

$$= \frac{\sum_i S_{I_i} P_{I_i}(D_I) P_{I_i}(v|D_I)}{\sum_i S_{I_i} P_{I_i}(D_I)} \quad \text{using Eqn.1}$$

At a LEAF node I using the Laplace estimator the conditional probability can be computed as follows

$$
\begin{aligned}
P_I(v|D_I) &= \frac{(c_v + 1)! \prod_{w \neq v} c_w!}{(\sum_w c_w + n)!} \Big/ \frac{\prod_w c_w!}{(\sum_w c_w + n - 1)!} \\
&= \frac{c_v + 1}{(\sum_w c_w + n)}
\end{aligned}
$$

In order to execute such an algorithm effectively it is only necessary to record the counts c and c_v on the leaf nodes and the weights $W_{I_i} \equiv S_{I_i} P_{I_i}(D_I)$ for each child I_i of an OR-node I. Given such a set of weights the recursive computation of $P_I(v|D_I)$ of a node I with children I_i can be summarized as

$$
P_I(v|D_I) = \begin{cases}
P_{I_i}(v|D_{I_i}) & \text{where } I \text{ is an AND node and } I_i \text{ is selected} \\
\dfrac{\sum_i W_i P_{I_i}(v|D_I)}{\sum_i W_i} & \text{where } I \text{ is an OR node} \\
\frac{c_v+1}{(c+n)} & \text{where } I \text{ is a LEAF node}
\end{cases}
$$

One difficulty with this approach is that the W_i can be too small to store in a standard floating point representation which potentially could slow the execution of the algorithm. Fortunately, they can be renormalized by any factor and the equation for conditional probabilities will remain unchanged. In OB1 they are normalized so that $\sum_i W_i = 1$, and stored in single precision floating point.

Typically OB1 is used in two phases. In the first phase training instances are supplied and the AND-OR tree is constructed together with the counts and weights. In the second phase test instances are supplied and the conditional probabilities are computed as above. The weights can be computed incrementally using an algorithm similar to that above. This relies on

$$
P(D) = \prod_{i=1}^{N} P\left(v_i \mid \{v_1, \ldots v_{i-1}\}\right),
$$

that is, the total probabilities can be computed incrementally as new data arrives. The procedure $W_I(v|D_I)$ below incrementally computes the weights and updates the counters on the leaves.

$W_I(v|D_I)$
    if I is an AND node and I_i is selected
        return $W_{I_i}(v|D_{I_i})$
    if I is an OR node
        for all I_i children of I $W_i := W_i * W_{I_i}(v|D_I)$
        return $t := \sum_i W_i$
        for all I_i children of I $W_i := W_i/t$ {renormalise weights}
    if I is a LEAF node
        $c_v := c_v + 1$
        $c := c + 1$
        return c_v/c

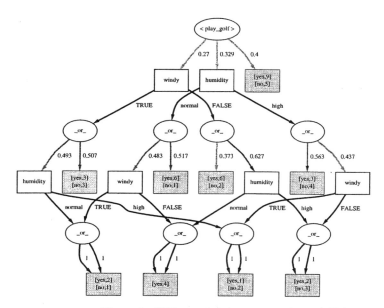

Figure 1: OB1 tree for the two attribute golf data set

The counts c are assigned and initialised to n and the counts c_v are initialised to 0. The weights W_i are initialized to the renormalising factors S_{I_i}. There is complete freedom to choose the S_{I_i} so long as they are positive and sum to one for the children of each OR-node. In fact they provide a very convenient way of specifying the priors. An approach that works well in practice is to set $S_{I_i} = 1/2$ when I_i is (the single) LEAF node, otherwise $S_{I_i} = 1/2l$ where l is the number of AND-children.

An example OB1 tree is shown in Figure 1 for a two attribute version of Quinlan's [11] golf data set. The tree depicts the set of hypotheses encompasing all value combinations represented in the training data. With such a restricted data set the single hypothesis with the highest weight (0.4) is the default hypothesis which simply reflects the distribution of class values in the training data. Children at level two in this tree are shared between level one parents. Such sharing can very significantly decrease memory usage.

Consider the classification of an instance with values (humidity = high, windy = false). The goal is to produce a probability distribution over the two classes (yes,no). We get contributions from all three hypotheses that emanate from the root node. The default hypothesis contributes $0.4 \times (\frac{10}{16}, \frac{6}{16})$. Recall that class probabilities at the leaves are given by Laplace estimators, so the probability of class=yes is $\frac{9+1}{14+2}$. The other two contributions trace down the tree to give $0.329 \times [0.563 \times (\frac{4}{9}, \frac{5}{9}) + 0.437 \times (\frac{3}{7}, \frac{4}{7})]$ and $0.27 \times [0.373 \times (\frac{7}{10}, \frac{3}{10}) + 0.627 \times (\frac{3}{7}, \frac{4}{7})]$. The sum of these three contributions gives a probability distribution of $(0.5343, 0.4657)$. So for this instance "yes" is assigned as the class value.

Dataset	NBayes	OB1 b0	OB1 b1	OB1 b2	OB1 b3
anneal	1.03	0.06 •	0.44 •	0.85 •	0.94 •
autos	−0.72	0.13 ∘	0.53 ∘	0.76 ∘	0.79 ∘
balance-scale	0.46	0.02 •	0.12 •	0.23 •	0.37 •
breast-cancer	−0.04	0.03 ∘	0.08 ∘	0.08 ∘	0.09 ∘
breast-w	0.52	0.01 •	0.64 ∘	0.75 ∘	0.75 ∘
colic	−0.29	0.01 ∘	0.25 ∘	0.34 ∘	0.35 ∘
credit-a	0.37	0.01 •	0.44 ∘	0.51 ∘	0.52 ∘
credit-g	0.11	0.01 •	0.09	0.11	0.11
diabetes	0.21	0.01 •	0.17 •	0.20	0.22
glass	0.88	0.12 •	0.56 •	0.78 •	0.83
heart-c	0.43	0.15 •	0.25 •	0.27 •	0.27 •
heart-h	0.26	0.15 •	0.35 ∘	0.35 ∘	0.35 ∘
heart-statlog	0.29	0.02 •	0.16 •	0.29	0.34
hepatitis	−0.13	0.03 ∘	0.09 ∘	0.10 ∘	0.12 ∘
hypothyroid	0.38	0.01 •	0.35 •	0.39 ∘	0.40 ∘
ionosphere	−0.98	0.02 ∘	0.37 ∘	0.54 ∘	0.58 ∘
iris	1.31	0.03 •	1.27	1.31	1.31
kr-vs-kp	0.58	0.00 •	0.21 •	0.48 •	0.71 ∘
labor	0.77	0.06 •	0.37 •	0.44 •	0.44 •
lymph	0.68	0.12 •	0.39 •	0.39 •	0.41 •

Table 1: $S_f i$ for naive Bayes and OB1 on discretised UCI datasets

3 Initial evaluation

Initial evaluation of OB1 involved a comparison with a naive Bayes classifier [8] on a variety of datasets from the UCI repository [9] using the WEKA workbench [7]. The performance measure used for evaluation is a MDL significance measure, S_f, [5] which gives a more accurate measure of the amount of information captured by a scheme than simple percentage correct. In essence, the S_f measure is the gain in bits when encoding the test instance class with respect to the scheme's predictions as opposed to encoding with respect to a naive method that produces predictions based only on the observed class frequencies during testing. Thus,

$$S_f = -\log_2(P(D)) + \log_2(P_{naive}(D)),$$

where $P_{naive}()$ is a naive Laplace estimator that ignores all the attributes.

Table 1 shows the S_f in bits per instance ($S_f i$) averaged over 25 trials. For each trial, the dataset was randomly divided into two thirds training and one third testing. All numeric attributes were discretised using Fayyad and Irani's [6] discretisation method. OB1 was evaluated with tree depth bounded to 0, 1, 2, and 3 attributes. Trees deeper than 3 attributes are not considered in these experiments because for many of the datasets we had insufficient memory to generate deeper OB1 trees. Where naive Bayes results are significantly worse (according to a two-tailed, paired t-test at the 95% confidence level) than OB1, this is postfixed with ∘, and where significantly better this is postfixed with •.

The most obvious result seen in Table 1 is that the performance of OB1 improves with added tree depth. Also, naive Bayes performs very well, and on some datasets (such as heart-c and labor) it performs considerably better than OB1.

Dataset	NBayes	OB1 b0	OB1 b1	OB1 b2	OB1 b3
anneal	1.03	0.06 •	1.03	1.03	1.08 ∘
autos	−0.72	0.13 ∘	0.52 ∘	0.78 ∘	0.95 ∘
balance-scale	0.46	0.02 •	0.46	0.48 ∘	0.50 ∘
breast-cancer	−0.04	0.03 ∘	0.08 ∘	0.07 ∘	0.07 ∘
breast-w	0.52	0.01 •	0.60 ∘	0.77 ∘	0.77 ∘
colic	−0.29	0.01 ∘	0.25 ∘	0.34 ∘	0.34 ∘
credit-a	0.37	0.01 •	0.44 ∘	0.51 ∘	0.52 ∘
credit-g	0.11	0.01 •	0.10	0.11	0.12
diabetes	0.21	0.01 •	0.21	0.22 ∘	0.23 ∘
glass	0.88	0.12 •	0.88	0.92 ∘	0.93 ∘
heart-c	0.43	0.15 •	0.43	0.49 ∘	0.49 ∘
heart-h	0.26	0.15 •	0.30	0.49 ∘	0.48 ∘
heart-statlog	0.29	0.02 •	0.29	0.32 ∘	0.34 ∘
hepatitis	−0.13	0.03 ∘	0.09 ∘	0.09 ∘	0.12 ∘
hypothyroid	0.38	0.01 •	0.38	0.40 ∘	0.42 ∘
ionosphere	−0.98	0.02 ∘	0.37 ∘	0.53 ∘	0.57 ∘
iris	1.31	0.03 •	1.31	1.32	1.32
kr-vs-kp	0.58	0.00 •	0.58	0.75 ∘	0.84 ∘
labor	0.77	0.06 •	0.76	0.74	0.73 •
lymph	0.68	0.12 •	0.69 ∘	0.68	0.67

Table 2: $S_f i$ results for naive Bayes and OB1 incorporating naive Bayes models using hold-one-out weighting on discretised UCI datasets

4 OB1 is omnivorous

At each OR-node in the OB1 tree, we can include a naive Bayes model that operates on all the attributes that have not been tested previously in the tree. The attribute-value counts needed for a naive Bayes model can be obtained by visiting the LEAF nodes attached to each OR node below each attribute split (thus these "free" naive Bayes models cannot be placed at the bottom level of an OB1 tree). The only extra storage associated with each naive Bayes model is its weight.

Since OB1 now includes naive Bayes models as competing hypotheses, it should never perform more than a couple of bits worse than naive Bayes alone using S_f. However it seems that this is not always the case. For example, the OB1 on the anneal dataset gives virtually identical results to those shown in Table 1, even though naive Bayes performs very well. The current hypothesis weighting method effectively measures hypothesis performance throughout training, rather than the expected performance on future data. In this case, the naive Bayes models within OB1 are penalized for poor performance during the early stages of training, even though naive Bayes performs well during testing. The next section describes a new weighting method that addresses this problem.

5 Hold-one-out hypothesis weighting

A common method of evaluating machine learning schemes is hold-one-out evaluation, where the scheme is trained on all instances but one, and tested on the remaining instance. This process is repeated until all instances have been tested. In the case of OB1 and naive Bayes, it is possible to compute the hold-one-out evaluation in a single pass by temporarily decrementing the counts for each instance. However, it cannot be computed incrementally for naive Bayes models. We have therefore opted to build the OB1 tree in one pass to collect counts, and compute the hypothesis weights in a second pass. In practice the total learning time is less than doubled, since the second pass does not require memory allocation.

The hold-one-out procedure provides a good estimate of the expected performance of a model, and thus can be used to replace the initial OB1 weighting method. Rather than the hypothesis weights representing the product of incremental predicted probabilities, the new weighting method forms the hypothesis weights from the product of the hold-one-out probabilities. For an OB1 tree without naive Bayes models, the new weighting method can be computed incrementally as a direct replacement for the original method.

Using the notation in Eqn.5 the probability of a data value v if one instance of it is held out is $P(v|D - \{v\}) = \frac{c_v}{c+n-2}$. Each symbol v is held out c_v times so the total contribution of that symbol to the probability is $\left(\frac{c_v}{c+n-2}\right)^{c_v}$. Thus

$$P(D) = \prod_v \left(\frac{c_v}{c+n-2}\right)^{c_v} = (c+n-2)^c \prod_v c_v^{c_v}$$

Table 2 shows the $S_f i$ for OB1 including naive Bayes models in the tree and using hold-one-out weighting. Experimental conditions are the same as for the previous experiments. The results are much improved over those in Table 1. OB1 always performs to within a small constant of the better of naive Bayes and the original OB1. It also performs considerably better than both methods alone on some datasets such as heart-c.

6 Single model performance

For the purposes of extracting a model that can be easily understood by humans, we can select the hypothesis with the highest weight. We can also produce predictions based only on the chosen hypothesis. Table 3 shows a comparison of the performance of the dominant hypothesis (pruned) with the performance of all hypotheses (unpruned), for each of the depth bounds. All runs incorporated hold-one-out weighting, and included naive Bayes models among hypotheses. Results marked with • indicate where the unpruned model performed significantly better than the pruned model, using a two-tailed, paired t-test at the 95% confidence level. In none of the cases did the pruned model perform significantly better than the unpruned model.

To confirm that selecting a single model can significantly degrade performance, we performed another comparison, this time with the optimal depth 1 and depth 2 hypotheses, as determined by T1 and T2 respectively [2]. Since T1

Dataset	b1	b1 Pr	b2	b2 Pr	b3	b3 Pr
anneal	1.03	1.03	1.03	1.00	1.08	1.01 •
autos	0.52	0.50 •	0.78	0.58 •	0.95	0.43 •
balance-scale	0.46	0.46	0.48	0.47 •	0.50	0.49 •
breast-cancer	0.08	0.07 •	0.07	0.03 •	0.07	−0.02 •
breast-w	0.60	0.59	0.77	0.71 •	0.77	0.69 •
colic	0.25	0.25	0.34	0.32 •	0.34	0.26 •
credit-a	0.44	0.44	0.51	0.48 •	0.52	0.49 •
credit-g	0.10	0.10	0.11	0.09 •	0.12	0.08 •
diabetes	0.21	0.21	0.22	0.22 •	0.23	0.22 •
glass	0.88	0.88	0.92	0.89 •	0.93	0.89 •
heart-c	0.43	0.43	0.49	0.47 •	0.49	0.47 •
heart-h	0.30	0.23 •	0.49	0.48	0.48	0.47 •
heart-statlog	0.29	0.29	0.32	0.28 •	0.34	0.28 •
hepatitis	0.09	0.02 •	0.09	−0.04 •	0.12	−0.10 •
hypothyroid	0.38	0.38	0.40	0.40 •	0.42	0.41 •
ionosphere	0.37	0.36 •	0.53	0.48 •	0.57	0.49 •
iris	1.31	1.31	1.32	1.31	1.32	1.31
kr-vs-kp	0.58	0.58	0.75	0.75	0.84	0.84
labor	0.76	0.76	0.74	0.72	0.73	0.72
lymph	0.69	0.69	0.68	0.65	0.67	0.65

Table 3: $S_f i$ for OB1 unpruned vs pruned (Pr) results

Dataset	OB1 b1	T1	OB1 b2	T2
anneal	80.77	83.40 ○	93.35	76.73 •
autos	47.94	45.77	61.54	65.89 ○
balance-scale	61.83	61.68	67.32	67.13
breast-cancer	70.19	67.96 •	71.63	67.05 •
breast-w	92.27	66.29 •	95.90	66.29 •
colic	79.81	79.46 •	84.54	81.31 •
credit-a	85.77	85.77	85.91	82.81 •
credit-g	69.11	70.84 ○	71.87	69.44 •
diabetes	74.02	74.02	74.90	73.95
glass	48.55	52.22	58.85	60.66 ○
heart-c	71.15	72.00	73.86	72.12 •
heart-h	78.40	54.00 •	78.72	78.20
heart-statlog	71.30	71.30	74.22	70.57 •
hepatitis	79.09	70.42 •	78.11	77.58
hypothyroid	96.61	86.88 •	98.48	98.43
ionosphere	82.55	83.76	89.78	88.71
iris	92.39	92.47	93.88	92.24 •
kr-vs-kp	66.30	67.74 ○	86.70	86.99
labor	79.58	57.47 •	84.63	83.79
lymph	74.40	73.44	73.28	73.20

Table 4: Percentage correct for OB1 full trees and the best tree from T1 and T2

Dataset	OB1	C5.0	C5.0B	1NN	5NN	NBayes	T2
anneal	1.08	0.94 •	0.95 •	0.94 •	0.92 •	1.03 •	0.41 •
autos	0.95	1.10 ○	1.34 ○	1.14 ○	1.06 ○	−0.72 •	0.68 •
balance-scale	0.50	0.29 •	0.34 •	0.21 •	0.36 •	0.46 •	0.12 •
breast-cancer	0.07	0.04 •	0.04 •	−0.02 •	0.08	−0.04 •	−0.05 •
breast-w	0.77	0.54 •	0.45 •	0.59 •	0.60 •	0.52 •	−0.08 •
colic	0.34	0.28 •	0.31 •	0.22 •	0.28 •	−0.29 •	0.24 •
credit-a	0.52	0.38 •	0.38 •	0.28 •	0.37 •	0.37 •	0.33 •
credit-g	0.12	0.07 •	0.10 •	−0.02 •	0.08	0.11	−0.03 •
diabetes	0.23	0.16 •	0.19 •	0.01 •	0.16 •	0.21 •	0.09 •
glass	0.93	0.80 •	0.71 •	0.37 •	0.89	0.88 •	0.37 •
heart-c	0.49	0.33 •	0.43 •	0.31 •	0.45	0.43 •	0.18 •
heart-h	0.48	0.33 •	0.46	0.24 •	0.44	0.26 •	0.24 •
heart-statlog	0.34	0.26 •	0.30	0.22 •	0.32	0.29 •	0.09 •
hepatitis	0.12	0.10	0.19 ○	0.13	0.21 ○	−0.13 •	0.02 •
hypothyroid	0.42	0.32 •	0.33 •	0.27 •	0.28 •	0.38 •	0.36 •
ionosphere	0.57	0.42 •	0.48 •	0.46 •	0.45 •	−0.98 •	0.40 •
iris	1.32	1.11 •	1.19 •	1.16 •	1.18 •	1.31	1.09 •
kr-vs-kp	0.84	0.71 •	0.69 •	0.50 •	0.52 •	0.58 •	0.43 •
labor	0.73	0.18 •	0.30 •	0.40 •	0.43 •	0.77 ○	0.25 •
lymph	0.67	0.37 •	0.50 •	0.45 •	0.51 •	0.68	0.22 •

Table 5: $S_f i$ for machine learning schemes, on discretised UCI datasets, relative to OB1 using hold-one-out weighting, naive Bayes models, with tree depth bound to 3 attributes

and T2 were not designed to produce probability distributions for each prediction, we use percentage correct rather than $S_f i$ for evaluation. The results are shown in Table 4. Where OB1 b1 performs significantly better than T1 this is postfixed with •, and where OB1 b1 performs significantly worse than T1 this is postfixed with ○ (similarly for T2 with OB1 b2).

The differences between T1 and OB1 b1 may not be considered large—T1 performs worse than OB1 b1 for seven datasets, and better for three. In contrast, T2 often performs significantly worse than OB1 b2 (9 out of the 20 datasets), and only significantly better twice.

OB1 was compared with C5.0 [11] (including boosted, denoted C5.0B), IB1 with 1 and 5 nearest neighbors [1], T2 [2], and a naive Bayes classifier [8], using default settings. OB1 settings are currently considered default: incorporating hold-one-out weighting, including naive Bayes models, and tree depth bound to three attributes.

Table 5 shows the $S_f i$ results, and Table 6 shows the percent correct results. Where a scheme performs significantly better than OB1 this is postfixed with ○, and where a scheme performs significantly worse than OB1 this is postfixed with •. In Table 5, the results are impressive. In only three datasets does any scheme capture significantly more domain information than OB1, in the majority of cases OB1 performs significantly better than the other schemes. The results in Table 6 are also impressive, with 19 cases where a scheme performs significantly better than OB1, and 65 cases where schemes perform significantly worse than OB1. The two schemes that have similar performance to OB1 are naive Bayes and boosted C5.0. Naive Bayes' good performance here indicates that in some cases it performs poorly at predicting class probabilities (and thus does not

Dataset	OB1	C5.0	C5.0B	1NN	5NN	NBayes	T2
anneal	97.27	98.36 ○	99.04 ○	98.03 ○	97.32	95.86 ●	76.73 ●
autos	66.97	68.91	77.49 ○	76.23 ○	59.66 ●	62.97 ●	65.89
balance-scale	76.28	75.75 ●	73.94 ●	71.58 ●	70.64 ●	76.60	67.13 ●
breast-cancer	70.85	69.98	70.27	69.07 ●	73.20 ○	72.12	67.05 ●
breast-w	96.29	94.87 ●	91.45 ●	96.10	96.67	97.28 ○	66.29 ●
colic	83.78	84.32	83.33	78.66 ●	80.00 ●	78.91 ●	81.31 ●
credit-a	86.21	85.43	85.43	79.97 ●	84.51 ●	86.08	82.81 ●
credit-g	73.05	71.01 ●	72.66	68.70 ●	71.80	74.00 ○	69.44 ●
diabetes	76.31	75.22 ●	75.60	68.93 ●	73.72 ●	76.15	73.95 ●
glass	64.77	62.90 ●	62.63 ●	57.48 ●	59.78 ●	64.60	60.66 ●
heart-c	80.62	76.35 ●	78.52 ●	76.82 ●	80.70	81.86 ○	72.12 ●
heart-h	81.80	78.32 ●	80.32 ●	75.04 ●	79.80 ●	82.32	78.20 ●
heart-statlog	80.48	78.65 ●	78.74	76.78 ●	80.00	81.43 ○	70.57 ●
hepatitis	78.87	80.68 ○	82.72 ○	81.43	85.36 ○	83.02 ○	77.58
hypothyroid	98.89	99.02 ○	99.20 ○	97.63 ●	96.94 ●	97.91 ●	98.43 ●
ionosphere	91.06	89.71	91.87	90.89	89.11 ●	89.11 ●	88.71 ●
iris	92.78	92.94	93.25	93.73 ○	93.02	92.78	92.24
kr-vs-kp	95.13	99.22 ○	99.54 ○	89.90 ●	94.90	87.72 ●	86.99 ●
labor	92.63	75.37 ●	79.37 ●	84.63 ●	86.74 ●	92.63	83.79 ●
lymph	81.60	74.24 ●	78.40 ●	78.64 ●	78.48 ●	82.48	73.20 ●

Table 6: Percentage correct for machine learning schemes, on discretised UCI datasets, relative to OB1 using hold-one-out weighting, naive Bayes models, with tree depth bound to 3 attributes

dominate the OB1 tree) even when it is able to accurately determine the most likely class. While boosted C5.0 produces deeper trees than OB1, it combines fewer alternative models, and these balance out to an extent, so the performance of OB1 and boosted C5.0 is similar.

7 Conclusions and future work

In this paper we have presented a new algorithm, OB1, which combines many possible decision trees by weighting their predictions. The basic algorithm can incorporate any scheme capable of inferring probability distributions. We described an implementation that includes decision trees, as well as naive Bayesian models.

The algorithm permits a single best tree with the highest weight to be selected from all the trees. However, experiments show that using this single tree never performs significantly better than the weighted sum and in many cases it performs much worse. Also when incorporating naive Bayesian models there are cases where OB1 performs better than either naive Bayes on its own or OB1 without naive Bayes models. This indicates that the weighted sum approach is effectively dealing with the problems of combining many models while at the same time avoiding overfitting.

OB1 was compared against a range of other techniques including both decision tree learners and instance based techniques. Using an information gain metric OB1 performs significantly better than any other technique on all of the tested data sets. Using accuracy as a comparison metric it performed significantly better than all algorithms except naive Bayes and boosted C5.0, which performed slightly worse than OB1. Overall these results indicate that OB1 is a strong robust learner. OB1 grows exponentially with the number of attributes and therefore on-going work will focus on pruning models with low weight to allow both the construction of deeper trees and also the handling of numeric attributes without discretisation. This is in addition to space saving achieved by sharing nodes. We envisage a system that will construct as much of the relevant model space as will fit within a user specified amount of memory.

8 Acknowledgements

The Waikato Machine Learning group, supported by the New Zealand Foundation for Research, Science, and Technology, has provided a stimulating environment for this research.

References

[1] D. W. Aha, D. Kibler, and M. K. Albert. Instance-based learning algorithms. *Machine Learning*, 6:37–66, 1991.

[2] Peter Auer, Robert C. Holte, and Wolfgang Maass. Theory and applications of agnostic PAC-learning with small decision trees. In Prieditis A. and Russell S., editors, *Proc. of the 12th International Conference on Machine Learning (ICML95)*, 1995.

[3] R.A. Baxter and J.J. Oliver. MDL and MML: Similarities and differences (introduction to minimum encoding inference—part III). Technical Report Technical Report 207, Department of Computer Science, Monash University, Australia, 1994.

[4] Wray Buntine. Classifiers: A theoretical and empirical study. In *Proc. of the 1991 International Joint Conference on Artificial Intelligence*, 1991.

[5] J. Cleary, S. Legg, and I. H. Witten. An MDL estimate of the significance of rules. In *Proc. of the Information, Statistics and Induction in Science Conference*, pages 43–53, Melbourne, Australia, 1996.

[6] Usama M. Fayyad and Keki B. Irani. On the handling of continuous-valued attributes in decision tree generation. *Machine Learning*, 8:87–102, 1992.

[7] G. Holmes, A. Donkin, and I. H. Witten. WEKA: A machine learning workbench. In *Proc. of the Second Australia and New Zealand Conference on Intelligent Information Systems*, Brisbane, Australia, 1994. [webpage at http://www.cs.waikato.ac.nz/~ml/].

[8] P. Langley, W. Iba, and K. Thompson. An analysis of Bayesian classifiers. In *Proc. of the Tenth National Conference on Artificial Intelligence*, pages 223–228, 1992.

[9] C.J. Merz and P.M. Murphy. *UCI Repository of Machine Learning Data-Bases*. University of California, Dept. of Information and Computer Science, Irvine, CA, 1996.

[10] W.J. Oates. *The Stoic and Epicurean Philosophers: The Complete Extant Writings of Epicurus, Epictetus, Lucretius, Marcus Aurelius*. Random House, New York, 1957.

[11] J. Ross Quinlan. *C4.5: Programs for Machine Learning*. Morgan Kaufmann, San Mateo, CA, 1994.

[12] R.E. Schapire, Y. Freund, P. Bartlett, and Wee Sun Lee. Boosting the margin: A new explanation for the effectiveness of voting methods. In *Proc. of the 14th International Conference on Machine Learning (ICML97)*, pages 322–330, 1997.

[13] P.A.J Volf. Deriving MDL-decision trees using the context maximizing algorithm. Master's thesis, Department of Electrical Engineering, Eindhoven University of Technology, 1994.

[14] Frans M. J. Willems, Yuri M. Shtarkov, and Tjalling J. Tjalkens. The context-tree weighting method: Basic properties. *IEEE Transactions on Information Theory*, 41(3):653–664, May 1995.

A Case Study of Strategic Induction: the Roman Numerals Data Set

David McSherry

School of Information and Software Engineering, University of Ulster, Coleraine BT52 1SA, Northern Ireland

Abstract

Strategist is an algorithm for decision-tree induction in which attribute selection is based on the evidence-gathering strategies used by doctors. The advantage is that in problem-solving applications of the induced decision tree, the relevance of a selected attribute can be explained in strategic terms. However, as we show in this paper, Strategist's policy of always giving priority to confirming the likeliest outcome class in the current subset of the data set can sometimes lead to the selection of attributes of limited discriminating power. We present a new version of Strategist in which a tactical approach to the selection of a target outcome class reduces its susceptibility to this problem. A new data set for the classification of Roman numbers as correct or incorrect provides a case study of strategic induction in which we examine the algorithm's behaviour with and without this refinement. The new algorithm tends to produce smaller decision trees than its predecessor and is shown to be comparable in accuracy to ID3 on certain data sets.

1   Introduction

There is general agreement that to be acceptable to users, intelligent systems must be able to explain their reasoning [1-3]. For example, a rule-based expert system can explain the relevance of any question it asks the user by showing the goal it is trying to prove and the rule it is attempting to fire. Often induced by machine-learning algorithms like ID3 [4], decision trees are increasingly used instead of rules to guide test selection in intelligent systems, for example in many applications of case-based reasoning [5]. However, problem-solving behaviour based on a decision tree in which attribute selection is based on information-theoretic measures can be difficult to explain.

Previously we have argued that for problem-solving behaviour based on an induced decision tree to be easily explained, the induction process should reflect the problem-solving strategies of a domain expert. It was this aim that motivated the development of Strategist [6], an algorithm for induction of decision trees in which attribute selection is based on the evidence-gathering strategies used by doctors, such as confirming a target diagnosis or eliminating a competing diagnosis [7]. The algorithm is *goal driven* in that the attribute it selects at any stage of the induction process depends on its target outcome class in the current subset of the data set and the evidence-gathering strategy, such as confirming the target outcome class, it is currently pursuing. It also differs from most decision-tree algorithms in its multiple-strategy approach to attribute selection. Instead of a single criterion like *information gain* in ID3, attribute selection in Strategist is based on a set of alternative strategies which are applied in order of priority.

Strategist's main advantage is that in problem-solving applications of the induced decision tree, the relevance of a selected attribute (or test) can be explained in strategic terms [6]. The algorithm is the basis of inductive retrieval in *CBR Strategist*, a prototype environment for interactive case-based reasoning in trouble-shooting and help-desk applications with support for mixed-initiative dialogue, explanation of reasoning, visual feedback on the impact of reported evidence, and sensitivity analysis [8].

In this paper, we examine a potential problem associated with Strategist's policy of always giving priority to confirming the likeliest outcome class in the current subset of the data set. We show that this can sometimes lead to the selection of attributes of limited discriminating power, which in turn may affect the size and accuracy of the induced decision tree. We present a new version of Strategist in which a tactical approach to the selection of a target outcome class reduces its susceptibility to this problem. The classification of Roman numbers as correct or incorrect provides a case study of strategic induction in which we examine Strategist's behaviour with and without this refinement and in comparison with ID3.

In Section 2, we introduce a data set for the classification of Roman numbers of up to three numerals in length. In Section 3, we describe the evidence-gathering strategies used in Strategist and the behaviour produced when the algorithm is applied to the Roman Numerals data set. In Section 4, we present Strategist-2, the new version of Strategist, and the results of its evaluation on the Roman Numerals and other data sets. In Section 5, we present a problem-solving consultation driven by Strategist-2 in lazy-learning mode, showing its ability to explain its reasoning and often to reach a conclusion when relevant data are missing.

2 The Roman Numerals Data Set

The Roman numerals M = 1000, D = 500, C = 100, L = 50, X = 5, V = 5 and I = 1 are still in everyday use, for example on clock faces and in copyright notices. In lower case, they are often used to label the items in a list. When the numerals are written in descending order, their collective meaning is unambiguous e.g.

$$MDCLXVI = 1000 + 500 + 100 + 50 + 10 + 5 + 1 = 1666$$

However, the interpretation of Roman numbers is complicated by the *subtractive* principle, according to which a smaller numeral before a larger one means that the smaller is to be subtracted from the larger e.g.

$$MCMXCIX = 1000 + (1000 - 100) + (100 - 10) + (10 - 1) = 1999$$

Algorithm convert(a)

```
if a ≥ 1000 then r := 'M' + convert(a - 1000)
 else if a ≥ 900 then r := 'CM' + convert(a - 900)
  else if a ≥ 500 then r := 'D' + convert(a - 500)
   else if a ≥ 400 then r := 'CD' + convert(a - 400)
    else if a ≥ 100 then r := 'C' + convert(a - 100)
     else if a ≥ 90 then r := 'XC' + convert(a - 90)
      else if a ≥ 50 then r := 'L' + convert(a - 50)
       else if a ≥ 40 then r := 'XL' + convert(a - 40)
        else if a ≥ 10 then r := 'X' + convert(a - 10)
         else if a ≥ 9 then r := 'IX' + convert(a - 9)
          else if a ≥ 5 then r := 'V' + convert(a - 5)
           else if a ≥ 4 then r := 'IV' + convert(a - 4)
            else if a ≥ 1 then r := 'I' + convert(a - 1)
             else r = ' '
```

Figure 1. Converting an Arabic number to an equivalent Roman number

Though widely used today, the subtractive principle was seldom adhered to by the Romans [9], who would often write VIIII instead of IX, or DCCCC instead of CM. However, noting that any departure from the subtractive principle produces a Roman number with at least 4 numerals, we will avoid this issue by focusing on Roman numbers of up to three numerals in length. Of the 399 possible permutations of one, two or three Roman numerals, most are illegal.

One convention that appears to be generally observed when an Arabic number is converted to an equivalent Roman number is that the thousands are dealt with first, then the hundreds, then the tens and finally the units [10]. According to this convention, for example, it is incorrect to write IM for 999, since:

$$999 = 900 + 90 + 9 = CMXCIX$$

or a much longer number if the subtractive principle is not applied. Similarly, IL, IC and ID are incorrect.

2.1 Converting an Arabic Number to a Roman Number

The algorithm shown in Figure 1 converts a given Arabic number $a \geq 1$ to an equivalent Roman number r. It follows the thousands-hundreds-tens-units convention and uses the subtractive principle at every opportunity, thus producing a legal representation of the Arabic number of shortest possible length.

2.2 Creating the Roman Numerals Data Set

Each example in the Roman Numerals data set, with *legal* or *illegal* as the associated outcome class, represents one of the 399 permutations of the Roman numerals of length less than 4. To identify the legal Roman numbers in the data

Table 1. Attributes in the Roman Numerals data set and frequencies of their values

Attribute		legal		illegal	
		true	false	true	false
A1	numerals are in descending order	95	36	24	244
A2	V, L or D appears more than once	0	131	60	208
A3	I appears before L, C, D or M	0	131	68	200
A4	V appears before V, X, L, C, D or M	0	131	90	178
A5	X appears before D or M	0	131	38	230
A6	L appears before L, C, D or M	0	131	68	200
A7	D appears before D or M	0	131	38	230
A8	third of 3 numerals is larger than first	0	131	147	121
A9	two matching numerals are separated by a larger numeral	0	131	21	247

set, the conversion algorithm was applied to all the Arabic numbers from 1 to 3,000. Note that no Arabic number greater than 3,000 can be represented by fewer than four of the seven numerals in use today, since for example:

$$3,001 = MMMI$$

It follows that the Roman numbers with 1, 2 or 3 numerals produced by the algorithm are the *only* legal Roman numbers with 1, 2 or 3 numerals. Of the 399 examples in the data set, 131 were identified as legal Roman numbers by this method and the remainder as illegal.

Nine of the ten attributes in the data set, A1-A10, are listed in Table 1. The frequencies of their values in the legal and illegal subsets are also shown. For example, A1 is the proposition that the numerals are in (not necessarily strictly) descending order. A3 is the proposition that I appears *anywhere* before L, C, D or M and is true for none of the 131 legal examples in the data set. Similar

Table 2. Attribute A10

no. of numerals	legal	illegal
one	7	0
two	31	18
three	93	250

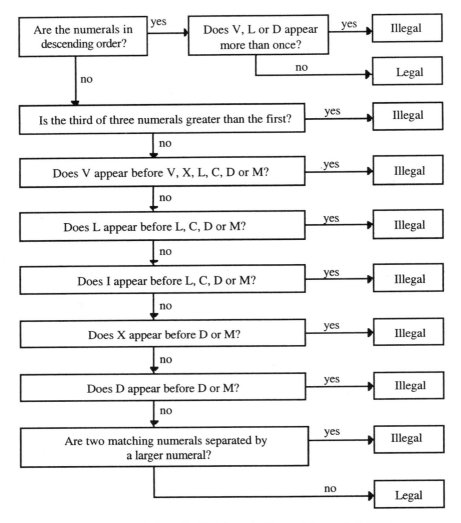

Figure 2. Tree induced by ID3 from the Roman Numerals data set

frequencies for A10 (no. of numerals), are shown in Table 2. Other relevant attributes can of course be identified, but the ten described here are more than adequate for correct classification of every example in the data set. The assignment of values of the ten attributes to each of the 399 examples was automated to ensure the absence of noise in the data set.

Figure 2 shows the decision tree induced by ID3, with attribute selection based on information gain, from the Roman Numerals data set. The only attribute that does not appear in the tree is A10. Thus in spite of its known preference for attributes that have more values, which led to the replacement of information gain by *gain ratio* in later versions [4], ID3 has ignored the only non-binary attribute in the data set.

3 Attribute Selection in Strategist

Attribute selection in Strategist is based on a collection of five strategies such as confirming a target outcome class or eliminating the likeliest alternative outcome class [6]. The attribute selected by Strategist at any stage depends on its target outcome class in the current subset of the data set and the evidence-gathering strategy, such as confirming the target outcome class, it is currently pursuing. Continually revised as the data set is partitioned, the target outcome class is the one that is most likely in the current subset of the data set. In order of priority, the algorithm's four main evidence-gathering strategies are:

CONFIRM : confirm the target outcome class

ELIMINATE : eliminate the likeliest alternative outcome class

VALIDATE : increase the probability of the target outcome class

OPPOSE : decrease the probability of the likeliest alternative outcome class

A fifth strategy called DISCRIMINATE (increase the probability of the target outcome class *relative* to the likeliest alternative outcome class) is available but seldom needed in practice. In a two-class induction task, CONFIRM and VALIDATE are the only strategies required, since for example the likeliest alternative outcome class can be eliminated only by confirming the target outcome class.

An attribute will support the CONFIRM strategy if, in the current subset of the data set, one of its values occurs only in the target outcome class. Initially in the Roman Numerals data set, the target outcome class, with a probability of 0.67, is ILLEGAL. Since A2 has a value (true) that occurs only in ILLEGAL, this attribute will support the CONFIRM strategy. Similarly, any of the attributes A3-A9 will support the CONFIRM strategy. An attribute will support the VALIDATE strategy if, in the current subset of the data set, one of its values is more likely in the target outcome class than in any alternative outcome class. With ILLEGAL as the target outcome class before the Roman Numerals data set is partitioned, A1 will support the VALIDATE strategy since $p(A1 = \text{false} \mid \text{ILLEGAL}) = 0.91$, while $p(A1 = \text{false} \mid \text{LEGAL}) = 0.27$.

3.1 Selecting the Most Useful Attribute

If more than one attribute is available to support the CONFIRM strategy, the attribute selected is the one whose *expected eliminating power* in favour of the target outcome class is greatest. In a given subset S of the data set, the eliminating power of an attribute value E, denoted by $elim(E)$, is the sum of the probabilities of the outcome classes surviving in S which are eliminated by E, or zero if none is eliminated. The expected eliminating power in S of an attribute A with values v_1, $v_2,..., v_n$, in favour of a target outcome class C_t, is:

$$\gamma(A, C_t) = \sum_{i=1}^{n} p(A = v_i \mid C_t) \, elim(A = v_i)$$

Unlike the expected eliminating power of an attribute, the eliminating power of an attribute value is independent of the target outcome class. Since A8 is true for none of the legal examples in the Roman Numerals data set, $elim(A8 = true) = 0.33$. On the other hand, neither outcome class is eliminated if A8 is false, so $elim(A8 = false) = 0$. Initially, the expected eliminating power of A8 in favour of ILLEGAL is therefore:

$$\gamma(A8, ILLEGAL) = p(A8 = true \mid ILLEGAL) \times 0.33 = 0.18$$

Expected eliminating power is also the measure of attribute usefulness in the ELIMINATE strategy, but a different measure is used in the VALIDATE, OPPOSE and DISCRIMINATE strategies. In a given subset S of the data set, the *expected weight of evidence* of an attribute A with values $v_1, v_2,..., v_n$, in favour of a target outcome class C_t, is:

$$\psi(A, C_t) = \sum_{i=1}^{n} \frac{p(A = v_i \mid C_t)^2}{p(A = v_i \mid C_a)}$$

where C_a is the outcome class which is the likeliest alternative to C_t in S. If the strategy of highest priority which can be applied is VALIDATE, OPPOSE or DISCRIMINATE, and two or more attributes are available to support it, then the attribute selected is the one for which $\psi(A, C_t)$ is greatest. Initially in the Roman Numerals data set, the expected weight of evidence of A1 in favour of ILLEGAL is:

$$\psi(A1, ILLEGAL) = \frac{0.09^2}{0.73} + \frac{0.91^2}{0.27} = 3.08$$

While an expected weight of evidence can never be less than one [11], it can easily be shown that $0 \le \gamma(A, C_t) < 1$ for any attribute A and target outcome class C_t.

3.2 The Strategist Tree

The decision tree induced by Strategist from the Roman Numerals data set is shown in Figure 3. With 36 nodes, the Strategist tree is much larger than the ID3 tree, which has only 19 nodes. As we now show, the difference in size of the induced trees can be attributed to Strategist's policy of always giving priority to confirming the likeliest outcome class in the current subset of the data set. With ILLEGAL initially the target outcome class, there is no shortage of attributes to support the CONFIRM strategy. Of the 8 attributes (A2-A9) with a value that will confirm ILLEGAL, the one whose expected eliminating power in favour of ILLEGAL is greatest is A8. However, in the subset of the data set for which A8 = false, the target outcome class changes to LEGAL as it is now the likeliest outcome class. Frequencies of the values of A1, A2 and A10 in this subset are shown in Table 3.

As the only attribute that will now support the CONFIRM strategy, A10 is given priority over all other attributes even though its expected eliminating power in favour of LEGAL, the target outcome class, is close to the minimum value:

$$\gamma(A10, LEGAL) = p(A10 = one \mid LEGAL) \times p(ILLEGAL) = 0.05 \times 0.48 = 0.02$$

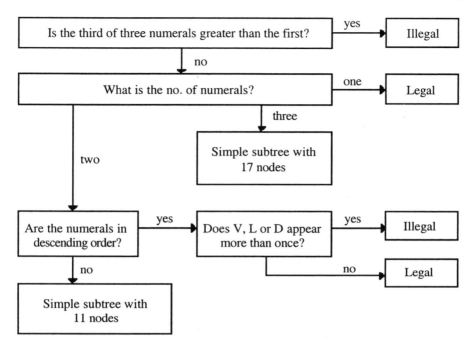

Figure 3. Tree induced by Strategist from the Roman Numerals data set

As previously noted, A10 is the only one of the ten available attributes not to appear in the ID3 tree. Though ignored at this stage by Strategist, A1 would be a reasonably strong supporter of the VALIDATE strategy since from Table 3:

$$\psi(A1, \text{LEGAL}) = \frac{0.73^2}{0.20} + \frac{0.27^2}{0.80} = 2.76$$

Thus by always giving priority to attributes that support the CONFIRM strategy, Strategist is sometimes forced to select attributes that are only weak supporters of the CONFIRM strategy when strong supporters of an alternative strategy are available. One reason for giving priority to the CONFIRM strategy is that the measure of attribute usefulness used in most of the other strategies (expected weight of evidence) can be applied only to attributes that do not support the CONFIRM strategy. The problem cannot therefore be solved simply by giving priority to the CONFIRM strategy only when supported by an attribute with an expected eliminating power that exceeds a predetermined threshold.

However, an important point to note is that Strategist's choice of attributes to support the CONFIRM strategy is restricted by its policy of always selecting the likeliest outcome class as the target outcome class. For example, if ILLEGAL were instead the target outcome class in the subset with A8 = false, several attributes would be available to support the CONFIRM strategy. One such attribute is A2. From Table 3, its expected eliminating power in favour of ILLEGAL is:

$$\gamma(A2, \text{ILLEGAL}) = p(A2 = \text{true} \mid \text{ILLEGAL}) \times p(\text{LEGAL}) = 0.35 \times 0.52 = 0.18$$

Table 3. Frequencies of the values of A1, A2 and A10 in the subset of the Roman Numerals data set with A8 = false

		legal	illegal
A1	(numerals in descending order)		
	true	95	24
	false	36	97
A2	(V, L or D appears more than once)		
	true	0	42
	false	131	79
A10	(no. of numerals)		
	one	7	0
	two	31	18
	three	93	103

which is nine times the expected eliminating power of A10 in favour LEGAL in the same subset. In the following section, we present a new version of Strategist in which a tactical approach to the selection of a target outcome class helps to increase the availability of attributes to support the evidence-gathering strategies of higher priority.

4   Attribute Selection in Strategist-2

Strategist's approach to attribute selection is first to select the likeliest outcome class as the target outcome class, then the evidence-gathering strategy of highest priority that is supported by at least one attribute, and finally the attribute that most strongly supports the selected strategy. Strategist-2 continues to prioritise its attribute-selection strategies in the same order as its predecessor, with CONFIRM given first priority as before. The difference is that either of the *two* most likely outcome classes in the current subset of the data set may now be selected as the target outcome class.

If C_1 and C_2 are the two most likely outcome classes, and at least one attribute has a value that confirms C_1 or C_2, then Strategist-2 chooses CONFIRM as its evidence-gathering strategy. It then identifies the outcome class C_t and attribute A for which $\gamma(A,C_t)$ is maximum, where $C_t \in \{C_1, C_2\}$, and A is an attribute with a value that confirms C_t. Finally, it selects C_t as the target outcome class and A as the attribute to partition the current subset of the data set. If no attribute has a value that confirms C_1 or C_2, then the CONFIRM strategy cannot be supported with C_1 or C_2 as the target outcome class. In this case, Strategist-2 resorts to the alternative strategy of highest priority that is supported by at least one attribute. With VALIDATE as the only alternative strategy in a two-class induction task, it

Step 1. Identify the two most likely outcome classes C_1 and C_2 in the current subset of the data set

Step 2. Select the evidence-gathering strategy of highest priority that is supported by at least one attribute with either C_1 or C_2 as the target outcome class

Step 3. Identify the outcome class C_t and attribute A for which the measure of attribute usefulness in the selected strategy is maximum, where $C_t \in \{C_1, C_2\}$ and A is an attribute that supports the selected strategy with C_t as the target outcome class

Step 4. Select C_t as the target outcome class and A as the attribute to partition the current subset of the data set

Figure 4. Selection of a target outcome class, evidence-gathering strategy, and most useful attribute in Strategist-2

selects the outcome class C_t and attribute A for which $\psi(A, C_t)$ is maximum, where $C_t \in \{C_1, C_2\}$. The general approach when there are more than two evidence-gathering strategies from which to choose is outlined in Figure 4.

The decision tree induced by Strategist-2 from the Roman Numerals data set, shown in Figure 5, is much smaller than the Strategist tree. At no point in the induction process is Strategist-2 forced to abandon the CONFIRM strategy. The target outcome class, initially ILLEGAL, remains unchanged at the second question node even though LEGAL is now the likeliest outcome class. This is the first point at which its behaviour differs from its predecessor's, resulting in the selection of an attribute that provides much stronger support for the CONFIRM strategy than the one selected by Strategist. At the third question node, the target outcome class changes to LEGAL because the expected eliminating power of A1 in favour of LEGAL exceeds the expected eliminating power of any attribute in favour of ILLEGAL. However, the target outcome class at the fourth question node is again ILLEGAL and remains the same at the rest of the question nodes. Though having the same number of nodes, and using the same attributes, the Strategist-2 tree is simpler in structure than the ID3 tree.

We now present the results of an empirical evaluation of Strategist-2 in comparison with Strategist and ID3 on the Roman Numerals data set and five data sets from the UCI Machine Learning Repository [12]. As currently implemented, neither Strategist-2 nor its predecessor can handle noise, missing values in the training set, or continuous attributes. For this reason, the selected data sets (Table 4) are noise free and have no continuous attributes or missing values. Though relatively small in size, Contact Lenses and Soybean Small were included as examples of data sets with 3 and 4 outcome classes respectively. Monks-1, Voting Records and Tic-Tac-Toe all have 2 outcome classes with majority class probabilities of 50%, 61% and 65% respectively. Each data set was randomly partitioned into training and testing sets containing 70% and 30% respectively of the instances in the full data set. Performance measures of interest were predictive

58

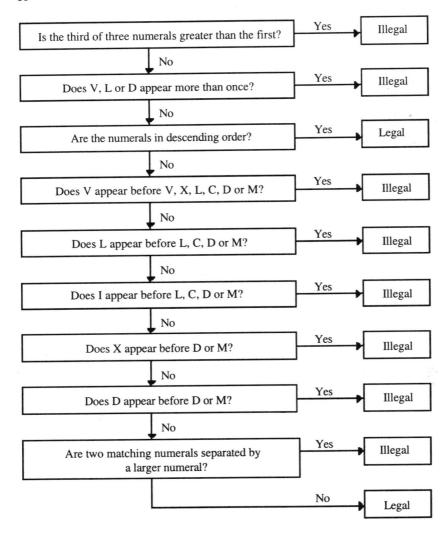

Figure 5. Tree induced by Strategist-2 from the Roman Numerals data set

accuracy and size of the induced decision trees. Average accuracy over 25 repeated trials is shown in Table 4. Average numbers of nodes in the induced trees are shown in brackets. Strategist-2 is comparable in accuracy to Strategist on the example data sets, though was outperformed by ID3 on three, with 3% on Contact Lenses the largest difference in accuracy. Though well known for its tendency to produce small decision trees [13], ID3's advantage over Strategist-2 in this respect is apparent only on Monks-1, Voting Records and Tic-Tac-Toe, with 4% the largest reduction in average number of nodes. However, the decision trees induced by Strategist-2 from Roman Numerals, Contact Lenses, Voting Records, and Tic-Tac-Toe were smaller on average than those induced by Strategist by up to 47%.

Table 4. Predictive accuracy (%) and size of induced classifiers

Data Set	ID3		Strategist-2		Strategist	
Roman Numerals	100	(19)	100	(18)	99	(34)
Contact Lenses	72	(11)	69	(11)	70	(12)
Soybean Small	93	(10)	94	(9)	94	(9)
Monks-1	94	(98)	94	(100)	94	(100)
Voting Records	95	(53)	94	(55)	93	(67)
Tic-Tac-Toe	85	(265)	84	(274)	84	(289)

5 Explanation of Reasoning in Strategist-2

We now present a problem-solving consultation driven by Strategist-2 in lazy-learning mode. In this mode, an explicit decision tree is not constructed by Strategist-2. Instead, it uses a problem case presented by the user to induce a single *path* in a conceptual decision tree. Another difference is that instead of creating a subset of the data set for each value of a selected attribute, Strategist-2 now asks the user for the value of the selected attribute and forms a single subset of the data set consisting of examples for which the attribute's value is the same as the reported value. As in other algorithms that run in lazy-learning mode [14-16], learning is incremental, in that immediate use of new examples can be made without restructuring an explicit decision tree. Freedom from commitment to an explicit decision tree also means that the algorithm can often tolerate missing data at problem-solving time simply by selecting the next best attribute when the value of the most useful attribute at a given node is unknown.

Before answering a question, the user can ask why it is relevant. The explanation provided by Strategist-2 depends on its target outcome class in the current subset of the data set and the evidence-gathering strategy it is currently pursuing. Where there are only two outcome classes in the data set, there are at most two distinct strategies to be explained. In the CONFIRM strategy, the user is shown the value of the selected attribute that will confirm the target outcome class, while in the VALIDATE strategy the user is shown the value of the selected attribute that will increase the probability of the target outcome class.

A problem-solving consultation based on the Roman Numerals data set is shown in Figure 6. As in an expert system, the user can answer *unknown* to any question. In this case, Strategist-2 selects the next most useful attribute, changing its target outcome class if necessary (and possible) to avoid using an evidence-gathering strategy of lower priority. This feature is illustrated in the example consultation. When the user first answers unknown, Strategist-2 changes its target outcome class to ILLEGAL, a tactic which enables it to continue pursuing the CONFIRM strategy. In fact, it is never forced to abandon this strategy in the example consultation. A positive answer to any of the next 5 questions would enable it to confirm ILLEGAL whether or not the numerals are in descending order.

Strategist-2:	The target outcome class is ILLEGAL. Is the third of three numerals greater than the first?
User:	why
Strategist-2:	Because if the third of three numerals is greater than the first this will confirm ILLEGAL. Is the third of three numerals greater than the first?
User:	no
Strategist-2:	Does V, L or D appear more than once?
User:	no
Strategist-2:	The target outcome class is LEGAL. Are the numerals in descending order?
User:	why
Strategist-2:	Because if the numerals are in descending order, this will confirm LEGAL. Are the numerals in descending order?
User:	unknown
Strategist-2:	The target outcome class is ILLEGAL. Does V appear before V, X, L, C, D or M?
User:	why
Strategist-2:	Because if V appears before V, X, L, C, D or M, this will confirm ILLEGAL. Does V appear before V, X, L, C, D or M?
User:	no
Strategist-2:	Does L appear before L, C, D or M?
User:	no
Strategist-2:	Does I appear before L, C, D or M?
User:	no
Strategist-2:	Does X appear before D or M?
User:	no
Strategist-2:	Does D appear before D or M?
User:	no
Strategist-2:	Are two matching numerals separated by a larger numeral?
User:	unknown
Strategist-2:	The target outcome class is LEGAL. What is the number of numerals?
User:	why
Strategist-2:	Because if the number of numerals is one or two, this will confirm LEGAL. What is the number of numerals?
User:	two
Strategist-2:	Have confirmed LEGAL

Figure 6. A problem-solving consultation driven by Strategist-2

On the second occasion when the user answers unknown, Strategist-2 has used all but one of the attributes in the data set, namely the no. of numerals. By changing its target outcome class to LEGAL, Strategist-2 can once again use the CONFIRM strategy, and this time the user's response enables it to confirm the target outcome class. An important point to note is that missing data at problem-solving time may necessitate the use of an attribute that was not required in the construction of an explicit decision tree, which usually makes no provision for missing data.

6 Conclusions

A new data set for the classification of Roman numbers has provided a case study of strategic induction which shows that always giving priority to confirming the likeliest outcome class can sometimes lead to the selection of attributes of limited discriminating power in Strategist. We have presented a new version of Strategist in which a tactical approach to the selection of a target outcome class reduces its susceptibility to this problem. Our results show that Strategist-2 tends to produce smaller decision trees than Strategist and is comparable in accuracy to ID3 on certain data sets. In lazy-learning mode, Strategist-2 shares with its predecessor the ability to explain its reasoning in strategic terms. Its use as a basis for question selection in intelligent systems may therefore help to increase their acceptability to users without significant loss of accuracy.

References

1. Breslow L, Aha D. Simplifying decision trees : a survey. Knowledge Engineering Review 1997; 12:1-40
2. Leake D. CBR in context : the present and future. In: Leake D (ed) Case-based reasoning: experiences, lessons & future directions. AAAI Press/MIT Press, 1996
3. Southwick R. Explaining reasoning: an overview of explanation in knowledge-based systems. Knowledge Engineering Review 1991; 6:1-19
4. Quinlan J. Induction of decision trees. Machine Learning 1986; 1:81-106
5. Watson I. Applying Case-based reasoning: techniques for enterprise systems. Morgan Kaufmann, San Francisco, 1997
6. McSherry D. Strategic induction of decision trees. Knowledge-Based Systems 1999; 12: 269-275
7. Elstein A, Schulman L, Sprafka S. Medical problem solving: an analysis of clinical reasoning. Harvard University Press, Cambridge, MA, 1978
8. McSherry D. Interactive case-based reasoning in sequential diagnosis. Applied Intelligence. In press
9. Conway J, Guy R. The book of numbers. Springer-Verlag, New York, 1996
10. The world book encyclopaedia. World Book International, London, 1996
11. McSherry D. Hypothetico-deductive data mining. Applied Stochastic Models and Data Analysis 1998; 13: 415-422
12. Blake C, Merz C. UCI Repository of Machine Learning Databases [http://www.ics.uci.edu/~ mlearn/MLRepository.html]. Irvine, CA: University of California, Department of Information and Computer Science, 1998
13. Mitchell T. Machine learning. McGraw-Hill, 1997
14. Friedman J, Kohavi R, Yun Y. Lazy Decision Trees. Proceedings of the Thirteenth National Conference on Artificial Intelligence, Portland, Oregon, August 1996, 717-724
15. McSherry D. Integrating machine learning, problem solving and explanation. Proceedings of ES95, Cambridge, England, December 1995, 145-157
16. Smyth B, Cunningham P. A comparison of incremental case-based reasoning and inductive learning. Proceedings of the Second European Workshop on Case-Based Reasoning, Chantilly, France, November 1994, 151-164

Selecting Optimal Split-Functions for Large Datasets*

Kilian Stoffel

IIUN, University of Neuchâtel

Pierre-à-Mazel 7

CH-2000 Neuchâtel (Switzerland)

Kilian.Stoffel@seco.unine.ch

Laura E. Raileanu

IIUN, University of Neuchâtel

Pierre-à-Mazel 7

CH-2000 Neuchâtel (Switzerland)

Laura.Raileanu@seco.unine.ch

Abstract

Decision tree induction has become one of the most popular methods for classification and prediction. The key step in the process of inferring decision trees is finding the right criteria for splitting the training set into smaller and smaller subsets so that, ideally, all elements of a subset finally belong to one class. These split criteria can be defined in different ways (e.g. minimizing impurity of a subset, or minimizing entropy in a subset), and therefore they emphasize different properties of the inferred tree, such as size or classification accuracy. In this paper we analyze if the split functions introduced in a statistical and machine learning context are also well suited for a KDD context. We selected two well known split functions, namely Gini Index (CART) and Information Gain (C4.5) and introduced our own family of split functions and tested them on 9,000 data sets of different sizes (from 200 to 20,000 tuples). The tests have shown that the two popular functions are very sensitive to the variation of the training set sizes and therefore the quality of the inferred trees is highly dependent on the training set size. At the same time however, we were able to show that the simplest members of the introduced family of split functions behave in a very predictable way and, furthermore, the created trees were superior to the trees inferred using the Gini Index or the Information Gain based on our evaluation criteria.

---

*This work was supported by grant number 2100-056986.99 from the Swiss National Science Foundation.

1   Introduction

Decision tree and decision rule induction has become a very popular method for classification and prediction in KDD. Breiman's CART [2] and Quinlans's C4.5 [8] are among the most popular decision tree systems. These systems were created to be used in a machine learning, respectively in a statistical context. Very often, exactly the same systems are applied in a KDD context. However, this approach is not as straight forward as one might conclude on a first glance. E.g. we realized that depending on the hardware and on the operating system, C4.5 does not induce identical decision trees for the same large database. A more thorough analysis of the underling inference algorithms shows why these differences can occur. The split function applied by C4.5 is using numerical unstable algorithms. This instability is mainly related to the size of the training data set. The larger the data set the higher is the probability to get unstable behavior of the split function. An obvious alternative to C4.5's split function would be the split function used by CART, but there are many more (Twoing Rule [2], Max Minority [4], Sum Minority [4], Sum of Variances [10], and MML [11]). A large number of comparative studies of these functions were conducted (e.g. [1, 7, 5, 3]), but most of them were not really conclusive, and more importantly, their main focus was not on the behavior of these functions in a KDD environment. The size of the underlying data set was not taken into consideration. In this paper we will study the structure and the inference capabilities of decision trees induced from data sets of various sizes. We did not restrict ourselves to a given set of split functions, but we will analyze a whole family of split functions which ranges from Gini Index (used by CART) to Information Gain (used by C4.5). This approach is based on the observation that the Gini Index function is identical to the first term of the Taylor development of the Information Gain function. In contrast to the above cited literature we will not only prospect the behavior of the two extrema (Information Gain and Gini Index), but also the intermediate terms. We will specially analyze their behavior as they are applied to a sequence of databases of growing size. The remainder of this paper is structured in the following way. The second section introduces the standard split functions. In the third section we introduce our own family of split functions. The fourth section describes the experimental setup and the fifth section presents the results, and then we conclude.

2   Analysis of Information Gain and Gini Index

In this section we will present a detailed analysis of the Gini Index and Information Gain function in order to evaluate their applicability in a KDD context. First, we have to introduce some notations and definitions. Let $\mathcal{L}$ be a learning sample of data, $\mathcal{L} = \{(\mathbf{x}_1, c_1), \ldots, (\mathbf{x}_{\|\mathcal{L}\|}, c_J)\}$, $\|\mathcal{L}\|$ representing the number of objects in $\mathcal{L}$, $\forall i = 1, \ldots, \|\mathcal{L}\|$, $\mathbf{x}_i$ being a measurement vector, $\mathbf{x}_i \in \mathcal{X}$, and $\mathcal{X}$ being the measurement space. $\forall i = 1, \ldots, J$, $c_i \in \mathcal{C}$, where $\mathcal{C} = \{\rfloor_\infty, \rfloor_\in, \ldots, \rfloor_\mathcal{J}\}$ is the set of classes. The prior probability that an object belongs to a given class c_i, is given by $p(c_i) = \frac{\|c_i\|}{\|\mathcal{L}\|}$. Given a test T, with n possible outcomes, t_i denotes the set of the objects in $\mathcal{L}$ having the outcome i. The probability that the test T has the outcome i is estimated by $p(t_i) = \frac{\|t_i\|}{\|\mathcal{L}\|}$. We note by $\|c_i, t_j\|$ the number of objects of $\mathcal{L}$ that lies in the class c_i and have the outcome j for the test T, the probability that an object lies in c_i and has the outcome j is $p(c_i, t_j) = \frac{\|c_i, t_j\|}{\|\mathcal{L}\|}$. The conditional probability $p(c_i|t_j)$ that an object lies in the class c_i, under the condition that the test T has the outcome t_j, is estimated by $\frac{p(c_i, t_j)}{p(t_j)}$. Obviously we have: $\sum_{i=1}^{k} p(c_i) = 1$, $\sum_{i=1}^{k} p(c_i|t_j) = 1$, $\forall j = 1, \ldots, n$ and $p(c_i), p(c_i|t_j), p(t_i) \in [0, 1]$ $\forall j = 1, \ldots, n$, and $\forall i = 1, \ldots, k$. The probabilities are related by the Bayes formula: $p(c_i|t_j) = \frac{p(c_i, t_j)}{p(t_j)}$. The fundamental idea in the construction of a tree is to select each split of a subset so that the data in each of the descendent subsets are "purer" than the data in the parent subset. These splits are based on the notion of impurity function. An impurity function is a function ϕ defined on the set of all k-tuples of numbers $(p(c_1), p(c_2), \ldots, p(c_k))$ satisfying $p(c_i) \geq 0$, $\forall i = 1, \ldots, k$ and $\sum_{i=1}^{k} p(c_i) = 1$ with the following properties: ϕ is a maximum only at the point $(\frac{1}{k}, \frac{1}{k}, \ldots, \frac{1}{k})$, ϕ achieves its minimum at the points $(1, 0, \ldots, 0), (0, 1, \ldots, 0), \ldots, (0, 0, \ldots, 1)$, and ϕ is a symmetric function of $(p(c_1), p(c_2), \ldots, p(c_k))$. The Gini Index introduced by Breiman et al. [2] is based on this concept. Given an impurity function ϕ, the impurity measure $i(t)$ of the node t is defined by: $i(t) = \phi(p(c_1|t), p(c_2|t), \ldots, p(c_k|t))$. The goodness of a split s for which we applied a test T is defined by: $\Delta i(s, t_j) = i(t) - \sum_{i=1}^{k} p(c_i|t_j) i(t_j)$, where t_j is the outcome of the test T. The impurity function of the Gini criterion assigns an example randomly selected from a node t to a class c_i with the probability $p(c_i|t)$. The estimated probability that the item is actually in class j is $p(c_j|t)$. Therefore, the estimated probability of misclassification under this rule is the Gini Index: $i(t) = \sum_{i=1}^{k} \sum_{j=1, j \neq i}^{k} p(c_i|t) p(c_j|t) = 1 - \sum_{j=1}^{k} (p(c_j|t))^2$. This function can also be interpreted in terms of variance. In a node t we assign to all examples belonging to class c_j the value 1, and to all other examples the value 0. The sample variance of these values is: $p(c_j|t)(1 - p(c_j|t))$. There are k classes, thus the corresponding variances are summed together: $i(t) = \sum_{j=1}^{k} p(c_j|t)(1 - p(c_j|t)) = 1 - \sum_{j=1}^{k} (p(c_j|t))^2$. Having a test T with n outcomes the goodness of the split is expressed using the Gini Index as follows:

$$gini(T) = 1 - \sum_{i=1}^{k} (p(c_i))^2 - \sum_{i=1}^{n} p(t_i) \sum_{j=1}^{k} p(c_j|t_i)(1 - p(c_j|t_i)).$$

The Gini Index criterion selects a test that maximizes this function. The Information Gain criterion [8] is based on the information theory. The information conveyed by a message depends on its probability and can be measured in bits as the negative logarithm to the base 2 of that probability. If we randomly select an example of a set and we announce that it belongs to the class c_j, the probability of this message is equal to $p(c_i) = \frac{\|c_i\|}{\|\mathcal{L}\|}$, and the amount of information it conveys is $-log_2(p(c_i))$. The expected information provided by a message in respect to the class membership can be expressed as: $info(\mathcal{L}) = -\sum_{i=1}^{k} p(c_i)log_2(p(c_i))$ bits. The quantity $info(\mathcal{L})$ measures the average amount of information needed to identify the class of a case in $\mathcal{L}$. This quantity is also known as the entropy of the set $\mathcal{L}$. We will consider a similar measurement after $\mathcal{L}$ has been partitioned in accordance with the n outcomes of a test T. The expected information requirement is the weighted sum over the subsets: $info_T(\mathcal{L}) = \sum_{i=1}^{n} p(t_i)info(T_i)$. The information gained by partitioning $\mathcal{L}$ in accordance to the test T is measured by the quantity: $gain(T) = info(\mathcal{L}) - info_T(\mathcal{L})$. We can rewrite the Information Gain as:

$$gain(T) = -\sum_{i=1}^{k} p(c_i) \log_2(p(c_i)) + \sum_{i=1}^{n} p(t_i) \sum_{j=1}^{k} p(c_j|t_i) \log_2(p(c_j|t_i)).$$

The Information Gain criterion selects a test that maximizes the Information Gain function. One should notice that in the Information Gain criterion, the logarithmic function is always applied to a probability that is in practice estimated by a frequency depending on the size of the training set or subset (see beginning of this section). E.g. if a class c has only one instance, it's probability is estimated by $p(c) = \frac{1}{\|\mathcal{L}\|}$. For a large data set this ratio will be very small, and therefore the value of the logarithmic function of this probability will tend to negative infinity. We would like to use a simpler function than the logarithmic function that allows us to manage exceptions occurring for small probabilities in a convenient manner. Instead of the logarithmic function we would prefer to use a polynomial function. An obvious candidate would be the Gini Index introduced previously. However, it was pointed out that the Gini Index is less optimal than the Information Gain (see e.g. [6, 9]). Thus, we are looking for a polynomial function that would approximate the logarithmic function. The most straight forward way to obtain such a function, is to replace the logarithmic function by its Taylor series development. We will now present this approach, introduce a new family of split functions and then analyze and compare them.

3   Taylor Series Development of the Information Gain

The Taylor series development is a generic approach that allows us to approximate a n-times derivable function by a polynomial function of degree n. Any function f satisfying the above constraint will be approximated in a point x_0 in the following way:

$$f(x) = f(x_0) + \frac{f'(x_0)(x - x_0)}{1!} + \frac{f''(x_0)(x - x_0)^2}{2!} + \ldots + \frac{f^{(n)}(x_0)(x - x_0)^n}{n!} + R_n$$

The logarithmic function can be derived infinitely often and therefore satisfies the necessary conditions to be developed in a Taylor series. For the development of the logarithmic function in the point $x_0 = 1$ we obtain:

$$ln(x) = 0 + \frac{\frac{1}{1}(x-1)}{1!} - \frac{\frac{1}{1^2}(x-1)^2}{2!} + \frac{\frac{2}{1^3}(x-1)^3}{3!} - \dots$$

This can be written as:

$$ln(x) = \sum_{i \geq 1} \frac{(x-1)^i}{i} = x - 1 - \frac{1}{2}(x-1)^2 + \frac{1}{3}(x-1)^3 - \frac{1}{4}(x-1)^4 + \dots$$

We will now substitute the logarithmic functions in the Information Gain by its developments, using the first term of the development, the first two terms, the first three terms etc. In this way we construct a whole family of split functions. A particularly interesting function in our family is the first one, constructed using only the first term of the development of the logarithmic function.

$$gain(T) = -\sum_{i=1}^{k} p(c_i) \log_2(p(c_i)) + \sum_{i=1}^{n} p(t_i) \sum_{j=1}^{k} p(c_j|t_i) \log_2(p(c_j|t_i))$$

$$\approx -\frac{1}{\ln(2)} \left[\sum_{i=1}^{k} p(c_i)(p(c_i) - 1) + \sum_{i=1}^{n} p(t_i) \sum_{j=1}^{k} p(c_j|t_i)(p(c_j|t_i) - 1) \right]$$

which can be written as:

$$\frac{1}{\ln(2)} \left[1 - \sum_{i=1}^{k} (p(c_i))^2 - \sum_{i=1}^{n} p(t_i) \sum_{j=1}^{k} p(c_j|t_i)(1 - p(c_j|t_i)) \right].$$

This represents nothing else then the Gini Index times a constant. Now, we have defined a family of split functions with a first member equal to the Gini Index, followed by an infinity of functions monotonically converging toward the Information Gain[1].

4 Experiments

In order to compare the split functions with a minimum of bias, we built our own decision tree induction system. This system is a variant of the C4.5 system with the possibility to select a split function within the function family defined previously. This is the only parameter of the system we varied during the tests, everything else (growing, pruning etc.) remained unchanged. More precisely, our system was parameterized in the following way: as split function we used

---

[1] Even though the Taylor series development of the logarithmic function converges very quickly, for the trees constructed by the split functions this is not necessarily the case. Empirical results of the convergence can be found in section 5. A theoretical analysis of this behavior is outside the scope of this paper.

the Information Gain (not Gain Ratio), the Gini Index and the first 49 functions of the previously defined family of split functions. In this paper, we are only interested in the influence of the different split functions on constructing decision trees, and not in their influence on pruning trees, and therefore we did not use any pruning algorithms. In order to conduct the tests we had to provide a large set of different databases. We were not able to find "real" data sets covering the whole spectrum of parameters we wanted to take into consideration. Therefore, we generated the necessary data sets according to our needs. For the construction of the databases we used the following parameters:

size: the number of tuples per data set (200, 500, 1,000, 2000, 5000, 7500, 10,000, 15,000, 20,000)

#attributes: the number of attributes per data set (between 5 and 20)

domain size: number of possible discrete values per attribute (between 10 and 20)

#classes: number of classes the tuples are belonging to (between 2 and 12)

#unclassifiable tuples: percentage of tuples per data set that can not be correctly classified (between 1% and 20%)

size of classes: two types of class membership distributions were used 1) all classes have the same size, 2) the size of each class is selected randomly.

For each of the nine possible values for *size* we generated 100 databases by varying the other parameters randomly within the intervals predefined for each of them.

4.1 Test Setup

In order to analyze the behavior of the different split functions on data sets of different size, we conducted a separate ensemble of tests for each set of the 100 databases generated per *size*. For each database we randomly sampled ten times 90% of the data as training set and we used the remaining 10% as test data. Overall, we created one thousand training and test sets for the nine possible values of *size*. We decided to evaluate 50 split functions (see parametrization of the system) on these test sets. Per training-test pair we generated 50 decision trees corresponding to the 50 different split functions selected above. In order to compare the 50 different trees we used the following three criteria:

1. tree size,

2. error rate for the training data,

3. error rate for the test data.

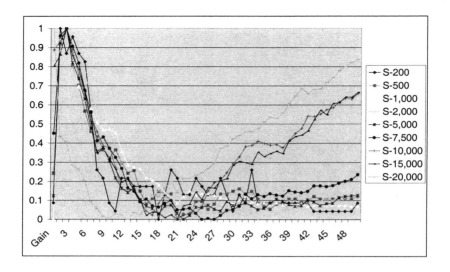

Figure 1: Ranks of size vs. split functions

For each training-test pair we created independent normalized ranks[2] for each of the three evaluation criteria. For the ten training-test data sets sampled from each database we calculated for each split function three average ranks corresponding to the three evaluation criteria. These average ranks are assigned to each split functions as its ranks for a given database.

5 Results

In the previous section we introduced three criteria, which now will be used to describe the behavior of the 50 split functions regarding databases of various sizes. The sizes of the generated decision trees is the first criterion used to present the behavior of the 50 split functions. We are specially interested in analyzing the influence of the size of the database on the created trees. In order to get one value for each split function, for each of the nine possible sizes of databases, we calculated the average rank achieved by each split function for the one hundred data sets per database size. These values are represented in Figure 1. The x-axes represents the Information Gain function, followed by the Gini Index function, and followed by the Taylor series developments using from 2 up to 49 terms. On the y-axes we can find the average rank

---

[2]The rank for a value v is calculated as follows: $rank(v) = \frac{v - min(values)}{max(values) - min(values)}$ where *values* stands for all possible values.

achieved by each split function with respect to the size of the inferred decision tree. For each database size we draw a line linking together the average ranks achieved by the 50 split functions. First of all, we can observe that the ranks of the split functions representing approximations of the Information Gain are slowly converging toward the rank of the Information Gain. For some databases even the split functions using 50 terms of the Taylor development still create trees different from those produced by the Information Gain split function. Secondly, we notice that the split functions based on the first few terms of the Taylor development are always creating relatively large trees. The smallest trees are always obtained for split functions using between 15 and 25 terms of the Taylor development. However, as the size of the database increases, the number of terms used in the split function that achieves the optimal rank decreases. Furthermore, we can observe that the rank of the Information Gain increases steadily with increasing database sizes. For small databases (up to 5,000 tuples) the rank of the Information Gain can always be found in the first quarter of all ranks. Then, the rank starts to increase until it reaches finally rank=1 for a 20,000 tuples database. In other words, compared to the other split functions, the relative size of the inferred trees by Information Gain is increasing; for the largest database the Information Gain functions creates the largest tree among the trees generated by all split criteria. In the second sequence of tests we analyze the behavior of the split functions with respect to the error rate on the training data. The results are resumed in Figure 2, which has the same layout as Figure 1, the x-axes represents the split functions, the y-axes represents this time the error-rate rank. As for the previous criterion (size of the inferred decision tree) we can observe that the ranks of the split functions based on the Taylor developments are converging towards the rank of the Information Gain function. With increasing database sizes we notice that the error-rate rank for the Information Gain is decreasing. This can be explained quite easily, by the increased relative size of the trees grown by the Information Gain (see Figure 1). However, for the split function based on the first, the first two and the first three terms of the Taylor development, we obtained always smaller ranks than for the Information Gain. This even holds for the cases in which the size of the trees grown by the split function based on the Taylor development was smaller than the size of the trees inferred by the Information Gain. The first three split functions based on the Taylor development achieved always the smallest ranks regardless of the database size. Now, we have to analyze how the split functions behave on unseen data. Figure 3 pictures the error-rate rank for unseen data. For this test set it is much harder to identify a general tendency. For most data sets we can not really observe any convergence. This might be related to the relatively small size of the test sets used to evaluate the split functions (10% of the original database, see section 4.1). However, it seems important to point out that for the nine database sizes used, in seven cases the first three split functions achieved smaller ranks then the Information Gain.

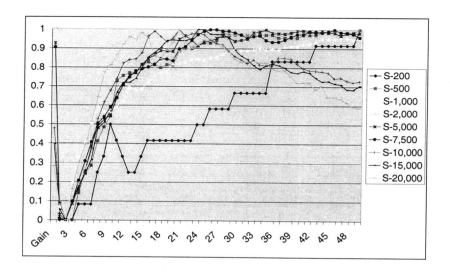

Figure 2: Ranks of error rate on training data vs. split functions

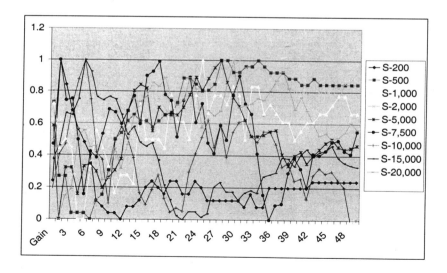

Figure 3: Ranks of error rate on unseen data vs. split functions

6 Conclusion and Future Work

Our main interest in this paper was to analyze if split functions introduced in a statistical or machine learning context remain applicable in a KDD context. We introduced a new family of split functions, the two extrema being the well known Information Gain (C4.5) and Gini Index (CART). We presented a wide range of tests based on a variety of 9,000 training and test data sets. The conducted tests have revealed that the size of the databases definitely influences the behavior of the split functions. Specially the widely used Information Gain is very sensitive to the size of the training set. On the other hand we were able to show, that the three simplest split functions of the introduced family behave in a very stable way and, furthermore, the created trees were superior to the trees inferred using the Gini Index or the Information Gain based on our evaluation criteria. This is important, especially in a KDD context as the size of the training sets can vary from very small to very large. In the future we will have to analyze how well the trees inferred by the different split functions are suited to post processing algorithms such as pruning, grouping etc. Furthermore, we are working on a decision tree induction system that supports multiple split functions. This is essential in order to adapt the decision tree to the context in which the system is used. A multi criteria optimization algorithm will be introduced in order to support the user in constructing optimal split functions.

References

[1] A. Babic, E. Krusinska, and J. E. Stromberg. Extraction of diagnostic rules using recursive partitioning systems: A comparison of two approches. *Artificial Intelligence in Medicine*, 20(5):373–387, October 1992.

[2] L. Breiman, J. Friedman, R. Olshen, and C. Stone. *Classification and regression trees*. Wadsworth International Group, 1984.

[3] J. Gama and P. Brazdil. Characterization of classification algorithms. In C. Pinto-Ferreira and N. Mamede, editors, *EPIA-95: Progress in Artificial Intelligence, 7th Portuguese Conference on Artificial Intelligence*, pages 189–200. Springer Verlag, 1995.

[4] D. Heath, S. Kasif, and S. Salzberg. Learning oblique decision trees. In *IJCAI-93: Proceedings of the 13th International Joint Conference on Artificial Intelligence*, pages 1002–1007, Chambery, France, 1993.

[5] Igor Kononenko. On biases in estimating multi-valued attributes. In Chris Mellish, editor, *IJCAI-95: Proceedings of the Fourteenth International Joint Conference on Artificial Intelligence*, pages 1034–1040, Montreal, Canada, August 1995. Morgan Kaufmann Publishers Inc, San Mateo, CA.

[6] Tjen-Sien Lim, Wey-Yin Loh, and Yu-Shan Shih. A comparison of prediction accuracy, complexity and training time of thirty-three old and new classification algorithms. *Machine Learning*, 1999. to apear.

[7] Usama M.Fayyad and Keki B. Irani. The attribute specification problem in decision tree generation. In *AAAI-92: Proceedings of the Tenth National Conference on Artificial Intelligence*, pages 104–110, San Jose, CA, July 1992. AAAI Press/ The MIT Press.

[8] J. R. Quinlan. *C4.5 Programs for machine learning.* Morgan Kaufmann Publishers, 1993.

[9] Y. Shih. Families of splitting criteria for classification trees. *Statistics and Computing*, 9:309–315, 1999.

[10] Steven Salzberg Sreerama K. Murthy, Simon Kasif. A system for induction of oblique decision trees. *Journal of artificial Intelligence research*, 2:1–32, August 1994.

[11] C.S. Wallace. Classification by minimum-message-length inference. In *Advances in Computing and Information*, pages 72–81, 1990.

Learning with C4.5 in a Situation Calculus Domain

Kamran Karimi and Howard J. Hamilton
Department of Computer Science
University of Regina
Regina, Saskatchewan
Canada S4S 0A2
{karimi,hamilton}@cs.uregina.ca

Abstract: It is desirable to automatically learn the effects of actions in an unknown environment. Using situation calculus in a causal domain is a very natural way of recording the actions and their effects. These could later be used for Automatic Programming purposes. A brute force approach to representing the situations involves recording the value of all the available variables. This is a combinatorial problem, and becomes unmanageable when the number of variables, or their domains, gets too large. A solution is to represent the situations and the transitions among the situations using first order logic formulas, which allows for generalizations and removal of irrelevant variables. But this usually requires a domain expert to act as a programmer. In this paper we look at the problem of automatic learning of causal and association rules in a situation calculus domain from observations, with little help from a domain expert. We feed C4.5 with temporal data generated in an Artificial Life environment, where the results of taking an action are not known to the creatures living in it. We show that C4.5 can discover causal rules, and has a good ability to prune irrelevant variables. We have modified C4.5 to generate Prolog rules as output, and show how the automatically learned rules can be used to make plan generators. The presented approach succeeds in generating plans in deterministic environments and needs less domain dependent preprocessing than techniques like Reinforcement Learning or Genetic Programming.

1.   Introduction

Situation Calculus [6] is a method of describing the effects of actions. Each situation can be considered a snapshot of the values of a set of variables. One can move from a situation to another by performing actions. This can result in a possibly cyclic graph with situations as nodes and actions as links between the nodes. One can interpret the transitions between the situations as the execution of rules. The starting situation forms the precondition of the rule, and the resulting situation forms the results. Planning is easy here: To go from the current situation to a desired situation, first make sure that they are both in the graph, and then find a path connecting them. Following this path can be regarded as executing the plan [8]. One problem with this brute-force approach to representing the effects of actions is that the number of possible situations grows exponentially as the number of variables increases or their domains become larger. This can make representing a graph very expensive or even impossible.

At the other end of the spectrum one can represent the situations and the transitions among them using first order logic formulas. [7] suggests that logic is a an appropriate way of representing knowledge. Suppose do(A, S) means performing action A in situation S, with the result being another situation. A statement like has(O, do(pick(O), S) would then mean that if in any situation the agent picks up an object O, then it has the object O in the next situation.

This method of representation allows us to generalise across variable values because the statement is true for many values of O and S. It also generalises across variables themselves, because the statement holds irrespective of what other variables (other than O and S) hold at the time. This form of representation has been used for programming purposes. For example, in [5] rules extracted in a situation calculus domain are considered as logic programmes. In GOLOG [3] which is a programming language based on Situation Calculus, the programmer writes code to specify the initial state of the environment, the preconditions and the effects of actions. This approach results in efficient representations of the domain. Our aim is to simplify the process of writing plans. We attempt to do this by deriving the rules of the environment automatically and then using them as parts of a plan generator.

Here the goal is to discover rules in a simplified world by using observational data and without programming. We will use C4.5 [9] for this purpose because it is widely available and produces the kind of rules that is suitable for a situation calculus domain. A situation transition can readily be represented by a simple **if-then** rule such as if{(<current situation> AND <action>)} **then** (<next situation>). We will see that if we give C4.5 enough information in the form of the relevant variables, it might be able to produce usable rules automatically. Though this may not result in very efficient representation in terms of the number of rules generated, it does remove the need for actual programming. The steady increase in computing power justifies the willingness to accept some redundancy in exchange for less work by the user.

The paper is divided into two main parts. First we show that C4.5 is suitable for discovering the effects of actions in a Situation Calculus domain. However, as individual rules, C4.5's results are of limited use, so we go on to show how Prolog can be used to turn C4.5's output into executable parts of a plan. The emphasis will be on reducing human involvement as much as possible.

The rest of the paper is outlined as follows. Section 2 describes our target domain, which is an Artificial Life [4] simulator. Section 3 shows how C4.5 performs when fed with temporal data generated in this simulator. The results show a strong generalization ability. Section 4 describes how C4.5's output in Prolog can be used to build plan generators. This turns C4.5's output into executable code. We will see how the temporal characteristics of the generated rules allow Prolog to perform recursive searches. The approach presented in this paper is not perfect, so in Section 5 we summarize some of its strong and weak points.

2. An Artificial Creature's Learning Problem

A state S_i is defined as a tuple of attributes $<x_{i1}, x_{i2},\dots x_{ij}>$. We go from one situation to another by performing actions over time. This means that we have a temporally ordered sequence of situation transitions caused by actions. We include the action as part of the situations in the sequence, and get records of the form $<x_{i1}, x_{i2},\dots x_{ij}, a_i>$. The aim is to know the effects of actions in different situations. We consider the *time window t* to be the number of situations that may be causally related. With a time window of 3, for example, the effects of an action taken in a situation will be known in the next 2 situations.

We use an artificial environment called URAL [11] as our source of data. The world in URAL is made of a two dimensional n by m board with one or more agents living in it. These are called *creatures* in Artificial Life literature. A creature moves around and if it finds food, eats it. There can be obstacles on the board. Food is produced by the simulator and placed at positions that are randomly determined at the start of each run. The creature can sense its position, humidity and temperature, and also the presence of food at that position. Humidity and temperature are constants that are assigned by the simulator to each location on the board. At each time-step the creature randomly chooses to move from its current position to either Up, Down, Left, or Right. The creature does not know the meaning or results of any of these actions, so for example it does not know that it's position may change if it chooses to go to Left (action L). It can not get out of the board, or go through the obstacles that are placed on the board by the simulator. In such cases, a move action will not change the creature's position. The creature can sense which action it takes in each situation. The goal is to learn the effects of the actions. This could later be used for making plans in the form of a series of movements from the set {U, D, L, R}, to reach food. URAL's creatures build situation calculus graphs and use them to store their observations of the world and to make plans for finding food.

For our creature time passes in discrete steps. At each time step it takes a snapshot of its sensors and randomly decides which action it should perform. This results in records such as $<x$ *position, y position, is food here?, temperature, humidity, action>* which the creature can log to a file. Listing 1(a) shows an example sequence of such records, with time passing vertically from top to bottom. These records can be used to find association among variable values. One example is the association between the presence of food and a specific location. Discovering causal rules, however, needs considering the passage of time, as in general the effects of an action such as moving appear at a later time. URAL can output more than one consecutive record as a single record, and set the last variable to any attribute. We call this operation *flattening* the records. C4.5 does not understand time, and this pre-processing step enables it to work on a window of two or more records instead of a single one. Thus time will be implicitly included in the records. Flattening the sequence in Listing 1(a) using a time window of size 2 and with x as the last variable would give us the records in listing 1(b). The subscripts show the time-step from which the variable was taken. We treat the last attribute specially because C4.5 considers it to be the decision attribute.

$<x, y, f, t, h, a>$	$<x_1, y_1, f_1, t_1, h_1, a_1, x_2>$
$<1, 3, false, 43, 24, L>$	$<1, 3, false, 43, 24, L, 0>$
$<0, 3, false, 26, 32, L>$	$<0, 3, false, 26, 32, L, 0>$
$<0, 3, true, 26, 32, D,>$	$<0, 3, true, 26, 32, D, 0>$
$<0, 4, false, 12, 65, U>$	
a	b

Listing 1. (a) A sequence of two records. (b) The flattened sequences.

In a sequence of flattened records, time passes horizontally from left to right as well as vertically from top to bottom. We have chosen a time window of 2 because we know that the effects of a move action will be known in the next time step. Here we have renamed the variables to remove name clashes. Flattening can be done for any attribute value of interest. Listing 2 shows the first two records in Listing 1(a) flattened with y, f, t, and h as the decision attribute.

$<x_1, y_1, f_1, t_1, h_1, a_1, y_2>$: $<1, 3, false, 43, 24, L, 3>$
$<x_1, y_1, f_1, t_1, h_1, a_1, f_2>$: $<1, 3, false, 43, 24, L, false>$
$<x_1, y_1, f_1, t_1, h_1, a_1, t_2>$: $<1, 3, false, 43, 24, L, 26>$
$<x_1, y_1, f_1, t_1, h_1, a_1, h_2>$: $<1, 3, false, 43, 24, L, 32>$

Listing 2. Flattening with a time window of 2 for different decision attributes.

3.   Rule Generation with C4.5

A creature needs to move to specific places. It cannot directly set the values of x and y to a desired value, but can perform actions through its actuators that change the values of x and y. What it needs is a set of rules to tell it when to apply a certain action to get closer to its goal. We are interested in finding rules for the next values of x and y, and also for the place of food. The correct condition attributes for x_2 are x_1 and a_1, and for y_2 they are y_1 and a_1. For f_2 any set of attributes from the second time step is correct, but the desired attributes are x_2 and y_2 because they are under indirect control. Humidity and temperature are constants for each location. This means that t and h have many of the same characteristics as x and y and could creep up into the rules, which is undesirable. In [1] we used C4.5 to generate correct rules for food and the next values of x and y. In that paper the creature was allowed to completely explore the world before its observations were fed to C4.5.

3.1 No Obstacles and a Time Window of 2

Here we investigate the effects of incomplete coverage of the world. The results for one typical run in a 15 by 15 board with no obstacles are shown in Table 1. "Correct" means having only a_1 and x_1 (for x_2) or a_1 and y_1 (for y_2) as condition attributes.

Moves	Nodes	Links	Decision	Rules	Correct
500	116	263	x_2	52	51
			y_2	47	47
1000	185	472	x_2	59	59
			y_2	60	60
1500	199	573	x_2	60	60
			y_2	60	60

Table 1. C4.5's results for a world with no obstacles.

Visiting more nodes and links increases the number of rules until they settle down at 60. For comparison, a brute force approach that only considered the x and y variables would have 225 nodes and a maximum of 900 (225 × 4) links. Each link would be equivalent to one rule. The rules for moving along the x and y axis are independent of each other, so the maximum number of distinct rules for each of x and y is 60 (15 × 4) which is the same as what we got. C4.5 did not need to visit all of the world to come up with rules that were correct everywhere because the same rules hold in all columns and rows. With smaller number of moves, most of the wrong rules looked like this: if $\{(x_1 = 9)\}$ then $(x_2 = 9)$, which suggests that C4.5 could not figure out how to move around in a certain column or row of the world because it was not explored enough.

We derived rules for the places of food too. Some of the rules discovered for f_2 contained t_2 and h_2 in addition to x_2 and y_2. There is no causality relation here, and these results are perfectly right from an association point of view. The problem is, there is no way for the creature to "affect" the temperature or humidity, and get to the food. This is what we call the *Association Problem*: C4.5, not knowing about the semantics of the domain, uses variables with strong association with the decision attribute in the rules it generates. C4.5's goal is not to come up with "meaningful" rules, but to use all available variables to come up with the shortest possible decision tree. Knowing that it is possible to change x and y only, the user can for example exclude temperature and humidity when outputting the flattened record for food. Since flattening is not necessary when looking for associations, URAL can be instructed to output records of the form $<x, y, a, f>$.

3.2 Obstacles and a Time Window of 2

We tried C4.5 when there were 10 randomly placed obstacles on the board. This resulted in an increase in the number of generated rules, as C4.5 now had to make rules that considered the exceptions to the general laws of moving around the board. The association problem was seen here too. C4.5 attempted to identify the position of the obstacles not only by their x and y values, but also by the humidity and temperature. We genereted new test data and allowed C4.5 to only choose from x_1, y_1 and a_1 variables. We expected an increase in the number of rules because C4.5 now had fewer variables to work with. However, there were not any significant increase in the number of rules. Results of two typical runs, one with all the variables, and one with only the position and action variables, come in Table 2(a) and 2(b), respectively.

Moves	Nodes	Links	Decision Attribute	Rules
500	101	231	x_2	63
			y_2	35
1000	165	405	x_2	64
			y_2	62
1500	175	460	x_2	64
			y_2	60
4000	215	731	x_2	79
			y_2	76
6000	215	763	x_2	80
			y_2	75
7000	215	763	x_2	83
			y_2	75

a

Moves	Nodes	Links	Decision Attribute	Rules
500	123	253	x_2	56
			y_2	62
1000	153	395	x_2	58
			y_2	66
1500	190	520	x_2	64
			y_2	70
4000	215	740	x_2	84
			y_2	78
6000	215	761	x_2	84
			y_2	82
7000	215	761	x_2	84
			y_2	82

b

Table 2. C4.5's typical results with obstacles on the board.

The number and correctness of the results depend heavily on not only the number of nodes visited, but also on the number of links travered. The number of links tell us how much the creature knows about ways to move between the situations. The more connections the creature is aware of, the better. In URAL, we can see which x and y values have been explored by looking at the creature's "brain" in a window as shown in snapshot 1. The move direction is usually determined randomly, but the user can also guide the creature to specific locations by "manual control" via on-screen buttons that instruct it to move in a specific direction. This is like allowing a robot to experience randomly with its actuators, but also having a joystick to guide it into performing certain interesting actions that it may have missed to perform on its own.

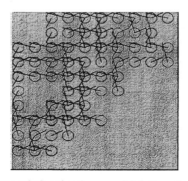

Snapshot 1. The creature's brain shows which locations have been explored.

Each circle in snapshot 1 denotes one (x, y) position in the world. The empty locations have not been explored. The lines show the paths taken by the creature as it has moved from one location to the next (the lines start at the centre of the source location). The denser this graph, the better the resulting rules. For the creature to find correct and general rules, it should have entered the same spot from all existing neighbours. That is when C4.5 will have enough knowledge to generate rules that are general enough to always work. In the case of an obstacle or at the borders of the world, the creature should have tried moving to the place of the obstacle, and experienced the failure. In these cases, C4.5 would create rules like **if** $\{(x_1 = 9)$ AND $(a_1 = R)\}$ **then** $(x_2 = 9)$. This is an exception to the general rule that moving to the right increases the value of x.

3.3 No Obstacles and Time Windows Greater Than 2

In order to see how sensitive the results are to the selected time window, we tried different time window values from 2 to 10 with no obstacles and all the condition variables present. The world was completely explored. The results are in Table 3. Only 3 cases are displayed because the results followed the same pattern for all other values of the time window. The subscripts of the variables designate the time step during which they were observed.

Window	Total Attributes	Decision Attribute	Condition Attributes
2	6	x_2	a_1, x_1
	6	y_2	a_1, y_1
6	30	x_6	a_5, x_5
	30	y_6	a_5, y_5
10	54	x_{10}	a_9, x_9
	54	y_{10}	a_9, y_9

Table 3. Condition attributes selected by C4.5 for different time windows.

With a time window of t, C4.5 consistently chose attributes from time step t-1 as the determining factors for the decision attribute. This shows that in the presence of a strong causal relation, the results are not sensitive to the time window.

3.4 Obstacles and Time Windows Greater Than 2

We evaluated the results after 7000 moves for time windows of 2 to 10. As in section 3.3, adding obstacles to the board did not affect C4.5's ability to choose the condition variables from time step t-1. The number of rules generated when C4.5 had access to all the previous variables varied slightly for different time steps, but they were the same when the available condition attributes were limited to x, y and a.

4.   Using Prolog for Plan Generation

Here we consider a plan and a programme to be the same. In the previous section we were concerned about learning the immediate effects of individual actions.

Now that we know these effects, we can combine the actions in the form of a plan and come up with more complex behaviours. Most other work on planning starts at this point, because they consider the problem of knowing the effects of actions as already solved. We have modified C4.5 to output the discovered rules in Prolog [10] statements that can be directly fed to a Prolog interpreter. A new option '-p' has been added to the c4.5rules programme that causes it to create a <file stem>.pl Prolog file in addition to its normal output. The generated Prolog statements are in the Edinburgh dialect.

There are two main problems in using Prolog to represent C4.5's rules. First, C4.5 assigns certainty values to the rules it outputs. These can not be represented in standard Prolog, and so are ignored. In a domain with little "surprises," the certainty value is very high and we expect this problem to be of minor consequence. This condition holds in URAL and many other industrial applications of robots. The second problem is that there is no concept of time in standard Prolog. But as explained later, using Prolog to represent the rules is especially appropriate in temporal domains, where the decision attribute is actually one of the condition attributes, seen at a later time. A temporal order is implicitly present in Prolog because it follows a rule's conditions from left to right. Table 4 shows parts of an example set of statements generated by the modified c4.5rules programme when the decision attribute is x_2.

class(A1, X1, 0) :- A1 = 2, X1 = 1.
class(A1, X1, 2) :- A1 = 3, X1 = 1.
class(A1, X1, 3) :- A1 = 2, X1 = 4.

Table 4. Three sample Prolog statements generated by c4.5rules.

In Table 4 a value of 2 and 3 for action *A1* could mean going to the left and right, respectively. Following C4.5's terminology, the results are designated by a predicate called "class." The condition attributes (action *A1* and position *X1* in this case) come first, and the value of the decision attribute (the next value of *x*) comes last. In the head of the rules, the condition attributes are used for the decision making process. In our example temporal data, *A1* and *X1* belong to the current time step, while the classification is done for the value of *x* in the next time step. To use such rules the user can issue queries like class(2, 4, X2) (where does the creature go from *x* = 4 if it moves Left?). If we are dealing with more than one sensor variable (*x* and *y* for example) we could rename "class" to something like "classx" to avoid name clashes.

Notice that the automatically generated Prolog statements use the unification operator (=) instead of the comparison operator (=:=). This allows the user to traverse the rules backward and go from the decision attribute to the condition attributes, or from a set of decision and condition attributes, to the remaining condition attributes. Some example queries are class(A1, 1, 2) (which actions take the creature from *x* = 1 to *x* = 2?) or class (A1, X1, 3) (which action/location pairs immediately leads to *x* = 3?). This makes C4.5's discovered rules generally more useful.

C4.5 can generate rules that rely on threshold testing and set membership testing. If we use the standard Prolog operators of =< and > for threshold testing, and implement a simple member() function for testing set membership, then we would not be able to traverse the rules backward, as they lack the ability to unify variables. So if we had a clause like: class(A, B, C) :- A =< B, member(A, C), then we would be unable to use a query like class(A, 3, [1, 2, 3]), because Prolog can not perform the test =< on variables that are not unified. Adding the unification ability to =<, > and member() will remove this limitation. For example, $X > 10$ would choose a value above 10 for X if it is not already unified, and member(X, [1, 2, 3]) would unify X with one of 1, 2, or 3 if it is not already unified. Both cases would always succeed if X is not unified, but could fail if it is. We have written some simple code to do just this and the results are shown in Table 5. We employed a deterministic method to choose the value of the variable that is going to be unified, but one could use a random method too. ule (unify less-equal), ug (unify greater) and umember() (unify member) are the unifying counter parts of =<, > and member(), respectively.

Name	Unifies?	Implementation
=<	No	Standard
>	No	Standard
member()	No	member(A, [A|_]). member(A, [_|B]) :- member(A, B).
ule	Yes	:- op(800, xfx, ule). A ule B :- var(A), $A = B$. A ule B :- A =< B.
ug	Yes	:- op(800, xfx, ug). A ug B :- var(A), A is $B + 1$. A ug B :- $A > B$.
umember()	Yes	umember(A, B) :- var(A), [X|_] = B, $A = X$. umember(A, B) :- member(A, B).

Table 5. Prolog operators and functions for planning.

If the argument to the left of ule is not unified, ule sets its value to be the same as its argument to the right, and returns with success. If the left hand side argument is already unified, then it does a =< test. The ug operator does the same with regard to >. If unification is needed, it sets the left hand side argument to the value of the right hand side argument plus 1. In both cases the right hand side argument should already have been unified. The function umember() unifies the first argument with the first member of the list if unification is needed. The second argument to this function should have already been unified. These conditions seem to hold for rules generated by C4.5. The modified c4.5rules programme can thus generate rules of the form class(A, B, C, 0) :- A = 1 , B ug 10, umember(C, [1, 2, 3]). As explained below, this unification ability has another advantage: it allows us to generate plans by moving backwards in the rules.

To create a Prolog plan generator, we have to make manual modifications in the Prolog statements generated by c4.5rules. The results will be a set of rules that search backward from a desired situation to the current situation, and if such a path is found, it prints the actions that have to be performed to get to the desired situation. The modifications should be done manually because we have made the changes to c4.5rules in a general manner and compatible with the normal output of C4.5. The Prolog clauses that are generated simply do a normal classification without caring about any "bigger picture" that may exist in a particular application such as planning. We now go over the modifications needed for planning. Suppose we start with the rule: class($A1, X1, 0$) :- $A1 = 2, X1 = 1$.

1) We have to make sure that Prolog does not get stuck in plans with cycles. To prevent this we keep track of the classes we have already visited. This is done by adding a list variable to the class() clause, and adding code for cycle-prevention. So now we have this rule: class($A1, X1, 0, P_1$) :- $A1 = 2, X1 = 1$, not(umember($X1, P_1$)), $P_2 = [X1|P_1]$.

   $X1$ is used to distinguish among the steps in the plan. If we do not find a value of $X1$ in our list, then we know we are not in a cycle. If this holds we add it to the list P_1 to get a new list P_2, and continue from there.

2) In a temporal domain one of the condition attributes may actually be the previous value of our decision attribute. In this example x has this property. We now have to make this fact explicit, because we want Prolog to make sure that we are actually in the previous situation before advancing to the next one. To do this we introduce the class() clause in the condition part of the Prolog statements. This will allow Prolog to use recursion and try all the paths that leads from one class to the next. So we now have: class($A1, X1, 0, P_1$) :- $A1 = 2, X1 = 1$, not(umember($X1, P_1$)), $P_2 = [X1|P_1]$, class($\_, \_, 1, P_2$).

   Notice that the value 1 in class($\_, \_, 1, P_2$) comes from $X1 = 1$, as in this example class() is C4.5's name for the x position. We would do the same for other sensor variables. Now Prolog can search for a way to get the robot from the starting state to a desired state.

3) We can add a statement to print the plan after it is generated. This is simple to do: class($A1, X1, 0, P_1$) :- $A1 = 2, X1 = 1$, not(umember($X1, P_1$)), $P_2 = [X1|P_1]$, class($\_, \_, 1, P_2$), printOut($A1, X1$).

4) Finally, we introduce the current situation as a class statement. For example, if we are currently at $X1 = 0$, we add the clause class($\_, \_, 0, \_$) to the set of rules. Intuitively this means we are currently at position 0, and we do not care how we got here.

Automating the above steps requires c4.5rules to know the previous value of the decision attribute. Conveying this information to c4.5rules is not very easy, so the transformation is done manually. The programme could of course be modified specifically for this problem to automatically generate rules of the form: class($A1, X1, 0, P_1$) :- $A1 = 2, X1 = 1$, not(umember($\#, P_1$)), $P_2 = [\#|P_1]$, class($\_, \_, *, P_2$), printOut($A1, X1$) and rely on the user to edit them and replace the '#' and '*' markers with the appropriate attributes.

Performing the above steps on the rules in Table 4 gives us the rules in Table 6. The helper functions not() and printOut() are also provided. The function umember() has already appeared in Table 5.

class($\_$, $\_$, 0, $\_$).
class($A1$, $X1$, 0, P_1) :- $A1$ = 2, $X1$ = 1, not(umember($X1$, P_1)), P_2 = $[X1|P_1]$, class($\_$, $\_$, 1, P_2), printOut($A1$, $X1$).
class($A1$, $X1$, 2, P_1) :- $A1$ = 3, $X1$ = 1, not(umember($X1$, P_1)), P_2 = $[X1|P_1]$, class($\_$, $\_$, 1, P_2), printOut($A1$, $X1$).
class($A1$, $X1$, 3, P_1) :- $A1$ = 2, $X1$ = 4, not(umember($X1$, P_1)), P_2 = $[X1|P_1]$, class($\_$, $\_$, 4, P_2), printOut($A1$, $X1$).
not(G) :- G, !, fail.   not(G).
printOut(A, X) :- write('Robot is at: '), write(X), write(', it does action: '), write(A), nl.

Table 6. Prolog rules modified for planning.

Using the above statements, the user can perform Prolog queries of the form class($\_$, $\_$, 7, []) to find a plan. He can include a position in the last argument of his query to prevent that position from showing up in the plan, as anything in that list will be avoided. Prolog will then print out the actions that should be performed to get from the current situation $x = 0$ to the desired situation $x = 7$.

The association rules for the presence or absence of food can use any condition variables, including the ones that do not make sense. One example is given in Table 7 below.

class(X, Y, 1) :- X = 6, Y = 7.
class(X, Y, 1) :- X = 2, Y = 7.
class(X, 0) :- X = 0.
class(Y, 0) :- Y = 0.
class(Y, 0) :- Y = 1.
class(A, 0) :- A = 1.

Table 7. Prolog rules for the presence of food.

Since we only care about the presence of food, the rules that will actually be executed are in the first two rows, with a 1 as the classification value. This means that the fact that the last rule does not make sense (it claims we can *not* find food if we perform an action) is not important. Such useless association rules are expected to be present, since in URAL it is the presence of food that follows a pattern of appearing at certain (x, y) positions, while this does not apply to the absence of food.

The first rule, when modified to form a plan, will look like: classf(1) :- classx($\_$, $\_$, 6, []), classy($\_$, $\_$, 7, []). This is an association rule, so there is no recursion here. Note that we have renamed the class() names to avoid clashes. Invoking the classf(1) command in Prolog will cause the planner to come up with a sequence of moves to get the creature to a place of food.

5. Concluding Remarks

For us ease of use is very important. With our approach very little pre-processing was needed to produce the rules that expressed the effects of actions in different situations. All we did was to feed the observed records directly to C4.5. All the pre-processing that was done involved choosing the decision attribute, and pruning unrelated condition attributes, so C4.5 would be able to come up with useful rules. In URAL this was done by clicking a few checkboxes before saving the observed records to a file, so there was no need to involve a programmer in the process. This is unlike some other Automatic Programming techniques like Reinforcement Learning or Genetic Programming where a domain expert must explicitly provide the system with high-level information. For Reinforcement Learning the work includes deciding on the behaviours that should be reinforced, and a payoff function, among others. For Genetic Programming one should determine sets of terminals and primitive functions and come up with a suitable fitness function. A discussion of this aspect of Genetic Programming and Reinforcement Learning appears in [2]. Implementing a system to actually produce the results comes next. There is no guarantee that performing these pre-processing steps will be easier than writing a program manually.

Our approach requires little explicit programming, which sets it apart from programming systems like GOLOG, which require the user to explicitly encode all the knowledge of the domain into Situation Calculus rules. The main problem with our approach is that a set of simple rules as generated by C4.5 may not have the ability to express the rules of a complex environment. This means that such rules are more suitable for expressing basic operations such as a single move action. As is evident in the case of the Prolog planner in this paper, going beyond the basic operators to write a programme that can guide a creature needs some manual work. Another problem is that for this approach to work, all situations of interest should have been experienced. This could be very hard or impossible to do as the search space becomes bigger. A programming approach like GOLOG is probably more suitable in very complex environments.

In the presented approach the domain expert can decide to write plans manually if it is necessary to do so. For example, doing a certain experiment may have undesirable consequences for the creature or the environment. In such cases the domain expert can opt to pre-programme the creature to avoid the problem, and let it discover other rules.

One thing to consider is that C4.5 can not generalise across variable values, so we will not have rules that literally look like: if $\{(x = \alpha) \text{ AND } (a = R)\}$ then $(x = \alpha + 1)$. This is not a bad thing when there are many exceptions to the rule, because then the generalised rules will have to deal with many special cases. C4.5 allows us to come up with rules that can handle the exceptions, otherwise a human programmer would have to write new rules or modify the existing rules for each randomly generated world because each will have a different set of exceptions. In an approach such as GOLOG, that would amount to manually rewriting a programme for each new environment in which a robot may have to function. It is more interesting to manufacture a robot once and then let it experience its new environment for a while. The observations would then be used to generate plans for the robot.

The modified c4.5rules programme retains backward compatibility, and its output is unchanged when the new option is not used. The modifications are available in the form of a patch file that can be applied to standard C4.5 Release 8 source files. It is available from http://www.cs.uregina.ca/~karimi or by contacting the authors.

Acknowledgements

We thank the anonymous referees for their useful comments.

References

[1] Karimi, K. and Hamilton, H. J. (2000). Finding Temporal Relations: Causal Bayesian Networks vs. C4.5. The 12th International Symposium on Methodologies for Intelligent Systems (ISMIS'2000), Charlotte, NC, USA.

[2] Koza, J. R. and Rice, J. P. (1992). Automatic Programming of Robots using Genetic Programming. The Tenth National Conference on Artificial Intelligence, Menlo Park, CA, USA.

[3] Levesque, H. J., Reiter, R., Lespérance, Y., Lin, F. and Scherl. R. (1997). GOLOG: A Logic Programming Language for Dynamic Domains. Journal of Logic Programming, 31, pp. 59-84.

[4] Levy, S. (1992). Artificial Life: A Quest for a New Creation. Pantheon Books.

[5] Lin F. and Reiter, R. (1997). Rules as actions: A Situation Calculus Semantics for Logic Programs. Journal of Logic Programming Special Issue on Reasoning about Action and Change, 31(1-3), pp.299-330.

[6] McCarthy, J. and Hayes, P. C. (1969). Some Philosophical Problems from the Standpoint of Artificial Intelligence. Machine Intelligence 4.

[7] Moore, R. C. (1985). The Role of Logic in Knowledge Representation and Commonsense Reasoning. Readings in Knowledge Representation, Morgan Kaufmann, pp. 335-341.

[8] Poole, D. (1998). Decision Theory, the Situation Calculus, and Conditional Plans. Linköping Electronic Articles in Computer and Information Science, Vol. 3 (1998): nr 3, http://www.ep.liu.se/ea/cis/1998/008.

[9] Quinlan, J. R. (1993). C4.5: Programs for Machine Learning. Morgan Kaufmann.

[10] Van Le, T. (1993). Techniques of Prolog Programming. John Wiley & Sons.

[11] http://www.cs.uregina.ca/~karimi/URAL.java

SESSION 2

CASE BASED REASONING

Incremental Footprint-Based Retrieval

Barry Smyth & Elizabeth McKenna
Smart Media Institute
Department of Computer Science
University College Dublin
Belfield, Dublin 4, Ireland
{Barry.Smyth, Elizabeth.McKenna@ucd.ie}

Abstract. Case-based reasoning systems solve new problems by retrieving and adapting problem solving experiences stored as cases in a case-base. Success depends largely on the performance of the case retrieval algorithm used. Smyth & McKenna [15] have described a novel retrieval technique, called footprint-based retrieval, which is guided by a model of case competence. Footprint-based retrieval as it stands benefits from superior efficiency characteristics and achieves near-optimal competence and quality characteristics. In this paper we describe a simple but important extension to footprint-based retrieval. Empirically we show that this new algorithm can deliver optimal retrieval performance while at the same time retaining the efficiency benefits of the original footprint-based retrieval method.

1   Introduction

The success of any case-based reasoning (CBR) system depends critically on the performance of its retrieval component. Smyth & McKenna [15] have previously presented a novel retrieval technique, *footprint-based retrieval* (FBR), which uses a model of case competence to guide retrieval, and which displays superior efficiency characteristics without significantly compromising retrieval competence or solution quality. However, FBR's efficiency benefits do result in minor competence and quality reductions (typically 1-5% below optimal levels), and since there are always situations where optimal competence and quality must be guaranteed, this means that there are certain situations where FBR, as it stands, is not applicable.

In this paper we describe a simple but important extension to the footprint-based retrieval algorithm. We demonstrate that this new algorithm (*incremental footprint-based retrieval* or iFBR) can guarantee optimal retrieval competence and quality while still offering significant efficiency gains. The next sections survey related work on retrieval and outline the competence model that forms the basis of the iFBR method, which itself is described and evaluated in the final sections.

2   Related Work

Retrieval has always received the lion's share of interest from the CBR community. All CBR systems have a retrieval component, and success depends on the efficient retrieval of the right case at the right time. Every retrieval method is the combination of two procedures; a similarity assessment procedure to determine the similarity between a case and target problem, and a procedure for searching the case memory in order to locate the most similar case. In this paper we are most interested in the latter.

To date research has focused on reducing the search needed to find the best case without degrading competence or quality [3,6,7,11,13,16,18]. The simplest approach is an exhaustive search of the case-base (the brute-force method), but this is not viable for large case-bases. Thus, the basic goal is to avoid the need to examine every case, for example by processing the case data in order to produce an optimised memory structure that facilitates a more directed search procedure.

One approach is to build a decision-tree over the case data (eg. [18]). Each node and branch of the tree represents a particular attribute-value combination, and cases with a given set of attribute-values are stored at the leaf nodes. Retrieval is implemented as a directed search through the decision tree. These approaches are efficient but may not be appropriate for case-bases with incomplete case descriptions, or where the relative importance of individual case features can change.

Spreading activation methods [3] represent case memory as a network of nodes capturing case attribute-value combinations. Activation spreads from target attribute-value nodes across the network to cause the activation of case nodes representing similar cases to the target. The approaches are efficient and flexible enough to handle incomplete case descriptions, however there can be a significant knowledge-engineering cost associated with constructing the activation network. Furthermore, spreading-activation methods may require specific knowledge to guide the spread of activation throughout the network. Related network-based retrieval methods are proposed by Lenz [7] and Wolverton & Hayes-Roth [19].

Perhaps the simplest approach to reduce retrieval cost is to search a *reduced* or *edited* case-base. This strategy is often used to improve the performance of nearest-neighbour techniques by editing training data to remove unnecessary examples (eg, [1,4,5]. Many powerful editing strategies have been developed, often preserving competence with a greatly reduced edited case-base.

With the above methods there is a risk in not examining every case during retrieval. The best case may be missed and this can result in a lower quality final solution when compared to the solution that would have been produced by adapting the best case. Even worse, it can mean a problem solving failure if the retrieved case is not close enough to the target for successful adaptation.

3 Model of Case Competence

In this section we briefly outline the important components of the competence model used to guide FBR methods (see also [8,13,15,16,17].

3.1   Local Competence Estimates

The local competence contributions of cases are characterised by two sets. The *coverage set* of a *case* is the set of *target problems* that this case can solve, while the *reachability set* of a *target problem* is the set of *cases* that can solve this target. It is not feasible to enumerate all possible future target problems, but by using the case-base (C) itself as a proxy for the target problem space we can efficiently estimate these sets as shown in Def. 1 and 2.

Def 1: $CoverageSet(c)=\{c' \in C: Solves(c,c')\}$

Def 2: $ReachabilitySet(c)=\{c' \in C: Solves(c',c)\}$

3.2   Shared Coverage & Competence Groups

Coverage and reachability sets provide local competence estimates, but to estimate the global competence of cases it is necessary to model the interactions between their local competences.

Def 3: $RelatedSet(c)= CoverageSet(c) \cup ReachabilitySet(c)$

Def 4:   For $c1, c2 \in C$, SharedCoverage(c1, c2)
            iff $[RelatedSet(c1) \cap RelatedSet(c2)] \neq \{\}$

Def 5:   For $G = \{c1,...,cn\} \subseteq C$, CompetenceGroup(G) iff
            $\forall ci \in G, \exists cj \in G-\{ci\}: SharedCoverage(ci,cj) \wedge$
            $\forall ck \in C-G, \neg \exists cl \in G: SharedCoverage(ck,cl)$

The related set of a case is the union of its coverage and reachability sets (Def. 3). If the related sets of two cases overlap they are said to exhibit *shared coverage* (Def. 4). Cases can be grouped into so-called *competence groups* which are maximal sets of cases exhibiting shared coverage (Def. 5). In fact, every case-base can be organised into a unique set of competence groups which, by definition, do not interact from a competence viewpoint – while each case within a given competence group must share coverage with another case in that group, no case from one group can share coverage with any case from another group (Fig. 1).

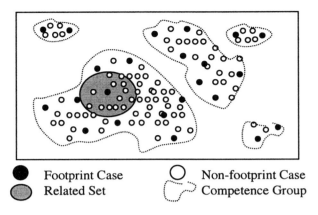

Fig. 1. A sample case-base showing competence groups, footprint cases, and related sets.

3.3 Footprint Cases & the Footprint Set

Every group makes a unique (and independent) contribution to competence, but not every case makes a positive competence contribution [13]. The cases that do are called *footprint cases* and the *footprint set* is that minimal set of footprint cases that collectively provides the same coverage as the entire group (see Fig. 1). This set is important because it is only these cases that we need to consider when estimating the competence properties of a given group or case-base (the footprint set of the case-base is the union of the footprint sets of its competence groups).

```
COV-FP(G)
R-Set ← cases in G
FP ← {}
While R-Set is not empty
   C ← case in R-Set with largest coverage set size
   FP ← FP ∪ {C}
   R-Set ← R-Set - CoverageSet(C)
   Update coverage sets of R-Set cases
EndWhile
Return (FP)
```

Algorithm 1. Computing the footprint set of a Group, G

The footprinting algorithm shown in Algorithm 1 operates by adding cases to the growing footprint set (FP). Each time a case is added, all of the cases that it covers are removed from the remaining case set (R-Set), and the next case to add is the one with the largest coverage set with respect to the remaining cases (see also [8, 15, 16,17]).

4 Incremental Footprint-Based Retrieval

Footprint-based retrieval was first introduced by Smyth & McKenna [15]. Its key innovation stems from its use of the above competence model to guide the retrieval process. In this section we outline the footprint-based retrieval algorithm and show how it can be extended to produce the iFBR method.

4.1 Footprint-Based Retrieval

Footprint-based retrieval is an edited-set retrieval method that uses the above competence model to edit the case-base with respect to a specific target problem. The algorithm (Algorithm 2) has two stages. Stage one identifies the local region of the case-base that contains the target problem. Stage two focuses the search in this region to locate the nearest case to the target. During each step the competence model is used to guide the search in the right way.

```
Target ← Current target problem
CB ← Case-Base, FP ← Footprint Set

FBR(Target, CB, FP)

  Stage 1
  RefCase ← closest case in FP to Target

  Stage 2
  RelSet  ← RelatedSet(RefCase)
  Case    ← closest case in RelSet to Target

  Return(Case)
```

Algorithm 2. The Footprint-Based Retrieval Procedure.

Stage 1: Retrieving from the Footprint Set. During the first stage the target problem is compared to each case in the footprint set of the case-base, in order to locate the case that best matches the target. This case is termed the *reference case* and acts as an index into the case-base for the next stage. The footprint set serves to mark out the principal regions of competence within the case space and thus is a useful structure to guide retrieval. Furthermore, the footprint set contains only a fraction of the case-base and therefore has a low associated search cost.

Stage 2: Retrieving from the Related Set. The reference case may, or may not, be able to solve the current target, it may even be the closest case to the target in the entire case-base – however, this cannot be guaranteed. This next stage of retrieval compares the target to related (non-footprint) cases in the case-base in order to locate the most similar case in the case-base. The related cases are those that are similar to the reference case, that is, those cases that are elements of its related set. During the second stage of retrieval each of the cases in the reference case's related set is compared to the target, a low-cost operation due to the small sizes of related sets.

4.2 Extending Footprint-Based Retrieval

One of the problems with the FBR method is that there are no guarantees that the best case in the case-base (closest to the target) will be contained within the related set of the reference case, and therefore this best case may not be retrieved. In fact in earlier experiments we have found this problem to occur in between 1% and 5% of retrievals [15]. This is the reason for the minor competence and quality degradation found for the footprint-based retrieval method when compared to the brute-force approach.

The new incremental FBR approach solves this problem by extending the second retrieval stage beyond the related set of a single reference case. So, during stage one, the k best footprint cases are selected to produce a *reference set*. Then stage two searches the union of the related sets of these k cases. This allows the new approach to "dig deeper" into the case-base in the region of the target and, for large enough values of k, guarantees that the best case is retrieved. By considering multiple reference cases in order of their similarity to the target we are effectively guiding the search in the target region. Note that k=1 is the original FBR method and k=0 corresponds to a footprint-based retrieval without stage two (that is, the reference case is retrieved).

```
Target ← Current target problem
CB ← Case-Base, FP ← Footprint Set

iFBR(Target,CB,FP)

   Stage 1
   RefSet ← k nearest FP cases to Target

   Stage 2
   For each c ∈ RefSet
     RelSet←RelSet ∪ RelatedSet(c)
   EndFor

   Case ← closest case in RelSet to Target

   Return(Case)
```

Algorithm 3. The Incremental Footprint-Based Retrieval Procedure.

4.3 Discussion

FBR and iFBR could be viewed as similar to other edited-set methods, as they search a subset of the available cases. However, the subset used by an edited-set technique such as CNN is computed eagerly, at training time, without reference to a specific target problem. In contrast, FBR and iFBR combine cases from a once-off subset of the entire case-base (the footprint set) with cases chosen (lazily) with respect to the target. This allows the FBR approaches to adapt their search space for the current target problem, thereby greatly improving retrieval competence and quality.

5 Experimental Studies

We claim that iFBR benefits from superior efficiency and optimal competence and quality characteristics. We support these claims by evaluating 3 retrieval algorithms: (1) **COV-FP**, iFBR using the footprinting method described in Algorithm 1; (2) **CNN-FP**, iFPR using the CNN footprinting method [5]; (3) **Standard**, a brute-force search of the case-base.

The experiments use two publicly available case bases: 1400 cases from the Travel domain (available from the Case base Archive at http://www.ai-cbr.org, [7]) and a 500 case case-base from the Residential Property domain (available from the UCI Machine Learning Repository). We also produced extra cases for each domain. For the Travel domain 400 duplicate cases and 400 near-miss (redundant) cases are added to generate a total of 2200 cases. For the Property domain 200 duplicates and 200 near-misses are added to give a total of 900 cases. These data-sets are processed to produce 30 different case-bases of size 700 with accompanying (non-overlapping) target problem sets of 200 cases.

We built CBR systems for these case-bases. For each system the solvability criterion was based on a similarity threshold; a target problem was successfully solved if the similarity between it and the retrieved case exceeded the threshold.

5.1 Retrieval Efficiency

The first experiment is concerned with evaluating the efficiency of the retrieval algorithms. Efficiency is measured as the inverse number of cases examined during retrieval. This is a fair measure since all four algorithms perform a simple search through a set of cases using the same standard weighted summed similarity operator; in other words there is no difference in the case similarity costs between the different retrieval methods.

Method: Each case-base is tested with respect to its target problem set and the average retrieval cost is computed. For the iFBR methods the value of k is increased until such time as CNN-FP and COV-FP retrieve the same case as the case retrieved by the standard, brute-force approach; This occurs are k = 3 and 4 (for COV-FP and CNN-FP) and at k = 5 and 6 (for COV-FP and CNN-FP), in the Travel and Property domains respectively.

Results: The results are shown in Fig. 2 as plots of efficiency (in terms of the average number of cases examined by each retrieval method) versus the reference set size. Notice that at k = 0 the CNN-FP and COV-FP methods are equivalent to a search of the footprint sets only (that is no stage 2 retrieval). Similarly, at k = 1 the CNN-FP and COV-FP methods are equivalent to the FBR method with its single reference case.

Discussion: Clearly the footprint-based methods significantly out-perform the Standard approach. In the Property domain, Fig. 2(b), for example, the COV-FP version of iFBR is between 4 and 6 times faster that the standard approach for values of k between 0 and 6. As expected, the efficiency of the footprint-based algorithms decreases for increasing values of k because of the larger sets of cases examined during the second stage of retrieval. However, the extra cost remains low with each increment of k. For instance, in the Travel domain, each increment of k contributes about 3 extra cases to the second stage of retrieval, and thus decreases efficiency by less than 1% for each increment; see also Section 6. In general, the COV-FP variant of iFBR performs consistently and significantly better than the CNN-FP variant since the footprints produced by COV-FP are smaller than those produced by CNN-FP.

In this experiment we have focused on efficiency for a 700 case case-base. We have carried out similar experiments for different case-base sizes, but due to lack of space we cannot report these results in detail here. However, very briefly, we have found that as the size of the case-base grows, so too does the speed-up achieved by iFBR (with k set for optimal retrievals). For example, in the Travel domain we achieve a speed-up of between 2.1 and 7.3 for case-bases ranging in size from 200 to 1400 cases; similar results have been observed in the Property domain.

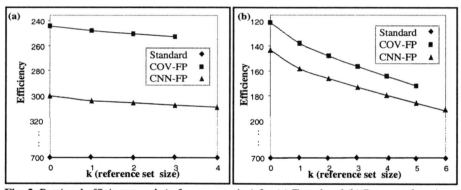

Fig. 2. Retrieval efficiency vs. k (reference set size) for (a) Travel and (b) Property domains.

5.2 Retrieval Optimality

The problem with FBR that motivates iFBR is that it does not guarantee the retrieval of the optimal case, that is, the best case for a given target. In this experiment we evaluate the optimality characteristics of iFBR and show how it can guarantee the retrieval of an optimal case.

Method: We follow the same experimental method discussed in Section 5.1, but this time, for each domain and algorithm we note the percentage of times that a sub-optimal case is retrieved for a target problem. We do this for increasing values of k until such time as no sub-optimal retrievals occur.

Results: The results are shown in Fig. 3 as a graph of the percentage sub-optimal targets retrieved versus k. Obviously, the Standard method has 0% sub-optimal retrievals since by definition it retrieves the best case every time (i.e. it achieves 100% optimality). Again note that k=0 and k=1 correspond to the results for the stage-one only and FBR retrieval methods, respectively.

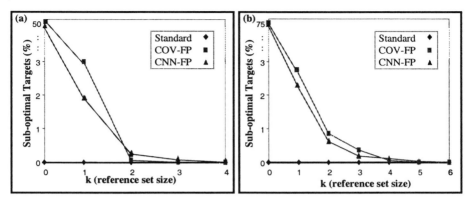

Fig. 3. Retrieval optimality vs. k (reference set size) for (a) Travel and (b) Property domains.

Discussion: As expected the iFBR variants perform poorly at k = 0, when only a stage-one retrieval is executed, the equivalent to searching a static edited set only. For example in the Travel domain the COV-FP and CNN-FP variants *fail* to retrieve the best case 56% and 48% of the time, respectively; see Fig. 3(a). At k=1, the standard FBR technique, the COV-FP and CNN-FP variants improve dramatically, with the failures dropping to 3% and 2% respectively. Very similar results are found in the Property domain as shown in Fig. 3(b). As the value of k increases beyond 1 we see that the iFBR variants quickly converge on an optimal result. For the Travel domain 100% optimality (matching the 0% failures of the Standard approach) is achieved at k=3 for COV-FP and at k=4 for CNN-FP. Similarly, for the Property domain, perfect optimality is achieved at k=5 for COV-FP and k=6 for CNN-FP. These results demonstrate that the additional iFBR stages do manage to actively reduce the number of sub-optimal retrievals, and indeed that 100% optimality can be achieved even for relatively small values of k where significant efficiency benefits are still available; for example, as shown the Property domain in Fig. 3(b), at k = 4 for COV-FP, we have reached 100% retrieval optimality by searching just over 20% of the case-base (that is, a speed-up of between 4 and 5 over the Standard method). In both domains we find that the COV-FP variant achieves 100% retrieval optimality at lower values of k than CNN-FP, indicating that the COV-FP footprinting technique is producing higher-quality footprint sets than CNN.

6 Discussion

The story so far is that we have introduced a simple but important extension to the successful footprint-based retrieval method. Before concluding we would like to address some of the concerns that have been raised about this extension recently.

a) "iFBR results in insignificant gains in retrieval optimality"

FBR on its own benefits from significant efficiency improvements but does suffer from a minor loss in retrieval competence and optimality (typically a 1%-5% loss as shown in [15]). In particular, there are no guarantees that the best available case will be retrieved, as would be the case in a standard brute-force search of the case-base. The point we have made is that sometimes the best available case *must* be retrieved, and in these situations the standard FBR method simply cannot be used. The incremental extension of FBR is a response to this, and although it is a relatively simple extension, we believe it to be an important one because it can be used in situations where FBR cannot; that is, in situations where optimal retrievals must be guaranteed. This point cannot be emphasised enough. The advantage of the new iFBR method is not so much that it leads to large improvements in retrieval optimality – after all, the standard FBR method delivers near optimal (95%+ of optimal) retrieval results to begin with. The point is that iFBR can deliver retrieval results that are 100% optimal (for a suitably chosen value of k), and even though the actual increase in optimality works out to be a small percentage, it can nonetheless be an important percentage, and it can make all the difference in domains where optimal retrievals are required.

b) "Retrieval time increases by a factor of k when examining k reference cases"

One of the criticisms that has been made against iFBR is that by looking at k reference cases rather than one, we are increasing the retrieval time by a factor of k, and therefore, that iFBR does not scale well with increasing values of k.

This is simply not true. On the face of it, it may appear to be true, because surely examining k related sets (or the k reference cases) will mean examining kn individual cases (where n is the average number of cases in a related set), and hence lead to a factor of k increase in retrieval time? However, the critical point is that nearby reference (footprint) cases will tend to have overlapping related sets, and therefore each new reference case will only contribute a fraction of its related set as new cases to be examined. For example, Fig. 4(a&b) show the percentage overlaps between pairs of overlapping related sets in the Travel and Property domain, respectively.

For example, we can see in Fig 4(a) that over 20% of the pairs of cases share identical related sets in the Travel domain. In fact, for pairs of cases with some overlap between their related sets, the average overlap values are 54% and 40% for the Travel and Property domain respectively. This means that, in the Travel domain for example, consecutive reference cases will have related sets that overlap by at least 54%, we say 'at least' here because consecutive reference cases are nearby to each other and therefore will have higher than average overlap.

Returning to the efficiency results (Section 5.1) we can see the effect of these overlaps. For example, in the Travel domain Fig. 2(a), the retrieval time for the COV-FP iFBR variant increases by roughly 3 cases per increment of k; that is, the related set of each new reference case contributes only 3 new cases to the retrieval process. Similar results are found for the Property domain, with each increment of k contributing between 7 and 10 new cases to the retrieval process (the Property domain has lower overlap characteristics than Travel). Therefore, the additional retrieval cost that comes with iFBR is not as significant as it might seem, and scales well with increasing values of k. Moreover, we argue that in many situations these minor increases in retrieval are acceptable given the benefits associated with the retrieval of an optimal case.

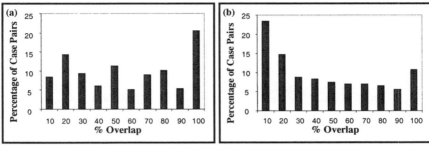

Fig. 4. Related set overlap characteristics for the (a) Travel and (b) Property domains.

c) "iFBR requires a competence model that is expensive to maintain"
The iFBR method relies on the availability of a comprehensive model of case competence and, of course, there is a cost associated with the construction and update of this model, and because of this there is an additional (and significant) cost associated with iFBR. While it is true that updating the competence model can involve a worst-case cost (of $O(n^2)$ in the size of the case-base), in recent work we have developed a new model building and update procedure that can significantly reduce this cost. In fact, the competence model can be constructed and maintained as a side-effect of iFBR, essentially removing the model-update cost altogether – the same basic computations are carried out in footprint-based retrieval and model update; see [17] for a complete description and evaluation of this update procedure.

7 Conclusions

We have described a competence-guided approach to retrieval (iFBR) that extends an earlier footprint-based retrieval method [15]. We have evaluated this new approach and demonstrated optimal retrieval results at a greatly reduced retrieval cost. iFBR is a general retrieval technique that makes no assumptions regarding the underlying CBR system, and that is generally applicable to any CBR system once a suitable similarity metric solvability criterion is available. Current and future work will continue to investigate the issue of performance modelling in CBR, and the role of these models in new solutions to problems such as case-base maintenance, case deletion, case-base construction, case-base visualization, and authoring support [8,9,10,14,16,17].

References

1. Aha, D.W., Kibler, D., and Albert, M.K. 1991. Instance-Based Learning Algorithms. *Machine Learning* 6. 37-66.
2. Agnar, A. and Plaza, E. 1994. Case-Based Reasoning: Foundational Issues, Methodological Variations, and System Approaches. *AI Communications* 7(1): 39-59.
3. Brown, M.G. 1994. An Underlying Memory Model to Support Case Retrieval. In *Topics in Case-Based Reasoning. Lecture Notes in Artificial Intelligence*, Vol. 837, 132-143. Berlin Heidelberg New York: Springer-Verlag.
4. Dasarathy, B.V. 1991. Nearest Neighbor Norms: NN Pattern Classification Techniques. Los Alamitos, Calif.: IEEE Press.
5. Hart, P.E.: 1967. The Condensed Nearest Neighbor Rule. *IEEE Transactions on Information Theory*, **14**: 515-516.
6. Leake, D.B., Kinley, A., and Wilson, D. 1997. Case-Based Similarity Asessment: Estimating Adaptability from Experience. *In Proceedings of the 14th National Conference on Artificial Intelligence*. Menlo Park, Calif.: AAAI Press.
7. Lenz, M. 1996. Applying Case Retrieval Nets to Diagnostic Tasks in Technical Domains. In *Advances in Case-Based Reasoning. Lecture Notes in Artificial Intelligence*, Vol. 1168, 219-233. Berlin Heidelberg New York: Springer-Verlag.
8. McKenna, E. and Smyth, B. 2000. Visualising the Competence of Case-Based Reasoners. *Journal of Applied Intelligence*. Forthcoming.
9. McKenna, E. and Smyth, B. 2000. Competence-Guided Case-Base Editing Techniques. In *Proceedings of the 5th European Workshop on Case-Based Reasoning*. Trento, Italy.
10. McKenna, E. and Smyth, B. 2000. Competence-Guided Editing Methods for Lazy Learning. In *Proceedings of the 14th European Conference on Artificial Intelligence*. Berlin, Germany.
11. Schaaf, J. W. 1996. Fish and Shrink: A Next Step Towards Efficient Case Retrieval in Large-Scale Case-Bases. In *Advances in Case-Based Reasoning. Lecture Notes in Artificial Intelligence, Vol. 1168*, 362-376. Berlin Heidelberg New York: Springer-Verlag.
12. Smyth, B. and Keane. M.T. 1998. Adaptation-Guided Retrieval: Questioning the Similarity Assumption in Reasoning. *Artificial Intelligence* **102**: 249-293.
13. Smyth, B. & Keane, M.T. 1995 Remembering to Forget: A Competence Preserving Deletion Policy for Case-Based Reasoning Systems. In *Proceedings of the 14th International Joint Conference on Artificial Intelligence*, 377-382. Morgan-Kaufmann.
14. Smyth, B. & McKenna, E. 1998. Modelling the Competence of Case-Bases. In *Advances in Case-Based Reasoning. Lecture Notes in Artificial Intelligence*, Vol. 1488, 208-220. Berlin Heidelberg New York: Springer-Verlag.
15. Smyth, B. and McKenna, E. 1999. Footprint-Based Retrieval. In *Case-Based Reasoning Research & Development. Lecture Notes in Artificial Intelligence, LNAI 1650*, 343-357. Berlin Heidelberg New York: Springer-Verlag.
16. Smyth, B. and McKenna, E. 1999. Building Compact Competent Case-Bases. In *Case-Based Reasoning Research & Development. Lecture Notes in Artificial Intelligence, LNAI 1650*, 343-357. Berlin Heidelberg New York: Springer-Verlag.
17. Smyth, B. and McKenna, E. 2000. An Efficient and Effective Procedure for Updating a Competence Model for Case-Based Reasoners. *Proceedings of the 11th European Conference on Machine Learning*. Barcelona, Spain.
18. Wess, S., Althoff, K-D., Derwand, G. 1994. Using k-d Trees to Improve the Retrieval Step in Case-Based Reasoning. In *Topics in Case-Based Reasoning. Lecture Notes in*

Artificial Intelligence, Vol. 837, 167 – 181, Berlin Heidelberg New York: Springer-Verlag

19. Wolverton, M., and Hayes-Roth, B. 1994. Retrieving Semantically Distant Analogies with Knowledge-Directed Spreading Activation. In *Proceedings of the 12th National Conference on Artificial Intelligence*, 56-61. Menlo Park, Calif.: AAAI Press.ernational Conference on Machine Learning (1992)

Macro and Micro Applications of Case-Based Reasoning to Feature-Based Product Selection

Guy Saward, Toby O'Dell
University of Hertfordshire
College Lane, Hatfield, Herts AL10 9AB, UK
{g.r.saward, t.odell}@herts.ac.uk

Abstract: This paper examines alternative applications of case-based reasoning to product selection. It is motivated by shortfalls in e-commerce solutions but addresses wider issues in the selection of case representations and reasoning strategies where solution requirements are negotiable and the number of potential features are large. Two approaches are examined: the micro approach uses the traditional CBR nearest-neighbour algorithm to augment product searches, while the macro approach is based on the traditional CBR-cycle but substitutes crisp constraint relaxation for similarity based retrieval. While the discussion is set against the background of a specific case study, the results have a wider applicability across a number of problem domains.

1. Introduction

The pivotal role of knowledge management in e-commerce applications is acknowledged at both a strategic level [PIU 1999] and at the level of individual applications. Many sites clearly fail to provide the knowledge[1] required to "help consumers make purchase decisions and buy products" [STA 99]. The inability of users to navigate a site easily and to correctly identify products that are relevant is highlighted as one of the most important issues for e-commerce [Shern & Crawford 1999]. The issue of product selection will become even more important as *e-tailers* (on-line retailers) "create new, large product databases that can be used to give online consumers a better choice of products than can be found off-line." [Jones et al, 1999].

The use of expert systems for product selection and configuration is a well-established idea (e.g. the R1 system used for configuring Dec VAXs [McDermott, 1980]). More recently, case base reasoning has been applied at a number of different levels. Fuzzy similarity based matching can be used (e.g. [Vollrath et al, 1998]) to provide a more graded response than that obtained by using crisp Boolean searches. This avoids the issue of getting too many results if the search is

---

[1] Using a teleological definition of knowledge as information likely to increase the probability of action [Nonaka 1994]

under constrained, or too few if the search is over constrained. Anther approach is to focus on the CBR cycle of retrieval, reuse, revision and retainment [Aamodt and Plaza, 1994]. This parallels work in the information retrieval domain, where iterative searching is becoming more important [Chen et al, 1998], and the convergence of case-based reasoning, information retrieval [Rissland and Daniels, 1996] and knowledge management processes [Saward, 2000]. Extensions of the CBR cycle have also been proposed to support product selection and sales [Wilke et al, 1999].

In this paper we separate out the use of similarity-based approaches from the CBR cycle. Although both approaches can still be characterised as case-based reasoning [Watson, 1997], we described the first as a *micro-application* of CBR that uses one of CBR's dominant techniques and the latter as a *macro-application* of CBR that is based on its underlying philosophy. In describing the macro approach we show how a query-based case representation can be used with crisp case matching to implement the standard CBR-cycle.

2. Products, Features and Cases

At a rational level the sales process can be viewed as a way of selecting a product that will best fulfil a customer's needs. One way of doing this is to translate product *features* into comparative *advantages* that will then deliver specific *benefits* to meet those needs [Kotler 2000]. However, in the main body of the paper we shall focus on product selection at the feature level. The justification for this is two-fold: first, the majority of large e-tailers are working at the feature level [Saward et al 2000]; second, the approach outlined here could easily be adopted through the use of a hierarchical case base structure.

2.1 Products as Cases

Taking a feature-based approach has the advantage of simplifying the sales process as there is no need to translate customer needs into product features. It also simplifies the knowledge representation as cases become simple relations. Taking a case as a situation-solution pair, each product becomes a single case. The product features F_i not only describe the product but also describe the customer feature requirements that the product would satisfy.

$C_i ::= <F_i , P_i>$

$F_i ::= <v_{1,i}, ..., v_{n,i}> \in A_1 \times ... \times A_n$

$C_i ::=$ case for ith product in case base

$P_i ::=$ product identifier for ith case

$F_i ::=$ feature values for ith product

$A_j ::=$ set of allowed values for jth feature

$v_{i,j} ::=$ value of ith feature of jth product

In general the product cases should be kept as simple and as descriptive as possible and focus on the product specification, rather than the requirements that a product may fit. For example, although a requirement for a red car may be met by cars that are maroon or scarlet, this information would not be captured in the car's colour attribute. The natural place to store this knowledge is in the functions used to assess similarity.

2.2   Assessing Similarity

The product feature case model fits easily with a relational database design and allows for easy extensions from Boolean queries, e.g. using SQL, to similarity based searches.

Similarity between any product case C_i and a customer's requirements R, expressed by a set of feature values, can be assessed using the standard nearest neighbour similarity function applied to the product features F_i.

$$\text{Sim}(R, F_i) = \frac{\sum_{j=1}^{n} w_j \times \sigma_j (r_j , v_{j,i})}{\sum_{j=1}^{n} w_j} \qquad \text{where}$$

$w_j ::=$ weighting for jth attribute

$\sigma_j : A_j \times A_j \to [-1,1] ::=$ similarity function for jth attribute used to assess degree of match between requirement value r_j and product feature value $v_{j,i}$

The similarity functions used in assessing a product's fulfilment of a specific customer requirement (i.e. a single attribute) may take many forms, both in terms of the type of data and the shape of the function. Using car selection as an example domain, the data used could be numeric (e.g. price), symbolic (e.g. 4-door or estate case) or some combination of the two via an encoding scheme (e.g. location or colour). The similarity functions could be:

- symmetric - e.g. for matching engine size

- upper bounded - e.g. for price

- lower bounded - e.g. for number of seats / passengers

- pair-wise relational - e.g. for colour matches between any pair of colours

The similarity functions defined above allows for easy extension of relational database queries to incorporate fuzzy retrieval of candidate products without reference to the revision or reuse parts of the CBR-cycle. For this basic approach, as with any other knowledge engineering task, the determination of the case attributes, similarity functions and attribute weightings would need to be determined by an analysis of the problem domain. However, there are generic issues with this basic approach that need to be addressed as discussed below.

2.3 Managing Choice

The main motivation of using CBR for product selection is to deal with the issue of search requirement specification. Using Boolean database queries, under-constrained search criteria will result in too many candidate products while over constrained criteria will result in too few. In principle the product feature case approach allows under- and over-specification to be managed by ranking candidate products according to degree of similarity.

In practice, the large number of product features and the size of the case base (i.e. number of potential products) make the specification, interpretation and use of similarity a non-trivial task. For example, when choosing a car one might have the option to specify values for major criteria such as:

- Make and Model

- Price

- Availability (i.e. delay in manufacture / delivery / time to market)

- Age and mileage (if not a new car)

- Body style

- Engine size

- Exterior and Interior colour

- Dealer location

- Equipment level, e.g. entry level, luxury, sporty etc

The choice generate by this list of features is substantial. This choice is compounded if one includes the specification of individual items of equipment such as entertainment (radio, tape, CD, PC) or other systems (trip computer, phone, navigation), safety systems (antilock brakes, air bags, fog lights), climate control (air conditioning, seat heating, quick clear windscreens) and so on.

The key issue with using the product feature case approach outlined above is the difficulty in specifying the notion of similarity so that the system can cope with the number of trade-offs and the subjectivity or personalisation involved in that assessment. For example, how might a consumer compromise their requirements if their ideal car is not going to be available for six months, and their closest alternatives are a larger, more expensive car or a two year old, lime green car at the other end of the country.

We have identified three distinct approaches for creating a solution that addresses this issue:

- An *adjusted weighting* model that focuses on the similarity measure to determine a weighting that provides the highest utility in ranking of cases;

- An *abstract feature* model that focuses on the case representation to reduce the number of cases, and thereby reduce the discrimination needed by the similarity measure;

- An *iterative relaxation* model that focuses on the CBR cycle to allow for iteration through selection cycle and identifies the best dimensions for compromise.

Figures1b-1d show the effect of each of these approaches on the CBR process through changes in the data, neighbourhood geometry and starting point of the basic product feature case approach.. Figure 1a shows an abstract representation of the product feature case approach in which similarity is assessed in two dimensions[2] to see which products (♦) best match / are closest to the specified requirements (o). In figure 1b, decreasing the importance of the price allows more variation in its value while maintaining the same similarity score[3]. Figure 1c shows the effect of using a more abstract feature representation in which the number of cases is reduced, while figure 1d shows the effect of revising the initial user requirements.

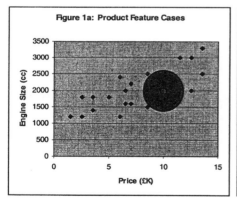
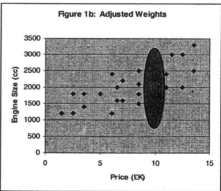

Figure 1: Alternative case representation and reasoning approaches

---

[2] A circle is used to represent a neighbour of equal similarity.

[3] This approach mirrors the stretching proposed by Dietrich et al [1997] for k-NN classifiers

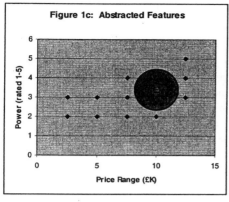 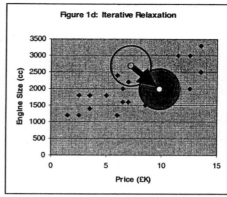

Figure 1: Alternative case representation and reasoning approaches

The differences in approach stem from the case representations used in each. In the adjusted weighting model, the case retains the product feature case with each individual product represented as a case. In the abstract feature model, each case is used to model a product exemplar in which individual features are used to derive more abstract attributes. For example, a car may be deemed sporty if it has a high power to weight ratio, alloy wheels and spoilers. Finally, in the iterative relaxation model, a case is used to model a previously successful query and CBR is used to determine which relaxation of requirements is likely to be most successful. The three types of case are increasingly abstract, and increasingly general or fuzzy about the exact product specification.

3.   Micro-CBR Approaches

The emphasis for micro-CBR approaches is on tuning the knowledge representation of the product cases and the retrieval algorithm in order to produce the best possible search results.

3.1   Adjusted Weighting

There are two basic approaches to refine the potentially arbitrary similarity function. The first is to abdicate responsibility of setting the weighting to the user. This then allows the user to set and adjust the relative importance of particular product attributes in an attempt to find the best match. This adjustment could take place during the search process and would allow users to evaluate "what if" scenarios. Although this allows the system to cater for the subjectivity and personal preference inherent in product selection, this does not present a systematic approach to managing the problem of choice. Moreover, this approach could be said to compound the problem as the user now has twice as much choice:. not only do they have to pick values for particular attributes, they have to rank or score the importance of that attribute.

The second approach is to allow the CBR system to adjusting the weightings automatically. This could either be done without intervention, using a maximum discrimination or entropy approach [Wilkes et al, 1999] or by allowing the user to pick the product that they perceive best matches their need. This user selection is then used as a training input to adjust the attribute weightings to reduce the error between the current system generated best selection and the user's best selection. There are various approaches that could be taken to this type of lazy learning where performance feedback (i.e. user perception of success) is used to tune the weighting of features [Dietrich et al, 1997]. One dimension of difference is that between on-line optimisers that adjust the weights after each use, and batch optimisers, e.g. those based on genetic algorithms that require training on a batch of stored data.

The simplest approach to feature weighting depends on the notion that there is a *single* best set of weightings. Although the case library is being used for only one purpose[4], the degree of subjectivity in assessing the user's best selection means that the system will only be able to arrive at a compromise weighting covering all users of the system. It would be possible to extend the system to allow it to be trained for individual users or groups of users. This would mean incorporating personal characteristics such as age, wealth, occupation etc into the case representation. Another change to the representation would be to allow different sets of features (i.e. variable weightings) to be used for different types of products [Domingos, 1997].

Other extensions would apply to the individual attributes' similarity function. These may also need to be adjusted as subjectivity is not only limited to trade-offs between features but is also inherent in the compromises for specific features. For example, sport enthusiasts might consider red and yellow very similar, while more conventional drivers would associate red with purple.

A final issue to consider here is the degree of independence between attributes and their weightings. For example, the amount of flexibility in the price a customer is prepared to pay is not a function of the users bank balance and the scale of the purchase. It will also relate to perceived benefit or "value for money" which in turn is a function of other product features [Hulthage & Stobie, 1998]. The result of this is that in some situations it is not possible to model the user preferences by adjusting the weightings of individual features so that the users preferred product becomes the highest ranked selection. Although techniques exist to tune models with interacting features, they either require domain specific knowledge to guide the learning process or result in representation that cannot be meaningfully interpreted [Dietrich et al, 1997].

3.2 Abstracted Features

---

[4] This is normally taken as an indicator of success [Kolodner 1993, p359],

The abstracted feature approach is based on the notion of reducing the number of features used in the case representation. This approach can also be extended to reducing the set of possible values for a particular feature, e.g. by mapping the size of the engine to a range of discrete values, say 1 - 5, or symbolic values such as *very powerful*. This approach is akin to exemplar based classification in which a single item is used to represent a class of similar objects. It is highly appropriate in this situation as the feature-rich products provide "well articulated models of the items (the system) is trying to match" which are reported to work well with this type of representation [Kolodner 19993, p482].

The abstraction that comes from using exemplars can be generated in two ways: it may be inherent in the configuration of standard products for sale; or it may be generated from the class of instances either through some kind of induction, or through explicit knowledge engineering within the domain. The former is exemplified by the purchase of new cars in which users can select the major characteristics such as model, body shape, equipment level and price band before tailoring their purchase through the selection of additional optional extras. The latter approach is akin to second hand car purchases where combinations of features might be used to determine if the car is nearly new (by age or mileage), and/or a family car (by number of seats and boot size). This distinction is also becoming important in the housing market where buyers of new houses have the opportunity to specify certain elements of the design while those purchasing existing houses must look for properties that meet their requirements be they a family house or a bachelor pad.

In general, using abstract features should help to manage choice as it reduces the number of degrees of freedom that the user has to work within. In practice, this will only happen if the abstractions are meaningful and generally applicable. This is not the case for example if one looks at car model designations where a range of options are packaged together. A top of the range Ford that includes almost all options could be branded a "GhiaX" while the equivalent Vauxhall would be a "CD". Other designations are more applicable, e.g. an "L" designation, but vary from one manufacturer to another. The fact that the same designation from the same manufacturer might also include different options over time will also decrease the meaningfulness of such abstractions.

4. Macro-CBR Approaches

The iterative relaxation approach is based on the notion that previous searches can be used to guide the modification or compromise of user requirements. In doing this, the underlying case representation is changed from the product feature case to a query requirements case. This is a fundamental change to the knowledge representation[5] and differs from a *use-adapted case retriever* in which the history is used to augment an existing case retrieval [Alterman and Griffin, 1996]. It also represents a departure from the CBR-cycle for electronic sales support applications proposed by Wilke et al [1999] of:

- **retrieve** products that match the initial user demands

- **reuse** products as the starting point for configuring an offer to meet the user's specific demands

- **revise**[6] view of products to establish list of evaluated products

- **refine** list of user requirements based on evaluated products

In the proposed iterative relaxation approach the product feature case is replaced by cases that are used to represent how users compromise their requirements. The single set of product features F_i used to represent both the product features and user requirements is replaced by two sets of product features. One set of features is used to represent the initial user query and the second represents the revised requirements that lead to a successful search. Both the initial query Q_i and the revised requirements R_i are expressed as sets of attribute values.

$$C_i ::= <Q_i , R_i>$$
$$Q_i ::= <v_{1,i}, ..., v_{n,i}> \in A_1 \times ... \times A_n$$
$$R_i ::= <v_{1,i}, ..., v_{n,i}> \in A_1 \times ... \times A_n$$

The standard CBR-cycle is then used to generate crisp database queries, with the result set used to judge the success or failure of the query. The search may be considered unsuccessful, if it returns too few, too many or simply the wrong type of product. In this situation, a case base search is undertaken to find the best adaptation of requirements, as shown in figure 2, using the traditional CBR cycle applied to the query cases:

- **retrieve** previous queries or searches that are similar to the initial user demands

- **reuse** queries by substituting variables as required

- **revise** query by trial execution to see if it represents a better solution

- **retain** query if it results in a successful search

---

[5] Although this is a fundamental change to the product feature case approach, the notion of storing local actions for optimal behaviour is not new, e.g. [Sycara and Miyashita, 1994]

[6] The original does not identify what is actually being revised - it is assumed that it is the customer's view of the product that it is revised.

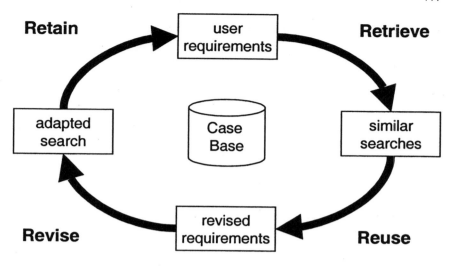

Figure 2: Iterative relaxation CBR cycle

As an example, suppose the user is looking for a green, 2 litre Ford Mondeo in Devon costing £10,000. If a search of the product database fails to retrieve any matching products then the user must compromise on their requirements. A search of the case base might reveal that similar requests had been met by an £8,000 blue Mondeo from Essex and a 1.8 litre from Coventry. Taking a simple majority voting approach over the previously relaxed attributes would indicate that the user should compromise on location first.

In practice, the inclusion of the reuse and revise phases of the CBR cycle will depend upon the ability to generalise from queries and apply specific rewrite rules. In the case of general query representations, the case will also need to have some measure of utility attached to it, so that the most successful query adaptations, i.e. most successful dimension for constraint relaxation, are attempted first.

5.   Implementation Issues

We are currently enhancing a nearest neighbour, product feature case application to investigate the comparative advantages and disadvantages of micro- and macro-CBR approaches. The application is based on an Access database and accessed via a combination of JavaScript, VBScript and ASP. Although the trial domain is used cars, the approach is equally applicable to other feature rich domains such as property, PCs, other consumer electronics and holidays. These sectors currently account for almost 50% of current e-commerce sales [Jones et al, 1999] as well as representing some of the high growth sectors. The system should also work equally well with new, "previously enjoyed" or auctioned goods. A key issue for the evaluation of the macro-approach to product selection will be the acquisition of sufficient customer data to allow for meaning constraint relaxation. This is currently being investigated with a number of major e-tailers.

Another key issue is that of case base maintenance. For the micro-approaches that use the product feature case, the case base must be maintained as new products are added and old products deleted. Where abstract features are used and the products represent exemplars of a product range this should be relatively straightforward as the product changes are less frequent than for concrete product feature cases. In the worst case where each case represents a single unique instance of a product, such as used cars, the case base indices and reasoning mechanisms must be maintained in real time as major dealers can buy and sell hundreds of products a day.

The changing stock of available products has less predictable consequences for the macro-CBR approach. The query cases show how the user requirements were modified at a particular point in time to meet a specific need. However, this compromise of requirements would have been done within the context of a particular set of choices, i.e. the products available within the product database at that specific point in time. The applicability of what was the best choice at that point in time will be reduced if the context has changed. The degree to which this affects the system usability can only be established through an on-going, long-term system evaluation.

6.   Conclusions

Feature based product selection is alive and well on the Internet and will continue to be so. However, it is clear that if e-commerce is to meet its explosive growth targets that e-tailers must provide systems to support less knowledgeable shoppers [Saward et al, 2000]. Case-based reasoning is an approach that can provide a number of different solutions to the problem of managing choice, all based on a simple underlying knowledge representation.   We have presented a range of alternatives from fuzzy database matching and the use of abstraction, to iterative approaches to searching.

There are other interesting CBR solutions for product selection and recommendation that have not been explored in this paper. They include:

- the combination of approaches outlined above for feature-based selection;

- the use of hierarchical or stratified CBR [Branting and Aha, 1995] to allow for the translation of user needs and benefits into product features for high ticket items;

- user classification into on-line communities such as reading circles and music channels for cross-selling related products for smaller ticket items.

The context of the work presented here has been limited to a small number of domains. However, the approaches outlined are widely applicable in an industrial context as well as providing a platform for exploring synergies between CBR, machine learning and information retrieval.

References

Aamodt A and Plaza E, 1994. Case-based reasoning: Foundational issues, methodological variations and system approaches, *AI Communications*

Aha, D.W., 1997. Lazy Learning, *Artificial Intelligence Review*, 11(1-5), pp1-423

Altman R and Griffin D, 1996. Improving Case Retrieval by Remembering Questions, *Thirteenth National Conference on Artificial Intelligence*, pp678-683

Branting L. and Aha D., 1995. Stratified Case-Based Reasoning: Reusing hierarchical Problem Solving Episodes, *Fourteenth International Joint Conference on Artificial Intelligence*, pp384-390.

Chen et al, 1998. Internet Browsing and Searching: User Evaluations of Category Map and Concept Space Techniques, *Journal of the American Society of Information Science*, July 1998, pp582-603.

Domingos P., 1997. Context-Sensitive Feature Selection for Lazy Learners, *Artificial Intelligence Review*, 11(1-5), pp227-253.

Hulthage I.E. and Stobie I, 1998. Countrywide Automated Property Evaluation System - CAPES, *Tenth Innovative Applications of Artificial Intelligence*, pp1039-1046

Jones I, Patel V, Beauvillain O and Neufeld E, 1999. <u>*European Online Shopping*</u>, Jupiter Communications, London.

Kolodner J., 1993. *Case-Based Reasoning*, Morgan Kaufman.

Kotler P., 2000. *Marketing Management*, Prentice Hall.

McDermott J., 1980. R1: an expert in the computer system domain, *Proc National Conference on Artificial Intelligence*, pp269-71.

Nonaka I., 1994. A Dynamic Theory of Organizational Knowledge Creation, *Organization Science*, 5(1), pp14-37.

PIU 1999. *E-commerce@its.best.uk*, Performance and Innovation Unit Report, UK Cabinet Office, September 1999.

Rissland E. and Daniels J, 1996. The Synergistic Application of CBR to IR, *Artificial Intelligence Review*, 10(1-2), pp441-475.

Saward G, 2000. The challenge for customer service: managing heterogeneous knowledge, in Schwatz D. (eds) *Internet Information Systems for Knowledge Management*, Idea Group Publishing

Saward G., Ambrosiadou V., and Polovina S., 2000. A FAB Approach to E-Commerce Knowledge Accessibility Requirements, Technical Report, University of Hertfordshire, forthcoming.

Shern S and Crawford F, 1999. *2nd Annual Internet Shopping Study*, Ernst & Young, New York.

STA, 1999. *Click Here Commerce*, Shelley Taylor Associates, February 1999, http://www.infofarm.com

Sycara K. and Miyashita K., 1994. Case-based acquisition of User Preferences for Solution Improvement in Ill-Structured Domains, *Twelfth National Conference on Artificial Intelligence*, pp44-55

Vollrath I., Wilke W., and Bergmann R, 1998. Case-based reasoning support for online catalogue sales, *IEEE Internet Computing*, July-August 1998

Wilke W., Bergmann R., and Wess., 1999. Negotiation During Intelligent Sales Support with Case-Based Reasoning, *German Workshop on CBR*

Wettschereck D., Aha D. and Mohri T., 1997. A review of Empirical Evaluation of Feature Weighting Methods for a Class of Lazy Learning Algorithms, *Artificial Intelligence Review*, 11(1-5), pp273-314

Formal Concept Analysis as a Support Technique for CBR [*]

Belén Díaz-Agudo and Pedro A. González-Calero
Dep. Sistemas Informáticos y Programación
Universidad Complutense de Madrid
email: {belend, pedro}@sip.ucm.es

Abstract. This paper shows how the use of Galois lattices and Formal Concept Analysis (FCA) can support CBR application designers, in the task of discovering knowledge embedded in the cases. FCA applied on a case library provides an internal sight of the conceptual structure and allows finding patterns, regularities and exceptions among the cases. Moreover, it extracts certain dependence rules between the attributes describing the cases, that will be used to guide the query formulation process.

1   Introduction

Our overall work is the development of a CBR shell, which provides support for the design process of knowledge intensive CBR applications. In a knowledge rich CBR approach, the domain knowledge can be used to provide with sophisticated CBR processes, by reasoning with the knowledge to get for example, semantic similarity measures or intelligent adaptation processes. Although this is our general line of work [4,7], we are not focusing on that in this paper, where we use specific knowledge extracted from the concrete cases to complement the general domain knowledge.

We consider that a concrete case library contains useful knowledge other than the individual specific pieces of problem solving experiences to be reused. We are considering the importance of the co-appearance of attribute values in the cases, i.e. regularities and exceptions among the cases. We propose the use of Formal Concept Analysis (FCA) as an inductive technique that elicits knowledge embedded in a concrete case library and enriches the domain conceptual taxonomy.

The dependency knowledge implicitly contained in the case base is captured during the FCA process in the form of dependence rules among the attributes describing the cases, that will guide the CBR query formulation process. Moreover the concept lattice resultant from the FCA application, can be used as a case organization structure: the formal concepts represent *maximal* groupings of cases with shared properties; within this structure we can

---

[*] Supported by the Spanish Committee of Science & Technology (CICYT, TIC98-0733)

access together all the cases sharing a set of properties with the given query, because they are grouped under the same concept. That facilitates a certain type of direct retrieval or inspection of the case set. The extracted knowledge is dependent from the case library and will be used to complete the knowledge already acquired by other techniques of domain modelling. The approach presented here complements other knowledge intensive CBR processes provided by our system, whose description is out the scope of this paper.

Next section introduces the basics of the Formal Concept Analysis technique. Section 3 describes how we are applying FCA for knowledge elicitation on case bases. Section 4 shows how the elicited knowledge can be used during the query formulation and retrieval tasks. Finally the related work and conclusions of our approach are discussed.

2 Formal Concept Analysis

FCA is a mathematical approach to data analysis based on the lattice theory of Garret Birkhoff [3]. It provides a way to identify groupings of objects with shared properties. FCA is especially well suited when we have to deal with a collection of items described by properties. This is a clear characteristic of the case libraries where there are cases described somehow by features. The formal concepts provide a method for structuring and displaying the relationships between the cases.

A (one-valued) *formal context* is defined as a triple (G, M, I) where there are two sets G (of objects) and M (of attributes), and a binary (incidence) relation $I \subseteq G \times M$, expressing which attributes describe each object[1] (or which objects are described using an attribute), i.e., $(g,m) \in I$ if the object g carries the attribute m, or m is a descriptor of the object g.

With a general perspective, a concept represents a group of objects and is described by using *attributes* (its intent) and *objects* (its extent). The extent covers all objects belonging to the concept while the intent comprises all attributes (or properties) shared by all those objects.

With $A \subseteq G$ and $B \subseteq M$ the following operator (*prime*) is defined as:

$$A' = \{m \in M \mid (\forall g \in A)\, (g,m) \in I \}$$
$$B' = \{g \in G \mid (\forall m \in B)\, (g,m) \in I \}$$

A pair (A,B) where $A \subseteq G$ and $B \subseteq M$, is said to be a *formal concept* of the context (G,M,I) if $A' = B$ and $B' = A$. A and B are called the *extent* and the *intent* of the concept, respectively.

It can also be observed that, for a concept (A,B), $A'' = A$ and $B'' = B$, what means that *all* objects of the extent of a formal concept, have *all* the attributes of the intent of the concept, and that there is no other object in the set G having all the attributes of (the intent of) the concept.

---

[1] See [6,12] for a complete description of Formal Concept Analysis.

The set of all the formal concepts of a context (G,M,I) is denoted by $\mathscr{B}(G,M,I)$. The most important structure on $\mathscr{B}(G,M,I)$ is given by the subconcept–superconcept *order* relation denoted by $\leq$ and defined as follows:

$$(A_1, B_1) \leq (A_2, B_2) \text{ if } A_1 \subseteq A_2 \text{ (which is equivalent to } B_2 \subseteq B_1 \text{ see [6])}.$$

BASIC THEOREM FOR CONCEPT LATTICES [11]
Let (G, M, I) be a context. Then $\langle \mathscr{B}(G,M,I), \leq \rangle$ is a complete lattice, called the concept lattice of the context (G,M,I), for which infimum and supremum can be described as follows:

$$\text{Inf } \mathscr{B}(G,M,I) \equiv \bigwedge_{\alpha} (A_\alpha, B_\alpha) = \left[\bigcap_\alpha A_\alpha, \left(\bigcup_\alpha B_\alpha \right)'' \right]$$

$$\text{Sup } \mathscr{B}(G,M,I) \equiv \bigvee_{\alpha} (A_\alpha, B_\alpha) = \left[\left(\bigcup_\alpha A_\alpha \right)'', \bigcap_\alpha B_\alpha \right]$$

Graphically, contexts are usually described by cross-tables (see Table 2) while concept lattices are visualised by a *Hasse diagram* (see Figure 2). The following sections illustrate how FCA is applied to different examples, and how the dependency knowledge is extracted from the concept lattice interpretation.

3 Knowledge Elicitation from a Case Base

What we propose is the application of FCA as an automatic technique to elicit the attribute dependency knowledge inside a case library, and use it to complete the knowledge already acquired by other techniques of domain modelling. Besides the dependence rules set, FCA application to a case library provides with a conceptual hierarchy, because it extracts the formal concepts and the hierarchical relations among them, where related cases are clustered according to their shared properties.

This section describes, through two examples, the process of knowledge elicitation, and next section describe how this knowledge can be applied for retrieval in CBR.

3.1 A First Example of FCA Application

We shall use an example domain that is a simplified view of the *Travel Agency Domain* [10], where the cases represent descriptions of the journeys offered by a travel agency. Figure 1 shows the slots used to describe the cases and the set of values that may be used for each slot in a case.

In CBR systems, cases are typically described by more complex structures than the simple tupla of the example domain. We will use this simplified view

Figure 1. Travel Agency Domain.

	DESTINATION	**HOLIDAY TYPE**	**TRANSPORTATION**	**SEASON**
Case 1	Spain	Education	Car	Summer
Case 2	New York	Skiing	Plane	Winter
Case 3	Spain	Education	Train	Summer
Case 4	England	Active	Car	Autumn
Case 5	Spain	Skiing	Plane	Winter
Case 6	England	Education	Train	Summer
Case 7	New York	Active	Plane	Spring

Table 1. Cases from the travel agency domain.

for the sake of an easier exposition of the FCA technique, but next subsection extends it to richer case representations.

We will consider a very simple case base made up of 7 cases described according to the structure given in Figure 1. Each case is described by the same attributes, i.e. we are using a *flat domain* [1], that can be represented in a table where the rows correspond to the cases and the columns to the attributes.

We interpret the data in Table 1 as a formal context. Actually, what we have is a *many-valued* formal context that is defined as an structure (G, M, W, I) where G is a set of objects, M is a set of attributes, W is a set of attribute values, and I is a ternary relation between G, M and W $(I \subseteq G \times M \times W)$; $(g,m,v) \in I$ is read as the object g has the value v for the attribute m, and $(g,m,v) \in I$ and $(g,m,w) \in I$ always implies that $v=w$. Note that, this property inhibits the FCA application when there are multi-valued attributes having more than one filler.

The Table 1 may be understood as a many-valued context for which G is the set of cases (whose names are heading the rows), M is the set of attributes (whose names are heading the columns), while W is a set containing all attribute values described by the entries in the table.

The many-valued formal context will be transformed to a one-valued context by *transformational scaling* [6,9,12]. By now we use the simplest way: *plain scaling*. Each attribute on the original many-valued context is substituted by a set of columns representing each one of the allowed values for the attribute. We obtain fifteen columns containing the same information that substitute the four original attributes. The crosses in the Table 2 indicate when an object has

	D::Spain	D::Egypt	D::England	D::New York	HT::Active	HT::Education	HT::Language	HT::Skiing	T::Car	T::Plane	T::Train	S::Summer	S::Winter	S::Autumn	S::Spring
Case 1	☑					☑			☑			☑			
Case 2			☑						☑		☑		☑		
Case 3	☑					☑				☑	☑				
Case 4		☑		☑					☑					☑	
Case 5	☑								☑		☑		☑		
Case 6		☑				☑				☑	☑				
Case 7				☑	☑						☑				☑

Table 2. Formal context for the travel agency domain.

an attribute, i.e. when a feature is a descriptor of a case. We abbreviate the attribute names by using their initial letter.

Obviously, the process of scaling results in a loss of information since scaled attributes are mutually independent, so that, in the example, there is the same relation between D::Spain and D::Egypt than between D::Spain and D::Car. Remember, however, that we are using FCA as a complementary technique, and not as the core representation mechanism.

We are extending our approach to more complex conceptual scaling processes where the choice of the attributes of the scale is purpose-oriented and reflects the understanding of an expert of the domain. That is used for example with numeric attributes where the attribute values are too specific and are replaced by more general attributes, for example the binary property of belonging (or not) to certain intervals chosen to reflect the view of an expert [9].

Besides the cross table representation, there is a graphical representation of formal contexts using a Hasse diagram of the concept lattice. Figure 2 shows the Hasse diagram of the concept lattice associated to the context given in Table 2. Each node in the diagram represents a formal concept of the context, and the ascending paths of line segments represent the subconcept-superconcept relation. The lattice contains exactly the same information that the cross table, so that the incidence relation I can always be reconstructed from the lattice.

In the Hasse Diagram, labels meaning attributes from the intent are marked by [ ] and labels meaning object from the extent are marked by {}. A lattice node is labelled with the attribute $m \in M$ if it is the upper node having m in its intent; and a lattice node is labelled with the object $g \in G$ if it is the lower node having g in its extent. Using this labelling, each label (attribute or object name) is used exactly once in the diagram. If a node C is labelled by the attribute $[m]$ and the object $\{g\}$ then all the concepts *greater* than C (above C in the graph) have the object g in their extents, and all the concepts *smaller* than C (below C in the graph) have the attribute m in their intents.

120

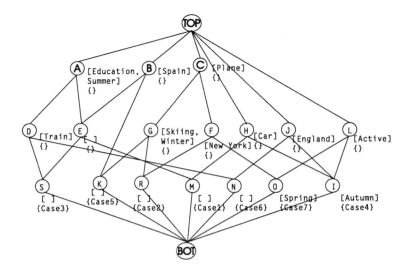

Figure 2. Hasse diagram for the travel agency domain.

In a Hasse diagram, the intent of a concept can be obtained as the union of the attributes in its label [ ] and attributes in the labels [ ] of the concepts *above* it in the lattice. Conversely, the extent of a concept, is obtained as the union of the objects in its label {} and attributes in the labels {} of the concepts *below* it in the lattice. Table 3 shows the complete extent and intent of the formal concepts in the diagram of Figure 2.

To reconstruct a row of the original incidence relation in Table 2, look for the unique concept C which label {} contains the object name heading the row and mark with a cross (in the row we are reconstructing) the column of each one of the attributes of the intent of C. For example, to reconstruct the cross table row of Case6, mark with a cross the columns corresponding to the intent of concept N: [Train, Education, Summer, England]. Dually, to reconstruct a Table 2 column, look for the concept C which label [ ] contains the attribute name heading the column, and mark with a cross the row of each one of the objects of the extent of C. For example, to reconstruct the column named Summer in the cross table, mark the rows corresponding to the concept A extent: {Case3, Case1, Case6}.

Besides the hierarchical conceptual clustering of the cases, the concept lattice provides with a set of *implications* between attributes. These implications are what we call *dependence rules*. A dependence rule between two attribute sets (written $M1 \rightarrow M2$, where $M1, M2 \subseteq M$) means that any object having all attributes in $M1$ has also all attributes in $M2$. We can read the dependence rules in the graph as follows:

– Each line between nodes *labelled with attributes* means a dependence rule between the attributes from the *lower* node to the *upper* one.

Formal Concept	Extent Case number	Intent
		_B_ (G,M,I) : Set of formal concepts
TOP	1,2,3,4,5,6,7	∅
A	1,3,6	Education, Summer
B	1,3,5	Spain
C	2,5,7	Plane
D	3,6	Education, Train, Summer
E	1,3	Spain, Education, Summer
F	2,7	NewYork, Plane
G	2,5	Skiing, Plane, Winter
H	1,4	Car
J	6,4	England
L	7,4	Active
M	1	Spain,Education,Car,Summer
R	2	NewYork, Skiing, Plane, Winter
S	3	Spain, Education, Train, Summer
I	4	England,Active,Car,Autumn
K	5	Spain, Skiing, Plane, Winter
N	6	England, Education, Train, Summer
O	7	NewYork, Active, Plane, Spring
BOT	∅	Spain, England, NewYork, Skiing, Education, Active, Plane, Car, Train, Summer, Winter, Autumn, Spring

Table 3. Formal concepts in the travel agency domain.

- When there are several attributes in the same label it means that there is a *co-appearance* of all these attributes for all the cases in the sample.

For example, the two attributes label [Skiing, Winter] means that in the case base all skiing travels are in winter time and vice versa, that all the travels in the winter season are for skiing activities. It induces a bi-directional dependence rule in the form Skiing ↔ Winter, that is separated in the two dependence rules Skiing → Winter and Winter → Skiing. The following set of dependence rules is extracted from the lattice:

{ Train → Education, Summer; New York → Plane;
  Skiing, Winter → Plane; Spring → New York; Autumn → Car;
  Autumn → England; Autumn → Active; Skiing → Winter;
  Winter → Skiing ; Education → Summer; Summer → Education }

The information about attribute implications represents knowledge from a concrete case library that will be used to help in the query definition process.

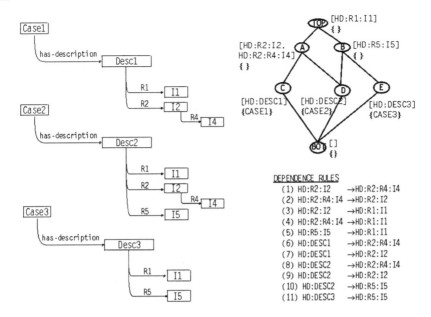

Figure 3. Cases, Hasse diagram and dependence rules.

	HD:DESC1	HD:DESC2	HD:DESC3	HD:R1:I1	HD:R2:I2	HD:R5:I5	HD:R2:R4:I4
CASE1	☑			☑	☑		☑
CASE2		☑		☑	☑	☑	☑
CASE3			☑	☑		☑	

Table 4. Context for the second example.

3.2 A Second Example of FCA Application

The travel agency example domain includes simple flat cases described by the same set of characteristics. We would like to apply FCA to more complex case bases with, for example, partially defined or complex structured cases.

When relational attributes are used to describe more complex and structured cases, we construct the sets G and M as follows: G is the set of cases; M is the set of case descriptors that is constructed over the case representation tree, level by level, obtaining partial paths of relations that lead to intermediate and final instances. The elements of M are made up with the subpaths from the case individual towards the leaves in the representation tree. Each descrip-

B (G,M,I) : Set of formal concepts		
Formal Concept	Extent	Intent
TOP	Case1, Case2, Case3	[hd:R1:**I1**]
A	Case1, Case2	[hd:R1:**I1**] [hd:R2:**I2**] [hd:R2:R4:**I4**]
B	Case2, Case3	[hd:R1:**I1**] [hd:R5:**I5**]
C	Case1	[hd:**desc1**][hd:R1:**I1**][hd:R2:**I2**] [hd:R2:R4:**I4**]
D	Case2	[hd:**desc2**] [hd:R1:**I1**] [hd:R5:**I5**] [hd:R2:**I2**] [hd:R2:R4:**I4**]
E	Case3	[hd:**desc3**] [hd:R1:**I1**] [hd:R5:**I5**]
BOT	∅	[hd:**desc1**] [hd:**desc2**] [hd:**desc3**][hd:R1:**I1**] [hd:R5:**I5**] [hd:R2:**I2**] [hd:R2:R4:**I4**]

Table 5. Formal concepts for the second example.

tor in M includes the relation subpath and the instance (internal or leaf) reached with this path from the case instance.

Table 4 shows the G and M sets (the row and column set names, respectively) for the set of 3 cases whose representation trees are given in Figure 3 (left). The has-description relation belongs to the CBR terminology provided by CBROnto [4], an ontology with generic CBR vocabulary. According to this ontology, each case is linked by means of the has-description relation, to an individual representing the description of this case. In the figures, HD abbreviates has-description. Correspondingly, there is a has-solution relation to join the case with its solution instance, but it is not represented because this case component doesn't take part in the FCA.

Figure 3 (right) shows the formal concept lattice and the dependence rules resulting from the FCA application; and Table 5 shows the intent and extent for each formal concept read from the lattice.

4   Case Retrieval

In the previous section we have defined and exemplified the extraction of dependence rules from a case library. FCA applied to a case library provides an internal sight of the structure and dependencies between its cases and allows capturing the specific dependencies and exceptions provided by this particular case library, apart from the general completion rules belonging to the domain model [2]. For example, the rule Autumn → Car, is not a general domain rule. Instead, it detects a regularity satisfied by *all* the cases in the library, but we cannot assure its applicability for every possible case in the domain. We will use this kind of rules to complete the user queries to search cases on this library.

Besides query completion, the explicit construction and use of the concept lattice to organise the cases in the library provides us with certain benefits. The concepts in the lattice represent maximal groupings of cases with shared properties. The utility of these groupings is that we can access all the cases that share properties with the query at the same time, because they are grouped under the same concept. The order between the lattice elements allows structuring the library according to the attributes describing the cases. The lower in the graph, the more characteristics can be said about the cases; i.e. the more general concepts are higher up than the more specific ones. The use of the concept lattice as a case organization structure corresponds with a representational approach to CBR [8] where the cases are organised in a structure where the proximity means *similarity*.

4.1 Direct Retrieval

The retrieval process begins with an incremental query description process, where the user provides with certain descriptors, while the system proposes other properties by using the dependence rules captured during the FCA.

When completing the query by using the dependence rules, intuitively, what we are doing is to guide the user towards more specific and defined concepts in the lattice. Note, this kind of retrieval over the lattice finds all the cases where the query descriptors appear, i.e. the cases retrieved as similar are those with the greater number of properties shared (with exactly the same value) with the query. This direct retrieval can be considered as a kind of exploration process over the case library where the formal concepts guide the search process. Our system is thus provided with a case search or inspection mechanism, easy to use and formally well founded, that complements other knowledge intensive CBR processes, including more sophisticated retrieval processes with semantic similarity measures.

The system uses the knowledge extracted from the case library, so the cases themselves are guiding the query formulation process. After that, the system explicitly constructs an individual with the query case description and classifies it in the lattice. We use a Description Logic (DL) system, LOOM [5], whose recognition module automatically classifies the new individual in its corresponding place in the lattice (belonging to the extent of certain formal concept). All instances classified under the most specific concept the query instance belongs to, are retrieved as similar. Moreover, as this concept will be typically specialized by other most specific concepts, the goal of the query definition module is to guide the user from general concepts towards their subconcepts. The DLs reasoning mechanisms are useful to automatically organize the concept lattice and to keep the cases automatically organized under them. Besides, the instance recognition mechanism is used for the direct retrieval of the siblings of the query individual.

```
Destination: Spain      HolidayType: Education  Transportation: Car    Season: Winter
Destination: Egypt      HolidayType: Language   Transportation: Plane  Season: Spring
Destination: England    HolidayType: Skiing     Transportation: Train  Season: Autumn
Destination: New York                                                  Season: Summer
```

Figure 4. Travel agency domain descriptors.

After the direct search, the retrieved cases could be ordered by other criterion, for example, minimizing the number of superfluous descriptors provided by the case but not asked in the query; but this process is not lattice or FCA dependent. Next subsections show retrieval examples using the lattice and dependence rule set elicited by FCA in Sections 3.1 y 3.2.

4.1.1   A First Retrieval Example

From the travel agency domain we extract the list of descriptors shown in Figure 4. To formulate a search query, the user selects a descriptor, for example, `HolidayType:Skiing`. The system then detects a dependency among the descriptors `HolidayType:Skiing` and `Season:Winter`, meaning that in the concrete case library we are managing, there are not cases of `skiing` in other season that `winter`. So, the query formulation process will guide the user towards these concrete cases. The following dependence rules are applied to complete the search query:

```
HolidayType:Skiing → Season:Winter
HolidayType:Skiing, Season:Winter → Transportation:Plane
```

and the completed query results to be:

```
HolidayType: Skiing
Season: Winter
Transportation: Plane
```

The search process in this point will create an instance that will be automatically classified under the concept G. The cases resulting from the current retrieval query are those from the G extent, i.e `Case2` and `Case5`.

If the user wants to choose another descriptor for the query it will be guided towards more specific concepts, i.e. K or R. The descriptor set offered to the user in this point is: [`Destination:New York`; `Destination:Spain`].

4.1.2   Another Retrieval Example

Related with the generic domain described in Section 3.2, lets suppose the user poses the queries whose representation graphs are shown in Figure 5. The dotted lines means the information derived from the dependence rules of Figure 3.

The system will construct the minimum query skeleton based on the CBROnto terminology (cf. Section 3). In this simple example the system will

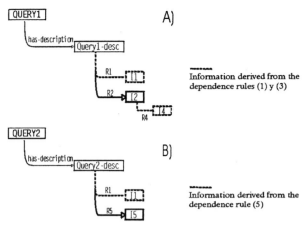

Figure 5. Query construction.

provide with an instance query linked by the `has-description` relation to a description individual (just created). The user should describe the description individual in each query.

In the query of Figure 5-A the user states that the query description individual `query1-desc` has the property `R2` filled by the instance `I2`, i.e. the query is assigned the descriptor `[HD:R2:I2]`. The query instance is completed by using the dependence rules (1) and (3) (Figure 3) and automatically classified (by the LOOM recognition module) under the concept A, because it satisfies all the properties on its intent, i.e. `[HD:R2:I2, HD:R2:R4:I4, HD:R1:I1]`; note that only the first one has been asserted by the user.

The search result would be the cases from the A extent, i.e. `Case1` and `Case2`. A finer similarity assessment could order them and select `Case1` as the more similar because it has less non-required descriptors than `Case2`.

In the query of Figure 5-B the user states that the query description instance `query2-desc` has the property `R5` filled by `I5`. The query is completed by using the dependence rule (5) and is automatically classified under the concept B because it satisfies the descriptors of its intent, i.e. `[HD:R5:I5, HD:R1:I1]`. The search result would be the cases from the B extent, i.e. `Case2` and `Case3`.

4.2   Query Formulation for Approximate Retrieval

The use of the dependence rules described in the examples, guides the query formulation towards exact matches with cases from the library. When using CBR, the retrieval process finds cases with similar (but not necessarily identical) descriptors, based on the use of similarity measures for the approximate matching.

In our system, the dependence rules also guide the query formulation process for the approximate case retrieval, but with some differences because, as it was described, the only allowed queries in direct retrieval are those for which we can find an exact matching case.

Suppose the rule R1:A → R2:B is elicited from the case library and the user uses R1:A as a query descriptor. The system proposes (and not imposes) the descriptor R2:B. If the user doesn't follow the system suggestion and changes R2:B, for example by the descriptor R2:C, the system will inform that an exact match won't be found in this library, but continue with the query formulation process and try the approximate retrieval. With this kind of queries, the user can formulate the query choosing from the complete descriptor set; note that during the exact retrieval, the descriptor set was reduced in each step to guide the query towards more specific concepts in the lattice.

For each descriptor given by the user, the system could propose others that can or cannot be accepted. When at least one of the suggestions is not accepted, we can assure the case base doesn't contain an exact match and approximate retrieval will be invoked. We are not describing here the approximate retrieval we are using but refer the interested reader to [7].

5   Conclusions and Related Work

The major contribution of this paper is the use of FCA as an automatic technique to elicit the attribute dependency knowledge inside a case library, and use it to complete the knowledge already acquired by other techniques of domain modelling.

FCA should be understood as a method to elicit patterns and regularities among the cases of a concrete case library apart from the general completion rules belonging to the general domain model [2]. The difference among the completion and dependence rules is that the former are general in the domain, and the latter are specific from a concrete case library. In particular, as every case on the library fulfils the completion rules, they represent a particular type of implication between the cases on this concrete library. That way, the completion rules are always a subset of the dependence rules set.

The concepts in the lattice represent maximal groupings of cases with shared properties, and their use to organise the cases reduces the effort to directly retrieve a case, when the user is able to make a precise query description (guided by the system) and a case exists in the case base satisfying it. This kind of direct and exact retrieval will be useful to explore a case library, and make use of the case library itself to guide the search. Nevertheless, we are providing with other retrieval processes that intensively use the domain knowledge within semantic and knowledge intensive similarity measures allowing approximate retrieval more than the syntactic similarity measure –the number of shared properties– codified by the concept lattice.

As the main drawback of our approach we cite it can not be applied to case bases where cases are described with multi-valued attributes, having more than one filler. Another point is the lattice recomputation when new cases are added to the library. What we do by now is to classify the new case on the lattice, and although the inclusion of a new case could provoke changes in the concepts, we only compute the lattice during a periodic maintaining phase performed off-line and not with each case added to the library. Nevertheless a new case is accessible through the concepts where it is classified in the lattice and the rest of the CBR processes.

FCA has been successfully used in many data analysis applications but we don't know of any use in the CBR area. We use it as a complementary technique to enrich the domain taxonomy, providing an alternative organization of the case library that facilitates a direct and guided access to the cases.

References

[1]   Althoff, K.-D., Auriol, E., Barletta R., & Manago, M., 1995. *A Review of Industrial Case-Based Reasoning Tools*, AI Intelligence, Oxford UK.

[2]   Bergmann, R., Wilke, W., Vollrath, I., & Stefan, W., 1996. "Integrating General Knowledge with Object-Oriented Case Representation and Reasoning". In *Procs. of the 4th German Workshop on CBR.*

[3]   Birkhoff, G., 1973. *Lattice Theory, third editon*. American Math. Society Coll. Publ. 25, Providence, R.I.

[4]   Díaz-Agudo, B., & González-Calero, P. A., 2000. "An Architecture For Knowledge Intensive CBR Systems". In *Procs. of the 5th European Workshop on CBR (EWCBR'00).*

[5]   Mac Gregor, R., & Bates, R., 1987. "The Loom Knowledge Representation Language". *ISI Reprint Series, ISI/RS-87-188*, Univ. of Southern California.

[6]   Ganter, B., & Wille, R., 1997. *Formal Concept Analysis. Mathematical Foundations*. ISBN 3-540-62771-5 Springer Verlag.

[7]   Gómez-Albarrán, M., González-Calero, P.A., Díaz-Agudo, B., & Fernández-Conde, C., 1999: "Modelling the CBR Life Cycle Using Description Logics", in *Case-Based Reasoning Research and Development: Third International Conference on Case-Based Reasoning*, LNAI 1650, Springer,

[8]   Porter, B.W., 1989. "Similarity Assessment: computation vs. representation". In *Procs. of DARPA CBR Workshop*, Morgan Kaufmann.

[9]   Prediger, S., & Stumme, G., 1999. "Theory driven logical scaling". In *Procs. of the International DLs Workshop*, CEUR Workshop Vol. 22.

[10]   Lenz, M., 1993. "CABATA–A hybrid CBR system". In *Procs. of the 1st European Workshop on CBR (EWCBR'93).*

[11]   Wille, R., 1982. "Restructuring Lattice Theory: an approach based on hierarchies of concepts". In Rival, I., (ed.), *Ordered Sets.*

[12]   Wille, R., 1992. "Conceptual Lattices and conceptual knowledge systems". *Computers and Mathematics with Apps.* Vol. 23, No. 6-9, pp. 493-515.

2D vs 3D Visualisation Techniques for Case-Based Reasoning

Barry Smyth, Mark Mullins and Elizabeth McKenna

Smart Media Institute, Department of Computer Science, University College Dublin, Belfield, Dublin 4, Ireland, email: {firstname.secondname}@ucd.ie

Abstract. Case-based reasoning systems solve new problems by retrieving and adapting the solutions to similar previously solved problem cases, and problem solving success depends critically on the quality of these cases. However, it is only relatively recently that researchers have begun to investigate ways of supporting the case-base authoring process in order to improve the quality of the resulting case-bases. In previous work we have argued that visualisation techniques have a valuable role to play in supporting a case-base author by helping the author to understand the structure of the evolving case-base. In this paper we compare and evaluate the 2D and 3D visualisation methods developed as part of the CASCADE case-based reasoning shell. We show that these visualisation methods are capable of producing accurate visual representations of complex case-bases.

1 Introduction

Case-based reasoning (CBR) systems solve new problems by retrieving and adapting the solutions of similar problem cases from a suitable case-base [9, 16]. The success of a case-based reasoner depends largely on the quality of the cases in its case-base, and the problem solving coverage that they provide. Recently the need to produce and maintain high-quality case-bases has been brought sharply into focus [14, 13] as CBR systems are deployed in the real-world. In turn the CBR community is beginning to recognise the need for new tools and techniques to support case-base authoring and maintenance processes [11, 17, 13]. We believe that visualisation techniques can play an important role in this respect since they provide the author with the means to perceive the structure of an evolving case-base and the relationships that exist between the individual cases. In this way, the author can readily recognise regions where cases are lacking, and thus where coverage is likely to be poor, as well as regions where there is an abundance of cases, and thus regions where there may be redundancy.

In earlier work we have demonstrated how force-directed visualisation techniques can be used to produce accurate 2D visual representations of complex case-bases [18]; according to a force-directed model, the positions of cases are influenced by attractive and repulsive forces between cases that are influenced by the inter-case similarity relationships. In this paper we build on this previous work by describing an extended visualisation technique capable of generating

3D visualisations. In addition we evaluate and compare the 2D and 3D methods according to their ability to reproduce visualisations that accurately reflect the relationships between cases.

The remainder of this paper is organised as follows. The next section surveys related work, focusing on the use of visualisation techniques within case-based reasoning. Section 3 outlines the CASCADE CBR shell and provides examples of its visualisation capability, while Section 4 describes CASCADE's force-directed visualisation technique in detail. Finally, before concluding, Section 5 describes the result of a comprehensive comparative evaluation of CASCADE's 2D and 3D visualisation methods focusing on their ability to accurately visualise complex case-bases under a variety of experimental conditions.

2   Related Work

Visualisation techniques are used in artificial intelligence, information retrieval, data analysis, and data mining to help users to discover patterns and trends in complex information spaces that might otherwise be missed [2–5, 7, 8, 12, 19].

However, to date there has been only limited use of visualisation techniques as part of the CBR problem-solving model. Some systems use graphical visualisations as a way to present case solutions that have a natural graphical form. For example, Macura & Macura [10] describe the MacRad case retrieval system for assisting the diagnostic process in radiology: cases contain medical image scans as part of their solutions structures.

Similarly, Wybo et al. [20] describe PROFIL, a CBR system for decision support in a design domain. Again cases contain a visual solution component - each case includes an annotated image of a given design. In addition, PROFIL uses a visualisation technique to present users with a representation of the cases retrieved for a given query. Cases are plotted on a two-dimensional graph of similarity (to the target query) versus solution quality (of a selected case); the target query is the graph's origin. Thus, the user can perceive the relationship between the target and similar cases. An important limitation of this visualisation technique is that while it preserves the similarity relationship between the fixed target query and retrieved cases, the similarity between the retrieved cases themselves is lost. Dissimilar retrieved cases can appear close on the screen. Therefore, this technique is not useful when it comes to visualising a case-base as a whole, where there is no fixed point of reference (such as a specific target query).

This problem of visualising a complete case-base is addressed by the work of Smyth & McKenna [11, 17]. A visualisation technique is described based on a novel model of competence for case-based reasoning systems. The model makes it possible to identify groups of cases that make shared contributions to overall system competence, and to measure the competence of these groups. The visualisation technique constructs a graphical representation of a case-base by plotting each group on a graph of group competence versus group size. Smyth & McKenna describe how the visualisation technique can be put to good effect as an intelligent support tool for case-base authors, by highlighting over-populated and under-populated regions of the case-base. One of the limitations with this technique is that the similarity relationship between cases (or groups of cases) does not translate into on-screen distances. For example, groups may appear close simply because they have similar sizes and competence contributions, but their constituent cases may be unrelated.

We believe that visualisation methods have an important part to play in case-based reasoning by facilitating an improved interaction between system and user. Moreover, given the importance of cases and the case-base in CBR, visualisation techniques that provide a user with a visual representation of the case-base are likely to prove useful in many stages during the CBR process. In the next section we will introduce a new method for visualising case-bases that is specifically designed to model the similarity relationships between cases as on-screen distances.

3 Cascade

The CASCADE (Case Authoring Support and Development Environment) system has been built to provide a test-bed for evaluating different ways in which authors can be intelligently supported in the construction of CBR systems. In its basic form CASCADE is a CBR shell providing users with all of the usual shell functionality: the ability to design case templates, feature types, similarity functions; the ability to add and edit cases. However, the real innovation in CASCADE is the way in which it actively supports the case-base author. In previous work we have described how CASCADE incorporates a competence model of an evolving case-base and uses this to help the author to optimise the case-base on the fly [17, 11]; the competence model explicitly models the solvability relationships between cases and facilitates an understanding of the competence contributions of individual cases. In this paper however we are interested in CASCADE's visualisation tools and the following sections focus on its force-directed visualisation techniques that allow the case author to view an animated visualisation of the entire case-base.

3.1 Architecture

The basic CASCADE architecture (shown in Fig. 1) is composed of the following components: (1) A case base and competence model; (2) An access process that provides the author with direct access to the cases in the case-base and to the details of the current competence model such as group and coverage information; (3) An update process that allows the author to change the case-base (by adding, deleting or editing individual cases), and ensures that the competence model is changed accordingly; (4) A visualiser process that allows the author to request certain types of visualisations and statistics from the evolving case-base, specifically competence-oriented visualisations as described in [17, 11] and the 2D and 3D force-directed case-base visualisations as described in this paper.

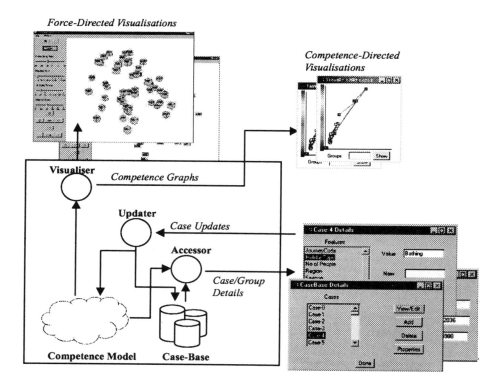

Fig. 1. The CASCADE Architecture.

3.2 Visualisation in CASCADE

We have already mentioned that one of the shortcomings of current CBR shells and toolkits is that they fail to provide the case author with any real comprehensive support services. We believe that the ability to visualise an evolving case-base is an important (if not vital) means by which the author can perceive and understand the ongoing evolution of the growing case-base, and in turn that this will help the author to build better case-bases.

Unfortunately, case-base visualisation is far from trivial. Cases are complex n-dimensional objects (a case is composed of n features), and the similarities between cases represent distances in an n-dimensional feature space. However, the visualisation space (the computer screen) is a two-dimensional one and thus the essence of the visualisation problem is how to map n-dimensional cases onto a two-dimensional screen while reproducing the similarity relationships between pairs of cases as on-screen distances.

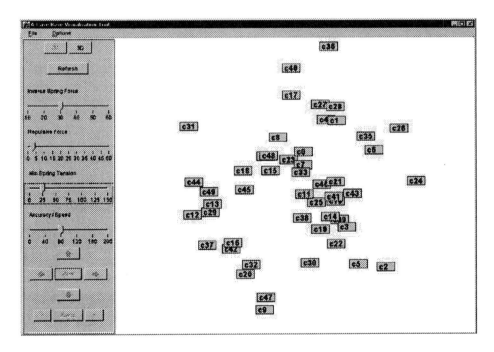

Fig. 2. 2D visualisation in CASCADE for a 50 case case-base.

In the next section we will describe how this problem is solved in CASCADE, but first we will demonstrate the results of CASCADE's case-base visualisation capabilities that are relevant in this paper. For example, Figures 2 and 3 show examples of CASCADE's 2D and 3D case-base visualisation facilities. In each screenshot an individual case is represented by a labeled node and the distance

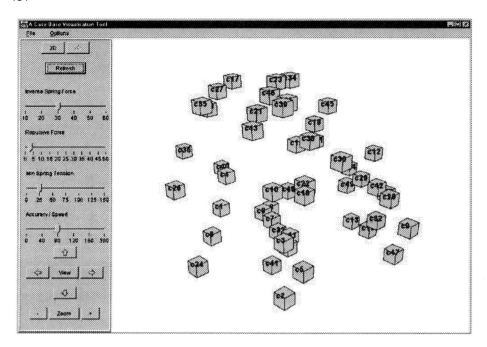

Fig. 3. 3D visualisation in CASCADE for a 50 case case-base.

between cases is designed to be a proxy for the similarity between cases. In the case of Figure 2 the case nodes are displayed on a 2D plane, while in Figure 3 a 3D visualisation is employed. The visualisation controls shown in each screenshot allow the user to adjust the various parameters that control the visualisation process; for example, visualisation speed, camera position, node sizes, etc.

Figures 3.2 and 3.2 show the final state of the visualisations, after the case nodes have settled in their equilibrium positions. Up until this point the nodes will have been in a state of animated flux as the visualisation engine adjusts their relative positions until an equilibrium state is found where the on-screen inter-node distances are an accurate representation of the inter-case similarities (see Sections 4 and 5).

4   Case-Base Visualisation

In the previous section we mentioned that the core problem to be solved with respect to visualisation is how to map n-dimensional cases onto a two-dimensional surface while preserving the similarity relationships between cases. In our research we have explored the use of a force-directed graph-drawing algorithm and in the following sections we describe the details of this algorithm and how it has been adapted in CASCADE for use as a 2D and 3D case-base visualisation technique.

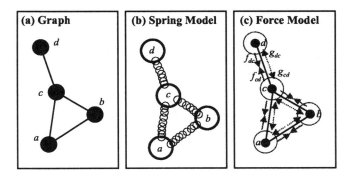

Fig. 4. The force-directed graph-drawing algorithm models a graph as a system of rings and springs under attractive and repulsive forces.

4.1 A Force-Directed Graph-Drawing Algorithm

Huang et al. [6] describe a force-directed algorithm for graph drawing that is suitable as the basis for our case-base visualisation technique. The algorithm models a graph, $G = (V, E)$, as a system of steel rings and springs: the vertices are steel rings and the edges are springs. The springs exert an attractive force between connected rings and the steel rings exert a repulsive force (figure 4).

During graph drawing, the position of a vertex is influenced by these attractive and repulsive forces. The graph-drawing algorithm is an iterative process that begins with a random configuration of vertices and proceeds to locate a minimum energy configuration by incrementally adjusting the relative positions of vertices in order to equalise forces. We proceed to outline the basic mechanics of this *spring-embedded* graph-drawing approach. Many of the details have been omitted and the interested reader is referred to [6] and also [1].

The Force Model The total force on a vertex v is given by (1), where f_{uv} is the attractive force exerted on v by the spring between u and v and g_{uv} is the repulsive force exerted between u and each of its neighbouring vertices; note, the set of edges of a vertex v is $N(v)$. The force f_{uv} follows Hooke's law and therefore is proportional to the difference between the distance between u and v and the zero-energy length of the connecting spring. The repulsive force between two nodes follows an inverse cubed law.

$$f(v) = \sum_{u \in N(v)} f_{uv} + \sum_{u \in V_i} g_{uv} \qquad (1)$$

If we denote the Euclidean distance between two points p and q by d(p,q), and suppose that the position of vertex v is denoted by $p_v = (x_v, y_v)$, then, from (1), the x component of the force $f(v)$ on v is $f_x(v)$ and is given by (2); the y component has a similar expression (as does the z component in the case of a 3D visualisation).

$$f_x(v) = \sum_{u \in N(v)} k_{uv}^{(1)} \frac{(d(p_u, p_v) - l_{uv})(x_v - x_u)}{d(p_u, p_v)}$$

$$+ \sum_{u \in V_i} k_{uv}^{(2)} \frac{(x_u - x_v)}{(d(p_u, p_v))^3} \qquad (2)$$

A number of new parameters are introduced by (2): l_{uv} is the zero-energy length of the spring between u and v, and $k_{uv}^{(1)}$ and $k_{uv}^{(2)}$ are the relative weights of the attractive and repulsive forces, respectively.

The Animation Model As mentioned above, the spring-embedded algorithm iteratively adjusts the positions of all vertices until a minimum energy configuration is found, leaving the vertices in an equilibrium force configuration. This produces a sequence of animation frames $D_1, .., D_n$ such that D_1 displays an initial random configuration of vertices while D_n is the final *equilibrium frame*; each D_i represents a configuration that is closer to equilibrium than D_{i-1}. During an iteration the algorithm moves from D_i to D_{i+1} by computing the appropriate change in the x and y positions of each vertex. In the remainder of this section we show how to compute this change for the x coordinate of v, that is, $\Delta_x(v)$; the computations for the y coordinate (and the z coordinate in the case of 3D visualisation) are analogous.

By Newton's second law of motion, $f_x(v) = m(v).a_x(v)$, where $m(v)$ is the mass of vertex v and $a_x(v)$ is its acceleration in the x direction, due to a force f. If we assume that each vertex has a mass of one then $f_x(v) = a_x(v)$, and in a few simple steps Huang et al [6] explain how $\Delta_x(v)$ can be written as shown in (3).

$$\Delta_x(v) = \frac{a_x(t_{j-1})}{2} \Delta_t^2 \qquad (3)$$

By substituting 3 into $f_x(v,) = a_x(v)$ we get,

$$\Delta_x(v) = \frac{f_x(v)}{2} \Delta_t^2 = C \bullet f_x(v) \qquad (4)$$

where Δ_t is the time period of one animation step and $C = \frac{\Delta_t^2}{2}$; normally we set $\Delta_t = 0.5$ seconds, so C = 1/200. Finally, we can transform the force model in (2) into the animation model in (5).

$$\frac{\Delta_x(v)}{C} = \sum_{u \in N(v)} k_{uv}^{(1)} \frac{(d(p_u, p_v) - l_{uv})(x_v - x_u)}{d(p_u, p_v)}$$

$$+ \sum_{u \in V_i} k_{uv}^{(2)} \frac{(x_u - x_v)}{(d(p_u, p_v))^3} \qquad (5)$$

As it stands, this animation model can produce jumps in vertex positions rather than smoothly interpolated transitions. Fortunately, a simple solution is to limit the maximum distance a vertex can move in a single iteration according to (6).

$$
\begin{aligned}
\triangle_x(v) = & -5 && if \quad \triangle_x(v) \leq -5 \\
& \triangle_x(v) && if \quad -5 \leq \triangle_x(v) \leq 5 \\
& +5 && if \quad 5 \leq \triangle_x(v)
\end{aligned} \tag{6}
$$

4.2 Modifications for Case-Base Visualisation

Two modifications are needed to use the above graph-drawing algorithm to visualise case-bases. First, a case-base is a fully connected graph. The cases correspond to the vertices of the graph and the similarity relations between cases correspond to the edges. Usually, it is possible to measure the similarity between each case and every other case and therefore every case can be linked to every other case by an edge. For this reason, there is no benefit in drawing the edges of the case-base graph, so only the graph vertices are drawn.

In the standard graph-drawing algorithm the principal presentation objective is to minimise the number of edges crossings in the graph [6]. This is not important however in our visualisation approach. The edges are not drawn for a start, so there can be no crossings, but more importantly the case-base should be drawn so that the screen distance between two cases corresponds to the similarity between these cases. Cases that are very similar should be drawn close together, and cases that are dissimilar should be drawn far apart. To achieve this we set the zero-energy length of the spring, which represents the relationship between two cases, to be a function of their inverse similarity. Thus, very similar cases will have a low zero-energy spring length to produce a higher attractive force between their corresponding on-screen vertices.

5 Evaluation

Our main objective is to develop a visualisation technique capable of representing a case-base of cases on a two-dimensional screen, while preserving the similarity relationships between cases as on-screen distances. If these relationships are not reliably preserved, that is, if there is a poor correlation between the similarity of a case-pair and the pair's screen distance, then the utility of the visualisation will be limited. Obviously the transformation from an n-dimensional space to a two-dimensional one will come at a cost. The relationship between similarity and screen distance will be impaired, and in this section we describe a series of experiments to investigate the nature and degree of this impairment with respect to the 2D and 3D visualisation tools.

In particular, in this work we are interested in comparing the 2D and 3D visualisation methods. Intuitively we would expect the 3D visualiser to outperform the 2D one because the extra degree of spatial freedom should make it possible to satisfy additional similarity constraints.

5.1   Similarity-Distance Correlation

We can measure the strength of the relationship between case similarities and screen distances by computing the correlation between the similarity values and the distance values of the case pairs (in the equilibrium frame). For example, in this experiment we use the Pearson's product-momentum correlation coefficient to measure the degree of linear relationship between the case similarities and screen distances produced during the visualisation.

Method: A publicly available case-base is used as a source of test data. The cases represent package holidays (in terms of 9 features such as holiday type, duration, location, etc.) and are available from the case-base archive at AI-CBR (www.ai-cbr.org). In total the case-base contains 1400 different cases. A standard weighted-sum similarity metric is used to measure case similarities.

In this experiment we investigate the 2D and 3D visualisations produced for case-bases of different sizes (10,25,50,100,200,300,400 cases). For each case-base size we randomly produce 20 case-bases from the original 1400 cases. A 2D and 3D visualisation is constructed for each case-base and the correlation coefficient between the similarities and screen distances is calculated. The 2D and 3D correlation coefficients are averaged to obtain a mean correlation for each visualisation technique across the different case-base sizes.

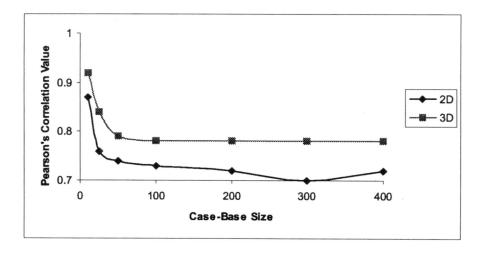

Fig. 5. Pearson's correlation coefficient results for 2D and 3D visualisation techniques.

Results: The results are plotted in Figure 5 as a graph of mean correlation versus case-base size. The results for both the 2D and 3D visualisations are very positive, indicating a strong correlation (> 0.7) between similarity and screen distance across the range of case-base sizes tested.

As expected the correlation values degrade for increasingly large case-bases - the limited visualisation space means that it becomes more and more difficult to layout large sets of cases in such a way that similarity relationships are preserved. These correlation coefficients are all significant at the 0.001 level and the results indicate that the visualisation technique is capable of producing accurate representations of real case-bases containing up to 400 cases.

As predicted the results for the 3D visualisations are superior to those produced for the 2D visualisation, indicating that the extra visualisation dimension is useful in resolving addition similarity constraints. In general, the 3D visualisation results in a correlation coefficient that is approximately ten percent greater that the equivalent 2D visualisation.

5.2 Rank Correlation

The correlation coefficient used in the previous experiment is designed to take account of the relative magnitude between case similarities and screen distances. In this experiment we consider an alternative evaluation function that examines the relative ranking of cases according to their similarities and screen distances. We would like our visualisation technique to preserve this relative ordering as far as possible so that, for example, the ith closest pair of cases in terms of screen distance is also the ith closest pair of cases in terms of case similarity.

Method: The experimental method used above is repeated except that instead of calculating Pearson's correlation coefficient we calculate Spearman's rank correlation coefficient, which is designed to explicitly examine the correlation between the relative ranking of paired data points. As before, a mean correlation coefficient is calculated for each case-base size.

Results: The results are plotted in Figure 6 as a graph of the mean rank correlation coefficient versus case-base size. Once again the results are very positive, indicating a strong correlation (> 0.7) between similarity and screen distance rankings for both 2D and 3D visualisations across the range of case-base sizes tested.

Once again the 3D visualisations benefit from superior correlation values when compared to the equivalent 2D visualisations. And as expected, the correlation values falls slowly as the case-base size increases, indicating that the visualisation method scales well with case-base size, and certainly produces accurate visualisations for case-bases of up to 400 cases. These results are significant at the 0.001 level.

6 Visual Authoring Support

From an authoring and maintenance viewpoint, the visualisation tool will help the user to: (1) understand and perceive the overall structure of an evolving

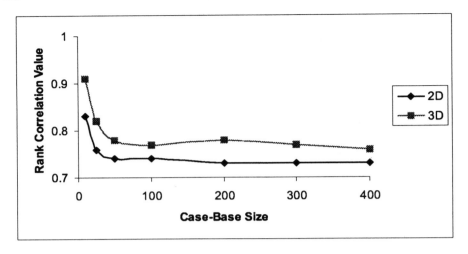

Fig. 6. Spearman's rank correlation coefficient results

case-base; (2) recognise emerging regions of competence within the case-base, that is, large clusters of cases; (3) recognise potentially redundant regions of the case-base, which contain densely packed clusters of similar cases; (4) recognise potential holes within the case-base indicating regions of poor competence; (5) recognise new regions of competence or exceptional cases that are outliers within the case-base.

Recently, we have integrated this visualisation tool with CASCADE's model of competence for case-base reasoning systems [11, 15, 17]. The competence model can be used to estimate the coverage properties of individual cases and as such can assign coverage values to particular cases. These values can be used to separate cases according to their competence contributions; for example, redundant cases have low values while important cases have higher values. The model can be used to enhance the visualisation output by annotating case nodes according to their coverage values to provide the author with a instant picture of the structural and coverage properties of a case-base.

In addition we have been able to verify that the 2D and 3D visualisations match closely with the competence model predictions. For example cases that fall within the same competence group are proximally related in the visualisation space. Cases that are densely packed according to the visualisation do correspond to regions of high competence and redundancy according to the model. And finally, holes in the visualisation space do reflect regions of poor competence according to the competence model.

Aside from improving the capabilities of authoring and maintenance systems, the visualisation technique also has applications in other parts of the CBR process. For example, it could provide a useful interface for presenting case retrieval results (see also [5]), allowing the user to perceive the relationship between retrieved cases at a glance. There are also many potential benefits to be gained from using a modified version of the visualisation tool as the basis for a large-scale case-base navigation tool.

7 Conclusions

Visualisation offers a powerful means of analysis that can help to uncover patterns and trends in data sets that may be missed by other non-visual methods. We believe that visualisation techniques may hold the key to the next generation of interactive case-based reasoning systems, by facilitating new modes of interaction between system and user, and by supporting more intelligent case-base authoring and maintenance strategies.

We have described and adapted a force-directed graph-drawing technique for use as a case-base visualisation technique - cases are represented as graph vertices and the screen-distances between cases are a proxy for similarity. In addition, we have evaluated the technique on a range of case-bases to show that it successfully preserves the n-dimensional similarity relationships between cases.

Our future work will continue to develop the above visualisation technique. We plan to further adapt the method to meet the specific needs of case-base visualisation, as outlined in Section 6.

Of course, in the context of advanced computer graphics research our visualisation technique is not ground-breaking, as many researchers have investigated similar graph-drawing techniques prior to this work [1, 6]. However, the work servers to introduce these visualisation techniques to the CBR community. We believe that there is much to be learned and we plan to investigate a range of visualisation techniques in the future that will serve as alternatives to the current two-dimensional graph-drawing method.

References

1. Battista, G. Di, Eades, P. , Tamassia, R. and Tollis, I. *Graph Drawing: Algorithms for the Visualization of Graphs*, Prentice Hall, 1999.
2. Bosch, R., Stolte, C., Tang, D., Gerth, J. Mendel Rosenblum, and Pat Hanrahan, 'The Information Mural: A Technique for Displaying and Navigating Large Information Spaces', *Computer Graphics*, (2000).
3. Devaney, M. and Ram, A. 'Visualization as an Exploratory Tool in Artificial Intelligence', in *Proceedings of the World Multiconference on Systemics, Cybernetics, and Informatics*, (1998).
4. Goel, A.K., Gomez de Silva Garza, G., Garza, S., Grue, N., Murdock, JW., Recker, MM. and Govindaraj, T. 'Explanatory Interface in Interactive Design Environments', in *Proceedings of the 4th International Conference on AI in Design*, (1996).
5. Hearst, MA. and Pedersen, J. 'Visualising Information Retrieval Results: A Demonstration of the TileBar Interface', in *Proceedings of Conference on Human Factors in Computing Systems '96*, eds., R. Bilger, S. Guest, and M.J. Tauber. ACM Inc., (1996).

6. Huang, ML., Eades, P. and Wang, J. 'On-line animated visualisation of huge graphs using a modified spring algorithm', *IEEE Transactions on Computers*, **9**, 623–645, (1998).

7. Jerding, D. and Stasko, J. 'The Information Mural: A Technique for Displaying and Navigating Large Information Spaces', *IEEE Transactions on Visualization and Computer Graphics*, **4(3)**, 257–271, (1998).

8. Keim, D. and Wills, G. 'Visualizing World-Wide Web Search Engine Results', in *Proceedings of the 1999 IEEE Symposium on Information Vizualisation*. IEEE Press, (1999).

9. Kolodner, J. *Case-Based Reasoning*, Morgan Kaufmann, 1993.

10. Macura, RT. and Macura, KJ. 'MacRad: Radiology Image Resource with a Case-Based Retrieval System.', in *Proceedings of the 1st International Conference on Case-Based Reasoning*, eds., M. Veloso and A. Aamodt, pp. 43–54. Springer Verlag, (1995).

11. McKenna, E, and Smyth, B. 'An Interactive Visualisation Tool for Case-Based Reasoners', *Applied Intelligence: Special Issue on Interactive Case-Based Reasoning*, (In Press).

12. Mukherjea, S. and Hara, Y. 'Visualizing World-Wide Web Search Engine Results', in *Proceedings of the International Conference on Information Visualization*. IEEE Press, (1999).

13. Smyth, B. 'Case-Based Maintenance', in *Tasks and Methods in Applied Artificial Intelligence. Lecture Notes in Artificial Intelligence*, eds., Angel Pasqual del Pobil, Jose Mira, and Moonis Ali, pp. 507–516. Springer Verlag, (1998).

14. Smyth, B. and Cunningham, P. 'The Utility Problem Analysed: A Case-Based Reasoning Perspective', in *Advances in Case-Based Reasoning. Lecture Notes in Artificial Intelligence*, eds., Ian Smith and Boi Falthings, pp. 392–399. Springer Verlag, (1996).

15. Smyth, B. and Keane, M.T. 'Remembering to Forget: A Competence Preserving Case Deletion Policy for CBR Systems', in *Proceedings of the 14th International Joint Conference on Artificial Intelligence*, ed., Chris Mellish, pp. 377–382. Morgan Kaufmann, (1995).

16. Smyth, B. and Keane, M.T. 'Adaptation-Guided Retrieval: Questioning the Similarity Assumption in Reasoning', *Artificial Intelligence*, **102**, 249–293, (1998).

17. Smyth, B. and McKenna, E. 'Modelling the Competence of Case-Bases', in *Advances in Case-Based Reasoning. Lecture Notes in Artificial Intelligence*, eds., B. Smyth and P. Cunningham, pp. 208–220. Springer Verlag, (1998).

18. Smyth, B., Mullins, M., and McKenna, E. 'Picture Perfect: Visualisation Techniques for Case-Based Reasoning', in *Proceedings of the 14th European Conference on Artificial Intelligence*, (2000).

19. C. Westphal and T. Blaxton, *Data Mining Solutions: Methods and Tools for Real World Problems*, Wiley, 1998.

20. Wybo, JL., Gefraye, R. and Russeil, A. 'PROFIL: A Decision Support Tool for Metallic Sections Design using a CBR Approach', in *Proceedings of the 1st International Conference on Case-Based Reasoning*, eds., M. Veloso and A. Aamodt. Springer Verlag, (1995).

SESSION 3

LEARNING II

An Instance-Based Approach to Pattern Association Learning with Application to the English Past Tense Verb Domain

Ray J. Hickey and Richard G. Martin
School of Information and Software Engineering
The University of Ulster at Coleraine
Coleraine, Co. Londonderry
Northern Ireland BT52 1SA
rj.hickey@ulst.ac.uk
www.infc.ulst.ac.uk/staff/rj.hickey

Abstract: We present a method for using instance-based learning to acquire pattern association rules and apply it to the English past tense verb domain. To retrieve exemplars, we introduce a distance metric for pattern association, PAMELA, which extends that used in PEBLS for classification. The associated pattern is then built by adapting that of the retrieved exemplar(s). We show that our algorithm IBPA-3, which uses exemplar distance weighting and attribute weighting, improves upon the C4.5-based SPA algorithm and, when tested on the difficult case of irregular verbs, out-performs the current state of the art algorithm for this problem, the relational learner, FOIDL.

1.   Introduction

In the pattern association (PA) task, a pattern - usually a vector of attribute values - must be mapped to another such pattern. Examples include sentence translation, converting a verb to its past tense and transforming an image. The PA task can be contrasted with the classification task: in the former there is usually a relatively small number of classes (typically less than 10) each of which can be regarded as a 1-dimensional 'pattern'. The essential distinction, between classification and PA task is that, in the latter, the target, i.e. associated object, is 'structured' rather than atomic.

This paper introduces a new method for learning pattern associations. It utilises instance-based learning (IBL) [1] together with an adaptation mechanism to produce an instance-based pattern association learner in a series of algorithms of increasing sophistication. These are evaluated on the well-known English past tense verb domain discussed below.

The PA task has been studied extensively by connectionists and cognitive scientists using artificial neural networks (see, for example [2]). Prominent amongst the applications experimented upon is the English past tense verb domain. Here a first person present tense verb is to be mapped to its past tense. Regular verbs dominate in the language and follow the rule: *add "ed"*, e.g. *push → pushed*. There are minor variants of this (still regular) such as: *if the present tense ends in y, then drop the y and add "ied"*, e.g. *hurry→ hurried*. There is a much smaller number of irregular verbs disobeying the general rule. These include non-generalisable (one-off) cases such as *go → went*, identity mapping as in *bid → bid* and adding different endings such as changing the present tense ending *eep* to *ept* as in *sleep → slept*.

The original Rumelhart-McClelland network [3] was superceded by that of MacWhinney and Leinbach [4]. The latter employed a representation of verbs involving a phonetic encoding system called UNIBET. Here ASCII characters are used to denote each of the 36 phonemes in English, of which 14 are vowels and 22 are consonants. Each phoneme is initially described in terms of several distinctive features relating to its vocalisation. For vowels there are eight such features: front, centre, back, round, high, middle, low and diphthong. For consonants there are 10 features: voiced, labial, dental, palatal, velar, nasal, liquid, trill, fricative and interdental. A fragment of the mapping from features present to the UNIBET ASCII character representation is shown below (the first three are vowels, the later two are consonants):

i ← front
E ← front, middle, low
3 ← front, high, low, diphthong
N← voiced, palatal, velar, nasal
s ← dental, fricative

Each word can now be represented as a vector of phonemes. For example, the association

arrange → arranged

would be represented, using vectors of length 15, as:

(6, r, e, n, d, Z, \$, \$, \$, \$, \$, \$, \$, \$, \$) → (6, r, e, n, d, Z, d, \$, \$, \$,\$, \$, \$, \$, \$)

where \$ represents a space.

Using UNIBET instead of the normal alphabet reduces the degree of irregularity in the task. MacWhinney and Leinbach [4] also employed a syllabic template, which assumes a trisyllabic structure for the verb.

The domain became a test-bed for comparison of connectionist and symbolic approaches within Artificial Intelligence, with MacWhinney and Leinbach [4] challenging the symbolic community to produce a system that out-performed theirs.

The challenge was answered by Ling and Marinov [5] and Ling [6]) who produced a symbolic pattern association learner, SPA. Using the UNIBET form, SPA treats each element of the target pattern as a class and learns, using a slightly modified version of C4.5 [7], a separate decision tree for that element. Each tree is built using all the attributes in the source pattern. Given any new source pattern, the associated target pattern is then simply the vector of all 'classes' obtained from applying the appropriate induced tree for each element.

SPA employed a novel heuristic for assigning a class at a leaf that contained no training examples. Normally, the default class in the training set would be assigned in such cases. It was argued in [5] and [6] that for pattern association it could be more appropriate, depending on local frequencies, to use the attribute value on the corresponding branch. This amounts to mapping a source value identically to the target and is referred to as *passthrough*. Using this selectively depending on local conditions yields an *adaptive default strategy*.

As shown in [6], SPA is able to substantially outperform, on the past tense problem, the neural network algorithm developed in [4].

An alternative symbolic approach to the learning of past tenses was provided in [8]. The first-order rule learner FOIL [9] was adapted to produce FOIDL which induced first-order decision lists (rather than 'if ... then' rules). FOIDL was able to learn with significantly fewer examples than both the connectionist algorithms and SPA. FOIDL can make use of background knowledge consisting of a predicate split(A,B,C) meaning that list A can be split into sublists B and C. This gives FOIDL a considerable advantage as it is provided a strong hint enabling it to easily learn the rule for regular verbs, in alphabetic representation, as

```
past (A,B) :- split (B, A, [e, d]).
```

where B is the past tense of A. FOIDL easily out-performs SPA when tested on unseen regular verbs.

A first attempt at an instance-based approach to PA was made in [10]. There the framework of SPA was adopted but with the IBL algorithm PEBLS [11] used instead of C4.5. This algorithm, PEBLS SPA, fared reasonably well against SPA based on unpruned trees but, when pruned trees were used, it was considerably out-performed.

SPA and PEBLS SPA can be regarded as *loosely coupled* PA learners in that they decompose the task into separate classification learning sub-tasks and subsequently combine the results of these. Our purpose here is to adopt a *more tightly coupled* or holistic approach to produce an instance based algorithm in which there is no separate classification learning of the target elements.

2. The Distance Metric PAMELA

Our basic algorithm is essentially a variation on PEBLS. The latter, like all instance-based concept learners, uses a measure of similarity to retrieve, from the exemplar base, an exemplar closest to a new instance. A distinguishing feature of PEBLS is that the similarity measure is itself derived from the training data in a first pass. The measure (based on the Value Difference Metric (VDM) in [12]) has, as its core notion, a value difference table of terms:

$$\delta(V_1, V_2) = \sum_{i=1}^{n} \left| \frac{C_{1i}}{C_1} - \frac{C_{2i}}{C_2} \right|^k \tag{2.1}$$

Here V_1 and V_2 are two possible values for an attribute used to describe the examples. C_{1i} (respectively C_{2i}) is the number of times, in the training set, that V_1 (V_2) was classified into category i; C_1 and C_2 are the total numbers of times value V_1 and V_2 occurred. n is the number of classes. k is a constant usually set to 1. Thus, two values of a particular attribute are judged 'similar' if they produce small discrepancies in relative frequency of incidence across the n possible classes.

The PEBLS metric is then the total distance, Δ, between two instances given by:

$$\Delta(X,Y) = w_X w_Y \sum_{i=1}^{N} \delta(x_i, y_i)^r \tag{2.2}$$

where X and Y represent two instances, with X being an exemplar in memory and Y a new example. The variables x_i and y_i are values of the ith attribute for X and Y, respectively, where each example has N attributes. w_X and w_Y are weights which reflect the reliability of an exemplar. Δ is called the Modified Value Difference Metric (MVDM). In [11], $k=1$ was adopted and $r=2$ was used mostly with $r=1$ being employed occasionally.

The PEBLS metric is not directly usable in pattern association because, in effect, the output patterns in the training set would each constitute a class. A simple alteration to (2.1) however, circumvents the difficulty. In the notation above, a classified example has the form $(x_1,..., x_N) \rightarrow i$ where i is a class. For a pattern association example the form is:

$$(x_1,..., x_N) \rightarrow (o_1,..., o_N) \tag{2.3}$$

where $(o_1,..., o_N)$ is the output pattern associated with input pattern $(x_1,..., x_N)$. A notion of value difference appropriate to pattern association can be defined by replacing the class relative frequencies in (2.1) by output value relative frequencies for the output attribute corresponding to the input attribute being considered. Thus the value differences for input attribute x_j, $j=1,...,N$ in (2.3) are based on values of o_j. For values V_1 and V_2 of x_j this leads to:

$$\rho(V_1, V_2) = \sum_{i=1}^{n} \left| \frac{F_{1i}}{F_1} - \frac{F_{2i}}{F_2} \right|^k \tag{2.4}$$

where F_{1i} (respectively F_{2i}) is the number of times, in the training set, that V_1 (V_2) was associated with the ith value of the jth output attribute; F_1 and F_2 are the total numbers of times value V_1 and V_2 occurred. n is the number distinct values of o_j (in general n may depend on j). Note that, for simplicity, we have suppressed the index j in (2.4). We will use $k=1$.

The new metric, PAMELA (Pattern Association Metric for Exemplar-based Learning Algorithms) is then the total distance, P, between two input description vectors X and Y given by:

$$P(X,Y) = \sum_{i=1}^{N} \rho(x_i, y_i)^r \qquad (2.5)$$

where each pattern has N features. We will use $r=1$.

3.   IBPA Algorithms

We can use PAMELA to develop instance-based pattern association (IBPA) learners. We begin with a simple algorithm IBPA-1 and extend it to create IBPA-2 and IBPA-3. Ideas will be illustrated using the past tense domain with a corpus in UNIBET form containing verbs up to eight characters in width (in contrast to the 15 mentioned above). This corpus was also employed in [6].

As is usual with the instance-based approach, we maintain an exemplar base of previous cases, which here will contain source patterns and their associated targets. Unlike in instance-based classification, simply retrieving the closest exemplar as judged by PAMELA and using its associated target as the required output vector for a new example is not sufficient. Unless the source pattern of the closest retrieved exemplar is identical to that of the new example, the latter target pattern will tend to be different to that of the exemplar. We cannot exploit the many-to-one nature of the classification problem.

Instead, the individual target attribute values associated with a retrieved exemplar must, usually, be adapted to yield the required target values for the new example. In some cases, however, it is appropriate to map an individual source attribute value identically to produce the target value - as was done for SPA using the passthrough strategy as noted above. To determine whether to map identically or change, it is necessary to retrieve and analyse m nearest neighbours.

Typically, amongst m retrieved exemplars, for a given attribute, some will have mapped the value of that attribute identically from source to target while others will have mapped it to a different value. If cases of identity mapping dominate amongst these exemplars, we should map that attribute identically in the new example. If not then we can map it to the most frequently occurring of the values in non-identity cases.

To illustrate the adaptation process, suppose we wish to construct the past tense of *admit*. This is represented as (6, d, m, I, t, \$, \$, \$) in the UNIBET format. Using $m=5$, suppose the closest exemplars as assessed by PAMELA are as shown in table 1. The frequency profiles for these matches across attributes are:

Attribute 1 → [identical/5]
Attribute 2 → [identical/5]
Attribute 3 → [identical/5]
Attribute 4 → [identical/5]
Attribute 5 → [identical/5]
Attribute 6 → [identical/2,I/3]
Attribute 7 → [identical/1,d/4]
Attribute 8 → [identical/4,d/1]

Table 1: Five closest exemplars in an exemplar base to the verb *admit*.

Ranking	Distance	Present Tense	Past Tense	English Form
1	2	(6,m,E,n,d,$,$,$)	(6,m,E,n,d,I,d,$)	amend
2	2	(6,s,E,n,d,$,$,$)	(6,s,E,n,d,I,d,$)	ascend
3	3	(6,b,1,n,d,$,$,$)	(6,b,1,n,d,I,d,$)	abound
4	4	(6,r,e,n,d,Z,$,$)	(6,r,e,n,d,Z,d,$)	arrange
5	4	(6,b,&,n,d,6,n,$)	(6,b,&,n,d,6,n,d)	abandon

For example, for attribute 8 there are four cases of identity and one that transforms to "$" to "d". The most common value is selected from each, yielding:

Attribute 1 → [identical/5]
Attribute 2 → [identical/5]
Attribute 3 → [identical/5]
Attribute 4 → [identical/5]
Attribute 5 → [identical/5]
Attribute 6 → [I/3]
Attribute 7 → [d/4]
Attribute 8 → [identical/4]

Therefore the past tense for *admit* is constructed as follows: take the first five input values and map them identically giving (6, d, m, I, t, ...). Next, change attribute 6 from "$" to "I", attribute 7 from "$" to "d" and leave attribute 8 as it is with the value "$". The resulting output vector is (6, d, m, I, t, I, d, $), which is the UNIBET form of the correct past tense, *admitted*.

Using PAMELA to retrieve the m closest exemplars and then applying the adaptation procedure described above yields our first algorithm, IBPA-1.. The pseudo-code is shown in table 2.

3.1   Evaluation of IBPA and Comparison with SPA and FOIDL

To evaluate IBPA-1 (and likewise the extensions to IBPA-2 and IBPA-3 to be discussed below) we used the eight UNIBET character corpus for the past tense domain. We report learning curve data based on 500 test examples for learning on i) samples of various sizes from the whole corpus and ii) samples from the sub-domain of regular verbs only (as was done in [8]). For i), the test results are given separately for regular and irregular verbs.

We trained SPA, FOIDL and the three IBPA algorithms on each example set. Code for SPA and FOIDL was supplied by the respective authors. SPA was used with pruning and with the adaptive default strategy setting [6] for assignment of classes in the leaves of the tree. For each sample size, 10 trials were performed and the results averaged. Initial investigations on the effect of m for IBPA-1 were carried out using $m = 5$, 10 and 20. Best results were obtained for $m=5$ and, accordingly, we used $m=5$ throughout.

For convenience and ease of comparison, all our results are presented in tables 3 and 4.

For learning on examples drawn from the whole corpus, table 3 (a) shows that IBPA-1 cannot compete with either SPA or FOIDL on test data consisting of unseen regular verbs. FOIDL is clearly superior to SPA (as was demonstrated in [8]) and SPA is superior to IBPA-1. As noted above, FOIDL possesses considerable background knowledge about the nature of the rule to be acquired in contrast to SPA and IBPA-1, which have none.

When tested on the learning of irregular verbs only, table 3(b) (illustrated in figure 1) shows that IBPA-1 is broadly comparable to FOIDL and improves considerably on SPA. For training on 450 and 500 examples, IBPSA-1's average is significantly better at the 5% level than FOIDL's and SPA's.

Table 2: Pseudo code for IBPA-1.

Initial Phase

Input: set of training examples
Output: value difference tables ; exemplar base

1. Construct value difference tables for each attribute using PAMELA (2.5)
2. Set exemplar base = {1st training example}
3. For each remaining training example do
   If training example $\notin$ exemplar base then add it to base

---
Association Phase

Input: source pattern vector; m (number of exemplars to be retrieved)
Output: associated (target) pattern vector

For each source pattern attribute in the retrieved exemplars do
    if all of the values in the corresponding target attribute are identical to their source
    then
        copy the source attribute value for the new example into the corresponding target attribute
    else
        calculate the frequency of identity mapping (FI) and, in non-identity cases the frequencies (FN) of the occurring target values and
        if $FI \geq \max\{FN\}$
        then
            copy the source attribute value for the new example into the corresponding target attribute
        else
            set the target value to be that with frequency $\max\{FN\}$ (or select randomly amongst ties)

For the second experiment involving the sub-domain of regular verbs, the results (see table 4) are similar to those in table 3(a) as might be expected since regulars dominate in the corpus. All the algorithms perform better on this much more straightforward domain.

Table 3: Average percentage correct past tenses on 500 test examples where training example sets (sizes 50 to 500) are drawn from whole corpus.

(a) Regular test verbs only					
Size	FOIDL	SPA	IBPA-1	IBPA-2	IBPA-3
50	93.0	25.6	24.6	24.9	42.6
100	98.0	36.5	31.2	32.0	59.7
150	99.0	54.6	39.4	40.0	69.8
200	100.0	59.6	45.3	47.2	75.6
250	100.0	66.7	47.0	49.0	77.5
300	100.0	69.4	49.6	52.6	84.6
350	100.0	72.8	51.3	55.7	86.6
400	100.0	76.7	52.6	56.8	87.4
450	100.0	79.4	55.4	57.8	88.0
500	100.0	81.5	57.1	60.9	90.1
(b) Irregular test verbs only					
Size	FOIDL	SPA	IBPA-1	IBPA-2	IBPA-3
50	2.6	4.0	3.4	8.9	12.2
100	12.2	12.1	15.2	16.5	17.5
150	18.1	15.6	18.9	21.0	22.3
200	22.3	17.9	20.2	24.2	25.2
250	21.5	20.2	24.2	26.2	28.4
300	25.6	21.5	25.4	27.2	33.0
350	26.2	22.4	26.7	28.7	35.4
400	29.2	23.1	29.4	30.1	35.6
450	27.9	24.2	34.2	30.5	36.7
500	30.1	25.6	33.2	32.3	39.9

Table 4: Average percentage correct past tenses on 500 test examples where training example sets (sizes 50 to 500) and test examples are drawn from the sub-domain of regular verbs.

Size	FOIDL	SPA	IBPA-1	IBPA-2	IBPA-3
50	94.8	42.5	36.4	37.8	52.6
100	98.6	55.4	42.5	44.7	67.4
150	99.5	69.4	46.7	47.8	72.6
200	100.0	74.0	53.2	52.3	77.9
250	100.0	72.4	51.6	53.6	81.9
300	100.0	73.2	54.8	57.9	89.9
350	100.0	79.8	56.7	60.2	90.2
400	100.0	83.7	56.2	59.9	91.3
450	100.0	87.6	57.6	61.3	90.2
500	100.0	89.7	57.9	62.9	91.8

4.   Weighting Exemplar Distance: IBPA-2

During the association phase in IBPA-1, the m nearest neighbours will, as seen in table 1, typically have different distances from the input vector of the new example. Yet, all m instances have equal 'voting rights' in determining what adaptation will be applied.

To attempt to improve upon the performance of IBPA-1, a weighting system can be introduced as part of the profiling of attribute values in the m nearest neighbours. An exemplar's weight can be determined from its PAMELA distance from the new case.

We introduce a simple inverse distance law: weights are calculated by placing the distance value as the denominator (plus 1 to cope with zero distances) and using 1 as the numerator. For the exemplars in table 1 the weights are therefore, 1/3, 1/3, 1/4, 1/5 and 1/5. Then, instead of counting the number of occurrences of each value, the associated weights are totalled. This allows for a more representative profile. The effect on the our worked example data is shown below:

Attribute 1 → [identical/1.31666]
Attribute 2 → [identical/1.31666]
Attribute 3 → [identical/1.31666]
Attribute 4 → [identical/1.31666]
Attribute 5 → [identical/1.31666]
Attribute 6 → [identical/0.53333,I/0.78333]
Attribute 7 → [identical/0.33333,d/0.98333]
Attribute 8 → [identical/0.98333,d/0.33333]

The most common value is then selected from each profile as for IBPA-1 yielding:

Attribute 1 → [identical/1.31666]
Attribute 2 → [identical/1.31666]
Attribute 3 → [identical/1.31666]
Attribute 4 → [identical/1.31666]
Attribute 5 → [identical/1.31666]
Attribute 6 → [I/0.78333]
Attribute 7 → [d/0.98333]
Attribute 8 → [identical/0.98333]

The resulting past tense is as for the unweighted IBPA-1 (which did form the correct association for *admit*) but it can be seen that the values in the profile more accurately reflect the mix of the data. For example, with attribute 6 the small difference between the "I" and the "identical" values indicate that the value for attribute 6 is harder to predict accurately than those for attributes 7 or 8.

The weighting scheme introduced here is entirely different to that used in PEBLS [11]. An exemplar weight in PEBLS reflects the performance history in classifying the training set during the second pass. PEBLS uses a single closest exemplar ($m=1$) so the notion of relative distance weighting is not appropriate.

4.1   IBPA-2 Results

For the whole corpus domain, table 3 (a) shows a small but fairly consistent improvement for IBPA-2 over IBPA-1 for unseen regular verbs. For the irregulars, table 3(b) shows a similar effect except that the performance of IBPA-2 falls beneath that of IBPA-1 at training set sizes of 450 and 500. It is not clear why this should be. Likewise, table 4 shows, for the regular sub-domain, a small improvement for IBPA-2 over IBPA-1. For sample sizes 300 and above, this is significant at 5%.

Overall the performance of IBPA-2 is disappointing. It may be that a more sophisticated approach to weighting for exemplar voting could produce greater improvement.

5.   Incorporating Attribute Weights: IBPA-3

In IBPA-1 and IBPA-2, all input attributes contribute on an equal basis to the assessment of distances as provided by PAMELA. An attribute weighting scheme would allow the experimenter to add a modest amount of background knowledge concerning the relevance of attributes. Here such a weighting will be applied manually although it could be automated. Each attribute will be assigned a weight between zero and 1. A value of zero will allow PAMELA to ignore that attribute.

The new definition of PAMELA with attribute weights is:

$$P(X,Y) = \sum_{i=1}^{N} \omega_i \rho(x_i, y_i)^r \qquad (5.1)$$

Where ω_i is the weight associated with attribute i. Again we set $r=1$.

Addition of this attribute weighting mechanism together with the inverse exemplar distance weighting of IBPA-2 yields our final algorithm IBPA-3.

5.1   IBPA-3 Results

A suitable attribute weight vector for the past tense domain might be:

(0.1, 0.2, 0.3, 0.5, 0.7, 0.9, 0.9, 0.8)

According to this vector, attributes 5, 6, 7 and 8 are more important than 1, 2, 3 and 4. No attribute, however, is irrelevant as none has a weight of zero. The algorithm is being told, essentially, that the latter attributes in the input are more important for retrieval. This is relevant information for both regular and irregular verbs but not nearly as specific or helpful as that provided to FOIDL by its splitting predicate. It does not provide any direct help in constructing the past tense.

With the addition of these attribute weights we see, from table 3, the most dramatic increase in accuracy for IBPA. For the whole corpus, IBPA-3 uniformly exceeds SPA for testing on regulars (table 3(a)). All differences of IBPA-3 and SPA along the learning curve are significant at the 5% level. IBPA-3, though, still cannot match the test performance of FOIDL on regulars. For irregulars, table 3(b) shows that IBPA-3 has a much clearer lead over FOIDL (significant at 5%) and therefore over SPA. On the regular sub-domain, IBPA-3 again performs better than SPA (table 4).

6.   Conclusion and Further Work

We have demonstrated that the instance-based paradigm, using the distance measure, PAMELA, can provide an effective means of learning pattern association rules. This adds a further 'answer' to the challenge of MacWhinney & Leinbach [4] that a system be produced to outperform their artificial neural network in learning English past tense tenses.

We have matched the performance of SPA while out-performing FOIDL, in spite of its superior background knowledge, on the most difficult task of all - learning the past tenses of irregular verbs. Such associations cannot be so readily captured in general rules. The 'case-based' nature of IBPA seems more appropriate.

FOIDL, as is to be expected, remains the best performing algorithm for learning regular past tenses. Away from this domain, however, it is not clear that FOIDL can be utilised effectively. It would be unusual to find real domains admitting such simple (and dominant) transformation rules as *add "ed"* In contrast, the IBPA approach would appear to possess the potential to be of general use across a variety of domains.

There are a number of ways in which the performance of the IBPA algorithms might be improved. In IBPA-2, it may be that allowing the number, m, of retrieved exemplars to be dynamic - perhaps adjusting to the size of the exemplar base - would be helpful. An additional weighing scheme to boost the contribution of exemplars with a good record of accomplishment (as is done in PEBLS) could also be developed. An automatic weighting for IBPA-3 would circumvent the difficulties in setting the attribute weight vector in domains where little is known about the mapping.

References

1. Aha, D.W., Kibler, D., and Albert, D.M.K. (1991). Instance-based learning algorithms. Machine Learning, 6, pp.37-66.
2. Rumelhart, D.E., McClelland, J.L. and the PDP Research Group (Eds.) (1986). Parallel Distributed Processing: Explorations in the microstructure of cognition, Vol. 1. Cambridge, MA: MIT Press.
3. Rumelhart, D.E., and McClelland, J.L. (1986). On learning the past tenses of English verbs. In, Parallel Distributed Processing: Explorations in the microstructure of cognition, Vol. 2, Rumelhart, D.E., McClelland, J.L. and the PDP Research Group (Eds.), pp.216-271, Cambridge, MA: MIT Press.
4. MacWhinney, B., and Leinbach, J. (1991). Implementations are not conceptualisations: Revising the verb model. Cognition, 40, pp.121-157.
5. Ling, C.X., and Marinov, M. (1993). Answering the connectionist challenge: a symbolic model of learning the past tense of English verbs. Cognition, 49, pp.235 – 290.
6. Ling, C.X. (1994). Learning the past tense of English verbs: The symbolic pattern associator vs. connectionist models. Journal of Artificial Intelligence Research, 1, pp.200-229.
7. Quinlan, J.R. (1993). C4.5 Programs for Machine Learning. San Mateo, CA: Morgan Kaufmann.
8. Mooney, R., and Califf, M. (1995). Induction of first-order decision lists: Results on learning the past tense of English verbs. Journal of Artificial Intelligence Research, 3, pp.1-24.
9. Quinlan, J.R. (1990). Learning logical definitions from relations. Machine Learning, 5, pp.239-266.
10. Martin, R.G, Hickey, R.J., and Bell, D.A. (1997). Loosely-coupled instance-based symbolic pattern association. In, Proceedings of the Sixth Scandinavian Conference on Artificial Intelligence, pp.240-248, Amsterdam, Netherlands: IOS Press.
11. Cost, S., and Salzberg, S. (1993). A weighted nearest neighbor algorithm for learning with symbolic features. Machine Learning, 10, pp.57-78.
12. Stanfill, C., and Waltz, D. (1986). Toward memory-based reasoning. Communications of the ACM, 29, pp.1213-1228.

Rule Generation Based on Rough Set Theory for Text classification

Yaxin Bi, Terry Anderson and Sally McClean
Faculty of Informatics, University of Ulster at Jordanstown,
Newtownabbey, Co. Antrim, BT37 0QB, N. Ireland, UK

Abstract

In this paper we describe an approach based on rough set techniques for decision rule generation applied to text classification. A minimal discriminating set – a reduct – for the original data set is achieved through analyzing the degree of dependency among attributes. To speed up the search for reducts, the *information gain* criterion is used to reduce the number of attributes considered and rank the attributes in decreasing order, and heuristic functions are incorporated into a range of rule generation algorithms.

1 Introduction

The rapid growth of the Internet has created a huge volume of online text documents. This has led to increased interest in machine learning methods for filtering and classifying documents. Various machine learning methods, in particular, statistical learning methods have recently been studied and applied to search engines, newswire filtering, text summarization and so forth. These include approaches such as regression modeling [1], nearest neighbor classification [2], naïve Bayes classification [3] and neural networks [4]. The common characteristic of these methods in assigning a document to predefined categories is based on a weighted combination of almost all the words in the document. In contrast, it is worth noting that another range of supervised learning methods, knowledge-based methods, is emerging as a promising approach in text classification. These mainly involve a range of inductive rule learning algorithms such as decision tree C4.5 [3], Ripper – a recent competitor to C4.5 [5] and rough set theory. The latter has not been extensively investigated in text classification. With such approaches, determining the categories of a document is through a set of 'keyword-spotting' rules, collectively making a rule-based classifier by using a small number of keywords. Also a rule-based classifier does not base a classification decision on word (term) frequency / inverse document frequency weighting (TF-IDF) [6], but only on the presence or absence of a word [5, 7]. With respect to this approach, an apparent advantage is that, like human-expressed knowledge, a rule-based classifier used in classifying text documents is explicitly interpretable.

A prior requirement for rule-based classifiers is to provide an effective method for extracting a set of decision rules from a large collection of documents. Rough set theory provides an effective mechanism for generating decision rules and can be used in different stages of the process of decision rule induction [8].

However, a common aspect of using the rough set approach lies in the utilization of the important concepts of *lower* and *upper approximations* in handling vagueness and uncertainty in determining the categories of an object using the limited available information. In other words, it is commonly the case that an object often can not be explicitly classified into one of the predefined categories based on a given training dataset. This therefore results in vagueness and uncertainty in constructing a rule classifier. Rough set theory [10] – a new mathematical tool – may provide an ideal solution to deal with such vagueness and uncertainty.

In generating decision rules using rough set techniques, dependency among the attributes of a data set will be analyzed. As a result, any redundant attributes will be removed and discriminating attributes will be preserved, constituting a minimal set of attributes that can be used to construct a rule classifier. This set of attributes is called a reduct*. For a dataset, more than one reduct may exist, but finding all reducts of a dataset often involves examining all combinations of attributes. This leads to a difficulty of 'combinatorial explosion', so that this approach can rarely be applied to a large collection of data [8].

Various attempts have been made to overcome this difficulty, for example, using genetic algorithms, which have achieved acceptable computational time for finding reducts [11]. However such approaches are still limited to a fairly small number of attributes, so they are not particularly appropriate for text classification.

In this work, we propose an approach to overcome this difficulty. First, using the *information gain* criterion reduces the number of attributes of a dataset, thus reducing the high dimensionality of a large dataset. Second, using heuristic functions for incorporating domain knowledge reduces the amount of computation in finding all reducts. We incorporate these ideas into a range of algorithms. The preliminary experimental results show an improvement in computational efficiency has been achieved. This work may provide an effective approach to constructing word-spotting rules for text classification.

2 The Data Model and Definition

First we introduce a data model of an information system (also called an attribute-value system) [10], which is able to represent textual information in a collection of documents, and facilitate the process of supervised learning based on a rough set approach for generating word-spotting rules.

---

* A special term in Rough Set Theory, see Definition 2.3

Let $S = <U, A, V, f>$ be an information system, where $U = \{u_1, \ldots, u_{|U|}\}$ is a finite set of objects, and $A = \{a_1, \ldots, a_{|A|}\}$ is a finite attribute set; $V = \{V_{a1}, \ldots, V_{a|A|}\}$ is a set of attribute values where $V_{a_i} = \{V_{a_{i1}}, \ldots, V_{a_{ik}}\}$ is the domain of attribute a_i; $V_{a_{ij}}$ is a categorical value and there is a mapping $f(u, a)$: $U \times A \rightarrow V_a$ which assigns the particular values from the domain of attributes to objects such that $f(u, a) \in V_a$, for all $u \in U$ and $a \in A$.

In practice, an information system can be extended to a decision table with a facility of supervised learning, where A consists of the condition attributes C and the decision attributes D such that $A = C \cup D$ and $C \cap D = \varnothing$. Typically, $D = \{d\}$ is a singleton set with a mapping $f(u, d)$: $U \times A \rightarrow V_d$, which gives the partition of the set of all objects over U, e.g. k disjoint classes $\{X_1, \ldots, X_k\}$ called *decision classes*. A decision table U constitutes a set of training examples.

The goal of learning a set of word-spotting rules – inducing decision rules – is to find a discriminating description of each decision class over U. These descriptions, composed of condition attributes that are non-redundant and the corresponding decision attributes, constitute a minimal set of decision rules. We introduce the definitions of several essential concepts below [10].

Definition 2.1: - With attribute $a \in A$, two objects $u, v \in U$ are defined as an *equivalence relation* over U if and only if $f(u, a) = f(v, a)$. An *equivalence relation* gives a group of partitions over U with respect to attribute a, denoted by U / a, and $U / a = \{X_1, \ldots, X_r\}$ such that any two objects u and v are in the same *equivalence class* X_i if and only if they have the same attribute value derived from V_a. Particularly, when $a = d$, the *equivalence class* also is called as *decision class*. For X_i, there are the following properties: $X_i \subseteq U, X_i \neq \varnothing, X_i \cap X_j = \varnothing$ for $i \neq j, i, j = 1, \ldots, r$ and $\cup X_i = U$.

Definition 2.2: - An *indiscernibility relation* is associated with every subset of attributes $B \subseteq A$ and is defined as $IR(B) = \{(u, v) \in U^2 \mid \forall a \in B, f(u, a) = f(v, a)\}$. Obviously, $IR(B)$ is an *equivalence relation* and is regarded as the intersection of all equivalence relations belonging to B. For $IR(B)$, it is alternatively written as $IR\{a_1, \ldots, a_k\}$, and for partitions over U with respect to attribute a, denoted by U / a, also $U / IR\{a\}$.

Definition 2.3: - Given a subset of attributes, $B \subseteq A$, if there is $Q \subseteq B$, $U / IR(B) = U / IR(Q)$, and Q is minimal among all subsets of B, then $IR(Q)$ is called a *reduct* of B, and the attributes within a reduct are significant so that none of them can be omitted. Note that B may have a group of reducts.

Definition 2.4: - For each subset $X \subseteq U$ with respect to decision attribute D, an *equivalence relation* $R \subseteq IR(B)$ with respect to condition attribute C, we associate two subsets:

$$\underline{R}X = \cup \{Y \mid Y \in U / R \wedge Y \subseteq X\}$$

$$\overline{R}\,X = \cup\,\{Y\,|\,Y\in\,U\,/\,R \wedge Y \cap X \neq \varnothing\}$$

called the *lower* and *upper approximation* of X respectively. *Lower approximation* $\underline{R}\,X$ also is called a positive region. In order to measure the accuracy of approximation, a formula is defined in [10] as follows:

$$\gamma_R = \frac{\left|\underline{R}X\right|}{\left|U\right|} \qquad\qquad (1)$$

In fact, this formula describes the dependency degree of condition attributes and decision attributes, as is also called the degree of support for decision classes from condition attributes [9]. If $\gamma_R = 1$, all the objects in a decision table U can be classified by using a subset of attributes R, for this case, $U\,/\,IR(R) = U$. If $0 < \gamma_R < 1$, only those objects which belong to the positive region can be classified by using R. In particular, if $\gamma_R = 0$, none of the objects of U can be classified using a set of attributes R.

3 Decision Rule Generation

A decision rule means an implication of the form $R \Rightarrow d$, where R is a subset of the condition attribute C, and d is a single decision class of the decision attribute D. The rule $R \Rightarrow d$ is satisfied in a decision table with the confidence factor $0 \le c \le 1$ if and only if at least c% of objects in the table that satisfy R also satisfy d. We will use the notion of $R \Rightarrow d\,|\,c$ to specify that the rule $R \Rightarrow d$ has a confidence factor c.

More specifically, let R be a conjunction of a set of condition attributes denoted by $R = c_1 \wedge \ldots \wedge c_k$, and let X be a subset of U. For any $x \in X$, $f(x, c_1) = V_{c_{1i}} \wedge, \ldots, \wedge f(x, c_k) = V_{c_{ki}}$ is in the same decision class d, then we say the subset of objects X satisfies the conditions represented by R and $X \subseteq U\,/\,IR(R)$. Also X is a non-redundant, minimal discriminating description of the decision class d over U. The cardinality of the subset of R is referred to as the support for the rule $R \Rightarrow d$, denoted by $|X|$, the proportion of the $|X|$ to $|U|$ of the set of objects is referred to as confidence factor.

To illustrate the process of rule reduction, we look at a decision table which consists of four condition attributes and one decision attribute with two decision classes (see Table 1). Since these objects do not all belong to the same decision class, we need a way to split them into subsets based on the condition attribute values. First, let us consider equivalent classes on attributes o and d, and whether the objects can be classified into the *Play* decision class (the following numbers in subsets are used to represent the corresponding objects in Table 1). With the definitions in Section 2, the equivalent classes can be represented in Figure 1.

U\A	Outlook (o)	Temperature (t)	Humidity (h)	Windy (w)	D'class(d)
1	Sunny	High	VH	False	Don't play
2	Sunny	High	VH	True	Don't play
3	Overcast	High	H	False	Play
4	Rain	Middle	VH	False	Play
5	Rain	Low	VH	False	Play
6	Rain	Low	H	True	Don't play
7	Overcast	Low	H	True	Play
8	Sunny	Middle	VH	False	Don't play
9	Sunny	Low	H	False	Play
10	Rain	Middle	VH	False	Play
11	Sunny	Middle	H	True	Play
12	Overcast	Middle	VH	True	Play
13	Overcast	High	H	False	Play
14	Rain	Middle	VH	True	Don't play

Table 1: A decision table (adapted from Quinlan's work)

$$U / IR\{o\} = \{ X_1^o, X_2^o, X_3^o \} = \{\{1, 2, 8, 9, 11\} \{3, 7, 12, 13\} \{4, 5, 6, 10, 14\}\}$$

$$U / IR\{d\} = \{ X_1^d, X_2^d \} = \{\{1, 2, 6, 8, 14\} \{3, 4, 5, 7, 9, 10, 11, 12, 13\}\}$$

Figure 1: Partitions on attributes o and d

Looking at the two subsets of equivalent classes of the equivalent relations $IR\{o\}$ and $IR\{d\}$, there only exists $X_2^o \subseteq X_2^d$, the equivalent classes X_1^o and X_3^o do not belong to either the decision classes X_1^d or X_2^d. This means that this subset can not be classified solely by using the attribute o. Hence we drop X_2^o and need other additional attributes for this subset to be discriminated between X_1^d or X_2^d. Similarly, we can evaluate each of the rest of the attributes over the decision table U until all objects over U are classified into the decision classes. Such a process of evaluating the classification power – dependency – of attributes can be viewed as a search for the minimal combinations of attributes or 'good model' in dividing all the objects with respect to the decision classes. The resulting combinations are reducts over U as defined in Definition 2.3.

Unfortunately, in some cases, some objects over U can not be successfully classified into the decision classes until all the combinations of attributes are exhausted. For example, in Table 1, if the value of the decision attribute for object *3*, *Play,* is substituted by *Don't play*, the objects *3* and *13* will not be characterized in terms of the limited available information in the decision table. This results in an uncertainty in determining a decision class for the objects *3* and *13*, making it impossible to induce decision rules for this. Recent research reveals that rough set theory is an effective approach for dealing with vagueness and uncertainty in rule induction. That is, this uncertainty concept is replaced by a pair of precise concepts – called *lower* and *upper approximations* of the uncertainty concept [10]. As a consequence of using the approximations, induced rules are categorized into *certain* (exact) and *approximate* (possible) ones depending on the *lower* and *upper approximations*, respectively [8].

As usual, in a decision table, more than one reduct may exist. Finding all reducts may need the evaluation of all the combinations of attributes in a table. However, the time to calculate all possible combinations of attributes increases exponentially with their number. Such calculations, in practice, are prohibitive, even unnecessary for many applications. For example, text analysis often involves the problem of high dimensionality. Use of prior knowledge can reduce the amount of information involved and hence the computational costs.

4 Information Reduction

A common representation for text documents is attribute-value pairs, as is typically done in the popular vector representation for information retrieval [6]. Using this representation, each document is regarded as an object of a decision table – a vector of attribute values. Each attribute represents a term (word) in a document, and attribute values – term weights – are computed using either the weighting formula TF-IDF or a Boolean formula. A decision table built in such a manner typically has a high dimensionality, such as ten or hundreds of thousands of terms. This is prohibitively high for a rough set based algorithm. It is very desirable to reduce the dimensionality of attributes to an acceptable number without sacrificing the accuracy of inducing rules before applying the rough set approach.

In this work, we have used two methods for attribute reduction. First, following the suggestions from information retrieval studies, terms with low or high frequencies are non-predictive, so that such terms will be removed. Second, we rank all of the terms according to their weights in decreasing order using the *information gain* criterion (see below) described in [12, 13] and pick the top ranking terms based on a predefined threshold. The decreasing order of attributes may speed up searches for a minimal set of attributes.

The *information gain* criterion ranks a set of attributes by measuring the number of bits of information. To calculate the *information gain* for each attribute in Figure 1 requires the average amount of information $In(U)$ and the expected information $In_a(U)$ (see Equation 2). The former measures the average amount of information needed to identify the class of an object within the partitions of a decision attribute, and the latter represents the weighted sum for each condition attribute based on its corresponding partitions. Therefore, for a decision table U, attribute $a \in A$ and the partitions $U / a = \{X_1, \ldots, X_r\}$, the information gain with respect to attribute a is defined as follows:

$$G(a) = In(U) - In_a(U) \qquad (2)$$

$$In_a(U) = \sum_1^n \frac{\left|X_i^a\right|}{|U|} \times In(X_i^a) \qquad (3)$$

$$In(X_i^a) = -\sum_1^n \frac{freq(x, X_i^a)}{\left|X_i^a\right|} \times \log_2\left(\frac{freq(x, X_i^a)}{\left|X_i^a\right|}\right) \qquad (4)$$

where $f(x, X_i^a) = V_{d_k}$

$$In(U) = -\sum_1^n \frac{freq(X_i^d, U)}{|U|} \times \log_2\left(\frac{freq(X_i^d, U)}{|U|}\right) \qquad (5)$$

A higher significant value for an attribute may indicate a greater interaction with decision attributes in a decision table.

Using attribute reduction, the dimensionality of a decision table is reduced to a relatively small, acceptable number of dimensions. But the question arises, what is the optimal one for a decision table? On the basis of empirical results discussed in [12], Yang and Pedersen argue that the number of attributes may lie in the range of 30-90 without degrading the accuracy of text classification. Another result described in [4] reveals that on average 20 terms yielded the best classification performance, and this number was consistent with the range of attribute set sizes used in [3]. Between 20 and 90 attributes then should be appropriate for determining the number of columns in a decision table.

5 The Algorithms for Computing Partitions and Intersections

5.1 A simple partition algorithm

As indicated in Section 2, for $a \in A$ and all $u \in U$, there is a mapping $f(u, a): U \times A \rightarrow V_a$, and $V_a = \{V_{a_1}, ..., V_{a_k}\}$ such that U can be partitioned into k subsets based on the k distinct domain values, denoted $U / a = \{X_1, ..., X_r\}$. With this in mind, we developed a partition algorithm as follows:

```
Procedure PartitionIntoSets //partitioning a decision table
Let A be a set of attributes over a decision table U;
Begin
  For i = 1 to |A| do
    Begin
      U/a_i ← MapTupleToSets(U [i]) // a column as input parameter
      Partitions ← Partitions + U/a_l
    End
  Return partitions;
End
```

```
Procedure MapTupleToSets(tuple L) //partitioning a tuple
Let Setarr be a array of sets; Let Set be a set; // the rows in a decision table;
Begin
  For i = 1 to |L| do
    Begin
      For k=i to |L| do
        Begin
          If L[i] == L[k];
          Set ← Set.add(k);
        End
      Setarr ← Setarr + Set;
    End
  Return Setarr;
End
```

Figure 2: A simple partition algorithm

5.2 An Intersection Algorithm

The problem of exponential complexity in finding reducts has been mentioned in Section 3. To cope with this, the first strategy adopted here is to use the *information gain* criterion to reduce the number of attributes to 20-30 and rank them in decreasing order. This order ensures that the combinations of the attributes with higher significance will be examined first, avoiding exhausting all attributes for any case. Arguably the best combination of attributes may not always be the combination of the attributes with decreasing order. But for statistical text analysis, the role of the order can be utilized for this end.

Another strategy attempts to reduce the amount of calculation in finding reducts. It is worth noting that if the domain of an attribute is made of many values, the equivalence classes belonging to the attribute set may have many small classes, and a rule will be based on a few objects only. Therefore its significance will be low, and its ability to classify new text documents is rather limited. We incorporate such prior knowledge – prior information – into the calculation procedure, removing such attributes to examine some, but not all, of the combinations.

Having determined the strategies, we now consider how the heuristic functions will be incorporated into the algorithm, consisting of three constraints:

- Given a singleton X, for any set $Y \neq \emptyset$, then $|X \cap Y| \leq |X|$ and $X \cap Y \subseteq X$.
- According to the results from information retrieval studies, any single case may be not predictive for text classification, thus such cases will be eliminated.
- Optimizing the calculation procedure of finding reducts, ensuring a unique subset to feed to the next iteration.

To show how heuristic functions play an important role in finding reducts, Figure 3 illustrates part of an algorithm for computing intersections. Given $|A|$ sets of partitions of objects over U, denoted by $U / a_1, \ldots, U / a_{|A|}$, the algorithm will calculate the intersections of any two sets of partitions U / a_i and U / a_j, $i \neq j$, three sets of partitions with respect to three attributes, and so on, until it finds all reducts or exhausts all sets of partitions with respect to all the attributes. Note that this algorithm only calculates the intersection of any two sets of partitions associated with two attributes. For the calculation of the intersections with respect to three attributes, as described in Definition 2.2, it is incrementally based on the resulting intersections of any two sets of partitions associated with two attributes. For each step in calculating intersections, the heuristic functions are applied to reduce the amount of calculation, avoiding 'combinatorial explosion'. Figure 4 shows an experimenting result on a data set called *bridge* [15]. It can be seen that an improvement in computing speed has been achieved. Evaluation of precision in finding reducts remains for future investigation.

```
Procedure CalculateIntersections
Let VT contain U/a_1 . . ., U/a_{|A|}
Begin
  VV ← VT[1];
  For i = 2 to |A| do
  Begin
    VV ← HyperIntersections (VT[i], VV);
  End
End
Procedure HyperIntersections(VT1, VT2){
Let RSCVT1 and RSCVT2 be sets of partitions
Begin
 For i = 1 to |VT1| do
  Begin
  For j = 1 to |VT2| do
    Begin
      RSCVT1 ← RSCVT1 + Intersection (VT1[i], VT2[j]);
    End
    RSCVT2 ← RSCVT2 + RemoveSingletons (RSCVT1);
    //heuristic function 1
  End
  RSCVT2 ← RemoveDuplicateSets (RSCVT2); //heuristic
  Function 2
  Return RSCVT2;
End
```

Figure 3: Calculating intersections

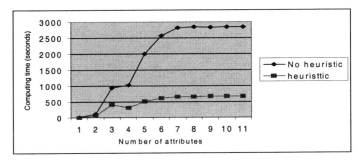

Figure 4: Evaluation of the performance

6 Finding Reducts, Lower Approximations and Decision Rule Generation

Going back to Definition 2.3, a reduct is a minimal set of attributes which discriminates objects in the same role as the full set of attributes, and preserves a maximal coverage for a decision table U. In general, more than one reduct exists for a given a decision table. We need, thus, to establish a method to acquire a reduct for constructing a rule-based classifier. Figure 5 illustrates an algorithm for finding a reduct based on the intersections of attributes. A reduct found using this algorithm is a set of attributes {o, t, w} and its partitions is presented in Figure 6.

```
Procedure FindingReduct
Let A_{N-1} be a set of the intersections of N-1 attributes;
Let A_N be a set of the intersections of N attributes;
Begin
    If |A_{N-1}| = |A_N| do
        For i = 1 to |A_{N-1}| do
            Begin
                If A_{N-1}[i] ∈ A_N do
                    A_N ← remove (A_{N-1}[i]) from A_N;
                Else
                    Return false
            End //for i
    Else
        Return false
    If |A_N| = 0 do
        Return A_{N-1} //a reduct
End
```

Figure 5: Finding a reduct

$$U / IR\{o, t, w\} = \{ X_1^{otw}, X_2^{otw}, X_3^{otw}, X_4^{otw}, X_5^{otw}, X_6^{otw}, X_7^{otw}, X_8^{otw},$$
$$X_9^{otw}, X_{10}^{otw}, X_{11}^{otw}, X_{12}^{otw} \} = \{\{4, 10\}, \{9\}, \{13, 3\}, \{8\}, \{7\}, \{6\}, \{5\}, \{14\},$$
$$\{12\}, \{11\}, \{2\}, \{1\}\}$$

Figure 6: Partitions based on the reduct {o, t, w}

When a reduct is found, the work of creating rules for the values of the decision attribute of a decision table is practically done. To transform a reduct into a set of rules, we have to bind the condition attribute values of the equivalent class from which the reduct originated to the corresponding decision attribute values. This involves use of the important concept of *lower* and *upper approximations*. In this paper, we confine our interest to the *lower approximation*. As indicated in Definition 2.4, a *lower approximation* gives a mechanism to measure how much support a decision class has from a set of condition attributes. The support from the combination of multiple condition attributes fits nicely with our needs of rule-based classifiers for text classification. Figure 7 gives an algorithm for calculating lower approximations, given a set of decision classes and a set of partitions with respect to a reduct. For example, taking the decision classes in Figure 1 and the partitions in Figure 6, the lower approximations are shown in Figure 8.

```
Procedure CalculatingLowerApproximation
Let D be a set of decision classes;
Let EC be a set of equivalent classes: U / IR(reduct);
Let LA be a set containing lower approximations
Begin
  For i = 1 to |D| do
        Begin
            For j = 1 to |EC| do
            Begin
                If EC[j] ⊆ D[i] do
                    LA[i]A_N ← EC[j]∪LA[i];
                End //for j
            End //for i
End
```

Figure 7: Calculating lower approximations

$$\underline{R}\ X_1^d = X_5^{otw} \cup X_8^{otw} \cup X_{11}^{otw} \cup X_{12}^{otw} \cup X_4^{otw} = \{6, 14, 2, 1, 8\}$$

$$\underline{R}\ X_2^d = X_6^{otw} \cup X_1^{otw} \cup X_7^{otw} \cup X_9^{otw} \cup X_{10}^{otw} \cup X_3^{otw} \cup X_4^{otw} = \{7, 4, 10, 5, 12, 11, 13, 3, 8\}$$

Figure 8: Two lower approximations for two decision classes in Figure 1

Once we have obtained lower approximations, we can transform them to rules. As described in Section 2 and 3, a mapping over a revised decision table can be rewritten as $f(u, a)$: $X_1^d \times$ reduct $\rightarrow V_d$, where $u \in X_1^d$, $a \in$ reduct $= \{o, t, w\}$ and V_d = "Don't play". This mapping is directly used to bind the condition attribute values and the corresponding decision attribute values to complete the generation of rules. For example, $f(6, o)$ =Sunny, $f(6, t)$ =High, and $f(6, w)$ =False, and so on. Similarly, this is done in the same way for the decision class X_2^d. The rules induced from Table 1 are as follows:

```
If(Outlook=Sunny)∧(Temperature=High)∧(Windy=False) then Don't play
If(Outlook=Sunny)∧(Temperature=High)∧(Windy=True)  then Don't play
If(Outlook=Rain)∧(Temperature=Low)∧(Windy=True)    then Don't play
If(Outlook=Sunny)∧(Temperature=Middle)∧(Windy=False)then Don't play
If(Outlook=Rain)∧(Temperature=Middle)∧(Windy=True) then Don't play
If(Outlook=Overcast)∧(Temperature=High)∧(Windy=False)   then play
. . .
```

Figure 9: Rules induced from the decision table shown in Table 1

In conjunction with the degree of support for the rules (according to Figure 8), as indicated in Definition 2.4, the cardinalities of $\underline{R}\ X_1^d$ and $\underline{R}\ X_2^d$ are 5 and 9 respectively. This means that the degree of support for decision *Don't play* is 5 and the confidence of its rules is referred as 5/14, as well as the degree of *Play* is 9 and its confidence is regards as 9/14.

7 Applied Model for Text Classification

In the previous sections, we have presented the approach established on rough set theory for inducing decision rules. In this section, we look at an application domain – text classification – that will fit this approach to inducing a set of rules for text classification. An adaptation of this approach for the purpose of text classification includes the following main processes:

- A collection of text documents is represented as a decision table. Condition attributes correspond distinct words, and a decision attribute is associated with topic categories. Instead of using Boolean values, attribute values are computed using the weighting function TF-IDF.
- Attribute values produced by TF-IDF typically have continuous values, which are not suitable for handling by the rough set approach. Therefore continuous-values have to be discretized to nominal values.
- All the attributes in a decision table will be ranked by the *information gain* criterion.
- A series of calculations will be carried out, including finding minimal reducts, calculating and generating a rule-based classifier, etc.

Given a task of text classification, most applications involve multiple classes that are not mutually exclusive. A document may thus be assigned to one or more of the categories simultaneously. In this work, one strategy taken is to decompose a decision table with a k-valued decision attribute to k sub-tables, where each is associated with one particular topic category. In this way, we can acquire k rule-based classifiers. Figure 10 shows an example of an induced rule set.

In order to evaluate the effectiveness and performance of this approach, the benchmark that will be used is a corpus of Reuters, the so-called Reuters-21578 collection [16]. This collection consists of the 12,902 stories that had been classified into 118 categories. We will follow the suggestion [4] in which 75% of the stories are used to build classifiers and the remaining 25% to test the accuracy of the resulting models in reproducing the manual category assignments. At the first experimental stage, we will use the top ten categories. These 10 categories account for 75% of the training instances, with the remainder distributed among the other 108 categories.

For this experiment, we will transform this ten-class problem to 10 two-class problems. This means that we have to construct 10 rule-based classifiers corresponding to the 10 topic categories. For example, with respect to the 'wheat' category, a classifier generated by a rule induction algorithm called Swap-1 [7] is shown in Figure 10. If any of these rules is satisfied, the document is classified as 'wheat'. Otherwise, the decision reverts to the default class of a 'non-wheat' topic.

```
If (w_{i1}=wheat)∧(w_{i2}=farm)                 then category wheat
If (w_{i1}=wheat)∧(w_{ir}=commodity)            then category wheat
If (w_{ij}=bushels)∧(w_{ik}=export)             then category wheat
If (w_{i1}=wheat)∧(w_{iq}=agriculture)          then category wheat
If (w_{i1}=wheat)∧(w_{is}=tonnes)               then category wheat
If (w_{i1}=wheat)∧(w_{ih}=winter)∧(w_{i2s}≠soft) then category wheat
```

Figure 12: Rule set for Reuters 'wheat' category

8 Summary and Further Work

In this paper, we provide an investigation of rule induction built on rough set theory for text classification. The algorithms described here have been implemented and preliminary experiments have been undertaken. The results show that an improvement in calculating reducts can be achieved through incorporating heuristic functions into the algorithms, but evaluation of the accuracy of calculating reducts remains for further study.

The characteristic techniques of the rough set-based approaches lie in analyzing the dependency of combining attributes of a data set to achieve a minimal set of the attributes – a reduct. Obviously, exhausting the combinations of attributes should give the best performance for reducts, but this does not mean that this is the best solution to finding reducts. Research on statistical learning methods for text categorization suggests that the significance of single words in a collection of documents is different with their different frequencies, which basically conforms to Zipf's law [17]. Thus we reduce the number of attributes using the *information gain* criterion and preserve an ordered and more informative set of attributes. This idea offers a potential solution to finding a reduct, but this remains to be verified in further work.

A reduct may provide evidence for the right combinations of attributes (terms), but this is based on the assumption that a decision table only has 20-30 attributes. We are also interested in exploring this correlation between the number of attributes and best combinations of attributes in text classification. Clearly these combinations are important to understanding text.

As mentioned in Section 6, a decision table may have more than one reduct, but we have not discussed methods for handling this situation. This work will involve the investigation of the intersection of all reducts and rule refinement methods in the future.

Acknowledgement

The authors are indebted to Professor Jiwen Guan for his valuable help on developing the algorithms for inducing rules.

References

1. Schütze H, Hull D and Pedersen JO. A comparison of classifiers and document representations for the routing problem. In proceedings of the annual international ACM SIGIR conference on research and development in information retrieval, 1995, pp229-237

2. Yang Y and Chute CG. An example-based mapping method for text categorization and retrieval. ACM transactions on information systems, 1994, 12(3), pp252-277

3. Lewis DD and Ringuette M. A comparison of two learning algorithms for categorization. In symposium on document analysis and information retrieval, pp81-93, 1994

4. Wiener EJ, Pedersen O and Weigend AS. A neural network approach to topic spotting. In symposium on document analysis and information retrieval, 1995, pp 317-332

5. Cohen WW and Yoram S. Context-sensitive learning methods for text categorization. In proceedings of the annual ACM SIGIR conference on research and development in information retrieval, 1996, pp307-315

6. Salton G, Allan J, Buckley C and Singhal A. Automatic analysis, theme generation, and summarization of machine-readable texts. Science. 1994, 264:1421-1426

7. Apté C, Damerau F and Weiss SM. Towards language independent automated learning of text categorization models. In proceedings of the annual international ACM SIGIR conference on research and development in information retrieval, 1994, pp24-30

8. Stefanowski J. On rough set based approaches to induction of decision rules. In Lech Polkowski and Andrzej Skowron (Eds) Studies in fuzziness and soft computing. Physica-Verlag, 1998, 1:500-529

9. Guang JW and Bell D. Rough computational methods for information systems. Artificial Intelligence 1998, 105:77-103

10. Pawlak Z. Rough Set: Theoretical aspects of reasoning about data. Kluwer Academic, 1991

11. Wroblewski J. Genetic algorithms in decomposition and classification problems. Polkowski, L. and Skowron, A. (Eds) Finding minimal reducts using genetic Algorithms. Rough set in knowledge discovery 2: applications, cases studies and software systems, Physica-Verlag, Heidelberg, 1998, pp472-492

12. Yang Y and Pedersen JP. A comparative study on feature selection in text categorization proceedings of the fourteenth international conference on machine learning, 1997

13. Quinlan JR. C4.5: Programs for machine learning. Morgan Kaufmann, 1993

14. Agrawal R, Imielinski T and Swami A. Mining association rules between sets of items in large databases. In proceedings of the ACM SIGMOD conference, 1993

15. The UCI KDD Archive. http://www.ics.uci.edu/~mlearn/

16. Lewis DD. Reuters-21578: http://www.research.att.com/~lewis/reuters21578.html

17. van Rijsbergen CJ. Information Retrieval (second edition). Butterworths, 1979

18. Yang Y. An evaluation of statistical approaches to text categorization. Journal of Information Retrieval, 1999, 1(1/2): 67-88

19. Bi Y, Murtagh F, McClean S and Anderson T. Text passage classification using supervised learning. Workshop on logical and uncertainty models for information systems, 1999, pp22-34

Grouping Multivariate Time Series Variables: Applications to Chemical Process and Visual Field Data

Allan Tucker, Stephen Swift, Nigel Martin and Xiaohui Liu

Department of Computer Science
Birkbeck College, University of London
Malet Street, London WC1E 7HX, United Kingdom
Email: [allan, swifty, nigel, hui]@dcs.bbk.ac.uk

Abstract

In many industrial and medical applications it is important to identify relationships in Multivariate Time Series (MTS) variables in as short a time as possible. Within this paper, we present a method for decomposing high dimensional MTS into mutually exclusive subsets of variables where within-group dependencies are high and between-group dependencies are low. The method involves the use of two evolutionary computation techniques, which find an approximate solution to an otherwise NP-hard problem. We apply the proposed method to two real-world datasets, a chemical process MTS from an oil refinery and an ophthalmic MTS regarding glaucomatous deterioration.

1. Introduction

There are many practical applications involving the partition of a set of objects into a number of mutually exclusive subsets. The objective is to optimise a *metric* defined over the set of all valid subsets: the term *grouping* has been often used to refer to this type of problem. Examples of grouping applications include bin packing, workshop layout design, and graph colouring [4]. Much research has been done on grouping problems in different fields, and it was established that many, if not all such problems, are NP-hard [7]. In the case of decomposing a high-dimensional multivariate time series (MTS) into a number of low dimensional MTS, the number of possible dependencies between time series variables becomes very large because one variable may affect another after a certain *time lag*. How to effectively utilise these dependencies becomes an important issue: using all possible dependencies in a variable grouping algorithm will be computationally infeasible for many, especially real-time, applications. This paper describes a methodology for variable groupings in MTS. In particular, we investigate a heuristic method for utilising the information regarding dependencies among MTS variables from chemical process and medical datasets. This method was developed and analysed in [20] using synthetic datasets and within this paper we apply the method to two real-world MTS.

2. Grouping in Multivariate Time Series

MTS data are widely available in different fields including medicine, finance, science and engineering. Modelling MTS data effectively is important for many decision-making activities. A MTS is a series of observations, $x_i(t)$, [$i=1,...,n;$ $t=1,...,T$], made sequentially through time. Here i indexes the different measurements made at each time point t. Although much research has been carried out on modelling MTS for different purposes, little has been done on an important pre-processing issue: the grouping of MTS. In [12] visual field variables are clustered but time delays are ignored. In [13] categorical data is segmented along the time axis and these segments are clustered. In [8] real valued MTS are clustered but expert knowledge is used to reduce the search space.

When dealing with an n dimensional MTS, it is desirable to model the data as a group of smaller MTS models as opposed to a single one since not all of the variables may be related, and also the number of parameters to be located in such a model would be very high. The process of breaking down the data into lower dimensional time series that are independent to some degree significantly narrows the search space allowing the speedier production of MTS models. Hence, we are interested in finding out how to decompose a high-dimensional MTS into groups of smaller MTS, where the dependency between variables within the same group is high, but very low with variables in another group. Note that this differs from *dimensionality reduction* techniques such as principal component analysis or factor analysis which are aimed at creating a smaller set of transformed and composite variables [14].

Our methodology consists of two stages. First, an approximate search over combinations of variables and time lags is carried out in order to construct a list Q with length Q_{len} of highly correlated variables. Each element of Q is a *triple* made up of two variables and a time lag, *lag*. For example, the triple *(x_1, x_2, 5)* represents the correlation between x_1 and x_2 with a time lag of 5. Essentially, the triples in Q represent the variable pairs that are deemed to be significantly correlated with the corresponding time lag. Stage two consists of a grouping algorithm applied to Q, where a specifically designed metric is used to group the variables in the original MTS based on the pairs of variables found in Q. Note that the lag portion of the triple is ignored once the grouping algorithm is applied since we wish to group highly correlated variables irrespective of the time lag between them.

2.1 Stage 1 - Correlation Search

The first stage of the methodology constructs Q which contains Q_{len} pairs of highly correlated variables over all possible integer time lags from zero to some positive maximum, *MaxLag*. We want to find these correlations after exploring a fraction of the search space. Previously, we have compared different methods for performing this task [17] and have found that for operations where speed is essential, an evolutionary programming approach performs best.

The correlation list generated using this method is then used in conjunction with the grouping strategy described below. Note that at time lag zero, the correlations represented by the triples $(x_i, x_j, 0)$ and $(x_j, x_i, 0)$ are effectively the same so duplicates are considered *invalid*. All triples of the form (x_i, x_i, lag) will also be considered invalid since these are auto-correlations and do not show relationships between different variables. All invalid triples are removed during the procedure.

In this paper we have chosen a *correl* that is a well established correlation coefficient - Spearman's Rank Correlation [16]. Spearman's Rank Correlation (SRC) measures linear and non-linear relationships between two variables, either discrete or continuous, by assigning a rank to each observation. We can calculate the SRC between two variables over differing time lags by shifting one variable in time. The equation incorporates the sums of the squares of the differences in paired ranks, according to the formula:

$$correl(x_i, x_j, lag) = 1 - \left(\frac{6 \sum_{t=1}^{T-lag} \left(rank(x_i(t)) - rank(x_j(t+lag)) \right)^2}{(T-lag)((T-lag)^2 - 1)} \right) \quad (1)$$

where T is the length of the MTS and $rank(x_i(t))$ is calculated from ordering and ranking every observation of the variable x_i on its value and recording the rank of the value at position t.

Note that the methods are in no way restricted to using this particular coefficient and others such as Pearson's [16] could have easily been used. We chose Spearman's Rank as it is well recognised and not restricted to finding linear dependencies.

Evolutionary Programming (EP) is based on a similar paradigm to the Genetic Algorithm (GA), [10]. However, the emphasis is on mutation and recombination is not used. The basic algorithm is outlined as follows [2, 5] where *MaxCalls* is the number of calls to the correlation function (some fraction of the search space), *RoundUp* is a function that rounds a value up to the nearest integer, and a triple's fitness is calculated using the absolute value of equation 1. The absolute value is taken since we are only interested in the magnitude of the correlation.

```
Input: X (a T×n MTS), MaxCalls, Q_len, Generations
Set Q = Empty List
Generate Q_len random triples and insert into Q
Generations = RoundUp(MaxCalls / Q_len) - 1
For g = 1 to Generations
        Set Children to Q
        Apply Mutate operator to Children
        Insert valid Children into Q
        Sort the Q according to the absolute value of equation 1
        Apply Survival operator to Q
End For
Output: Q of length Q_len
```

Traditionally, EP algorithms use *Tournament Selection* [1] during the survival stage. However, it was decided that the entire population would be the solution for our EP method. That is, each individual chromosome would represent a single correlation (a triple) while the population would represent the list of correlations found (*Population Size=Q_{len}*). Hence, the survival operator consisted of keeping the best Q_{len} individuals. This therefore required a check for any duplicates after mutation, and for any invalid chromosomes. Although the entire population would represent the solution, it must be noted that the fitness of each individual would still be independent of the rest of the population. Each individual would try to maximise the correlation coefficient that it represents. This in turn would maximise the population's fitness by improving the list of correlations represented by the population.

Within the EP, a gene is either x_i ,x_j, or the *lag*. We have used the idea of *Self-Adapting Parameters* [2] in this context. Here each gene, *gene$_i$*, in each chromosome is given a parameter, σ_i. Mutation is defined as follows:

$$gene_i = gene_i + N(0,\sigma_i) \qquad (2)$$

$$\sigma_i = \sigma_i \cdot e^{(s+s_i)} \qquad (3)$$

$$s = N\left(0, \frac{1}{\sqrt{2len}}\right) \qquad (4)$$

$$s_i = N\left(0, \frac{1}{\sqrt{2\sqrt{len}}}\right) \qquad (5)$$

Note that s is constant for each gene in each chromosome but different between chromosomes, and s_i is different for all genes in all chromosomes. Both parameters are generated each time mutation occurs. Each chromosome consisted of three parameters and their corresponding σ_i values. The value of *len* is the size of each chromosome, i.e. three. Each gene within a chromosome is mutated according to the Normal distribution with mean zero and standard deviation equal to the gene's corresponding standard deviation, σ_i, in equation 2. Each σ_i is then mutated according to equation 3. Essentially equation 2 is a Normally distributed offset.

2.2 Stage 2 - The Grouping Algorithm

The second stage consists of grouping the MTS variables based on the triples discovered using the EP and some metric. This partition metric, which we define below, is used to group variables together which have strong mutual dependency and to separate them into different groups where the dependency is low.

Let n be the number of variables, G be the list of groups and $m = |G|$ (the number of groups). Let g_i be the ith member of the list G where $1 \leq i \leq m$ and let $k_i = |g_i|$. The notation g_{ij} refers to the jth element of the ith list of G. G is restricted such that

$$\bigcup_{i=1}^{m} g_i = \{x_1..x_n\} \text{ and } g_u \cap g_v = \phi, \forall u \neq v \text{ where } k_i \geq 1. \text{ Therefore } \sum_{i=1}^{m} k_i = n.$$ It

is clear that in all cases $m \leq n$. The *partition metric* for any fixed list G, $f(G)$, is defined as follows, where $corr(x_i, x_j)$ returns true if there exists in Q any triple of the form (x_i, x_j, lag) or (x_j, x_i, lag) for any valid lag.

$$f(G) = \sum_{i=1}^{m} h(g_i) \qquad (6)$$

$$h(g_i) = \begin{cases} \displaystyle\sum_{\substack{\forall a,b \\ a \neq b \\ 1 \leq a < b \leq k_i}} L(g_{ia}, g_{ib}) & \text{if } k_i > 1 \qquad (7) \\ 0 & \text{otherwise} \end{cases}$$

$$L(g_{ia}, g_{ib}) = \begin{cases} 1 & \text{if } corr(g_{ia}, g_{ib}) \qquad (8) \\ -1 & \text{otherwise} \end{cases}$$

The metric has the following characteristics (proofs for these can be found in [20]):

i) If there are no correlations, the maximum value is obtained when all variables are in separate groups.
ii) If a correlation exists for each pairing of variables (the search space), then the maximum fitness is obtained when all of the variables are in one group.
iii) If the data generating the correlations came from a mixed set of MTS observations, then the metric will be maximised when the variables within the same group have as many correlations within the list Q as possible and variables within differing groups contain as few correlations as possible.

We have previously looked at various methods for maximising the metric outlined above in the context of grouping MTS [20]. This analysis has shown that the best search method for this sort of problem is the Grouping Genetic Algorithm (GGA) introduced by Falkenaeur [4]. We apply this algorithm, described below, to the different MTS variables and score the candidate groupings against the triple list using the Partition metric. The general outline for a genetic algorithm, first introduced by Holland, is defined below where the fitness is calculated using equation 6. There then follows a description of the representation and the operators used in the GGA.

```
Input: Q and the parameters from Table 2
Generate Population random chromosomes and calculate their fitness
For i = 1 to Generations do
    For j = 1 to CrossoverRate x Population do
            Set Parent1 and Parent2 to two different  random¹ chromosomes
            Crossover Parent1 and Parent2 to generate Child1 and Child2
            Apply Mutation Operator to Child1 and Child2
            Insert Child1 and Child2 into the population
            Sort the population according to Fitness
            Retain Population fittest chromosomes
    End For
End For
Output:  G (a list of groups, constructed from the fittest individual
         from the final population)
```

For the GGA, the representation of a chromosome consists of two parts. In the first part, each gene represents a variable in the domain. The value of the gene determines which group the variable is a member of. In the second part, each gene represents the actual groups without any information about their contents. Hence, the chromosome is of variable length since the number of groups can vary. For example, 8 variables to be placed into the following 3 groups:

Group 0: 0 3 4   Group 1: 1 2 6   Group 2: 5 7

This would be represented by the following chromosome: 01100212:012. It is the second part of the chromosome (after the colon) that crossover is applied to. Crossover works as follows:

i)   Select two random crossing sites, delimiting the crossing sites in each of the two parents, denoted as:
[Parent start position, Parent end position].

ii)   Inject the contents of the crossing section of the first parent at the first crossing site of the second parent.

iii)   Remove any elements that are repeated from the groups that were members of the first parent.

iv)   Remove any empty groups and reinsert any unassigned variables to existing groups.

v)   Repeat (i) to (iv) to produce the second child by reversing the roles of the first and second parent.

Example for first child: Parent 1: 0 1 1 0 0 2 1 2 : 0 1 2
                           Parent 2: 4 5 3 4 5 6 3 6 : 3 4 5 6

i)   The crossing sites for Parent 1 = [0,1] and for Parent 2 = [1,3]

ii)   Inject group 0 into position 1:   0 ? ? 0 0 ? ? ? : 3 0 4 5 6

iii)   Remove group 4 and 5 due to repeats: 0 ? 3 0 0 6 3 6 : 3 0 6

iv)   Reinsert variable 1 into random group (6):   0 6 3 0 0 6 3 6 : 3 0 6

A '?' denotes an unallocated variable (adapted from [4]).

---

¹ Fitter chromosomes are chosen with higher probability.

Mutation involves randomly mutating genes within the chromosome according to the *Mutation Rate*. Each gene has Mutation Rate probability of being mutated to a value from a uniform distribution $U(0,n-1)$. This mutation is only applied to the first part of the chromosome and the second part, after the colon, is updated accordingly. Falkenauer proves [4] that this method allows the schema theory to hold even for grouping problems. In contrast, other proposed representations appear to collapse when applied to grouping problems.

3. The Experiments

In this section we apply our proposed methodology to two real-world datasets. We briefly describe the application and associated datasets in section 3.1. In section 3.2 we describe the procedure for applying our methodology to these datasets.

3.1 The Applications

Oil Refinery Process Data - Many complex chemical processes record MTS data every minute. This data is characterised by a large number of interdependent variables (in the order of hundreds per process unit). There can be large time delays between causes and effects (over 120 minutes in some chemical processes) and some variables may have no substantial impact on any others. Correlations can change within the system depending on how the process is being controlled. The dataset used in this paper is from a Fluid Catalytic Cracker (FCC) [15] and contains a subset of 50 variables from a total of approximately 300. Learning models such as Dynamic Bayesian Networks [3,6] for this dataset would be very time consuming due to the search spaces involved, especially as the time lags can be very large. Therefore, we wish to group the MTS variables into distinct lower-dimensional MTS to enable separate models to be learnt for the data in as close to real time as possible. See Table 1 for the FCC dataset's characteristics.

Visual Field Data - The second dataset is a section of normal tension glaucoma visual field (VF) data. Glaucoma [9] is the name given to a family of eye conditions. The common trait of these conditions is a functional abnormality in the retina, leading to loss of visual field. This vision loss is usually only part of the visual field, but untreated glaucoma can lead to blindness. Once diagnosed, a patient undergoes frequent outpatient appointments where their visual field is tested. The forecasting of a patient's visual field is important in order to diagnose, monitor and control the progression of glaucoma. Correlation between points at different time lags can play a useful role in the monitoring of the disease's progression since many mathematical methods for time series forecasting need the correlations between variables to complete the models. Again, it is important that correlations are grouped in as short a time as possible to enable the models to be

built and diagnostic decisions made during a patient's regular consultation. The VF
dataset consists of 82 patients' right eyes measured approximately every six months
for between five (a time series length of ten) and 22 years (a time series length of
44). The particular test used for this dataset results in 76 points being measured,
which correspond to 76 variable time series. See Table 1 for details.

Dataset	Variables	Length	Max Lag
FCC	50	3000	75
VF	76	18.2 (mean)	5

Table 1. Characteristics of the Datasets

From table 1, one can see that both datasets are high dimensional, however the
length of each MTS is very different. It is worth noting that there is just one MTS
for the FCC data but 82 MTS for the VF data, corresponding to the 82 patients.

3.2 Application of Methodology to the Datasets

For each dataset we have applied the proposed algorithm using the following
parameters (detailed in section 2):

Dataset	Population	Generations	Crossover Rate	Mutation Rate	Search Space	MaxCalls	Q_{len}
FCC	150	150	0.8	0.1	184975	56250	500
VF	150	150	1.0	0.1	31350	8664	1000

Table 2. Method Parameters

Within table 2, the first four GA parameters have been described in section 2.2. As
described in section 2.1, Q_{len} is the number of correlations being searched for (the
length of Q), *Search Space* is how many possible correlations exist within the
dataset and *MaxCalls* is the maximum number of correlation calls permitted (a
fraction of *Search Space*). These parameters were chosen to optimise the
performance of the algorithm for each dataset.

For the oil refinery dataset, the algorithm was applied and the resultant groupings
were investigated in respect to feedback from control engineers who have a good
knowledge of the process in question. This involved looking at individual groups
and the raw data plots of variables within them as well as looking for known
relationships that were expected in the process.

For the visual field dataset, the algorithm was applied to each patient's time series
and the resulting groupings for each patient are analysed. The groups are compared
between patients, using a pre-defined metric. The intention is to ascertain if there
are any similarities between groups based upon a similar level of severity of the
condition.

4. Results

Oil Refinery Data. The results of the grouping algorithm are displayed in table 3. This illustrates the nine groups and the variables associated with each one. The fitness of the individual that represented these groupings was 488.

Group	Variable ID - Variable Name	Group	Variable ID - Variable Name
A	2 ABSORB REFLUX TRAY-1	H	28 GAS FLOW TO ABSORB
B	17 ABSORB TAIL-GAS H2 CHROM	H	30 F8 I/STAGE DRUM LEVEL
B	27 M/FRACT TOP REFLUX	H	33 ABSORB SPONGE OIL TRAY11
C	22 DE-PROP FEED	H	34 M/F TOP REFLUX PRESS CTRL
D	25 WASH WATER	H	35 DEBUT DIF PRESS TRAY1/19
E	32 J17-COMP SUCTN. PRESSURE	H	38 J17-COMP SPEED
F	40 ABSRB STRIPPER BOTTOM	H	41 C11/3 INLET
G	4 ABSORB TAIL-GAS	H	42 J17 SUCTN.
G	24 C3/C4 EX CDU3	H	43 J17 I/STAGE
G	36 AUTO/MAN STN TO GAS MAIN	H	44 J17 DISCH
G	37 AUTO/MAN STN TO GIRBOTOL	I	7 ABSORB PRESSURE CONTROL
H	0 FRESH FEED A-PASS	I	11 ABSORB STRIPPER O/HDS
H	1 FRESH FEED B-PASS	I	13 ABSRB STRIP RBOIL OUTLET
H	3 DEBUT FEED EX ABSORB	I	14 E4 OVERHEADS - C3
H	5 ABSORB REFLUX TO TRAY-13	I	15 ABSORB TAIL-GAS PCT C3
H	6 ABSORB STRIPR WATER LVL	I	16 ABSORB T/GAS METH CHROM
H	8 REACTOR INLET A	I	19 ABSORB. H2 METHANE RATIO
H	9 REACTOR INLET B	I	29 ABSORB BASE LEVEL
H	10 SPONGE OIL	I	31 ABS/STRP TRAY-10
H	12 ABSRB LEAN-OIL TO TRAY11	I	39 ABSORB STRIPPER TRAY-6
H	18 DEBUT O/HDS PCT C2	I	45 M/FRACT TOP REFLUX D/OFF
H	20 DEBUT OVERHEADS - C2	I	46 M/FRACT TOP TO C06
H	21 F8 H/CARBON TO ABSORB	I	47 ABSORB STRIPPER FEED
H	23 PROPENE PRODUCT EX J102	I	48 ABSORB STRIPPER TRAY-36
H	26 REFRIDGE A201 TOTAL FEED	I	49 ABSRB STRIP RBOIL OUTLET

Table 3. The Discovered Groupings from the Oil Refinery MTS

The discovered groupings compared very favourably to the information elicited from the control engineers. Only 5 of the 50 variables were singled out as independent of the others. This was expected as there are a lot of strong relationships amongst most of the dataset's variables. Whilst one of these, variable ID 22, was expected to be included in group H (and a raw data plot supports this hypothesis), the remaining variables upon inspection appear to be extremely noisy. This is the most likely reason for them being excluded from any groups. A small number of variables were found to be grouped in unexpected groups. For example, variable with variable ID 4, was placed in a small group (Group G) separated from any tray temperatures which was unexpected. However, upon inspection of the raw data plots for this group, the variables were all very highly correlated together.

The most interesting result concerns the two main groups, H and I, which contained a large number of strongly correlated variables, mostly temperatures and flow rates within the main fractionator column. The two groups appear to separate out variables with certain characteristics. For example, group I seems associated more with variables towards the top of the fractionator column such as the higher tray temperatures and the top product quality. Group H, in contrast, is more associated with the lower trays and the bottom product flow and quality. What is more, those variables which are not located in either of these areas of the fractionator but are associated with one or the other, appear in the group where they hold most influence. For example, within this section of data, the variables with variable ID 0 and variable ID 1 (the flow rates of the main feed to the FCC) have a strong effect on the bottom product flow (variable ID 3) and these are included with the associated group (H).

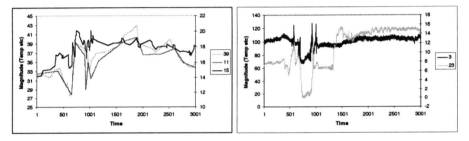

Figure 1. Sample Variable Plots from Group I and from Group H

There are of course some exceptions to the lower trays / upper trays split such as variable ID 48, which is a low tray temperature yet is found in group I. However, in general these two groups have fairly consistently separated these two systems. Figure 1 highlights the different shaped plots and characteristic features of some variables from two sample groups, I and H. Looking at the two graphs in figure 1, it can be seen that the variables plotted within each group appear to follow the same general trends.

4.2 Visual Field Data

The visual field data results are very different from those produced by the FCC dataset. Where the FCC data produces one grouping arrangement, there are 82 patients, thus 82 sets of groupings. It would make no sense to try and average these groupings, as the results are expected to be different between some patients. As a whole, the fitness of the groups generated by the method ranged from 66 to 216, with an average of 84. The low fitness can be explained by there being, on average, approximately 30% of the points ungrouped (i.e. univariate). A higher fitness has a direct correlation with average group size: where the fitness is low there are many small groups, and at the other extreme, there are one or more large groups (20 or more variables per group). The large groups that have been found cover whole portions of the eye, namely, the variables are located together in a cluster.

On examination of these large groups, one finds that they consist of points suffering from extreme visual loss, e.g. corresponding to tunnel vision. Figure 2 shows an example of a group that was found for patient number 11, containing four variables where *point sensitivity*, i.e. how well a patient can see at a specific location in the visual field, is measured over time. The four variables seem to be following the same general trends, hence one may conclude that they are highly correlated. The variables have a high variation, which is an indication that a section of the eye has severe glaucomatous damage. Other groups that were inspected visually have been found to contain variables that followed the same trends.

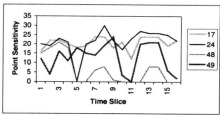

Figure 2. A Four Variable Group for Patient 11

One of the aims of this work was to see if the patients can be classified on their groupings, i.e. are there any collection of groups for patients at the same stage of the condition. In order to get an initial view on this, a similarity metric is needed to compare two groups. This is defined as follows:

```
Input: Two groups, G₁ and G₂
Remove all of the univariate groups from G₁ and G₂
Let n be the number of unique variables remaining in both groups
Let EVM = 0
For i = 1 to n - 1
    For j = i + 1 to n
        Let g₁ be the group within G₁ containing i
        Let g₂ be the group within G₂ containing j
        If j in g₁ and i in g₂ then EVM = EVM + 1
        If j not in g₁ and i not in g₂ then EVM = EVM + 1
    Next j
Next i
Divide EVM by 0.5 × n(n - 1)
Output: EVM
```

The last update in this algorithm ensures that this metric is between zero and one inclusive. This metric removes all of the univariate groups before determining the similarity; this is because we are only interested in related variables. The metric works by generating all pairs of variables. It then gives credit where, for both groupings, each pair is assigned to the same group or each pair is assigned to different groups. The patients are then reordered according to average sensitivity, this being a rough measure of how far the condition has progressed for a patient. The new patient 1 corresponds to the lowest average sensitivity and the new patient 82 the highest. Figure 3 shows the results of the metric applied to all patient pairings.

There are ten scales, white to black. White corresponds to the highest metric results and black to the lowest. The remaining eight grey scales correspond to metric scores somewhere in between, i.e. lighter means a higher metric score. The white diagonal is where a patient's grouping is compared with itself, the two sides of this line are effectively the same, i.e. patient a and b are compared above the line, whilst below it is patient b with a.

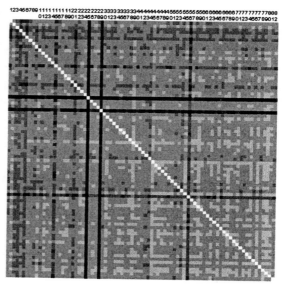

Figure 3. Comparison of Patient Groupings using the Metric

The graph in figure 3 goes from light in the bottom right hand corner to a darker shade in the top left hand corner. This indicates that those patients with high sensitivity have similar groups; these groups tend to be smaller in size (on inspection). Those with lower sensitivity tend not to have any similar groupings to any other patient; their groups tend to be quite large.

This can be explained by those with good sensitivity and hence good vision being more consistent during the visual field tests, which would result in similar grouping between those points that are related. With the low sensitivity (and low vision) patients, the results of the visual field test tend to be more variable. This is due to each field point corresponding to a large section of the retina, hence any glaucoma damage may only affect part of a point. The visual field test does not consistently test the exact same spot, but somewhere in the same vicinity, i.e. the visual field test light source does not fill the test point exactly, and hence may be testing different collections of cells on each test.

Additionally, the deterioration does not follow exactly the same path for each patient: two patients may have the condition with the same severity but have totally differing parts of the eye affected, and hence different groupings.

In short, the visual field data generates groups that make good sense: the groups are low in size and similar for patients with good vision, and large in size and varied for those with low vision.

5. Concluding Remarks

The problem of decomposing a high-dimensional MTS into a number of low-dimensional MTS is a challenging one. The number of possible dependencies between the variables is very large because one variable can affect another after a certain time lag. In this paper we have proposed a MTS variable grouping methodology based on cross-correlation search and evolutionary computation. This method has been applied to two real-world data sets with encouraging results.

For the FCC data the grouping algorithm allows us to model the system as approximately three independent sub-systems (groups G, H and I in table 3). What is more, these groupings have been generated very quickly allowing the algorithm to be used as a pre-processing stage for a model-building algorithm, developed previously for explaining new data [19].

For the VF data, the groups make an ideal starting point for modelling the visual field deterioration through statistical models such as the Vector Auto-Regressive (VAR) process [11] as has been previously investigated in [17]. This model has a large number of parameters, which is proportional to the square of the number of variables being modelled. Decomposing the visual field data into several smaller and highly related subsets of variables will make this model easier to deal with, which will form a significant part of the further work arising from this paper.

An area of particular interest which we are pursuing in further work is the identification of relationships in genomic data. Currently, we are in the process of applying our methodology to the grouping of gene expression data with the aim of building models from subsets of closely related genes.

Acknowledgements

The authors wish to thank the project sponsors: the Engineering and Physical Sciences Research Council, UK; Moorfields Eye Hospital, UK; Honeywell Technology Centre, USA; and Honeywell Hi-Spec Solutions, UK. We would also like to thank BP-Amoco, UK for supplying the oil refinery dataset.

184

References

[1] T. Bäck, G. Rudolph, H.-P. Schwefel, "Evolutionary Programming and Evolution Strategies: Similarities and Differences", editor: D. B. Fogel, W. Atmar, Proceedings of the Second Annual Conference on Evolutionary Programming, 11-22, 1993.

[2] T. Bäck, "Evolutionary Algorithms: Theory and Practice", Oxford Uni. Press, 1996.

[3] P. Dagum, A. Galper, E. Horvitz, A. Seiver, "Uncertain Reasoning and Forecasting", International Journal of Forecasting 11, pp 73-87, 1995.

[4] E. Falkenauer, "Genetic Algorithms and Grouping Problems", Wiley, 1998.

[5] D. B. Fogel, "Evolutionary Computation - Toward a New Philosophy of Machine Intelligence", IEEE Press, 1995.

[6] N. Friedman, K. Murphy, S. Russell, "Learning the Structure of Dynamic Probabilistic Networks", Proceedings of the 14th Conference on Uncertainty in AI, pp 139-147, 1998.

[7] M. Garey, D. Johnson, "Computers and Intractability - A Guide to the Theory of NP-Completeness", W.H. Freeman, San Francisco, 1979.

[8] C. Goutte, P. Tofte, E. Rostrup, F. Å. Nielsen, L. K. Hansen, "On Clustering fMRI Time Series", NeuroImage 9, pp. 298-310, 1999.

[9] M. J. Haley (editor), "The Field Analyzer Primer", Allergan Humphrey, 1987.

[10] J. H. Holland, "Adaptation in Natural and Artificial Systems", University of Michigan Press, 1995.

[11] H. Lutkepohl, "Introduction to Multiple Time Series Analysis", Springer-Verlag, 1993.

[12] S. Mandava, M. Zulauf, T. Zeyen, J. Caprioli, "An Evaluation of Clusters in the Glaucomatous Visual Field", American Journal of Ophthalmology 116, pp. 684-691, 1993.

[13] T. Oates, P. R. Cohen, "Searching for Structure in Multiple Streams of Data", Proceedings of the 10th International Conference in Machine Learning, 1996.

[14] D. Pena, G. Box, "Identifying a Simplifying Structure in Time Series", Journal of American Statistical Association 82, pp 836-843, 1987.

[15] R. Sadeghbeigi, "Fluid Catalytic Cracking Handbook", Gulf Publishing, 1995.

[16] G. Snedecor, W. Cochran, "Statistical Methods", Iowa State University Press, 1967.

[17] S. Swift, X. Liu, "Modelling and Forecasting of Glaucomatous Visual Fields Using Genetic Algorithms", Proceedings of the Genetic and Evolutionary Computation Conference, Morgan Kaufmann, pp. 1731-1737, 1999

[18] S. Swift, A. Tucker, X. Liu, "Evolutionary Computation to Search for Strongly Correlated Variables in High-Dimensional Time-Series", Proceedings of Intelligent Data Analysis 99, LNCS 1642, Springer-Verlag, pp 51-62, 1999.

[19] A.Tucker, X. Liu, "Extending Evolutionary Programming to the Learning of Dynamic Bayesian Networks", Proceedings of the Genetic and Evolutionary Computation Conference, Morgan Kaufmann, pp. 923-929, 1999.

[20] A. Tucker, S. Swift, X. Liu, "Variable Groupings in Multivariate Time Series via Correlation", Technical Report BBKCS-9909, Department of Computer Science, Birkbeck College, University of London, 1999.

Genetic Algorithm Behaviour in the Task of Finding the Multi - Maximum Domain

A. Takahashi and A. Borisov

Technical University of Riga, 1 Kalkyu St., Riga LV-1658, Latvia

arita.takahashi@delfi.lv

aborisov@egle.cs.rtu.lv

Abstract: The present study examines the genetic algorithm behaviour. A hypothesis is suggested that the genetic algorithm can be used not only to find a single global optimum point but also to determine a whole parameter region. Parametric optimisation task is solved and the behaviour of several different real-number genetic algorithms is compared during the solution process. Real number genetic algorithm steps are described and their meaning is explained. Populations are compared graphically, after a definite number of generations (after the 1st, 8th, 16th, and the 100th generation). Differences in the algorithm behaviour and for causes of such differences are explained.

1.   Introduction

The behaviour of the classic genetic algorithm is determined by the nature or properties of its operators. Each operator of the genetic algorithm performs some particular function. Tasks, which the classic genetic algorithm is able to solve, are well known. Therefore it is worthwhile to analyse the behaviour of the genetic algorithm in solving harder and less investigated tasks.

One of the issues to be investigated may be the following: How will the genetic algorithm behave in finding maxima of the function depicted in Fig. 1?

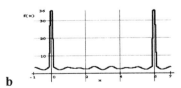

a   b

Figure 1 Function for which the genetic algorithm behaviour will be analysed in searching for maxima: a - three dimensional pattern; b - section in X-Y plane

This is the function of two parameters and there are four global maxima of the value 36 in the parameter value region under consideration. The function has multiple local maxima and is described by equations:

$$f(x_1, x_2) = \left(2 + f_1(x_1, x_2)\right) \cdot \left(5 + 4 \cdot \Phi\left(f_1(x_1, x_2) - 2 + 0.1\right)\right) \quad , \text{ where}$$

$$\Phi(x) = \begin{cases} -1 & \forall x < 0 \\ 0 & x = 0 \\ 1 & \forall x > 0 \end{cases}$$

$$f_1(x_1, x_2) = \cos(x_1 \cdot \frac{\pi}{3}) \cdot \cos(2 \cdot \pi \cdot x_1) + \cos(x_2 \cdot \frac{\pi}{3}) \cdot \cos(2 \cdot \pi \cdot x_2)$$

For simplicity, the global maximum of this function was considered to be found as soon as its value in the region of parameters exceeded 35.

2. Analysis of Behaviour of the Classic Genetic Algorithm

To start space searching based on the genetic algorithm, one should first generate an initial population. Let us assume, that it is generated in the form of random numbers. It means, that the following cases are possible:

1. The initial population does not contain any global maximum points.
2. The initial population contains a single global maximum point.
3. The initial population contains several global maximum points.
4. The initial population contains several points belonging to one maximum.
5. Situation (4) appears in the initial population with several global maxima.

Cases (1) and (2) are often met in experiments with the population of the size 200. If the initial population does not contain global maximum point, then, the 2nd, 3rd or 5th generations are most likely to contain it. After the maximum point has been found the further behaviour of the classic genetic algorithm can be the following:

1. Points will "disappear" in the next generation (besides, for different values of the function this is unlikely).
2. The next generation will have multiple descendants of these points.
3. This point will be inherited by the next generation only in one sample.

In the experiments the points of global maxima will be designated as A, B, C, and D. Afterwards, by preserving generation states, it was possible to examine, how many times each global maximum appears in each generation. The frequency of global maximum appearance is illustrated by Fig. 2. In diagrams letters A, B, C and D are replaced, correspondingly, by designations "1", "2", "3" and "4".

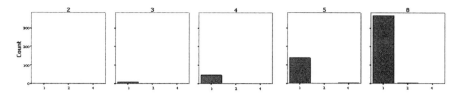

Figure 2 The number of maximum height points in generations

From Fig.2 it follows, that none of generations contain the maximum "3". Points belonging to the maximum "2" appear in the substantial number in the 3rd generation. In the 4th generation their number increases. Note, that the number of points belonging to the maximum "1" has been multiplied in the 5th generation. Moreover, in the 5th generation a point belonging to the maximum "4" appears, however it is lost later. We can also see, that in the 8th generation a point belonging to the maximum "2" was found, however it will very likely be lost in further generations.

It can be seen from Fig.2, that due to the preservation by the algorithm of one important piece of information and its inheritance, the other information of the same importance is lost. The reason, why there cannot be balance between Y maxima, is explained by principles of performance of the classic genetic algorithm operators. This phenomenon can be called assimilation, as a result of which one set of features in the population is passed over with large numerical overbalance from previous generations and others disappear in spite of being equally successful or even more successful.

Now let's examine Fig. 3 illustrating the condition of points preserved by the algorithm in the function maxima in generations.

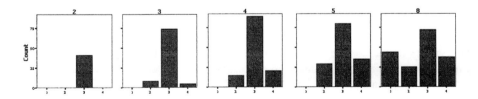

Figure 3 The number of maximum height points in generations pertinent to the modified genetic algorithm (terrene-dependent search)

In the process of the search for maximum the modified genetic algorithm at first finds the global maximum "3" and the information of parameters corresponding to this maximum is then passed over to further generations. Parameter sets corresponding to the maxima "2" and "4" are found later. Information of these sets is reproduced through descendants. In the 4th generation this takes place at account of non-optimum points. The contrary pattern is seen in the 5th generation - the number of points belonging to the maximum "3" has decreased to assist to fix inherited information of the maxima "2" and "4". It seems, that also at this stage operation of the algorithm can not be considered as completed, since the 8th generation itself contains descendants belonging to maximum "1". Having considered operation of such algorithm, it is difficult to define a condition corresponding to completion of the process of search since the algorithm does not know, if the maximum "5" not found previously is hidden elsewhere. May be, it is worth to consider as completion of the process of search by the algorithm an event, when after m generations no global maximum has been found. Hence, the algorithm can assume, that no more global maxima exist in the parameter space.

3. Hypothesis of function parameters optimisation for multiple solution case

Let us analyse the finding of a set of maximum value points of the function depicted in Figure 4. The function is of a volcanic shape and its equation is as follows:

$$f(x_1, x_2) = -10 + F_B + \left(-10 + F_B\right) \cdot \left(-1 + 0.9 \cdot \Phi(-10 + F_B)\right) + 11 \quad , \text{ where}$$

$$F_B = 7.9 \cdot \sqrt{x_1^2 + x_2^2} \qquad \Phi(x) = \begin{cases} -1 & \forall x < 0 \\ 0 & x = 0 \\ 1 & \forall x > 0 \end{cases}$$

The domain of the function parameter changes is:

$$-2 \leq x_1 \leq 2$$
$$-2 \leq x_2 \leq 2$$

The values of the function increase in accordance with the conical equation but around point (0; 0) they suddenly start decreasing. If the classic genetic algorithm had to solve this task, it would fizzle out in all cases.

The task of the genetic algorithm is to find a set of the most suitable parameter values, i.e. a circumference (circle line) around which the values of the function are maximal. Note that the classic genetic algorithm is able to find a circle, the circumference of which contains the optimal points, it, however, is unable to escape from the points in the middle of the circle. In later generations, at some circumference border the points start disappearing due to the assimilation. The disappearance of the points increases in the direction of the function's centre until the population is concentrated around a single circumference point (see also experimental results in [2]).

Figure 4 The volcanic shape function

The classic genetic algorithm is capable of finding only one global maximum point out of a whole set of points belonging to the circumference (see Figure 5). From this it follows that the classic genetic algorithm is unable to converge simultaneously in various parameter space directions. It can only converge in the direction in which the population elements reach the numerical dominance. Moreover, sometimes the concentration happens in a point lower than global maximum.

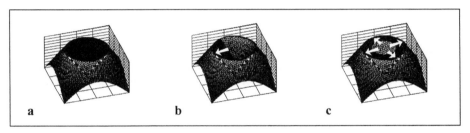

a   b   c

Figure 5 The behaviour of the classic genetic algorithm: (a) ability to find the points belonging to the circle, (b) non-ability of simultaneous multidirectional searching. To find a set of optimal points, the algorithm's behaviour shown in case c is necessary

Let us build up the following hypothesis: by modifying the genetic algorithm so that its behaviour varies, one can achieve that searching takes place in several parameter space directions simultaneously (see Figure 5, case c). The hypothesis will be tested experimentally by analysing the behaviour of the modified genetic algorithm.

4. Genetic algorithm operators on real numbers

As shown by Wright [1] in his study, binary-coded string operators may be transformed to similar operators that handle real numbers.

The following operators were formulated:

1. Crossover. For phenotypes $X = (x_1, x_2, x_3, ... x_n)$ and $X' = (x'_1, x'_2, x'_3, ... x'_n)$ a descendant is the phenotype whose parameters in the real numbers domain are located in the region limited by planes parallel to thee co-ordinates axis drawn through points X and X'. The descendant is located within a parallelepiped and various combinations of co-ordinates form the apexes of the parallelepiped. As described in [2], the first co-ordinate of the descendant is a random number lying between x_1 and x'_1, the second co-ordinate is a random number between x_2 and x'_2 and so on.

2. Crossover with inversion. For phenotypes $X=(x_1, x_2, x_3, \ldots x_n)$ and $X'=(x'_1, x'_2, x'_3, \ldots x'_n)$ an inverted descendant is the phenotype, whose parameters in the area of real numbers are located outside the area limited by those planes.

3. Mating operator. Phenotypes' rank numbers are ordered so that the best phenotype is with the rank number 1, the next (as good or worse) having the rank number 2, etc. The crossover is performed in a deterministic way not randomly. The first phenotype according to the rank is crossed with the second. The third is crossed with the forth. The mating operator sets the same order number to both phenotypes assigning a couple number. If the identical successful phenotypes get in one couple then for one of them one parameter is changed in a random way. It protects population from premature shrinking, due to which a large part of the region could be left unexplored.

4. Selection operator. This operator selects the further population out of parents' and children's group. Each phenotype has been selected for fitness a proportional number of times (as the rotating wheel stops against the appropriate phenotypes more frequently). The selection operator performs elimination of the unsuccessful sets of function parameters and accumulation of the successful sets of function parameters.

5.   Localised search

The idea of a localised parameter space search in the multi-criteria optimisation may be illustrated by the following example. The functional dependence of two criteria on two parameters is shown in Fig. 6. In between the break lines of the two surfaces, there is a Pareto set to be found by the genetic algorithm.

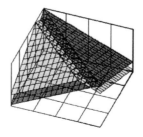

Figure 6 Simultaneous maximisation of two criteria

Let's have the genetic algorithm search strategy modified by imposing restrictions as to which phenotypes may be selected for the emergence of an offspring. The analysis of marriage models in the human environment will show a variety of restrictions. For instance, in geographical terms, there will be a biological restriction imposed by a human race: there are individuals who are unable to get accustomed to very cold weather conditions because their body is adapted to life in a hot climate, and vice versa. In their turn, restrictions for mutual contacts and understanding may be imposed by the mother tongue or nationality. Assume that a population consists of two races, with either race comprising two nations. If there are n phenotypes in the population, then each race will include $int(n/2)$ phenotypes. The remainder will be assigned to the latest race. If a race consists of m phenotypes, then each nation will include $int(m/2)$ phenotypes. The remainder will be assigned to the latest nation in each race.

The example shown in Fig. 6 relates to the two-parameter x_1, x_2 space (see Fig. 7). Parameter x_1 varies from x_{1min} to x_{1max}, while parameter x_2 varies from x_{2min} to x_{2max}. First, phenotypes are ordered in the ascending sequence of the parameter x_1 values; the first $n/2$ phenotypes which are the nearest to x_{1min} will be assigned to the first race, and the remaining ones will be ascribed to the second race. Then, phenotypes are ordered in the ascending sequence of the parameter x_2 values; the first $m/2$ phenotypes of the first race will be assigned to the first nation, and the remaining ones will be ascribed to the second nation. Thus, each phenotype will be assigned the *race* and *nation* ordinal numbers. Essentially, this algorithm may be repeated indefinitely. The principal idea here is that phenotypes may be crossed over only within the limits of one *nation* and one *race*. The *nation* layout can be seen in Fig.7. The third restriction for marriage is presented by the so-called *estate*, meaning that a person belonging to a specific estate marries a person of the same estate. Therefore, all phenotypes of a nation are arranged in the descending sequence of criterion values Y. Value Y is one of the several criterion values. It will be identical to the first criterion's functional value $f_1(x_1,x_2)$ when a random number generated specifically for Y definition is $n_{rand}<0.5$, and it will be identical to the second criterion's functional value $f_2(x_1,x_2)$ when the random number is $n_{rand}\geq0.5$. The random Y determination may be used in case of more than two criteria optimisation. It looks as if a play with the random number yields one fuzzy criterion whose real value cannot be defined.

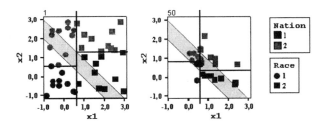

Figure 7 Sample population subdivision for a local search: the 1st generation and the 50th generation.

For better experimental convergence, value Y is substituted for $Y-Y_0$, where Y_0 is the population's minimum value Y, or "relative zero". Once the phenotypes are ordered by Y values, they are coupled - the first best phenotype with the second best one, the third with the fourth, and so on. The two parents will by all means have k (say, 2) children. After that, the parents together with the children take part in the competitive activity for survival.

6. Algorithm with localised search (race/nation)

Steps 3 through 10 describe the multilayer genetic algorithm, whereas steps 1 through 10 describe the race/nation algorithm.

First, an initial population comprising n phenotypes is randomly generated. Then, the following steps are performed as a cycle:

1) The entire population is arranged in a parameter x_1 ascending sequence, each phenotype being assigned its *NrOfRace* race number, so that

$$1 \le NrOfRace \le RaceCount$$

Phenotypes with smaller x_1 values are assigned lower *NrOfRace* values. Phenotype count will be *n/RaceCount*.

2) Each race's phenotypes are arranged in a parameter x_2 ascending sequence similar to the x_1 sequence. Each phenotype is assigned a *NrOfNation* nation number:

$$1 \le NrOfNation \le NationCount$$

3) In the race cycle and nation cycle, phenotypes are arranged in the Y value descending sequence.

Each phenotype is assigned a *CoupleNr* couple number: 1 to the first two phenotypes, 2 to the second two phenotypes, and so on. The highest *CoupleNr* couple number will correspond to the nation phenotype count divided by 2.

4) In the race cycle and the nation cycle, for each phenotype couple with identical *CoupleNr* make ordinary crossover. If one phenotype's parameter values are $x1_{mother}$ and $x2_{mother}$, and if the second phenotype's parameter values are $x1_{father}$ and $x2_{father}$, and if $x1_{mother} < x1_{father}$, and if $x2_{mother} < x2_{father}$, then the crossover will result in children having parameter values $Child1=(x1_{child1}, x2_{child1})$ and $Child2=(x1_{child2}, x2_{child2})$. For *Child1*:

$$x1_{mother} \le x1_{child1} \le x1_{father}$$

$$x2_{mother} \le x2_{child1} \le x1_{father}$$

The obligatory children count for a couple may be specified as a natural number. In the experiment, the children count used was two.

5) If $x1_{mother} = x1_{father}$ and $x2_{mother} = x2_{father}$, then two "foster-children" will be generated for this couple. For *Child1*, there will be the following parameter values:

$$x1_{min} \leq x1_{child1} \leq x1_{max}$$

$$x2_{min} \leq x2_{child1} \leq x2_{max}$$

A random number n_{rand} is generated. If $n_{rand} < 0.5$, a new $x1_{mother}$ value is generated:

$$x1_{min} \leq x1_{mother} \leq x1_{max}$$

If $n_{rand} \geq 0.5$, a new $x2_{mother}$ value will be generated.

6) Compute value Y for all *mother*, *father*, *child1* and *child2* phenotypes. In case of one criterion (function of two parameters) optimisation:

$$Y = f(x1, x2)$$

In case of multi-criteria optimisation (two criteria – two functions f_1 and f_2) - a random number n_{rand} is generated. If $n_{rand} < 0.5$ and if *CoupleNr* is the couple number, then

$$Y = f_1(x1, x2)$$

If $n_{rand} < 0.5$ and if *CoupleNr* is an odd number, then

$$Y = f_2(x1, x2)$$

If $n_{rand} \geq 0.5$, then $Y = f_2(x_1, x_2)$ in case where *CoupleNr* is an even number; otherwise $Y = f_1(x_1, x_2)$.

7) Find minimum value Y_0 of Y.

8) Compute value $Y_{relative}$ for all *mother*, *father*, *child1* and *child2* phenotypes:

$$Y_{relative} = Y - Y_0$$

9) Compute the value $Y_{relative}$ sum for the population. Then, compute probabilities and cumulative probabilities.

10) Generate the random number cyclically n count times to define the phenotype selection for the next generation.

7. Terrene-Dependent Algorithm

Since the experiments with the above mentioned algorithms have revealed inconsistency of population individuals, it was also required to check the effect of different additional modifications. The idea of the terrene-dependent algorithm has appeared, since values of parameters x_1 and x_2 depend on geographic longitude and latitude. The function to be maximised, in its turn, represents nature products consumed by individuals for their life. Hence, territories where the density of population is high are not so favourable for the reproduction of new individuals due to the restricted access to natural sources in comparison with the territories characterised by low density of population. This means, that each individual belonging to a population has to take into consideration the area of land he is allowed to occupy. As the numerical equivalent of this value there has been assumed the sum of all distance difference squares. For an individual described by parameters x_{self1} and x_{self2} it will look as follows:

$$Terrene_{self} = \sum_{j=1}^{pop\_size} \left((x_{self1} - x_{j1})^2 + (x_{self2} - x_{j2})^2 \right) \qquad (7.1)$$

This value will be applied to perform one additional selection of each genetic operator execution cycle. Respectively, the operator of the terrene-dependent algorithm consists of two sub-selection operators. The first sub-selection operates as in the above described algorithm, yet the number of selected individuals is not n, but $2n$. Afterwards, the second sub-selection is applied to the population obtained, however in this case the calculation of the value of the function Y is replaced by the calculation of the value of "Terrene". The second sub-selection is performed only n times selecting n individuals for the next population

The shortcoming of this newly developed algorithm is that it has no parameter able to regulate the intensity of the second sub-selection influence on searching. In case of solving different optimisation tasks the influence of the second sub-selection was too strong. This is seen in Fig. 8 depicting the population consisting of 200 individuals. There are the 1st and the 50th generations fixed with a simultaneous maximisation of the functions presented in Fig. 6. The sub-selection maximising the distance between individuals is too powerful and therefore the location of population is inadequate to the location of parameters of the best value.

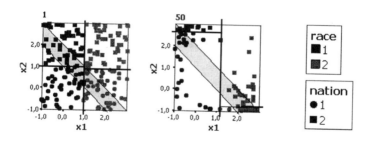

Figure 8 Sample population subdivision for a terrene-dependent search: the 1st generation and the 50th generation

8. Extinction-Dependent Algorithm

This algorithm is similar to the previous one with the difference, that individuals in the second sub-selection are selected not for life, but for extinction. Extinction takes place due too high density of individuals. The rate of extinction can be determined by the equation:

$$k_{EXTINCTION} = \frac{Decedent\_count}{Alive\_count} \qquad (8.1)$$

Two values for experiments have been specified: the rate of extinction (the numerical value 0.25) and *Alive_count=Pop_size* (the population size *Pop-size* of the numerical value 200).The first sub-selection has been performed *Pop_size* + *Pop_size*k* times (correspondingly, 250 times). The intermediate population calculated in this way was larger by the number of individuals needed to keep the reserve for extinction. The density of population for each individual described by parameters x_{self1} and x_{self2} was calculated by formula

$$Density_{self} = \frac{\left(Pop\_size \cdot (1+k)\right)^2}{Terrene_{self}}$$ (8.2)

where the value of *Terrene_{self}* was calculated by Equation 7.1. Further selection was performed by applying the method of roulette *k*Pop_size* times and marking (for deleting) each selected individual. In case the marked element was selected, selection was repeated. After all cancellations the number of population elements remained equal to the given *Pop_size*. Fig. 9 illustrates the states fixed by this algorithm for the 1st, 50th and the 100th generation.

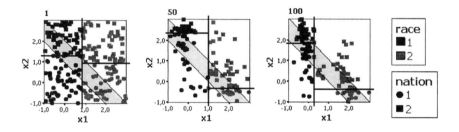

Figure 9 Sample population subdivision for a extinction-dependent search: 1st, 50th and 100th generations

9. Experimental Results

Searching for the maximum of the volcanic shape function (see Section 3) was performed by five different algorithms:

1. The classic genetic algorithm.
2. The multilayer genetic algorithm.
3. The race/nation algorithm.
4. The terrene-dependent algorithm.
5. The extinction-dependent algorithm.

In all the experiments the size of population was 200. The number of children of each pair of parents was 2, the probability of crossing was assumed to be 1, yet the probability of inverse crossing was assumed to be 0. The behaviour of the algorithm was investigated in the course of 100 generations. The extinction rate for the fifth algorithm was assumed to be 0.25. In the race/nation algorithm, the number of races was equal to 5 but the number of nations was assumed to be 3 like in the terrene-dependent and the extinction dependent algorithm. The results have been obtained by fixing data for the 1st, 8th, 16th, 24th 50th and 100th generation for each experiment. After that population states were analysed graphically. The data for the 1st, 8th, 16th and 100th generation are depicted in this paper.

The classical genetic algorithm always searches for one particular maximum point, whereas the other algorithms search for a set of maximum points. This specific result has been achieved during the time interval between the 50th and 100th generation (see Fig. 10).

The multilayer algorithm finds a set of solution with poorly defined boundaries, optimisation is weak since the difference between the initial population and later populations is weakly expressed. The process of convergence comes through the first 16 generations. Moreover, it then becomes asymmetrical and is not smoothed over all parameter domains (see Fig. 11).

The race/nation algorithm is smoother since the restriction of crossing prevents the assimilation of the population in any direction of the domain. Convergence is achieved to approximately 16th generation (see Fig. 12.).

The terrene-dependent algorithm is the poorest with regard to the achievement of the end of the task since the second sub-selection being proportional to the size of the territory of each point multiplies boundary points which are poorly valuable (see Fig.13). In addition, this algorithm has a very time-consuming processing cycle in the program.

Similarly, the extinction-dependent algorithm is time consuming. However, the processes of assimilation are not specific to it as compared to other algorithms and therefore it finds the maximum point set with the highest precision. The process of convergence completes already on the 16th generation. Due to the features characteristic of this algorithm it preserves the acquired information also for further generations (see Fig. 14).

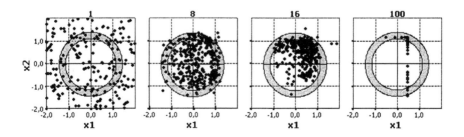

Figure 10 Classic genetic algorithm

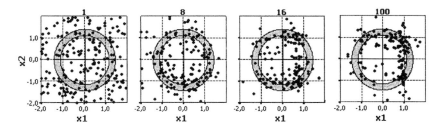

Figure 11 The multilayer genetic algorithm

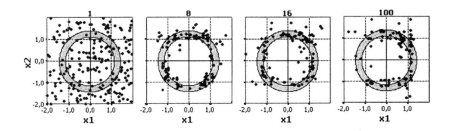

Figure 12 Race/nation genetic algorithm

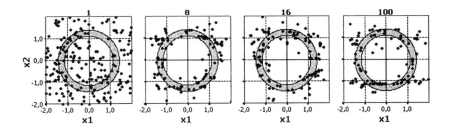

Figure 13 Terrene dependent genetic algorithm

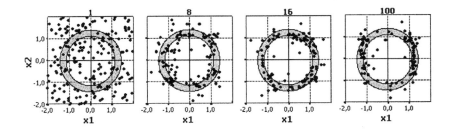

Figure 14 Extinction-dependent genetic algorithm

10. Conclusion

The experiments performed have demonstrated that the multilayer algorithm, as well as the terrene-dependent algorithm does not achieve the goal specified. In contrast, the race/nation algorithm and the extinction-dependent algorithm solve the problem completely. Thus, the suggested hypothesis that the modified genetic algorithm can perform searching in the space, moving in several domain directions simultaneously, has been confirmed.

More experiments need to be performed analysing the differences in the optimisation of specific functions. The improvement of the fitness calculation [3] strategy in the multi-criteria optimisation task may change behaviour of algorithms considerably.

References

[1]   Wright, A. H. (1991). Genetic Algorithms for Real Parameter Optimization. In *Foundations of GA*, Gregory J.E. Rowlins, ed., Morgan Kaufmann Publishers, 205-218.

[2]   Takahashi, A. (2000). Using Genetic Algorithms to Search for Maximum of the Multimodal Function. In Proceedings of the 6th International Conference on Soft Computing MENDEL 2000, Brno University of Technology, Brno, Czech Republic, 159-164.

[3]   Takahashi, A. (2000). Genetic Algorithm Behaviour in the Multi-criteria Optimisation Task. In Proceedings of the Fourth International Conference on Knowledge-Based Intelligent Engineering Systems & Allied Technologies KES'2000, University of Brighton, Sussex, U.K, 514-520.

A Modified Perceptron Algorithm for Computer-Assisted Diagnosis*

A. ALBRECHT

Dept. of Computer Science, Univ. of Hertfordshire,
Hatfield, Herts AL10 9AB, UK

M. LOOMES

Dept. of Computer Science, Univ. of Hertfordshire,
Hatfield, Herts AL10 9AB, UK

K. STEINHÖFEL

GMD–National Research Center for Information Technology,
Kekuléstr. 7, 12489 Berlin, Germany

M. TAUPITZ

Faculty of Medicine, Inst. of Radiology, Humboldt University of Berlin,
Schumannstraße 20/21, 10117 Berlin, Germany

Abstract

We present a new stochastic learning algorithm and first results of computational experiments on fragments of liver CT images. The algorithm is basically an extension of the Perceptron algorithm by a special type of simulated annealing. The fragments of CT images are of size 119×119 with 8 bit grey levels. From 220 positive (focal liver tumours) and 220 negative examples a number of hypotheses of the type $w_1 \cdot x_1 + \cdots + w_n \cdot x_n \geq \vartheta$ were calculated for $n = 14161$ and then tested with a voting function on various sets of 50 additional positive and negative examples, respectively. The input to the algorithm is derived from the DICOM standard representation of CT images. The simulated annealing procedure employs a logarithmic cooling schedule $c(k) = \Gamma / \ln (k + 2)$, where Γ is a parameter that depends on the underlying configuration space. In our experiments, the parameter Γ is chosen according to estimations of the maximum escape depth from local minima of the associated energy landscape.

Key words:
Perceptron Algorithm, Simulated Annealing, Logarithmic Cooling Schedule, Threshold Functions, CT Images, Focal Liver Tumour.

---

*Research partially supported by the AIF Research Programme under Grant No. FKV 0352401N7 and by BerCom GmbH, Berlin.

1   Introduction

Since the seminal paper [5] by ASADA ET AL., there has been a rapidly growing interest in new, unconventional types of medical knowledge-based systems which are designed as artificial neural networks, trained by examples ("positive" and "negative") related to a specific diagnostic problem. So far, the research has been concentrating on digital X-ray-based medical diagnosis [15, 17, 24, 35, 36, 37], although there are applications in different medical branches, for instance, in electrocardiographic measurement and clinical laboratories; see [14, 26].

The paper [32] introduces the assignment of fractal dimensions to tumour structures. The fractal dimensions are assigned to contours which have been extracted by commonly used filtering operations. In fact, these contours represent polygonal structures within a binary image. For example, the fractal dimensions $D_1 = 1.13$ and $D_2 = 1.40$ are assigned to the boundary and the interior, respectively, of a glioblastoma.

A high classification rate of nearly 98% is reported in [28], where the Wisconsin breast cancer diagnosis (WBCD) database of 683 cases is taken for learning and testing. The approach is based on feature extraction from image data and uses nine visually assessed characteristics for learning and testing. Among the characteristics are the uniformity of cell size, the uniformity of cell shape, and the clump thickness.

In the present paper, we utilise an extension of the Perceptron algorithm by a simulated annealing-based search strategy [13, 23] for the automated detection of focal liver tumours. The only input to the algorithm are the image data without any preprocessing. Since focal liver tumour detection is not part of screening procedures like the detection of microcalcifications [18, 21, 25, 28, 30], a certain effort is required to collect the image material. To our knowledge, results on neural network applications to focal liver tumour detection are not available in the literature. Therefore, we could not include comparisons to related, previous work in our paper.

During the last decade, research on the classical Perceptron algorithm has been revitalised by a number of papers, see, e.g., [6, 7, 10, 16, 19, 33]. The research on this type of classification algorithms has a long history and goes along with the efforts to find fast and reliable algorithms that solve systems of linear inequalities $l^j(\vec{z}) = \vec{a}^j \cdot \vec{z} + b^j \geq 0$, $j = 1, \ldots, m$. AGMON [2] proposed in 1954 a simple iteration procedure that starts with an arbitrary initial vector $\vec{z}_0$. When $\vec{z}_i$ does not represent a solution of the system, then $\vec{z}_{i+1}$ is taken as the orthogonal projection of the farthest hyperplane which corresponds to a violated linear inequality: $\vec{z}_{i+1} := \vec{z}_i + t \cdot \vec{a}^{j_0}$, where $t = -l^{j_0}(\vec{z}_i)/\mid \vec{a}^{j_0} \mid^2$ and $\vec{a}^{j_0}$ maximises $-l^j(\vec{z}_i)/\mid \vec{a}^j \mid^2$ among the violated $l^j(\vec{z}_i)$.

Basically the same method is known as the classical Perceptron algorithm [31]. If the set of points can be separated by a linear function, the following convergence property can be proved for the Perceptron algorithm [27]: Let S denote the set of positive and negative input vectors and $\vec{w}^*$ be a unit vector solution to the separation problem, i.e., $\vec{w}^* \cdot \vec{x} > 0$ for all $[\vec{x}, +] \in S$ and $\vec{w}^* \cdot \vec{x} < 0$

for all $[\vec{x}, -] \in S$. Then the Perceptron algorithm converges in at most $1/\sigma^2$ iterations, where $\sigma := \min_{[\vec{x}, \eta] \in S} |\vec{w}^* \cdot \vec{x}|$, $\eta \in \{+, -\}$. The parameter σ has the interpretation of $\cos(\vec{w}^*, \vec{x})$ for the angle between $\vec{w}^*$ and $\vec{x}$ and the value of σ can be exponentially small in terms of the dimension n.

But in general, the much simpler Perceptron algorithm performs well even if the sample set is not consistent with any weight vector $\vec{w}$ of linear threshold functions (see, e.g., [19, 33]). When the sample set is linearly separable, BAUM [6] has proved that under modest assumptions it is likely that the Perceptron algorithm will find a highly accurate approximation of a solution vector $\vec{w}^*$ in polynomial time.

Variants of the Perceptron algorithm on sample sets that are inconsistent with linear separation are presented in [7, 9, 10, 16]. For example, if the (average) inconsistency with linear separation is small relative to σ, then with high probability the Perceptron algorithm will achieve a good classification of samples in polynomial time [9, 10].

Our simulated annealing procedure employs a logarithmic cooling schedule $c(k) = \Gamma/\ln(k+2)$, i.e., the "temperature" decreases at each step. With the modified Perceptron algorithm, we performed computational experiments on fragments of liver CT images. The fragments are of size 119×119 with 8 bit grey levels. From 220 positive (with focal liver tumours) and 220 negative examples we calculated independently $X = 5, \ldots, 19$ hypotheses of the type $w_1 \cdot x_1 + \cdots + w_n \cdot x_n \geq \vartheta$ for $n = 14161$. Then, we performed tests on various sets of 50 positive and negative examples, respectively, that were not presented to the algorithm in the learning phase. When $> X/2$ hypotheses voted for a positive (negative) classification, the corresponding output was taken as the result.

The input to our algorithm was derived from the DICOM standard representation of CT images [22].

The choice of the crucial parameter Γ is based on estimations of the maximum escape depth from local minima of the associated energy landscape. The estimations of Γ were obtained by preliminary computational experiments on CT images. We used this method before in [34] where logarithmic simulated annealing was applied to job shop scheduling.

2 Basic Definitions

The simulated annealing-based extension comes into play when the number of misclassified examples for the new hypothesis is larger than that for the previous one. If this is the case, a random decision is made according to the rules of simulated annealing procedures. When the new hypothesis is rejected, a random choice is made among the misclassified examples for the calculation of the next hypothesis.

To describe our extension of the Perceptron algorithm in more detail, we have to define the configuration space together with a neighborhood relation (more information about simulated annealing generally and its application in diverse areas can be found in [1, 12, 29]).

The configuration space consists of all linear threshold functions with rational weights w_i represented by pairs of binary tuples each of length $d : w_i \in (\pm 1) \cdot \{0,1\}^d \times \{0,1\}^d$, $i = 1, ..., n$. We assume that the elements of the configuration space do have a fixed n^{th} coordinate, i.e., w_n represents the threshold. We denote the configuration space by

$$\mathcal{F} = \{ f(\vec{x}) : f(\vec{x}) = \sum_{i=1}^{n} w_i \cdot x_i, \ w_i \in (\pm 1) \cdot \{0,1\}^d \times \{0,1\}^d \}.$$

The neighborhood relation depends on the sample set S, where

$$S = \{ [\vec{x}, \eta] : \vec{x} = (x_1, ..., x_n), \ x_i = (p_i, q_i), \ p_i, q_i \in \{0,1\}^d,$$
$$x_n = 1, \ \text{and} \ \eta \in \{+, -\} \},$$

and, additionally, on the number of examples that are misclassified by the current configuration $f(\vec{x})$. This number corresponds to the set

$$S\Delta f(\vec{x}) := \{ [\vec{x}, \eta] : f(\vec{x}) < 0 \ \& \ \eta = + \ \text{or} \ f(\vec{x}) \geq 0 \ \& \ \eta = - \},$$

and the objective function is defined by

$$\mathcal{Z}(f) := |S\Delta f(\vec{x})|. \tag{1}$$

The set of potential neighbors $\mathcal{N}_f$ is derived from $S\Delta f(\vec{x})$ in accordance with the Perceptron algorithm:

$$\mathcal{N}_f := \{ f' \mid w_i' := w_i - \frac{\sum_{i=1}^{n} w_i \cdot x_i}{\sqrt{\sum_{i=1}^{n} w_i^2}} \cdot x_i, \ \vec{x} \in S\Delta f \} \cup \{f\}. \tag{2}$$

In our approach, we use a non-uniform generation probability which is derived from the Perceptron algorithm: When f is the current hypothesis, we set

$$U(\vec{x}) := \begin{cases} -f(\vec{x}), & \text{if } f(\vec{x}) < 0 \text{ and } \eta(\vec{x}) = +, \\ f(\vec{x}), & \text{if } f(\vec{x}) \geq 0 \text{ and } \eta(\vec{x}) = -, \\ 0, & \text{otherwise.} \end{cases} \tag{3}$$

The f' in (2) are related to the $\vec{x} \in S\Delta f$ and therefore it is justified to define

$$G[f, f'] := \frac{U(\vec{x})}{\sum_{\vec{x} \in S\Delta f} U(\vec{x})}. \tag{4}$$

Thus, preference is given to the neighbors that maximise the deviation.

The acceptance probabilities $A[f, f']$, $f' \in \mathcal{N}_f$ are derived from the underlying analogy to thermodynamic systems [1]:

$$A[f, f'] := \begin{cases} 1, & \text{if } \mathcal{Z}(f') - \mathcal{Z}(f) \leq 0, \\ e^{-(\mathcal{Z}(f') - \mathcal{Z}(f))/c}, & \text{otherwise,} \end{cases} \tag{5}$$

where c is a control parameter having the interpretation of a *temperature* in annealing procedures. The actual decision, whether or not f' should be accepted for $\mathcal{Z}(f') > \mathcal{Z}(f)$, is performed in the following way: f' is accepted, if

$$e^{-(\mathcal{Z}(f') - \mathcal{Z}(f))/c} \geq \rho, \tag{6}$$

where $\rho \in [0, 1]$ is a uniformly distributed random number. The value ρ is generated in each trial if $\mathcal{Z}(f') > \mathcal{Z}(f)$.

The probability of performing the transition between f and f' is given by

$$\mathbf{Pr}\{f \rightarrow f'\} = \begin{cases} G[f, f'] \cdot A[f, f'], & \text{if } f' \neq f, \\ 1 - \sum_{g \neq f} G[f, g] \cdot A[f, g], & \text{otherwise,} \end{cases} \tag{7}$$

where $G[f, f']$ denotes the generation probability and $A[f, f']$ is the probability of accepting f' once it has been generated by f.

Let $\mathbf{a}_f(k)$ denote the probability of being in the configuration f after k steps performed for the same value of c. The probability $\mathbf{a}_f(k)$ can be calculated in accordance with

$$\mathbf{a}_f(k) := \sum_h \mathbf{a}_h(k-1) \cdot \mathbf{Pr}\{h \rightarrow f\}. \tag{8}$$

The recursive application of (8) defines a Markov chain of probabilities $\mathbf{a}_f(k)$, where $f \in \mathcal{F}$ and $k = 1, 2, \ldots$. If the parameter $c = c(k)$ is a constant c, the chain is said to be a *homogeneous* Markov chain; otherwise, if $c(k)$ is lowered at any step, the sequence of probability vectors $\vec{a}(k)$ is an *inhomogeneous* Markov chain.

Finally, we have to define how the temperature $c = c(k)$ changes with increasing k. Unlike standard simulated annealing procedures, where a relatively large number of transitions is performed at a fixed temperature, we consider the case of inhomogeneous Markov chains, i.e., the temperature is lowered at each step. We have chosen a logarithmic cooling schedule as discussed in the next section.

3 The Logarithmic Cooling Schedule

We are focusing on a special type of inhomogeneous Markov chain where the value $c(k)$ changes in accordance with

$$c(k) = \frac{\Gamma}{\ln(k + 2)}, \quad k = 0, 1, \ldots, \tag{9}$$

The choice of $c(k)$ is motivated by HAJEK's Theorem [20] on logarithmic cooling schedules for inhomogeneous Markov chains. To explain Hajek's result, we first need to introduce some parameters characterizing local minima of the objective function:

Definition 1 *A configuration $f' \in \mathcal{F}$ is said to be reachable at height h from $f \in \mathcal{F}$, if $\exists f_0, f_1, \ldots, f_r \in \mathcal{F}(f_0 = f \wedge f_r = f')$ such that $G[f_u, f_{u+1}] > 0$, $u = 0, 1, \ldots, (r-1)$ and $\mathcal{Z}(f_u) \leq h$, for all $u = 0, 1, \ldots, r$.*

We use the notation $height(f \Rightarrow f') \leq h$ for this property. The function f is a *local minimum*, if $f \in \mathcal{F} \setminus \mathcal{F}_{\min}$ and $\mathcal{Z}(f') > \mathcal{Z}(f)$ for all $f' \in \mathcal{N}_f \setminus f$.

Definition 2 *Let $g_{\min}$ denote a local minimum, then $depth(g_{\min})$ denotes the smallest h such that there exists a $g' \in \mathcal{F}$, where $\mathcal{Z}(g') < \mathcal{Z}(g_{\min})$, which is reachable at height $\mathcal{Z}(g_{\min}) + h$.*

The following convergence property has been proved by B. HAJEK:

Theorem 1 [20] *Given a configuration space $\mathcal{F}$ and a cooling schedule defined by*

$$c(k) = \frac{\Gamma}{\ln(k+2)}, \ k = 0, 1, \ldots,$$

the asymptotic convergence $\sum_{f \in \mathcal{F}} \mathbf{a}_f(k) \xrightarrow[k \to \infty]{} 1$ of the stochastic algorithm, which is based on (5) and (7), is guaranteed if and only if

(i) $\forall g, g' \in \mathcal{F} \exists g_0, g_1, \ldots, g_r \in \mathcal{F}(g_0 = g \wedge g_r = g')$: $G[g_u, g_{u+1}] > 0$, $u = 0, 1, \ldots, (r-1)$;

(ii) $\forall h : height(f \Rightarrow f') \leq h \iff height(f' \Rightarrow f) \leq h$;

(iii) $\Gamma \geq \max\limits_{g_{\min}} depth(g_{\min})$.

Hence, the speed of convergence of the logarithmic cooling schedule (9) is mainly defined by the value of Γ. The condition *(i)* expresses the connectivity of the configuration space.

Unfortunately, we cannot apply HAJEK's convergence result to our simulated annealing procedure since we cannot guarantee that the conditions *(i)* and *(ii)* are valid for $\mathcal{N}_f$.

For a theoretical analysis, one can introduce a generalised neighborhood relation where *all* possible changes of weights are allowed:

$$f' \in \widehat{\mathcal{N}_f} \iff \exists i \left(w_i' := w_i \pm \frac{p}{q}, \ p, q \in \{0, 1\}^d \right). \tag{10}$$

We note that $\widehat{\mathcal{N}_f}$ covers the transitions performed by the Perceptron algorithm. To describe the convergence for $[\mathcal{F}, \widehat{\mathcal{N}_f}]$, we introduce the set of functions with minimum error on S:

$$\mathcal{F}_{\min} := \{ f : \forall f'(f' \in \mathcal{F} \to \mathcal{Z}(f) \leq \mathcal{Z}(f')) \}.$$

When S is generated by a linear threshold function, then the error is zero on $\mathcal{F}_{\min}$. Obviously, $\widehat{\mathcal{N}_f}$ satisfies *(i) and (ii)* and therefore Theorem 1 implies

Corollary 1 *The inhomogeneous Markov chain which is based on (3) till (9) and the neighborhood $\widehat{\mathcal{N}_f}$ tends to the probability distribution* $\displaystyle\lim_{k\to\infty} \sum_{f\in\mathcal{F}_{\min}} \mathbf{a}_f(k)$.

The convergence analysis from [4] indicates a time complexity of $n^{O(\Gamma)}$. To speed up the local search for optimum solutions, we employ the neighborhood $\mathcal{N}_f$ from (2) together with the non-uniform generation probability (4) where the transitions are forced into the direction of the maximum deviation. The approach is motivated by the computational experiments on equilibrium computations from [3]: For the implementation of simulated annealing-based heuristics a significant speed-up was obtained when transitions were performed into the direction of maximum local forces.

Our heuristic utilises the Perceptron algorithm in the generation probabilities and can be summarised in the following way:

1. The initial hypothesis is equal to zero: $w_i = 0$, $i = 1, 2, \dots n$.

2. For the current hypothesis, the probabilities $U(\vec{x})$ are calculated; see (3).

3. To determine the next hypothesis f_k, a random choice is made among the elements of $\mathcal{N}_{f_{k-1}}$ according to (3).

4. When $\mathcal{Z}(f_k) \leq \mathcal{Z}(f_{k-1})$, we proceed with the new hypothesis f_k.

5. In case of $\mathcal{Z}(f_k) > \mathcal{Z}(f_{k-1})$, a random number $\rho \in [0,1]$ is drawn uniformly.

6. If $e^{-(\mathcal{Z}(f_k)-\mathcal{Z}(f_{k-1})/c(k)} \geq \rho$, the function f_k is the new hypothesis. Otherwise, we return to 3 with f_{k-1}.

7. The computation is terminated after a predefined number of steps L.

Thus, instead of following unrestricted increases of the objective function, our heuristic tries to find another "initial" hypothesis when $\mathcal{Z}(f_k) - \mathcal{Z}(f_{k-1}))$ is too large.

4 Computational Experiments

In most applications, simulated annealing-based heuristics are designed for homogeneous Markov chains where the convergence to the Boltzmann distribution at fixed temperatures is important for the performance of the algorithm; see [1]. We utilised the general framework of inhomogeneous Markov chains described in [4] for the design of a pattern classification heuristic. In particular, we paid attention to the choice of the parameter Γ which is crucial to the quality of solutions as well as to the run-time of our heuristic.

The heuristic was implemented in C^{++} and we performed computational experiments on SUN Ultra 5/333 workstation with 128 MB RAM.

4.1 Evaluation on n-dimensional Vectors

We evaluated the heuristic by comparison to the classical Perceptron algorithm. For this purpose, we generated sample sets S from polynomials of the type

$$w_1 \cdot x_1^{a_1} + \cdots + w_{n-1} \cdot x_{n-1}^{a_{n-1}} \geq \vartheta.$$

The poynomials itself were generated by a random procedure. We used an upper bound Max_Coeff for the weights and the threshold: $|w_i|, \vartheta \leq$ Max_Coeff. A similar bound was used for the exponents: $0 < a_i \leq$ Max_Exp. In our experiments, the number of positive examples is the same as the number of negative examples.

n = 256	Max_Exp = 5 Max_Coeff = 100.0 $\Gamma = 17, ..., 48$							
L	15000				30000			
Number	LSA		Perceptron		LSA		Perceptron	
of	Error	Time	Error	Time	Error	Time	Error	Time
Samples	(%)	(Sec.)	(%)	(Sec.)	(%)	(Sec.)	(%)	(Sec.)
1024	11.4	512	12.2	511	11.2	1022	12.0	1020
2048	21.4	1153	22.6	1149	20.1	2301	23.2	2299
4096	23.6	2316	26.8	2313	21.8	4629	26.8	4624
8192	25.5	4689	29.2	4682	23.4	9375	28.7	9382

Table 1

The parameter Γ was estimated by test runs on several polynomials with fixed parameters, except for the number of examples. During the simulated annealing procedure, we calculated the maximum number of increases of the objective function before a decrease of $\mathcal{Z}(f)$ occurred. The maximum values were taken as Γ for the definition of $c(k)$ in (9).

In Table 1, we present typical outcomes of runs with an increasing number of examples and two values L for the number of changes of hypotheses. During a single run on the same data, the smallest error was stored for both the LSA and Perceptron algorithm. The error is about $\approx 5\%$ smaller for our LSA heuristic on sample sets of size $|S| \geq 4096$ when $L = 30000$.

4.2 Classification of CT Images

The results presented in Section 4.1 encouraged us to apply the LSA heuristic to liver tissue classification. Since focal liver tumour detection is not part of screening procedures like the detection of microcalcifications [18, 25, 28], a certain effort is required to collect the image material. We present first results of classifications on the limited number of examples that are currently available.

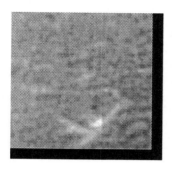

Figure 1: An example of normal liver tissue (negative example).

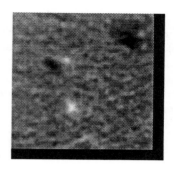

Figure 2: An example of tumour tissue (positive example).

The computational experiments were performed on fragments of liver CT images of size 119×119 with 8 bit grey levels. From 220 positive (with focal liver tumours) and 220 negative examples several independent hypotheses of the type $w_1 \cdot x_1 + \cdots + w_n \cdot x_n \geq \vartheta$ were calculated for $n = 14161$. We tested the hypotheses simultaneously on 50 positive and negative examples, respectively. The test examples were not presented to the algorithm during the training phase. A voting function on the output of the hypotheses defined the final classification.

$n = 14161$	$|POS| = |NEG| = 50/220$ $\quad \Gamma = 37 \quad |T\_POS| = |T\_NEG| = 50$				
Number X of Voting Functions	Changes of Weights	Total Run-Time (Min.)	Errors on		Total Errors
			T_POS	T_NEG	
5	65135	248	7	6	13%
11	198044	551	4	5	9%
19	335160	947	5	4	9%

Table 2

The input to the algorithm was derived from the DICOM standard representation of CT images [22]. In Figure 1 and Figure 2, examples of input instances are shown in the DICOM format. From these 128×128 images we calculated grey level representations of size 119×119 as inputs to our algorithm.

The results of our computational experiments on fragments of CT images are summarised in Table 2 and Table 3. The entries are values for $X = 5, 11, 19$ independent calculations of threshold functions. Each function was trained on a random sample of 50 + 50 (Table 2) and 75 + 75 (Table 3) examples out of 220 + 220 examples. This is indicated by the notations 50/220 and 75/220 in Table 2 and Table 3, respectively. The random samples are different for each hypothesis. All examples were learned with zero error after about 14000 to 19000 changes of the hypothesis for a single threshold function. The classification rate of $\approx 90\%$ seems to us promising for further studies on larger sample sets. As can be seen, the results do not change for random samples of size 50 and 75 when $X = 11, 19$. For larger random samples, e.g., of size 150, the classification rate even decreases because the random choice of samples becomes nearly the same for the independently calculated hypotheses.

$n = 14161$		$|POS|=|NEG|= 75/220$	$\Gamma = 48$	$|T\_POS|=|T\_NEG|= 50$	
Number X of Voting Functions	Changes of Weights	Total Run-Time (Min.)	Errors on T_POS T_NEG		Total Errors
5	156329	570	5	6	11%
11	399512	1212	4	6	10%
19	703836	1983	4	5	9%

Table 3

To our knowledge, results on neural network applications to focal liver tumour detection are not reported in the literature. Therefore, we cannot include a direct comparisons to related, previous work in our paper. In [25] the detection of microcalcifications by neural networks was studied. After training a total number of almost three thousand examples, a classification rate of $\approx$ 88% was achieved on about the same fraction of test examples as in our case of 220 + 220 learning examples and 50 + 50 test examples. In [28], a database of 683 cases is taken for learning and testing. The approach is based on feature extraction from image data and uses nine visually assessed characteristics for learning and testing. Consequently, the classification rate is much higher and lies between 97.1% and 97.8%. For our approach, we intend to include information about several slices at different depths of the same location of liver tissue. From this information we expect a significant improvement of the results presented in Table 2 when a large sample set is available.

5 Concluding Remarks

We performed computational experiments with an extension of the Perceptron algorithm by a simulated annealing-based heuristic that employs the logarithmic cooling schedule $c(k) = \Gamma/\ln(k + 2)$, where Γ is a parameter of the underlying configuration space. The experiments were performedon on fragments of liver CT images. The image data are the only input to the algorithm, i.e., no feature extraction or preprocessing is performed. The fragments are of size 119×119 with 8 bit grey levels. From 220 positive (with focal liver tumours) and 220 negative examples several hypotheses of the type $w_1 \cdot x_1 + \cdots + w_n \cdot x_n \geq \vartheta$ were calculated for $n = 14161$ and random samples of size $50 + 50$ and $75 + 75$ out of $220 + 220$ examples. The result was tested on $50 + 50$ additional test examples, where a voting function on the independent hypotheses defined the final outcome. For $5, ..., 19$ independent hypotheses we obtained a correct classification between 87% and 91%. Further research will be based on larger sample sets and we intend to include information about image slices at different depths of the same location of liver tissue.

6 Acknowledgement

The authors would like to thank Eike Hein and Daniela Melzer for preparing the image material.

References

[1] E.H.L. Aarts and J.H.M. Korst. *Simulated Annealing and Boltzmann Machines: A Stochastic Approach*, Wiley & Sons, New York, 1989.

[2] S. Agmon. The Relaxation Method for Linear Inequalities. *Canadian J. of Mathematics*, 6(3):382 – 392, 1954.

[3] A. Albrecht, S.K. Cheung, K.S. Leung, and C.K. Wong. Stochastic Simulations of Two-Dimensional Composite Packings. *J. of Comput. Physics*, 136(2):559 – 579, 1997.

[4] A. Albrecht and C.K. Wong. On Logarithmic Simulated Annealing. In: J. van Leeuwen, O. Watanabe, M. Hagiya, P.D. Mosses, T. Ito, editors, *Proc. IFIP International Conference on Theoretical Computer Science*, pp. 301 – 314, Lecture Notes in Computer Science (LNCS), vol. 1872, 2000.

[5] N. Asada, K. Doi, H. McMahon, S. Montner, M.L. Giger, C. Abe, Y.C. Wu. Neural Network Approach for Differential Diagnosis of Interstitial Lung Diseases: A Pilot Study. *Radiology*, 177:857 – 860, 1990.

[6] E.B. Baum. The Perceptron Algorithm is Fast for Nonmalicious Distributions. *Neural Computation*, 2(2):248 – 260, 1990.

[7] A. Blum, A. Frieze, R. Kannan, and S. Vempala. A Polynomial-Time Algorithm for Learning Noisy Linear Threshold Functions. *Algorithmica*, 22(1/2):35–52, 1998.

[8] A. Blum and R.L. Rivest. Training a 3-Node Neural Network is NP-Complete. *Neural Networks*, 5(1):117 – 127, 1992.

[9] T. Bylander. Learning Linear Threshold Functions in the Presence of Classification Noise. *Proc. 7th ACM Workshop on Comput. Learning Theory*, pp. 340 – 347, 1994.

[10] T. Bylander. Learning Linear Threshold Approximations Using Perceptrons. *Neural Computation*, 7:370-379, 1995.

[11] O. Catoni. Rough Large Deviation Estimates for Simulated Annealing: Applications to Exponential Schedules. *Annals of Probability*, 20(3):1109 – 1146, 1992.

[12] O. Catoni. Metropolis, Simulated Annealing, and Iterated Energy Transformation Algorithms: Theory and Experiments. *J. of Complexity*, 12(4):595 – 623, 1996.

[13] V. Černy. A Thermodynamical Approach to the Travelling Salesman Problem: An Efficient Simulation Algorithm. Preprint, Inst. of Physics and Biophysics, Comenius Univ., Bratislava, 1982 (see also: *J. Optim. Theory Appl.*, 45:41 – 51, 1985).

[14] W.K. Chan, K.S. Leung, and W.S. Wong. An Expert System for the Detection of Cervical Cancer Cells Using Knowledge-Based Image Analyser. *Artificial Intelligence in Medicine*, 8:67 – 90, 1996.

[15] L.P. Clarke. Computer Assisted-Diagnosis: Advanced Adaptive Filters, Wavelets and Neural Networks for Image Compression, Enhancement and Detection. In: *Proc. Meeting of the Radiological Society of North America*, p. 225, 1994.

[16] E. Cohen. Learning Noisy Perceptrons by a Perceptron in Polynomial Time. In: *Proc. 38th IEEE Symp. on Foundations of Computer Science*, pp. 514 – 523, 1997.

[17] K. Doi, M.L. Giger, R.M. Nishikawa, H. McMahon, R.A. Schmidt. Artificial Intelligence and Neural Networks in Radiology: Application to Computer-Aided Diagnostic Schemes. In: *Digital Imaging*, eds. W. Hendee and J.H. Trueblood, pp. 301 – 322, 1993.

[18] D.B. Fogel, E.C. Wasson III, E.M. Boughton and V.W. Porto. Evolving Artificial Neural Networks for Screening Features from Mammograms. *Artificial Intelligence in Medicine*, 14(3):317, 1998.

[19] S.I. Gallant. Perceptron-Based Learning Algorithms. *IEEE Trans. on Neural Networks*, 1(2):179 – 191, 1990.

[20] B. Hajek. Cooling Schedules for Optimal Annealing. *Mathem. of Operations Research*, 13:311 – 329, 1988.

[21] H. Handels, Th. Roß, J. Kreusch, H.H. Wolff and S.J. Pöppl. Feature Selection for Optimized Skin tumour Recognition Using Genetic Algorithms. *Artificial Intelligence in Medicine*, 16(3):283 – 297, 1999.

[22] R. Hindel. *Implementation of the DICOM 3.0 Standard*. RSNA Handbook, 1994.

[23] S. Kirkpatrick, C.D. Gelatt, Jr., and M.P. Vecchi. Optimization by Simulated Annealing. *Science*, 220:671 – 680, 1983.

[24] X. Li, S. Bhide, M.R. Kabuka. Labeling of MR Brain Images Using Boolean Neural Network. *IEEE Trans. on Medical Imaging*, 15(5):628 – 638, 1997.

[25] S.B. Lo, Y.C. Wu, M.T. Freedman, S.K. Mun, A. Hasegawa. Detection of Microcalcifications by Using Adaptive-sized Neural Networks. In: *Proc. Meeting of the Radiological Society of North America*, p. 171, 1994.

[26] L.J. Mango. Computer-Assisted Cervical Cancer Screening Using Neural Networks. *Cancer Letters*, 77:155 – 162, 1994.

[27] M.L. Minsky and S.A. Papert. *Perceptrons.* MIT Press, Cambridge, Mass., 1969.

[28] C.A. Pea-Reyes and M. Sipper. A Fuzzy-genetic Approach to Breast Cancer Diagnosis. *Artificial Intelligence in Medicine,* 17(2):131 – 155, 1999.

[29] F. Romeo and A. Sangiovanni-Vincentelli. A Theoretical Framework for Simulated Annealing. *Algorithmica,* 6(3):302 – 345, 1991.

[30] A.L. Ronco. Use of Artificial Neural Networks in Modeling Associations of Discriminant Factors: Towards an Intelligent Selective Breast Cancer Screening. *Artificial Intelligence in Medicine,* 16(3):299 – 309, 1999.

[31] F. Rosenblatt. *Principles of Neurodynamics.* Spartan Books, New York, 1962.

[32] C. Roßmanith, H. Handels, S.J. Pöppel, E. Rinast, and H.D. Weiss. Computer-Assisted Diagnosis of Brain Tumors Using Fractals, Texture and Morphological Image Analysis. In: H.U. Lemke, ed., *Proc. Computer-Assisted Radiology,* pp. 375 – 380, 1995.

[33] J. Shavlik, R.J. Mooney, and G. Towell. Symbolic and Neural Learning Programs: An Experimental Comparison. *Machine Learning,* 6(2):111 – 143, 1991.

[34] K. Steinhöfel, A. Albrecht, and C.K. Wong. On Various Cooling Schedules for Simulated Annealing Applied to the Job Shop Problem. In: M. Luby, J. Rolim, and M. Serna, eds., *Randomization and Approximation Techniques in Computer Science,* pp. 260 – 279, LNCS, vol. 1518, Springer-Verlag, Barcelona, 1998.

[35] R. Tawel, T. Dong, B. Zheng, W. Qian, and L.P. Clarke. Neuroprocessor Hardware Card for Real-time Microcalcification Detection at Digital Mammography. In: *Proc. Meeting of the Radiological Society of North America,* p. 172, 1994.

[36] Y.C. Wu, K. Doi, M.L. Giger. Detection of Lung Nodules in Digital Chest Radiographs Using Artificial Neural Networks: A Pilot Study. *J. Digital Imaging,* 8:88 – 94, 1995.

[37] Y. Zhu and H. Yan. Computerized tumour Boundary Detection Using a Hopfield Neural Network. *IEEE Trans. on Medical Imaging,* 16(1):55 – 67, 1997.

SESSION 4

KNOWLEDGE REPRESENTATION

Uniform Representation of Content and Structure for structured document retrieval

Mounia Lalmas

Department of Computer Science, Queen Mary College, University of London
London, United Kingdom

Abstract

Documents often display a hierarchical structure. For example, a SGML document contains a title, several sections, which themselves contain paragraphs. In this paper, we develop a formal model to represent in a uniform manner structured documents by their content and structure. As a result, querying structured documents can be done with respect to their content, their structure, or both. The model is based on a possible worlds approach, modal operators and uncertainty distributions.

1 Introduction

In traditional information retrieval (IR) systems, documents are retrieved as atomic units. However, documents often display a *hierarchical structure*; they are composed of hierarchically organised *components*. For example, a large corporate report will contain a title page, introductory material, several chapters, each composed of sections, themselves composed of subsections. From the user's point of view, presenting only some components of documents can make it easier to distinguish potentially relevant documents from irrelevant ones. It can also make it easier for a user to target which components of the document and what types of components may be most useful. Therefore, with *structured documents*, the retrievable units should be the document components as well as the whole document [1, 2, 3, 4, 5, 6]. Also the retrieval process should return various levels of composite parts, for example, a section when only that section is relevant, a group of sections, when all the sections in the group are relevant, or the document itself, when the entire document is relevant. Finally, querying should be with respect to content (seeking parts relevant to an information need), and to structure (selecting which types of structure to retrieve).

Many authors (e.g., [7, 4, 8]) argue that to allow for an effective retrieval of structured documents, the IR model must exploit not only the content of documents, but also the structural knowledge associated with the documents. Querying structured documents without considering the links between document components wastes user time since related components (e.g., a chapter and its section) will most probably be displayed at distant location in the retrieved result. A more effective display of retrieval results (e.g. [9, 7, 8]) is to return best entry points, which correspond to relevant document components from which users can browse to retrieve further relevant document components. Best entry points can be determined by defining the representation of a document component as the *aggregation* of the representations of its sub-components [10]. This also makes it possible to return various levels of composite parts.

In [11, 8], we developed a model for representing structured documents based on the Dempster-Shafer theory of evidence [12]. The model allows only content retrieval (e.g., relevant document components should be about "German white wine"), and not structure retrieval (e.g., relevant information should be contained in a title). In this paper, we present a **uniform model to represent structured documents that enables retrieval by content and structure**. In particular, we concentrate on the aggregation of representations yielding the representation of components based on that of their sub-components. The proposed representation enables to describe in a uniform manner the content, the structure, and both the content and structure of document components. As a result, the relevance of document components are comparable, thus better reflecting relative relevance of document components whether retrieval is by content, structure, or both.

The model is based on *evidential reasoning* [13], a theory based on a possible worlds approach, modal operators, and uncertainty distributions. Evidential reasoning is used because representing content and structure necessitates two indexing vocabularies for describing, respectively, the content and the structure of documents, which cannot be represented with a model based on Dempster-Shafer theory. However, evidential reasoning is a generalisation of the Dempster-Shafer theory of evidence, hence it possesses properties similar to those of the Dempster-Shafer theory, which were shown in [8, 11] compatible with those advanced by [10] regarding the representation and retrieval of structured documents.

The outline of the paper is as follows. In Section 2, we present the model to represent structured documents. In Sections 3 and 4, we apply the model to describe, respectively, the content and the structure of document components. In Section 5, we apply the model to describe both content and structure. In Section 6, we show how relevance of document components can be estimated using the obtained representation. We finish with conclusions and thoughts for future work.

2 The Model

In this work, the structure of a document corresponds to a tree whose nodes, referred to as *objects*, are the components of the document and whose edges represent the composition relationship (e.g., a chapter contains several sections). The *leaf* objects comprise the raw data (e.g., a title, a paragraph), and any non-leaf object is referred to as a *composite* object. We call $\mathcal{O}$ the set of objects. We describe the model for representing objects, where the representation can be about content or structure. The representation is modelled by an *object indexing model*. For space constraints, theorems and proofs are omitted.

2.1 Object indexing model

To represent an object o of $\mathcal{O}$, an indexing vocabulary is used, which elements are symbolised by propositions forming a *proposition space P*. For content representation, terms (after removal of stop words and stemming) extracted from the content of objects in the collection would constitute the proposition space. For structure representation of, for instance, XML documents, XML tags related to structure would compose the proposition space. An object can be described by a proposition, the combination of propositions, or by stating that it is not described by a proposition or a combination of them; all these form *sentences*.

Definition 2.1 *The sentences that can be used to describe an object o constitute a* sentence space S *defined as follows:* (1) $\top$ *and* $\bot$ *are sentences of S;* (2) *any proposition in P is a sentence of S; and* (3) *if ϕ and ψ are sentences of S, then so are $\phi \vee \psi$, $\phi \wedge \psi$, and $\neg\phi$.*

To express which sentences of S describe o, the sentence space is extended to a *modal sentence space S^I* with the introduction of a unary operator I referred to as a *modal operator*.

Definition 2.2 *The* modal sentence space S^I *is the set of sentences* Iϕ *for* $\phi \in S$.

For instance, the modal sentence I*is_section* where *is_section* is a sentence of the sentence space would be used to express that the object is a section.

We have syntactically defined sentences that can be used to describe an object o. The semantics is expressed with a possible worlds approach, assigning truth values to propositions and sentences with respect to possible worlds of a given set W.

Definition 2.3 $v : W \times P \to \{true, false\}$ *assigns truth values to propositions of P in W and $\pi : W \times S \to \{true, false\}$ defines the truth values of sentences in S using v and the rules of standard classical logic.*

We also have the classical *logical implication* $\Rightarrow$ and *logical equivalence* $\Leftrightarrow$.

Truth values are assigned to modal sentences with respect to worlds to express which sentences of S describe an object o. The assignment is modelled by the mapping π^I defined upon a given set $BASE \subseteq S$. This set contains sentences, referred to as *basic sentences*, for which there is *explicit evidence* (e.g., extracted by the indexing process applied to the object) that they describe the object. For instance, for content representation of a text object, $BASE$ would contain sentences (e.g., terms and their conjunction and disjunction, etc.) that were explicitly extracted from the analysis of the content of the text.

Definition 2.4 *Let $\pi^I : W \times S^I \to \{true, false\}$ such that for all $w \in W$ and $\phi \in S$*

$$\pi^I(w, I\phi) = \begin{cases} \pi(w, \phi) & \text{if } \phi \in BASE^*, \\ false & \text{in all other cases.} \end{cases}$$

where $BASE^*$ is the transitive closure of $BASE$ with respect to conjunction and logical implication.

All true modal sentences are sentences that describe the object o. For instance, if *fish* and *wine* are in $BASE$ for content representation, then the object is described by *fish*, *wine* and *fish* $\wedge$ *wine*, and any sentence implied by *fish*, *wine* and *fish* $\wedge$ *wine*. This is modelled by having (1) in the worlds in which *fish* is true, I*fish* true, (2) in the worlds in which *wine* is true, I*wine* true, and (3) in the worlds in which *fish* and *wine* are true, I(*fish* $\wedge$ *wine*), I*fish* and I*wine* true.

In IR, indexing elements are usually weighted to reflect their uncertainty or importance in describing an object [14, 15]. Uncertainty is modelled by way of a *mass function* (a distribution function) that assign weights (mass values) to *most specific sentences*.

Definition 2.5 *A sentence $\phi \in S$ is said to be the* most specific sentence *for a world $w \in W$ iff (1) $I\phi$ is true in w, (2) ϕ corresponds to the conjunction of the sentences in $BASE$ that are true in w, and (3) for every sentence $\psi \in S$, $I\psi$ is true in w iff $\phi \Rightarrow \psi$.*

(2) ensures that only sentences forming $BASE$ and their conjunction (i.e. sentences explicitly extracted by the indexing process, and their conjunction) are weighted. For instance, let *has_section* and *is_chapter* be in $BASE$ for structure representation. Weights are then assigned to *has_section*, *is_chapter* and

has_section ∧ *is_chapter* if these correspond to most specific sentences. The weights reflect the uncertainty of *has_section*, *is_chapter* and *has_section* ∧ *is_chapter* in describing the structure of the object.

Definition 2.6 *The uncertainty of the representation of an object o is modelled by a mass function* $m : S \to [0, 1]$ *such that:*

$$\sum_{\phi \in MSS} m(\phi) = 1$$

where $MSS \subseteq S$ *is the set of most specific sentences for the object o.*

m represents the uncertainty of the representation of the object. For $\phi \in S$, $m(\phi)$ is the exact (or explicit) belief that ϕ describes appropriately (the content or structure of) the object. The higher $m(\phi)$, the higher ϕ is considered a good description of the object o. If $m(\phi) = 0$, then there is no explicit evidence that ϕ describes the object. There may be implicit evidence that ϕ describes the object. This happens if there exists a sentence $\psi \in S$ such that $m(\psi) > 0$ and $\psi \Rightarrow \phi$. This can be captured by the belief function associated with the mass function (Section 6). For content representation, assume that $m(fish \wedge wine) > 0$. This means that there is explicit evidence that $fish \wedge wine$ describes the content of the object. There may be implicit evidence that $salmon \wedge sauvignon$ describes the content of the object if it can be proven that $fish \wedge wine \Rightarrow salmon \wedge sauvignon$.

How the mass values are obtained depends on the type of representation (e.g. content, structure) and how the representation is generated. This is discussed in later sections.

We have introduced all entities forming the representation of an object o. These entities constitute an *object indexing model* $OIM = \langle P, S, S^I, BASE, I, W, v, \pi, \pi^I, m \rangle$. If o is a leaf object, the object indexing model is constructed upon the indexing vocabulary symbolised by the proposition space P, and the set $BASE$ and the mass values for m (the latter two are outcomes of the indexing process applied to the raw data of the object). If o is a composite object, the object indexing model is constructed upon the *aggregation* of object indexing models symbolising the representations of its sub-component objects.

2.2 Aggregation of object indexing models

Objects representations are aggregated in two cases. In the first case, the representation of a composite object is defined as the aggregation of the representation of its component objects, as proposed in [10]. In the second case, the full representation (content and structure) of an object is defined as the aggregation of the content representation and the structure representation of that object. As a result, the proposed model provides a uniform approach to aggregate the various representations. In both cases, object indexing models are aggregated. The aggregation yields an *aggregated object indexing model*.

Let

$$OIM_A = \langle P_A, S_A, S_A^I, BASE_A, I_A, W_A, v_A, \pi_A, \pi_A^I, m_A \rangle$$

and

$$OIM_B = \langle P_B, S_B, S_B^I, BASE_B, I_B, W_B, v_B, \pi_B, \pi_B^I, m_B \rangle$$

be two object indexing models. The aggregation of the two indexing models, denoted $OIM_A \oplus OIM_B$, yields the aggregated object indexing model $OIM = \langle P, S, S^I, BASE, I, W, v, \pi, \pi^I, m \rangle$.

P, referred to as the aggregation of P_A and P_B, is defined as the union of P_A and P_B. The aggregation of S_A and S_B yielding S is defined as follows: if ϕ is a sentence of S_A or S_B, then it is a sentence of S, and clause (3) of Definition 2.1 defining well-formed sentences over S. Sentences forming the modal sentence space S^I are defined in Definition 2.2, the modal operator being I.

The set of possible worlds W for OIM is built from the *compatible* aggregation of worlds of W_A and W_B. To construct W, we need to know which sentences in S_A are "informationally related" to which sentences in S_B, and vice versa. By informationally related, we mean sentences that informationally imply others. This data can be extracted from thesauri, dictionaries, more sophisticated knowledge bases, or can be determined manually. We assume that the data is available and is expressed by the relation $inf : S \times S$. For example, in some applications, we would have $(boat, ship) \in inf$ for $boat$ and $ship$ sentences of S. We assume that, with respect to sentences in S_A informationally related to sentences in S_B and vice versa, inf satisfies logical implication and equivalence in W_A and W_B. W can be defined as follows.

Definition 2.7 *For any world $w^A \in W_A$ and $w^B \in W_B$, if for all $\phi^A \in S_A$ and $\phi^B \in S_B$, and vice versa, either (1) if $(\phi^A, \phi^B) \in inf$ and $\pi_A(w^A, \phi^A) = true$ then $\pi_B(w^B, \phi^B) = true$, or (2) $(\phi^A, \phi^B) \notin inf$, then a world $w \in W$ is created. The set of created worlds constitutes W. The relation between w^A and w^B, and the created world w is expressed by the function $\otimes : W_A \times W_B \to W$, where $\otimes(w^A, w^B) = w$.*

Following from the previous example, let w_A and w_B in which $boat$ and $ship$ are true, respectively. Let us assume that no other pairs of sentences (ϕ^A, ϕ^B) in inf are true in w^A and w^B, respectively. In this case, a world w would be created such that $\otimes(w^A, w^B) = w$.

The mappings assigning truth values to propositions of P and sentences of S in worlds of W are defined below. The truth values remain the same with respect to a world w^X in W_X and the world w in W that are related by the function $\otimes$ (for $X = A, B$).

Definition 2.8 *For* $w \in W$ *such that* $\otimes(w^A, w^B) = w$: *(1) for all propositions* $p \in P_X$, *for* $X = A, B$, $v(w,p) = v_X(w^X, p)$; *(2) for all sentences* $\phi \in S_X$, *for* $X = A, B$, $\pi(w, \phi) = \pi_X(w^X, \phi)$; *and (3) the truth values of all other sentences are given by clause (2) of Definition 2.3.*

Following from our previous example, both sentences *boat* and *ship* would be true in world w.

In the aggregation, sentences of S_A and S_B describing o_1 and o_2 may require *transformation* when describing o. For instance, suppose that the structure of o_1 is described by the sentence *is_section* (e.g., the object is a section). This sentence, when used to describe the structure of o, should be transformed to reflect that o is composed of o_1 which is a section. Therefore, the sentence *has_section* should be part of the description of the structure of o, and not the sentence *is_section*. The transformation of sentences is expressed by the functions $prop_X : S_X \to S$ for $X = A, B$, each *transforming* sentences of S_X into corresponding sentences of S. How $prop_X$ is defined depends on the type of representation. When no transformation is performed, $prop_X$ corresponds to the identity function.

The aggregated set of basic sentences $BASE$ can then be defined as

$$prop_A(BASE_A) \cup prop_B(BASE_B)$$

where $prop_X(BASE_X)$ for $X = A, B$ is the function $prop_X$ applied to all elements of $BASE_X$ (the image of $BASE_X$ by $prop_X$). The basic sentences for the aggregated object indexing model come from the union of the basic sentences of the object indexing models being aggregated, "modulo" the transformation. The aggregated mapping π^I is defined as follows.

Definition 2.9 *For all* $w \in W$ *such that* $\otimes(w^A, w^B) = w$ *and* $\phi \in S$

$$\pi^I(w, \mathrm{I}\phi) = \begin{cases} true & \text{if there exist } \psi^A \in S_A \text{ and } \psi^B \in S_B, \\ & \text{such that } \mathrm{I}_A\psi^A \text{ is true in } w^A \text{ and} \\ & \mathrm{I}_B\psi^B \text{ is true in } w^B \text{ and} \\ & prop_A(\psi^A) \land prop_B(\psi^B) \Rightarrow \psi; \\ false & \text{otherwise.} \end{cases}$$

The truth values of a modal sentence is based on the existence of two modal sentences in S_A^I and S_B^I which conjunction, modulo the transformation, logically implies the modal sentence. Suppose that $\psi^A = dog$ and $\psi^B = cat$ for the content representation (see Section 3), where $prop_A(dog) = prop_B(cat) = animal$. If in worlds w^A and w^B, $\mathrm{I}_A dog$ and $\mathrm{I}_B cat$ are true, respectively, and $\otimes(w^A, w^B) = w$ (the worlds w^A and w^B are compatible) then $\mathrm{I}animal$ is true in w. That is, the content of object o is described by *animal*, which encompasses the content descriptions of objects o_1 and o_2, which are respectively, *dog* and *cat*, and where o is composed of o_1 and o_2.

The next step is the aggregation of the uncertainty, that is the computation of m based on m_A and m_B. In this work, we assume that the representations of objects o_1 and o_2 are independent. Such a scenario will often if not mostly be the case for structured documents[1]. With the independence assumption, the mass function m is calculated upon m_A and m_B as follows.

Definition 2.10 *For all $\phi \in S$:*

$$m(\phi) = \frac{1}{\mathcal{K}} * \sum_{(\phi^A, \phi^B) \in \Gamma(\phi)} m_A(\phi^A) * m_B(\phi^B)$$

where

- $\mathcal{K} = \sum_{(\phi^A, \phi^B) \in S_A \times S_B} m_A(\phi^A) * m_B(\phi^B)$, *ensuring that m is a mass function.*

- *The function $\Gamma : S \to \wp(S_A \times S_B)$ maps every sentence ϕ in S to sentence pairs (ϕ^A, ϕ^B) with $\phi^A \in S_A$ and $\phi^B \in S_B$, such that $prop_A(\phi^A) \wedge prop_B(\phi^B) \Leftrightarrow \phi$ in W.*

Given a sentence $\phi \in S$, its weight $m(\phi)$ is computed upon the weights of pairs of sentences $\phi^A \in S_A$ and $\phi^B \in S_B$ such that $prop_A(\phi^A) \wedge prop_B(\phi^B)$ is logically equivalent to ϕ. Such pairs of sentences is given by the set $\Gamma(\phi)$. Sentence pairs (ϕ^A, ϕ^B) with high weights lead to a high weight of ϕ. Also, the more such sentence pairs, the higher the weight of ϕ. It can be showed that such sentences ϕ^A and ϕ^B are most specific sentences with respect to the object indexing models OIM_A and OIM_B. Also, for $m(\phi) > 0$, ϕ is the most specific sentence for the aggregated object indexing model.

For the above example, assume that $\Gamma(animal) = \{(dog, cat), (lion, tiger)\}$. In this case, $m(animal) = \frac{1}{\mathcal{K}}(m_A(dog) * m_B(cat) + m_A(lion) * m_B(tiger))$.

We use the aggregation to determine the object indexing model for representing a composite object. Let o be composed of l objects $o_1 \ldots o_l$. Let OIM be the object indexing model associated with o, and let OIM_i be the object indexing model associated with object o_i, for $i = 1, l$. We have $OIM = OIM_1 \oplus \ldots \oplus OIM_l$[2]. How aggregation is used to defined the full representation of an object is describe in Section 5.

---

[1]Evidential reasoning [13] allows for the dependent case to be taken into account.

[2]Note that the aggregation operator $\oplus$ is commutative and associative. See [11, 8] for a study of the properties of $\oplus$ with respect to the Dempster-Shafer theory of evidence.

3 Representing content

We apply the model to represent the content of objects. We discuss first the content representation of leaf objects, then the content representation of composite objects. Only what is specific to representing content is discussed.

3.1 Content representation of leaf objects

The content representation of an object o is modelled by an object indexing model $OIM_c = \langle P_c, S_c, S_c^I, BASE_c, I_c, W_c, v_c, \pi_c, \pi_c^I, m_c \rangle$. The elements of the indexing vocabulary, modelled by the proposition space P_c, can be keywords, phrases, sentences, concepts, etc. For example, the terms "wine" and "salmon" are symbolised by the propositions $wine \in P_c$ and $salmon \in P_c$, respectively. The sentence $wine \wedge salmon \in S_c$ can be used to express that an object is about both "wine and salmon".

The set $BASE_c$ is the set of sentences extracted by the indexing process applied to the raw data of the object. For instance, if the terms "white" and "wine" symbolised, respectively, by $white$ and $wine$ have been extracted from the indexing process, then $white$ and $wine$ are in $BASE_c$. If $wine$ and $salmon$ are in $BASE_c$, then the object is described by $wine$, $salmon$ and $wine \wedge salmon$. With more sophisticated algorithms, bags of terms or phrases may be extracted. For instance, $white \wedge wine$ would be in $BASE_c$ if the noun-phrase "white wine" was extracted by the indexing process.

The uncertainty is modelled by assigning weights to sentences of S_c to reflect how well they describe the object content. The mass function m_c can be constructed from the output of the indexing process applied to the raw data of o. This can be done using standard IR weighting mechanisms [16] based on frequency (the number of occurrences of a sentence in an object) and inverse component frequency (the number of components described by a sentence).

3.2 Content representation of composite object

Let o be composed of two objects o_1 and o_2. Let the object indexing models for o_1 and o_2 be, respectively, $OIM_{c_1} = \langle P_c, S_c, S_{c_1}^I, BASE_{c_1}, I_{c_1}, W_c, v_c, \pi_c, \pi_{c_1}^I, m_{c_1} \rangle$ and $OIM_{c_2} = \langle P_c, S_c, S_{c_2}^I, BASE_{c_2}, I_{c_2}, W_c, v_c, \pi_c, \pi_{c_2}^I, m_{c_2} \rangle$.

Some entities are common to the three objects, others are not. The former is because one common indexing vocabulary is used for all objects with respect to representing content; therefore, the proposition space and the sentence space are common to the three objects. Also the set of possible worlds, and the mappings associating truth values to propositions and sentences (but not modal sentences) can be defined to be common to all objects.

The "transformation" function that relates sentences describing the content of o_1 and o_2 to those describing the content of o could capture that more general sentences could be used to describe the content of o than those used for o_1 and o_2 (e.g., "animal" vs "cat", "dog" and "horse"). The only difference is that sentences are transformed to ones in the same sentence space. The transformation function can be constructed upon a thesaurus, a knowledge base, an ontology, or manually. The aggregation also requires the instantiation of the relation $inf : S_c \times S_c$, stating the sentences of S_c that are informationally related with each other. As for the transformation function, a thesaurus may be used for implementing the relation inf.

4 Representing structure

We apply the model to represent the structure of objects. The application is similar to that for the content representation, the main difference being that we are dealing with structure. We discuss the structure representation of leaf objects, then that of composite objects.

4.1 Structure representation of leaf objects

An object can be a paragraph, a section, a chapter, an article, etc. This is expressed by a function $struct : \mathcal{O} \to \mathcal{ST}$ where $\mathcal{ST}$ is a set of structures (for example, extracted from XML Data Type Definition related to structure). Let $o \in \mathcal{O}$ be a leaf object. Its structure representation is modelled by an object indexing model $OIM_s = \langle P_s, S_s, S_s^I, BASE_s, \mathbf{I}_s, W_s, v_s, \pi_s, \pi_s^I, m_s \rangle$.

Examples of propositions could include is_d, has_d and has^*_d, where d stands for $section, paragraph, title, chapter$, that is the elements of $\mathcal{ST}$. has_d symbolises that an object is directly composed of an object of type (discourse) structure d; has^*_d symbolises that an object is indirectly composed of an object of type structure d. For example, the sentence $is\_chapter \wedge has\_section \in S_c$ can be used to express that the object "is a chapter and has a section".

For a leaf object, the sentences forming $BASE_s$ come from the indexing process (e.g., an SGML parser) applied to the raw data of the object. For instance, if the SGML parser identifies that the object is a section, then the sentence $is\_section \in BASE_s$. Furthermore, $BASE_s$ contains one sentence $struct(o)$ because the raw data is contained in leaf objects only. The fact that an object is composed of two objects will be derived from the aggregation operation applied to the structure representations of the two objects (see next section). As a result, the only true modal sentence (except for tautologies) for a leaf object is $Istruct(o)$ (plus all sentences that are logically implied by $struct(o)$, if any). Furthermore, the most specific sentences forming the set MSS are $struct(o)$ and the true sentence $\top$ (in all worlds in which $struct(o)$ is false).

For a leaf object o, the mass function m_c is constructed from the output of the indexing process applied to the raw data of o. This can be done based on empirical studies reflecting the importance attached to each structure/discourse. For example, in a scientific paper, titles and abstracts may be considered more important than conclusions. This could be reflecting by assigning higher mass values to most specific sentences is_title and $is\_abstract$. It may also happen that the nature of the structure may not always be correctly identified (e.g., in PDF documents). In this case, the mass values may be based on empirical studies providing statistics on incorrect identifications, together with risk functions.

4.2 Structure representation of composite objects

Let an object o be composed of two objects o_1 and o_2. The representation of o is defined as the aggregation of the representation of o_1 and o_2. Let OIM_{s_1} and OIM_{s_2} be the object indexing models for the structure representation of o_1 and o_2, respectively. Similar considerations arise with respect to having one proposition space, sentence space, etc. than that for representing content.

Suppose that o_1 is a section (i.e., $is\_section \in BASE_{s_1}$), then the structure of o, with respect to o_1, is that o has a section (i.e., $has\_section \in BASE_s$), o_1 itself. To capture this, we can define $prop_{s_X}$ for $X = 1, 2$ as follows: $prop_{s_X}(is\_d) = has\_d$, $prop_{s_X}(has\_d) = has^*\_d$ and $prop_{s_X}(has^*\_d) = has^*\_d$. In our example, $has\_section$ is in $BASE_s$ because $prop_{s_1}(is\_section) = has\_section$. Note that this is one possible implementation of the transformation functions. In general, the implementation will depend on practical and pragmatic issues.

5 Representing content and structure

Representing both the content and the structure of an object is essential for retrieval by content and structure (e.g., "chapter about wine"). We have two approaches, both equivalent, due to the commutativity and associativity of $\oplus$. The difference stems from the order in which we perform the aggregation of object indexing models. We therefore only describe one of them.

The content and structure of an object o are modelled separately, each by an object indexing model, respectively OIM_c and OIM_s. The full representation of the object o, denoted $OIM_{c \oplus s}$, is obtained by aggregating the two object indexing models: $OIM_c \oplus OIM_s$. The transformation functions $prop_c$ and $prop_s$ are defined as the identity function, since here the aggregation is with respect to the representations of the same object. The relation inf is set to the empty set, unless some sentences regarding content are informationally related to some sentences regarding structure (e.g., only some keywords can be used in titles). If o is composed of o_1 and o_2, then the content representation of o is given by $OIM_c = OIM_{c_1} \oplus OIM_{c_2}$ and its structure representation is given by $OIM_s = OIM_{s_1} \oplus OIM_{s_2}$, where OIM_{c_X} and OIM_{s_X} are the object indexing models corresponding to the content representation and structure representation of object o_X for $X = 1, 2$.

6 Relevance of document components

The retrieval of a structured document must return to users those objects in the document that are most relevant to their information needs, and are of the specified structure. Querying can be with respect to content or structure. The returned objects are displayed to the users, and then constitute entry points from where the users can decide to browse the structure if needed. In this section, we show how the relevance of each object is computed.

Let OIM_c, OIM_s and OIM be the object indexing models for representing, respectively, the content, the structure, and the content and structure of an object o. We discuss first retrieval by content and structure, that is using the object indexing model OIM.

An information need, as phrased in a query, is represented as a sentence q of the aggregated sentence space S. The relevance of an object to the query is expressed in terms of belief functions [12].

Definition 6.1 *The relevance of any object $o \in \mathcal{O}$ to a query $q \in S$ is given by the function $Rel : \mathcal{O} \times S \to [0, 1]$ defined as follows:*

$$Rel(o, q) = \sum_{\psi \Rightarrow q, \psi \in MSS} m(\psi)$$

The quantity $Rel(o, q)$, when not null, indicates that the object o contains information that concerns q with respect to its content and/or structure. This is because $Rel(o, q)$ is based on the description of the object o (the most specific sentences of o, MSS, that support the sentence q). It also takes into account the uncertainty associated to their use; the higher the mass values, the higher the relevance. Also, the greater their number, the higher the relevance. For instance, if $Rel(o, q) < Rel(o_1, q)$, the object o_1 contains more information pertinent to the query q than does the object o, so is more relevant to the query than o is. Objects can then be ranked according to R, and then fed to a process that determines the best entry points, thus taking into consideration that objects are related[3].

If the query is with respect to content only, then the relevance of the object can be calculated using directly the content representation OIM_c. The same holds

---

[3] How to determine the best entry points is discussed in [16, 8]. The techniques used are not specific to evidential reasoning, but are made possible with our representation of structured documents based on evidential reasoning.

with respect to the structure representation. The same ranking is obtained. This is because it can be shown that for any sentence that describes the content only, or the structure only, the value $Rel(o, q)$ is the same as that obtained with the content representation only, and the structured representation only, respectively (the proof is omitted). Consequently, the retrieval results are comparable, whether the retrieval is by content, structure, or both. This was achievable because we are having a uniform model for representing content, structure, and both.

7 Conclusion

We presented a model for representing structured documents based on evidential reasoning. The model is uniform, so it can be applied to model the representation of content only, structure only, and both content and structure of document components. As as result, querying can be with respect to content, structure, or both.

By being uniform, the model proposes a "clean" formalism, where we can clearly identify and study various aspects in representing content and structure. For instance, we can formally investigate aspects that result from the outcome of the indexing process, or natural language issues for the relationships between indexing elements. A uniform model also allows us to separate the content representation and the structure representation of document components, but also to combine the two representations when and if necessary.

In this paper, many aspects of the model, in particular, when applied to representing content and structure, were not formally presented. In future work, we will define all aspects formally, thus providing a complete and sound representation of document components. Only then, can we fully discuss the expressiveness of our approach at the theoretical level. We will also implement our model using real data (e.g., collection of SGML and XML documents) to evaluate its effectiveness and efficiency in a real environment.

References

[1] S.H. Myaeng, D. H. Jang, M. S. Kim, and Z. C. Zhoo. A flexible model for retrieval of SGML documents. In *Proceedings of ACM-SIGIR Conference on Research and Development in Information Retrieval*, pages 138–145, Melbourne, Australia, 1998.

[2] S. Abiteboul, S. Cluet, V. Christophides, T. Milo, G. Moerkotte, and J. Simeon. Querying documents in object databases. *International Journal on Digital Libraries*, 1:1–9, 1997.

[3] R. Wilkinson. Effective retrieval of structured documents. In *Proceedings of ACM-SIGIR Conference on Research and Development in Information Retrieval*, pages 311–317, Dublin, Ireland, 1994.

[4] Y. Chiaramella and A. Kheirbek. An integrated model for hypermedia and information retrieval. *Information Retrieval and Hypertext*, 1996.

[5] G. Salton, J. Allan, and C. Buckley. Approaches to passage retrieval in full text information systems. In *Proceedings of ACM SIGIR Conference on Research and Development in Information Retrieval*, pages 49–58, Pittsburgh, USA, 1993.

[6] T. Roelleke and N. Fuhr. Retrieval of complex objects using a four-valued logic. In *Proceedings of ACM-SIGIR Conference on Research and Development in Information Retrieval*, pages 206–214, Zurich, Switzerland, 1996.

[7] T. Roelleke. *POOL: Probabilistic Object-Oriented Logical Representation and Retrieval of Complex Objects - A Model for Hypermedia Retrieval*. Shaker Verlag, Aachen, 1999. Phd Thesis.

[8] M. Lalmas and I. Ruthven. Representing and retrieving structured documents with Dempster-Shafer's theory of evidence: Modelling and evaluation. *Journal of Documentation*, 54(5):529–565, 1998.

[9] M.E. Frisse. Searching for information in a hypertext medical handbook. *Communications of the ACM*, 31(7):880–886, 1988.

[10] Y. Chiaramella, P. Mulhem, and F. Fourel. A model for multimedia information retrieval. Technical Report Fermi ESPRIT BRA 8134, University of Glasgow, 1996.

[11] M. Lalmas. Dempster-Shafer's theory of evidence applied to structured documents: modelling uncertainty. In *Proceedings of ACM SIGIR Conference on Research and Development in Information Retrieval*, pages 110–118, Philadelphia, PA, USA, 1997.

[12] G. Shafer. *A Mathematical Theory of Evidence*. Princeton University Press, 1976.

[13] E. H. Ruspini. The logical foundations of evidential reasoning. Technical Report 408, SRI International, 1986.

[14] C. J. van Rijsbergen. *Information Retrieval*. Butterworths, London, 2 edition, 1979.

[15] R. Baeza-Yates and B. Ribeiro-Neto. *Modern Information Retrieval*. Addison Wesley, 1999.

[16] M. Lalmas and E. Moutogianni. A Dempster-Shafer indexing for the focussed retrieval of hierarchically structured documents: Implememtation and experiments on a web museum collection. In *RIAO*, 2000.

Implementing Metadata on the Web: A Conceptual, NKRL-based Approach

Gian Piero Zarri

Centre National de la Recherche Scientifique (CNRS)
Paris, France
zarri@ivry.cnrs.fr

Abstract: We introduce some of the data structures proper to NKRL (Narrative Knowledge Representation Language), a language expressly designed for representing, in a standardised way, the semantic content (the 'meaning') of complex narrative documents. We will emphasise, in particular, some characteristics of the new version of NKRL, implemented in Java and XML/RDF compliant.

1.   Introduction

In this paper, we describe some of the main data structures proper to NKRL (Narrative Knowledge Representation Language), see [1, 2]. NKRL is a language expressly designed for representing, in a standardised way, the narrative 'meaning' of complex natural language (NL) and multimedia documents. NKRL has been used in European projects like Nomos (Esprit P5330), Cobalt (LRE P61011), and WebLearning (GALILEO Actions). It is presently used in the new CONCERTO (Esprit P29159) and EUFORBIA (IAP P2104) projects to encode the 'conceptual annotations' (*metadata*) that must be added to Web documents to facilitate their 'intelligent' retrieval and processing. A new version of NKRL, implemented in Java and XML/RDF compliant, has been realised in a CONCERTO's framework.

According to its name, NKRL is restrained to the conceptual representation of 'narratives', i.e., of situations relating the actual situation of some actors (or characters, personages etc.), or their real or intended behaviour. These actors try to attain a specific result, experience particular situations, manipulate some (concrete or abstract) materials, send or receive messages, buy, sell, deliver etc. NKRL is able, in particular, to deal with most of the complex problems that make particularly uncomfortable the computer processing of narratives (indirect speech, implicit and explicit enunciative situations, behaviours, wishes and intentions, plural situations, second order relationships like goal and causality, modalities, etc.). Moreover, we can note that:

- A considerable amount of the natural language (NL) information that is relevant from an industrial point of view deals, in reality, with narratives. This is true, of course, for the news stories, but also for most of the corporate information (memos, policy statements, reports, minutes etc.), to say nothing of a large percentage of information stored on the Web.

- In the narrative documents, the actors or personages are not necessarily human beings. We can have narrative documents concerning, e.g., the vicissitudes in the journey of a nuclear submarine (the actor, subject or character) or the various avatars in the life of a commercial product. This 'personification' process can be executed to a very large extent, allowing then using NKRL tools to deal with documents apparently very remote from a 'human' context.

- It is not at all necessary that the narrative situation to deal with be recorded in a NL document. Let us consider a collection of Web pictures or of JPEG images, where one represents "Three nice girls are lying on the beach". This narrative situation can be directly represented making use of the NKRL tools; as an alternative, an 'NL annotation' formed by the sentence above can be associated with the picture, and then 'translated' into NKRL format, see [3]. The same is, obviously, possible for narrative situations described in video or digital audio documents.

In this paper, we describe first, Section 2, the general organisation of NKRL; Section 3 gives some simple examples of the actual use of this language. Section 4 discusses the problems encountered when translating into RDF the NKRL data structures and the solutions adopted in this context. RDF (Resource Description Format) is a recommendation of the WWW Committee (W3C) for the implementation of metadata. Section 5, Conclusion, includes a short comparison with other possible solutions for dealing with narrative information.

2. The architecture of NKRL

NKRL is organised according to a two-layer approach. The lower layer consists of a set of general representation tools that are structured into four integrated components, the definitional, enumerative, descriptive and factual components.

The definitional component of NKRL supplies the tools for representing the important notions (*concepts*) of a given domain. In NKRL, a concept is, substantially, a frame-like data structure associated with a symbolic label like `human_being, location_, city_`, etc. The NKRL concepts are inserted into a generalisation/specialisation hierarchy that, for historical reasons, is called H_CLASS(es), and which corresponds well to the usual ontologies of terms.

A fundamental assumption about the organisation of H_CLASS concerns the differentiation between notions which can be instantiated directly into enumerable specimens, like "chair" (a physical object) and notions which cannot be instantiated directly into specimens, like "gold" (a substance). The two high-level branches of H_CLASS stem, therefore, from two concepts labelled as `sortal_concepts` and `non_sortal_concepts` [4], see also Figure 6. The specialisations of the former, like `chair_, city_` or `european_city`, can have direct instances (`chair_27, paris_`), whereas the specialisations of the latter, like `gold_`, or `colour_`, can admit further specialisations, see `white_gold` or `red_`, but do not have direct instances.

The enumerative component of NKRL concerns then the formal representation of the instances (`lucy_, taxi_53, paris_`) of the sortal concepts of H_CLASS. In NKRL, their formal representations take the name of *individuals*. Throughout this paper, we will use the italic type style to represent a `concept_`, the roman style to represent an `individual_`.

The representation of the 'events' proper to a given domain — i.e., the coding of the interactions among the particular concepts and individuals that play a role in the contest of these events — makes use of the descriptive and factual tools.

The descriptive component concerns the tools used to produce the formal representations (*predicative templates*) of general classes of narrative events, like "moving a generic object", "formulate a need", "be present somewhere". In contrast to the dyadic structures used for concepts and individuals, templates are characterised by a complex threefold format connecting together the *symbolic name* of the template, a *predicate* and its *arguments*. These, in turn, are linked with the predicate through the use of a set of named relations, the *roles*. If we denote then with L_i the generic symbolic label identifying a given template, with P_j the predicate used in the template, with R_k the generic role and with a_k the corresponding argument, the NKRL data structures for the templates will have the following general format:

$$(L_i \, (P_j \, (R_1 \, a_1) \, (R_2 \, a_2) \, ... \, (R_n \, a_n))) \, .$$

see the examples in subsection 3.1. In other terms, a predicative template is formed by a set of triples having a common 'left' term, the predicate; the set is reified via the symbolic name of the template. Presently, the predicates pertain to the set {BEHAVE, EXIST, EXPERIENCE, MOVE, OWN, PRODUCE, RECEIVE}, and the roles to the set {SUBJ(ect), OBJ(ect), SOURCE, BEN(e)F(iciary), MODAL(ity), TOPIC, CONTEXT}. Templates are structured into an inheritance hierarchy, H_TEMP(lates), which corresponds, therefore, to a taxonomy (ontology) of events.

Moreover, the expressiveness of the above format is enhanced by the use of two additional tools:

- the AECS 'sub-language', see Sections 3 and 4 below, that allows the construction of complex (structured) predicate arguments;

- the second order tools (binding structures and completive construction, see Section 3) used to code the 'connectivity phenomena' (logico-semantic links) that, in a narrative situation, can exist between single narrative fragments (corresponding to single NKRL predicative structures).

The instances (*predicative occurrences*) of the predicative templates, i.e., the representation of single, specific events like "Tomorrow, I will move the wardrobe" or "Lucy was looking for a taxi" are, eventually, in the domain of the last component, the factual one.

The upper layer of NKRL consists of two parts. The first is a *catalogue* describing the formal characteristics and the modalities of use of the well formed, basic templates of the H_TEMP hierarchy (like "moving a generic object" mentioned above). By means of proper specialisation operations is then possible to obtain from the basic templates the derived templates that could be needed to implement a particular application. The second part is given by the general concepts that belong to the *upper level* of H_CLASS, such as sortal_concepts, non_sortal_concepts, physical_entity, modality_, event_, etc., see again Figure 6. They are, as the basic templates, invariable.

3.   A brief survey of some important NKRL features

3.1   Factual and descriptive components

Figure 1 supplies a simple example of *factual* NKRL code. It translates a fragment of a fictitious news story: "This morning, the spokesman said in a newspaper interview that, yesterday, his company has bought three factories abroad", which is represented according to the rules for encoding plural situations in NKRL [1].

```
c1)   MOVE     SUBJ       (SPECIF human_being_1 (SPECIF spokesman_
                                                  company_1))
               OBJ        #c2
               DEST       newspaper_1
               MODAL      interview_1
               date-1:  today_
               date-2:

c2)   PRODUCE  SUBJ       company_1
               OBJ        (SPECIF purchase_1 (SPECIF factory_99
                              (SPECIF cardinality_ 3))): (abroad_)
               date-1:    yesterday_
               date-2:

[ factory_99
     InstanceOf  :   factory_
     HasMember   :   3 ]
```

Figure 1 An example of NKRL code

Two predicative occurrences (*factual component*), identified by the symbolic labels c1 and c2 and instances of basic NKRL templates, see also Figure 4 below, bring out the main characteristics of the event. The arguments human_being_1, company_1, newspaper_1, interview_1, purchase_1, factory_99 are individuals (enumerative component); today_ and yesterday_ are two fictitious individual introduced here, for simplicity's sake, in place of real or approximate dates [2], see also Figure 2. spokesman_, cardinality_ and abroad_ are concepts (definitional component). The attributive operator, SPECIF(ication), is one of the AECS operators used to build up structured arguments (or *expansions*) [1]; the SPECIF lists, with syntax $(SPECIF\ e_i\ p_1\ ...\ p_n)$, are used to represent some of the properties which can be asserted about the first argument e_i, concept or individual, of the operator, e.g., human_being_1 and spokesman_ in c1. The arguments, and the templates/occurrences as a whole, may be characterised by the presence of particular codes, determiners or attributes, which give further details about their significant aspects. For example, the location attributes, represented as lists, are linked with the arguments by using the colon operator, see c2 (abroad_).

The last item of Figure 1 supplies an example of *enumerative data structure*, explicitly associated with the individual factory_99. The non-empty

HasMember slot in this structure makes it clear that the individual factory_99, as mentioned in c2, is referring in reality to several instances of *factory_*. Individuals like factory_99 are 'collections' rather then 'sets' (all the NKRL concepts can be interpreted as sets), given that the extensionality axiom (two sets are equal iff they have the same elements) does not hold here [5]. In Figure 1, we have supposed that the three factories were, *a priori*, not sufficiently important in the context of the news story to justify their explicit representation as specific individuals, e.g., factory_1, factory_2 etc. Note that, if not expressly required by the characteristics of the application, a basic NKRL principle suggests that we should try to avoid any unnecessary proliferation of individuals.

Finally, we will remark that the basic, MOVE template (descriptive component) at the origin of c1 — see Figure 4 below — is systematically used to translate any sort of explicit or implicit transmission of an information ("The spokesman said..."). In this context, it is used according to a particular syntactic construction (*completive construction*, a second order structure), where the filler of the OBJ(ect) slot in the occurrence (here, c1) which instantiates the 'transmission' template is a symbolic label (here, c2) that refers to another occurrence, i.e. the occurrence bearing the informational content to be spread out (" ...the company has bought three factories abroad").

To supply now some details about the representation of temporal data in NKRL, and to introduce the concept of search pattern, let us examine the code of Figure 2, that translates an information like: "On June 12, 1997, John was admitted to hospital" (upper part of the Figure). From this, we see that temporal information in NKRL is represented through two 'temporal attributes', date-1 and date-2. They define the time interval in which the event represented by the predicative occurrence 'holds'. In c3, this interval is reduced to a point on the time axis, as indicated by the single value, the timestamp 2-july-93, associated with the temporal attribute date-1; this point represents the 'beginning of an event' because of the presence of begin (a temporal modulator). The temporal attribute date-1 is then represented 'in subsequence' (category of dating)[2].

```
c3) EXIST SUBJ    john_:  (hospital_1)
          { begin }
          date-1: 2-june-1997
          date-2:

( ?w     IS-PRED-OCCURRENCE
                 :predicate    EXIST
                 :SUBJ         john_
                 (1-july-1997, 31-august-1997))
```

Figure 2 Coding of temporal information, and a simple example of search pattern

Predicative occurrences like those of Figure 1 and 2 are usually collected in a knowledge base that can be questioned directly making use, in case, of complex inference procedures [6]. The basic data structures used in this context are called *search patterns*: search patterns represent the general framework of information to be searched for, by filtering or unification, within an NKRL knowledge base.

A simple example of search pattern, in the style of: "Was John at the hospital in July/August 1997?" is given in the lower part of Figure 2. The two timestamps associated with the pattern constitute the 'search interval' that is used to limit the search for unification to the slice of time that it is considered appropriate to explore. In the case of Figure 2, occurrence c3 can be successfully unified with the pattern: in the absence of explicit, negative evidence, a given situation is assumed to persist within the immediate temporal environment of the originating event [2].

As a further example of factual structures, we give now, Figure 3, a fragment of the conceptual annotation associated with a CONCERTO document that can be rendered in natural language as : "We notice today, 10 June 1998, that British Telecom will offer its customers a pay-as-you-go (payg) Internet service".

```
c4) (GOAL   c5   c6)

c5)   BEHAVE   SUBJ   british_telecom
      { obs }
      date1:   10-june-1998
      date2:

*c6)  MOVE     SUBJ   british_telecom
               OBJ    payg_internet_service_1
               BENF   (SPECIF customer_ british_telecom)
               date1: after-10-june-1998
               date2:
```

Figure 3 Representation in NKRL of 'acting to obtain a result'

To translate then the general idea of 'acting to obtain a given result', we use:

- A predicative occurrence (c5 in Figure 3), instance of a basic template pertaining to the BEHAVE branch of the template hierarchy (H_TEMP), and corresponding to the general meaning of "focusing on a result". This occurrence is used to express the 'acting' component, i.e., it allows us to identify the SUBJ(ect) of the action, the temporal co-ordinates, possibly the MODAL(ity) or the instigator (SOURCE), etc.

- A second predicative occurrence, c6 in Figure 3, with a different predicate and which is used to express the 'intended result' component. This second occurrence, which happens 'in the future' with respect to the previous one (BEHAVE), is marked as hypothetical, i.e., it is characterised by the presence of an uncertainty validity attribute, code '*'. Expressions like after-10-june-1998 are concretely rendered as a date range [2].

- A 'binding occurrence', c4 in Figure 3, linking together the previous predicative occurrences and labeled with GOAL, an operator pertaining to the taxonomy of causality of NKRL [2].

As already stated, binding structures — i.e., lists where the elements are symbolic labels, c5 and c6 in Figure 3 — are second-order structures used to represent the logico-semantic links (connectivity phenomena) that can exist between (predicative) templates or occurrences. The general schema for representing the 'focusing on an intended result' domain in NKRL is then:

c_α) (GOAL c_β c_γ)
c_β) BEHAVE   SUBJ   <human_being_or_social_body>
*c_γ) <predicative_occurrence, with any syntax

In Figure 3 obs(erve) is, like begin and end, a temporal modulator [2]. obs is used to assert that the event related in the occurrence 'holds' at the date associated with date-1 without, at this level, giving any detailed information about the beginning or end of this event. Note that the addition of a ment(al) modulator in the BEHAVE occurrence, c_β, that introduces an 'acting to obtain a result' construction should imply that no concrete initiative is taken by the SUBJ of BEHAVE in order to fulfil the result. In this case, the 'result', *c_γ, reflects only the wishes and desires of the SUBJ(ect).

Figure 4 reproduces the MOVE template (*descriptive component*) at the origin of occurrence c1 of Figure 1. Optional roles and fillers are in square brackets. 'Structured information' means that the information transmitted is not simply a concept or an individual, but (at least) a complete predicative occurrence. Note that the constraints on the variables are expressed by means of concepts of the H_CLASS hierarchy (*definitional component*).

```
name : Move:StructuredInformation
father : Move:TransmitInformation
position : 4. 42
NL description : 'Transmit a Structured Information'

              MOVE    SUBJ   var1: [(var2)]
                      OBJ    var3
                      [SOURCE var4: [(var5)]]
                      [BENF   var6: [(var7)]]
                      [MODAL  var8]
                      [TOPIC    var9]
                      [CONTEXT var10]
                      { [ modulators ], ≠abs }

  var1 = <human_being_or_social_body>
  var3 = <symbolic_label_>
  var4 = <human_being_or_social_body>
  var6 = <human_being_or_social_body>
  var8 = <action_name> | <information_support>
  var9 ≠ <property_>
  var10 = <event_> | <action_name>
  var2, var5, var7 = <physical_location>
```

Figure 4 An example of template

Figure 5 represents a fragment of an actual H_TEMP hierarchy (*descriptive component*), namely, the H_TEMP hierarchy used in the CONCERTO project. For clarity's sake, and in view of the space constraints, this representation has been severely abridged. Several branches (e.g., the BEHAVE, EXIST etc. branches pertaining to the first level of H_TEMP, or the "Receive:IntellectualResource" (7.2) branch in the RECEIVE sub-tree and the "Move:AnimateDisplacement" (4.31) branch in the MOVE sub-tree) have been suppressed, and a lot of intermediate nodes (e.g., 5.11, 5.12, 4.31 etc.) are missing. Each node of Figure 5 corresponds then to a *template*, i.e., to a structure in the style of the MOVE predicate shown in Figure 4 above.

3.2 Definitional and enumerative components

Figure 6 gives a simplified representation of the upper level of H_CLASS (hierarchy of concepts, *definitional component*). From this Figure, we can note that substance_ and colour_ are examples of non-sortal concepts [1]; the terminology of Guarino *et al.* [4] has been adopted for their generic terms, pseudo_sortal_concepts and characterising_concepts.

The data structures used for (concepts and) individuals, *enumerative component*, see also Figure 1 above, are essentially frame-based structures and their design is relatively traditional. These structures are composed of an OID (object identifier), and of a set of characteristic features (slots). Three different types of slots are used, 'relations', 'attributes', and 'procedures', see again [1] for more details.

4. Implementation notes: NKRL and RDF

The RDF model [7], implemented in XML, makes use of Directed Labelled Graphs where the nodes, that represent any possible Web *resource* are described using *properties*, i.e., named attributes (characteristics, features) of the resource. The values associated with the properties may be text strings, numbers, or other resources. In knowledge representation terms, the basic RDF data structure can be assimilated to a *triple* where two resources are linked by a property that behaves like a *dyadic* conceptual relation. In this way, a resource identified by the URI (Uniform Resource Identifier) "http://www.foo.com/J.Smith" and having two properties, firstName=John and lastName=Smith, is linked via a third property fatherOf with the resource "http://www.foo.com/K.Smith" having the properties firstName=Karen and lastName=Smith. The schema language RDFS (Resource Description Framework Schema), see [8], supplies a specialised vocabulary to model class and properties hierarchies, to define a set of core properties, to define domain and range restrictions about properties, etc.

The first, general problem we had to solve for implementing the XML/RDF-compliant version of NKRL has concerned the very different nature of the RDF and NKRL data structures. The simple RDF triples built up via dyadic conceptual relations are very different from the complex threefold constructions used in NKRL to represent predicative templates and occurrences, see Section 2 above. To assure the conversion, we have then split the NKRL data structures into intertwined dyadic 'tables', see Figure 7 that describes the RDF-compliant, general structure of an NKRL template. For simplicity's sake, this figure does not take into account the hierarchical relations between templates or the relationships between templates and occurrences.

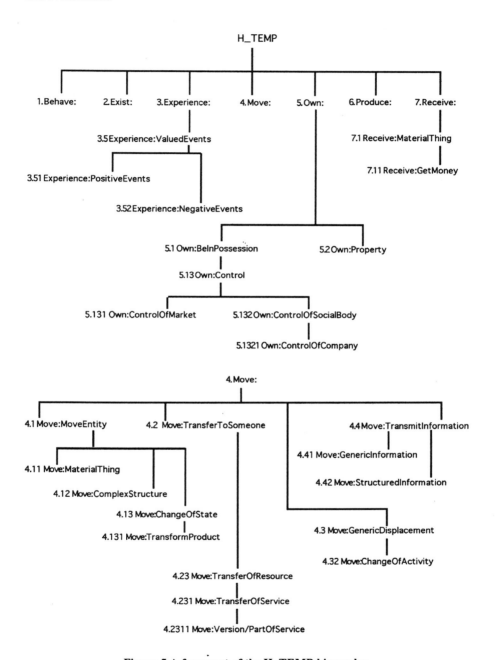

Figure 5 A fragment of the H_TEMP hierarchy

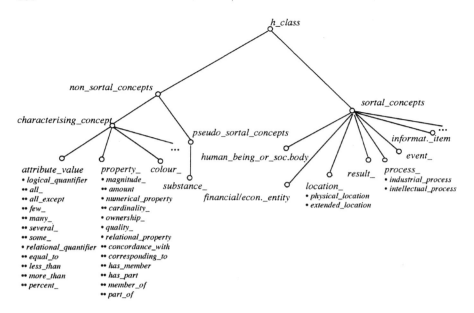

Figure 6 An abridged view of the 'upper level' of H_CLASS

More specific problems have concerned the limited set of knowledge representation tools that are presently associated with RDF. To give only an example, let us consider the solutions that, making use of the RDF containers [7], we have adopted in order to reproduce the semantics of the so-called AECS sublanguage [1] of NKRL. The AECS operators are used to build up structured arguments (or 'expansions') like those included in Figures 1 and 3 above.

AECS includes four operators, the disjunctive operator (ALTERNative = A), the distributive operator (ENUMeration = E), the collective operator (COORDination = C), and the attributive operator (SPECIFication = S). The semantics of SPECIF(ication) has already been explained in Section 3.1 above; the semantics of ALTERN(ative) is evident. The difference between COORD(ination) and ENUM(eration) consists in the fact that, in a COORD expansion list, all the elements of the expansion take part (necessarily) together in the particular relationship with the predicate defined by the associated role. As an example, we can imagine a situation similar to that described in Figure 3 above, where British Telecom *and* French Telecom want *together* offer a payg service to their customers: the SUBJ of BEHAVE would be, in this case: (COORD british_telecom french_telecom). In an ENUM list, each element satisfies the same relationship with the predicate, but they do this separately. RDF defines on the contrary three types of containers:

- 'Bag', an unordered list of resources or literals, used to declare that a property has multiple values and that no significance is associated with the order in which the values are given;

- 'Sequence', Seq, an ordered list of resources or literals, used to declare that a property has multiple values and that the order of these values is significant;

- 'Alternative', Alt, a list of resources or literals that represent alternative for the (single) value of a property.

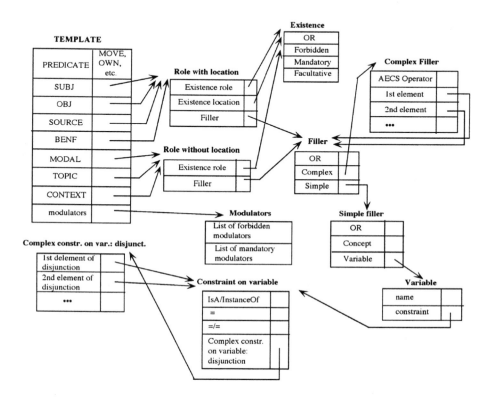

Figure 7 General structure of an NKRL template according to a 'dyadic' view

Of these, only Alternative presents a very precise coincidence with an AECS operator, obviously, ALTERN; moreover, we have at our disposal only *three* container constructions to represent *four* NKRL operators. We can note, however, that the use of a Bag construction is an acceptable approximation to represent the semantics of COORD. For example, in the RDF Model and Syntax Specification report [8], the use of Bag is associated with the representation of the sentence: "The committee of Fred, Wilma and Dino approved the relation". As the editors of the report say, "...the three committee members *as a whole* voted in a certain manner...". This situation corresponds certainly in NKRL to a COORD situation. As a first conclusion, we can then state that:

- The ALTERN constructions are described making use of the RDF container Alt.

- The COORD constructions are represented making use of the RDF container Bag.

With respect now to the RDF representation of the ENUM and SPECIF constructions, we make use of a 'liberal' interpretation of the semantics of Seq containers. Seq introduces an *order relation* between the elements of a list. In Section 3.1, we have seen that the operator SPECIF introduces, on the contrary, a 'partial order' relationship, where the order of the properties specifying the first element e_i of the list is indifferent. We can then include these properties in an (implicit) Bag, and insert e_i and this Bag in a Seq list. The same solution has been adopted for the ENUM operator, with the (only) difference that an explicit 'enum' identifier is inserted in the first position of the Seq list. We can say that:

- For the SPECIF constructions, we use the RDF operator Seq followed directly by the elements of the SPECIF list. Of these, the elements representing the 'properties' are to be considered as inserted into a Bag; to simplify the RDF code, this Bag list is considered as an 'implicit' one, and the Bag operator is not explicitly mentioned.

- The ENUM constructions are coded by using a Seq container where the first element is the identifier 'enum'.

As an example, let us consider, Figure 8, the RDF representation of occurrence c3 of Figure 2 where we have slightly modified the formulation of the SUBJ filler by assuming that John and Peter have been admitted *together* (COORD) to the hospital. The RDF text associated with each predicative occurrence is composed by several tags, all nested within the <CONCEPTUAL_ANNOTATION> tag and belonging to two different namespaces, rdf and ca. The first describes the standard environment under which RDF tags have to be interpreted. The second describes specific tags defined in the context of an application, in this case, the CONCERTO project. The tag <ca:Template*i*> denotes that the predicative occurrence is an instance of Template*i*. The other tags specify the various roles of the predicative occurrence, together with the associated value; a tag for each additional information concerning a role is nested inside the role tag. Additional tags are used to represent temporal information and modulators used in the context of the considered predicative occurrence. The code li means 'list item', and it was chosen in RDF to be mnemonic with respect to the corresponding HTML term.

For the solutions adopted to fully represent in RDF the variables and the constraints of the NKRL templates see, e.g., [9]. We can compare the effectiveness of this sort of solutions with other, more uncertain suggestions (see, e.g., [10]) for making an actual use of RDF containers.

5. Conclusion

We can conclude with some short remarks about two knowledge representation systems that have been sometimes used to represent narrative-like information, frame systems (descriptive logics included) and conceptual graphs.

```
<?xml version="1.0" ?>
<!DOCTYPE DOCUMENTS SYSTEM "CA_RDF.dtd">
<CONCEPTUAL_ANNOTATION>
    <rdf:RDF xmlns:rdf="http://www.w3.org/1999/02/22-rdf-syntax-ns#"
    xmlns:rdf="http://www.w3.org/TR/1999/PR-rdf-schema-19990303#"
    xmlns:ca="http://projects.pira.co.uk/concerto#">
      <rdf:Description about="occ3">
      <rdf:type resource="ca:Occurrence"/>
          <ca:instanceOf>Template2.31</ca:instanceOf>
          <ca:predicateName>Exist</ca:predicateName>
          <ca:subject rdf:ID="Subj2.31" rdf:parseType="Resource">
          <concerto:filler>
            <rdf:Bag>
              <rdf :li rdf:resource="#john_"/>
              <rdf :li rdf:resource="#peter_"/>
            </rdf:Bag>
          </concerto:filler>
            <concerto:location>hospital_1</concerto:location>
          </ca:subject>
          <ca:listOfModulators>
              <rdf:Seq><rdf:li>begin</rdf:li></rdf:Seq>
          </ca:listOfModulators>
          <ca:date1>02/06/1997</ca:date1>
      </rdf:Description>
    </rdf:RDF>
</CONCEPTUAL_ANNOTATION>
```

Figure 8 The RDF format of a predicative occurrence

For the first, we can simply note that frame systems have been sometimes 'forced' to represent elementary classes of events, e.g. "buy-sell" events; however these systems, based on the traditional hierarchical and property-value principles, are not suitable when it becomes necessary to represent wishes and beliefs, causality, modalities, 'plural' situations, conditions, complex relationships among several actors, etc. Moreover, it is well known that the 'uniqueness syndrome' (which leads one to represent all reality making use of only one representational principle) can only lead to particularly awkward results, very difficult to interpret and disambiguate.

With respect now to CGs, we can note firstly the bewildering amount of (sometimes arcane) formalism that CGs researchers consider as absolutely necessary to supply sound logic foundations to their theories, see [11]. The result of this premature hyper-formalisation is that many, more mundane aspects of the CGs endeavour have often been neglected see, to give only an example, the ambiguities that still concern the choice between ATTR (Attribute) and CHRC (Characteristic), or AGNT (Agent) and EXPR (Experiencer). Moreover, even if CGs have the possibility of defining structures of a general import, similar to the NKRL templates, an exhaustive and authoritative list of these structures ("canonical graphs") have never been supplied, and the constitution of such a list has never been planned. The practical consequence of this state of affairs concerns then the need, whenever a concrete application of the CGs theory must be created, of constructing *ex novo* a list of canonical graphs for this application. On the contrary, a fundamental (and apparently unique) characteristic of NKRL is given by the fact that a catalogue of 'basic templates' is part and parcel of the definition of the language. This approach is particularly important for practical applications because it implies, in particular, that: i) a system-builder does not have to create himself the structural knowledge needed to describe the events proper to a (sufficiently) large class of narrative texts and documents; ii) it becomes easier to secure the reproduction or the sharing of previous results.

References

[1] Zarri, G.P. (1997). NKRL, a Knowledge Representation Tool for Encoding the 'Meaning' of Complex Narrative Texts. Natural Language Engineering, 3, pp.231-253.

[2] Zarri, G.P. (1998) Representation of Temporal Knowledge in Events: The Formalism, and Its Potential for Legal Narratives. Information & Communications Technology Law, 7, pp.213-241.

[3] Zarri, G.P. (1995) Knowledge Acquisition from Complex Narrative Texts Using the NKRL Technology. In: Proceedings of the 9th Banff Knowledge Acquisition for Knowledge-Based Systems Workshop, Gaines, B.R., and Musen, M. (Eds.), vol. 1. Department of Computer Science of the University, Calgary.

[4] Guarino, N., Carrara, M., Giaretta, P. (1994) An Ontology of Meta-Level Categories. In: Proceedings of the 4th Int. Conference on Principles of Knowledge Representation and Reasoning. Morgan Kaufmann, San Francisco.

[5] Franconi, E. A Treatment of Plurals and Plural Quantifications Based on a Theory of Collections (1993) Minds and Machines, 3, pp.453-474.

[6] Zarri, G.P., Azzam, S. Building up and Making Use of Corporate Knowledge Repositories (1997). In: Knowledge Acquisition, Modeling and Management - Proceedings of EKAW'97 Plaza, E., Benjamins, R. (Eds.). Springer-Verlag, Berlin.

[7] Lassila, O., Swick, R.R. (Eds.) (1999) Resource Description Framework (RDF) Model and Syntax Specification (Technical Report). W3C, Available at <URL: http://www.w3.org/TR/REC-rdf-syntax/>.

[8] Brickley, D., and Guha, R.V. (1999) Resource Description Framework (RDF) Schema Specification (Technical Report). W3C, Available at <URL: http://www.w3.org/TR/PR-rdf-schema/>.

[9] Marin, B., and Laradi, D. (2000) A Solution to the Problem of Fully Representing NKRL Variables and Constraints in RDF (Technical Note NRC-2). CNRS, Paris.

[10] Noy, N.F., Fergerson, R.W., and Musen, M.A. (2000, in press) The Knowledge Model of Protégé-2000: Combining Interoperability and Flexibility. In: Proceedings of the 12th EKAW Conference, EKAW'2000. Springer-Verlag, Berlin, Available at <URL: http://smi-web.stanford.edu/pubs/SMI_Abstracts/SMI-2000-0830.html>.

[11] Sowa, J.F. (1999) Knowledge Representation: Logical, Philosophical, and Computational Foundations. Brooks Cole Publishing Co., Pacific Grove (CA):

Design and development of a decision support system to support discretion in refugee law.

Tunde Meikle[1] and John Yearwood[2]
School of Information Technology and Mathematical Sciences
University of Ballarat, Ballarat, Victoria, Australia
[1] imcu00tzm@students.ballarat.edu.au [2] jly@ballarat.edu.au

Abstract

From our research into decision making in the discretionary domain of refugee law two important concepts emerge. Consistency and discretion are examined in terms of their operational meanings and relationship as well as the implications for decision support system design. We briefly describe our system, EMBRACE and discuss how the system attempts to support the exercise of discretion in refugee law. We also present a framework (MODDE) for a Model Of Decision support system Design and Evaluation that uses three continuous dimensions to represent the field of system aims and performance. These three dimensions, *predictive-descriptive, strong-weak discretion* and *low-high consistency* divide the field into octants into which we place EMBRACE. It is proposed that MODDE will have utility for clarifying system aims as well as evaluating system performance.

1.   Introduction

Our ongoing research into decision making in discretionary domains is focused here on the special domain of refugee law. The decision makers at the Refugee Review Tribunal (RRT) have provided a field in which key concepts important to decision support system (DSS) design and evaluation have been identified.

Two of these concepts are *consistency* and *discretion*. An understanding of the operational meaning of them, and their interrelationship are important to a full understanding of the way decisions are made in discretionary domains. Another important concept relates to the autonomy of legal decision makers and their desire to maintain control over crucial subjective decisions rather than have them automated.

The implications of these understandings for DSS design and evaluation are of particular relevance to our commitment to the development of the EMBRACE system. We are designing this system to support discretion and enhance consistency while maintaining individual autonomy.

We begin this paper by examining the nature of refugee law as a discretionary domain and the way decisions are made at the RRT. The concepts of discretion and consistency as evident in law in general and refugee law in particular are then discussed. We then consider some of the perceived problems with DSS, followed by the proposed framework for a Model Of DSS Design and Evaluation (MODDE). Finally our system, EMBRACE is described and the way it attempts to address the earlier issues raised is discussed.

2. Decision making in this discretionary domain

2.1 Law is a discretionary domain

The general domain of law is considered discretionary due to its *open texture* [1]. Open texture means that a term may not be defined in advance of it being used in practice [2]. Where a specific practice of law is governed by legislation that contains many open textured terms, agreed rules are unlikely to be generated. While decision makers would try to apply the law reliably, it is difficult to do so because of this characteristic.

Refugee law is characterised by many open textured terms and as such can be considered a discretionary domain. Terms are open to interpretation at the discretion of the decision maker. It is apparent that this feature is both a strength of the domain and a weakness. Laws that are too rigid can be cumbersome and do not permit individual considerations, while laws that are too vague risk being interpreted in widely differing ways among practitioners and over time. These problems relate directly to the central issues of discretion and consistency explored later in this paper.

2.2 Decision making in refugee law

Decision making in refugee law may be thought of as a form of judicial decision making. It shares many characteristics common to judicial decision making in other contexts, as well as the particular relationship judicial decision making has with artificial intelligence (AI), (see [3]).

In the context of the RRT, decision makers include both trained lawyers and non-lawyers. They generally begin as novices in this specific practice and develop the skills of applying the provisions of refugee law to an applicant's case as well as the skills of legal writing. Gale [4] stresses the unique character of legal writing as a genre, and the special challenge it poses to the non-lawyer. This is an important consideration of the design of a DSS in this domain.

The RRT member has the task of reviewing a decision from an applicant that was not granted refugee status by the primary decision maker. In the main, they may set aside, or confirm the primary decision maker's determination, or they may refer the case to the Minister on humanitarian grounds.

Refugee law is a domain with few rules and many broad guidelines that are derived from the ***United Nations Convention relating to the Status of Refugees, 1951*** to which Australia is a signatory. From the Convention a refugee is a person who

> *"...owing to a well-founded fear of being persecuted for reasons of race, religion, nationality, membership of a particular social group or political opinion, is outside the country of his nationality and is unable or, owing to such fear, is unwilling to avail himself of the protection of that country, or who not having a nationality and being outside the country of his former habitual residence as a result of such events, is unable, or owing to such fear, is unwilling to return to it."* [5]

2.3   Discretion as exercised in refugee law

One experienced domain expert has characterised *discretion* as the practice of *not being directed towards a specific outcome*. This does not mean that a decision maker acts without any constraints. In the commentary of McHugh [6] even judicial law-making is not without constraints. He cites a High Court judgement in *Breen v Williams* [7] in which he and Gaudron J said:

> *"Judges have no authority to invent legal doctrine that distorts or does not extend or modify existing legal rules or principles. Any changes in legal doctrine, brought about by judicial creativity, must 'fit' within the body of accepted rules and principles. The judges of Australia cannot, so to speak, 'make it up' as they go along."* (p 47)

Discretion has also been seen as a continuum [8], as involving power relationships [9] and as the ability to reason toward one of a number of possible conclusions [10]. Dworkin [11] identified three basic types of discretion that exemplified different conclusions inferred in different ways: two types of weak discretion and a type he characterised as strong.

Strong discretion characterises that reasoning involving the liberty, on the part of the reasoner to incorporate standards of his or her own choosing. Dworkin [11] proposes that this is the nature of the position of the judge in a situation where usual standards or rules do not apply. Weak discretion of type one exists when one's decision is bound by standards that may inherently have variable interpretations, but nevertheless, those rules apply. The second type of weak discretion exists when a decision is made according to applicable rules and standards but the decision maker's decision stands as final, as in an umpire's call.

2.4   Discretion and 'hard' and 'easy' cases

Some DSS, have as one function, the filtering of cases into those that the system can 'solve' and those that are beyond the capacity of the system. This filtering is a form of case *triage* and is evident in systems like that proposed by Gardner [12] and Popple [13]. To avoid the folly of treating a 'hard' case as though it were an 'easy' one [14], these systems attempt to distinguish hard cases from others and refer them to an expert human decision maker. In the case of the RRT, the members must make decisions on all cases before them, both hard and easy although they are reluctant to refer to difficult cases as 'hard'. They respond to a differentiation of case complexity with an appropriate reallocation of resources in order to make a decision, as though all cases are demanding (or 'hard'), just some moreso.

A domain in which decisions are made in instances that are all 'hard' in the sense that they do not have outcomes directed by clear rules, can be said to also demand strong discretion from its decision makers, and can be described as a discretionary domain. Discretion is not restricted to the choice of final outcomes for there are cascades of subjective choices to be made, each of which affects another in uncertain ways.

2.5   Decision making under uncertainty

Our domain experts report that subjectivity is evident in their judgements about an applicant's credibility and the level of *satisfaction* about findings of fact. Although fact-finding may appear unambiguous, involving tasks such as matching dates, locations, and events there is no reliable calculus to guide how they are to be combined or used. Therefore which facts will be found and how significant they may be continues to be a major source of *uncertainty*.

The challenge for DSS design that is posed by the complexity of decision making under uncertainty is recognised by many authors in AI (e.g.[3],[15],[16], [17],[18]). Krause & Clarke [16] in particular suggest a relationship between inconsistency (the possible converse of consistency, an important concept in this domain) and uncertain knowledge.

2.6   The problem of consistency of legal decisions

Experts in our domain feel they are sometimes perceived as lacking in *consistency* between decision makers. They describe this view is often held by naïve observers that see the issue of making decisions as being based on only a few factors such as country of origin or membership of a political group only. Certainly on these few criteria some decisions may appear not to be consistent, not everyone from country X gains refugee status.

Domain experts cite instances of differences of opinion on the weight of specific facts in an applicant's case. For example, member's opinions vary on whether the non-issuing of a health care card in a particular country is evidence of persecution. Differences of opinion can mean that who reviews an applicant's case can be a significant influence on the outcome. One decision maker may feel and argue cogently for refugee status (a 'set-aside' decision) whereas another may not.

Gardner [12] questions the expectation that legal agreement is a norm and describes the legal system as one that "*makes institutional provision for expert disagreement*". She goes on to ask whether there would be "*any class of cases as to which all competent lawyers would reach the same conclusion?*"

These variations compromise the intention of deciding *similar* cases in a *similar* manner and is related to the legal principle of *stare decisis*, that emphasises the binding nature of precedents. Tata [17] asks what is meant by 'similarity'. He implies that there may be a form of similarity that may suffice for legal reasoning that may not conform to the ideal of 'sameness' as described by what he terms a *legalistic* or *analytical* viewpoint. He attributes what he sees as the prevailing legalistic and analytical conceptualisation of judicial decision making to the way computers themselves require knowledge to be represented in order to work best.

This is a non-trivial issue and poses a DSS design challenge for retaining human autonomy and discretion, while maintaining consistency. It would be beneficial for a DSS to incorporate the capacity for a sense of personal or internal consistency. Tata [17] goes some way to describing how this may be done within the domain of sentencing and criminal law with reference to a narrative model, and Meikle [19] suggests that the narrative analogy may be a useful conceptualisation in refugee law.

2.7   Rationality and consistency of judgements

Judgement writing serves several purposes. As explained by Doyle [20] referring to Sir Frank Kitto, these include (1) to explain how and why the result was reached; (2) exposure of the judge's reasoning on matters of fact and law for the benefits of an appellate court; (3) exposure of a defect in the law or its administration; (4) exposure of any error or deficiency in public administration where relevant; (5) exposure of individual wrongdoing when necessary to decide a case; and (6) exposure of the administration of justice to the public gaze.

McHugh [6] lists only three purposes with much the same intentions, including (1) the parties must be permitted to see the extent to which their arguments have been understood and accepted, and with reference to Lord MacMillan, a reasoned judgement should not only do but seem to do justice; (2) they must clearly explain the reasoning process and thereby further judicial accountability; and (3) the reasons must declare and apply a principle or rule at a level of generality that transcends the facts of the case and enables other courts to decide other cases, identical in principle but not in detail, in the same way. All these purposes also serve to demonstrate the rationality of judicial decisions.

Increased rationality, as Lovegrove [21] argues is also on the path to ensuring greater consistency. Particularly if consistency is reflected in the way a judge is able to articulate how this case instance is similar to or different from another, or how the law does or does not apply to this instance. This is in sympathy with the view of domain experts that consistency is largely a matter of applying the law in the same way in each case, rather than something achieved by comparing outcomes.

3.   Core and penumbra concepts of discretion and consistency

Derived from investigations into the decision makers at the RRT the complexity of the operational meanings of consistency is suggested in Figure 1. It is represented as a penumbra of concepts surrounding a core. For consistency, the core concept of *similarity* is reflected in each of the operational penumbra. Also in that figure is a representation of the core and penumbra operational concepts for discretion. The core concept for discretion, *interpretation*, is reflected in each of the operational penumbra.

We propose that these concepts operate through the exercise of choice (about similarity, and about interpretation). It is also proposed that the ability to exercise choice is moderated by organisational arrangements (such as the degree of autonomy, or legitimate authority given to a decision maker, and whether they make decisions individually or as a group). In the design of our DSS we aim to preserve these essential core qualities.

4.   Perceived success of legal decision support systems

Leenes and Svensson [22] criticise the outcomes that lawyers were led to believe would follow from LKBS. They point to a decrease in successful real-world implementations and an increase in research into knowledge modeling and representations explaining these observations as being the result of two main factors. One factor is the incapacity of current generations of LKBS to adequately represent and actually reason as an expert lawyer. This leads to lack of acceptance and interest by lawyers to adopt LKBS even as assistants The other factor is the prevailing need that lawyers have for support in their decision making via access to wide-ranging information, not just precedents.

Wall and Johnstone [23] suggest that lawyers may be culturally resistant to the use of technology because progress in information technology has moved far from the way lawyers and their world actually work. They also suggest the training of new lawyers is deficient in the way information technology is introduced and taught alongside legal knowledge and skills.

Tata [17] and Leith [24] also note that there is a continuing tension relating to judicial acceptance of decision support systems. Oskamp & Tragter [25] discuss the related problem of the effects of systems that are not well designed from the point of view that they lack transparency to the users. They argue that poor attention to this aspect in design can have very negative unintended regulatory consequences for those the system is meant to serve. In the specific domain of sentencing law for example, there are legal practices in place that vary from the vague to the numerically specific (as in US sentencing guidelines), and the cases are about criminal matters that raise concerns about the public good. It is to be

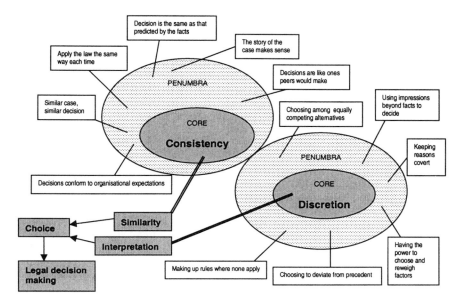

Figure 1. Suggested core and penumbra operational concepts for consistency and discretion, and their relationship to legal decision making.

expected that judges may view with suspicion LKBS that may be illconceived and attempt to intrude upon their exercise of discretion.

An increasingly common critical focus is on the nature of the specific legal domain in which one is trying to assist decision makers (e.g. [17],[24],[25],[26],[27]). This involves setting aside the assumptions and limitations that follow from a traditional computer model where decisions are at their simplest and most effective when they follow *modus ponens* ('if p then q', etc), and which inevitably sends most systems designs along a positivist road of legal rules.

We propose that an important problem for the design of a DSS is how it may still provide support for the exercise of discretion without diminishing the ability to exercise it. A concern about this effect is also expressed by Taruffo [3]. This is also similar in sentiment to the requirement expressed by Leith [24] when he says that, *"The design of a decision support system should not detract from the discretionary elements which are at the heart of notions of 'justice'."* This implies that system designs of the past may not have achieved this aim. He goes on to describe the shift in emphasis in the design of computerised systems, from *'expert systems'* (in vogue in the 1980's) to *'decision support systems'*. The move away from systems that tried to behave like 'experts' seems to be due in part, he proposes, to their having failed to reliably perform as promised.

5.   The MODDE framework

DSS design should be responsive to the needs of decision makers in a domain. It is this responsiveness that ideally leads to the formulation of well-formed aims for a DSS design. The specific aims will be unique to the context for which the DSS is intended, but in terms of the legal domain, it is proposed that the aims may be an attempt to balance three important generic operational goals. These goals are represented as continuous dimensions that divide the potential space into octants.

- the *predictive-descriptive* dimension is the extent to which a system should be an 'outcome predictor'. *Predictive* systems are designed to converge on an outcome 'solution'. *Descriptive* systems are designed to provide a diverse range of methods to access and manipulate information and knowledge in the domain without converging on a specific outcome.

- the *strong – weak discretion* dimension is the extent to which a system intends to support discretion. *Strong discretion* implies that the decision maker has complete autonomy to come to a decision or seek unfettered information, and depart from the DSS processes or 'solution' (if it has one), at the extreme this dimension approaches irrational arbitrariness. *Weak discretion* implies that the decision maker has no ability to alter the decision of the system, or no decision may be required (as in statistical analysis)

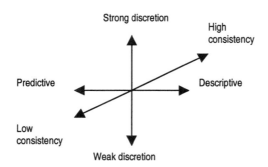

Figure 2. The field of decision support systems aims is divided into octants

- the *high – low consistency* dimension is the extent to which a system must ensure 'similarity' of output or process. *High consistency* implies that there is a requirement for reliability and predictability of process or outcome. *Low consistency* describes decision makers that have the liberty to produce different outcomes regardless of situation and input where unpredictability may be desired.

The dimensions are normative and represent ordinal concepts rather than discrete or continuous numerical variables. It is the intention to further develop the model to formulate indicators for each of the dimensions. This will make the model useful as a guide to DSS design as well as a mean to frame evaluation. The assumption is that evaluation is not applied simply at the end of DSS production, but must be anticipated at the start. One part of evaluation must be to answer the question "Has this system met its stated aims?" It is expected that MODDE will have utility to articulate those aims by providing one part of the guidance required when collaborating with domain experts towards system design. Consequently it contributes to evaluation by providing a means to frame the performance of systems against those aims.

A system may be located in this three-dimensional space, for example Ashley's HYPO [28] would be somewhere in the *strong discretion/predictive/high consistency* octant. HYPO produces 'solutions' and applies processes the same way each time, but does permit the user to manipulate the outcome rather than be bound by it. The 'Lex Mulder' system for collecting traffic fines described by Oskamp and Tragter [25] would be somewhere in the *weak discretion/predictive/high consistency* octant. The system produces reliable binding outcomes and users are not expected to adjust factors or rules or the use made of outcomes. Sentencing information systems (SIS) such as LIST [29] provides wide access to potentially divergent information and data sources which the user may make extensive use of as they wish. Those features would place this system in the *weak discretion/descriptive/low consistency* octant.

The EMBRACE system [30] is being developed with aims that would place it into the *strong discretion/descriptive/high consistency* octant. In providing support in the complex discretionary domain of refugee law it permits divergent processes and outcomes.

6.   EMBRACE

There is evidence to suggest that the integration of reasoning (whether modelled as arguments or not) with information retrieval (IR), drafting and tutoring leads to performance improvements over independent systems. For example, Rose [31] describes limitations for information retrieval that arise when human computer issues are ignored and knowledge about documents is not represented. The IR improvements made by Daniels and Rissland [32], Moens, Uyttendaele and Dumortier [33] and Yearwood [34] attribute improvements over keyword matching to the integration of more sophisticated representation of knowledge of documents with statistical techniques.

Four systems, PLAID [35], ARMOR [36], CATO [37],[38] and EMBRACE [30] attempt some level of integration of information retrieval with reasoning and drafting. Each system does not represent a fixed line of reasoning but models argumentation. Each system responds to user direction. The systems differ in their application domains, the structure of underlying knowledge, human-computer interaction design and inferencing methods though all claim sophisticated performance results.

Stanieri, Yearwood and Meikle [39] propose that discretion, in being intimately linked with reasoning, is necessarily dependent on the way in which knowledge is represented. This point is particularly salient for computer based systems that must artificially represent knowledge. Discretion manifests in a different way if knowledge is represented as a set of rules than it does if knowledge is represented as a series of modified Toulmin [40] arguments, or as default logic clauses.

In EMBRACE an argument is represented using a frame that is based on, but not identical to, the structure proposed by Toulmin [40]. This frame explicitly represents as a generic argument, the claims, the data items on which the claim is based, the inference procedure, the reasons for relevance of each data item and the reasons for the appropriateness of the inference procedure. For a particular argument which is an instance of a generic argument a reason for the claim value is also incorporated to conceptually integrate the information retrieval task with the reasoning. This structure is illustrated in Figure 3.

Data elements in Figure 3 are the one or more elements such as *"Recently the practices and policies...in the country of origin"*, that comprise the data component of the argument. Each data element has possible data element values. For example, the data element *"Recently the practices and policies...in the country of origin,"* can take values on a 2 point scale, either *"has changed substantially "* or *"has not changed substantially"*. The claim element in this argument is *"Severe practices and policies of harassment that target the applicant are..."*, and the claim element values are either *"prevalent"*, *"probable"*, *"possible" or " unlikely"*. Information retrieval of evidence for claim values is sourced from the information base in a way that is structured and contextualised to support the reasoning.

EMBRACE consists of 4 major modules: the knowledge base, which we refer to as the generic argument structure, repositories, an I/O module and an inferencing module. The knowledge base or generic structure is a framework of the arguments that are found in the domain. It is central to all components of EMBRACE. The repositories consist of a database of symbolically represented arguments, a database of text fragments corresponding to these arguments, a database of the full text of the cases that these arguments were extracted from, a repository of inference procedures and an information base of full-text country information and reports from Amnesty International, World Council of Churches, US State Reports and Reuters.

As a result of the Toulmin [40] representation we discern three ways that a decision maker, in the process of reasoning by constructing an argument can apply discretion (see also [39])

1.   *The decision maker has discretion to add (or remove) data item factors*

2.   *The decision maker has discretion to use an inference procedure of his/her own choosing to infer a claim value from data item values*

3.   *The decision maker has the discretion to leave data items, reasons for relevance, inference procedure, and reasons for the appropriateness of inference procedures implicit.*

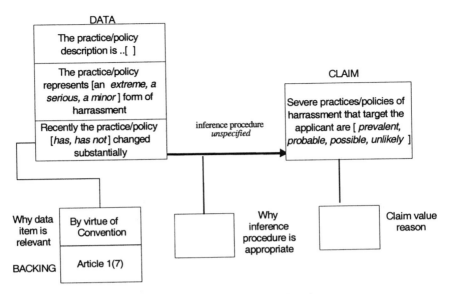

Figure 3. Generic argument structure

EMBRACE is planned to permit the exercise of discretion in that it allows the above as well as the addition of new instance arguments. It is also expected to support discretion by providing the generic argument structure, allowing variations of this and by providing free as well as directed access to relevant information sources. Articulated in the generic argument framework for each argument are reasons for relevance of the data items and reasons for relevance of the inference process used. When the decision maker constructs new arguments there is also a responsibility to articulate reasons for the relevance of new data items and reasons for relevance of the inference procedures.

It does not however attempt to model or support the user in choosing alternative data items or in supporting the extra legal problem solving and reasoning skills that maybe required in the exercise of discretion [17]. It will be able to carry out symbolic argument retrieval as well as full text, structured text and fragment retrieval which are important aspects of providing comparable case and argument information. These capacities combine to support the requirement of RRT members to fully articulate the reasons for their decisions, and so aligns with the views of authors that emphasise the benefits of rationality to legal decision making, (e.g. [6],[20],[41])

The first stage of EMBRACE, a shell that allows the development of arguments, is now complete. The argument shell consists of the following components:

- A generic argument editor that enables a knowledge engineer to enter a tree of generic arguments within a domain
- An actual argument editor that enables a user to enter actual arguments made by participants

- An information retrieval engine. This engine is invoked during the construction of a new actual argument when a user is seeking sources of information to use as warrants or claim value reason components of an argument

- A document generation facility that generates a document that represents the reasoning captured in a series of actual arguments. We have shown that a document with an acceptable structure can be generated with the use of a simple heuristic that avoids complex discourse analysis methods [30].

- An inference engine that can infer a value for a claim from data item values by invoking the procedure embedded in an argument. In refugee law, no machine inferences are made at all, whereas in predicting property outcomes in family law, neural and rule inferences are used.

- A dialogue generator that models the relationships between arguments such as A supports B, A rebuts C and D, A extends G; This is important for modeling the way in which two or more parties apply arguments in a dialogue.

7.   Conclusion

This paper presents an brief consideration of the implications for our DSS design that arise from our research into generic and specific aspects of legal decision making in refugee law. From this work we have proposed a framework for a Model Of DSS Design and Evaluation (MODDE) that will be developed further. It is hoped that it will be useful for guiding knowledge engineers in their work with domain experts in the design phase by providing a systematic way in which to construct system aims. This should directly support evaluation of systems when matching system performance to the articulated aims.

In the design of EMBRACE we have planned to provide support for the exercise of strong discretion, as well as allowing a divergent approach to the work of an RRT member. We acknowledge that potential exists for any system to diminish the capacity for discretion, but by systematic attention to the needs of domain users and the detailed nature of the decision making in that domain we anticipate this risk is minimised. Ongoing feedback from domain experts is encouraging, but given the cautious tone of authors (e.g. [3],[17],[24],[25]) about the success of implementations in the field, we are modest in our aims. We also anticipate that the use of the MODDE framework will lead directly to the evaluation necessary to operationally validate the system.

8.   Acknowledgments

The authors appreciate the ongoing assistance and support of the members of the Refugee Review Tribunal and Victorian Legal Aid.

9.   References

1.   Stranieri, A. (1998) *Automated legal reasoning in discretionary domains.* PhD thesis, La Trobe University.
2.   Hart, H.L.A. (1961) *The concept of law.* Oxford: Clarendon Press
3.   Taruffo, M. (1998) Judicial decisions and artificial intelligence. *Artificial Intelligence and Law.* **6**, p 311-324
4.   Gale, F.G. (1996) Logic, rhetoric and legal writing. *Journal of Business & Technical Communication.* **10**, 2, p 203-213
5.   Hathaway. J.C. (1991) *The law of refugee status.* Toronto: Butterworths
6.   McHugh, M. H. (1999) The judicial method. *The Australian Law Journal.* **73**, p 37-518.
7.   *Breen v Williams* (1996) 186 CLR 71 at 115 per Gaudron and McHugh JJ
8.   MacCormack, D.N. (1981) *H.L.A.Hart.* Edward Arnold
9.   Christie, G. C., (1986). An Essay on Discretion. *Duke Law Journal.* P 747-778
10.   Bayles, M. D. (1990) *Procedural Justice. Allocating to Individuals.* Dordrecht: Kluwer
11.   Dworkin, R. (1977) *Taking rights seriously.* London: Duckworth
12.   Gardner, A. (1987) *An artificial intelligence approach to legal reasoning.* Cambridge, Massachusetts: The MIT Press
13.   Popple, J.D. (1993) SHYSTER: A pragmatic legal expert system. PhD thesis, The Australian National University.
14.   Smith, T. (1995) *Legal expert systems: Discussion of theoretical assumptions.* Oslo: Tano
15.   Bench-Capon, T.J. M. (1997) Argument in artificial intelligence and law. *Artificial Intelligence and Law.* **5**, p 249-261
16.   Krause, P.J. and Clarke, D.A. (1993) *Representing uncertain knowledge.* Dordrecht: Kluwer
17.   Tata, C. (1998) The application of judicial intelligence and 'rules' to systems supporting discretionary judicial decision-making. *Artificial Intelligence and Law.* **6**, p 203-230
18.   Zeleznikow, J. (1999) Building decision support systems in discretionary legal domains. (*in press*)
19.   Meikle, T.Z. (1999) A decision support architecture in refugee law. Paper presented at the 2nd *AustLII Conference on Computerisation of Law via the Internet*, University of Technology Sydney, July.
20.   Doyle, J. (1999) Judgement writing: Are there needs for change? *The Australian Law Journal.* **73**, p 737-742
21.   Lovegrove, A. (1999) Statistical information systems as a means to consistency and rationality in sentencing. *International Journal of Law and Information Technology.* **7**, 1, p 31-72
22.   Leenes, R. and Svensson, J. (1997) Supporting the legal practitioner: LKBS or Web? *Information & Communication Technology Law.* **6**, 3, p 217-229
23.   Wall, D.S. and Johnstone, J. (1997) Lawyers, information technology and legal practice: The use of information technology by provincial lawyers. *International Review of Law, Computers and Technology.* **11**, 1, p 117-128
24.   Leith, P. (1998) The judge and the computer: How best 'decision support'? *Artificial Intelligence and Law.* **6**, p 289-309
25.   Oskamp, A. and Tragter, M.W. (1997) Automated legal decision ssystems in practice: The mirror of reality. *Artificial Intelligence and Law.* **5**, p 291-322
26.   Oskamp, A., Tragter, M. W. and Groendijk, C. (1995) AI and law: What about the future? Letter to the Editor, *Artificial Intelligence and Law.* **3**, p 209-215

27. Santos, I. And Carvalho, J.A. (1998) Computer-based systems that support the structural, social, political and symbolic dimensions of work. *Requirements Engineering*. **3**, p 138-142

28. Ashley, K. (1991) Reasoning with cases and hypotheticals in HYPO. *International Journal of Man-Machine Studies*. **34**, p 753-796

29. Hogarth, J. (1988) *Computer and the law: Sentencing database system, user's guide*. Vancouver: LIST Corporation

30. Yearwood, J. and Stranieri, A. (1999) Integration of retrieval, reasoning and drafting for refugee law: A third generation legal knowledge based system. In Proceedings of *Seventh International Conference on Artificial Intelligence and Law, ICAIL' 99*. Oslo, July.

31. Rose, D.E. (1994) *A symbolic and connectionist approach to legal information retrieval*. San Francisco:Lawrence Erlbaum Associates

32. Daniels, J. and Rissland, E. (1997) Finding legally relevant passages in case opinions. In Proceedings of *the Sixth International Conference on Artificial Intelligence and Law, ICAIL '97*, University of Melbourne, Melbourne, July. p 29-38

33. Moens, M., Uyttendaele, C. and Dumortier, J. (1997) Abstracting of legal cases: The SALOMON experience. In Proceedings of the *Sixth International Conference on Artificial Intelligence and Law, ICAIL '97*. University of Melbourne, Melbourne, July. p 114-122

34. Yearwood, J. L. (1997) Case-based retrieval of Refugee Review Tribunal text cases. In Oskamp, A., De Mulder, R. V., van Noortwijk, C., Grtters, C. A. F. M., Ashley, K. and Gordon, T. (Eds) *Legal Knowledge Based Systems. JURIX: The Tenth Conference*, p 67-83.

35. Bench-Capon, T.J.M. and Staniford, G. (1995) PLAID – Proactive Legal Assistance. In Proceedings of the *Fifth International Conference on Artificial Intelligence and Law, ICAIL '95*, College Park, Maryland, May. p 81-87

36. Matthijssen, L. (1996) A task-based hyperindex for legal databases. In Kralingen van, R.W., Henrik van den, H.J., Prins, E.J., Sergot, M. and Zeleznikow, J. (1996) *Legal knowledge based systems: Foundations of legal knowledge systems. Jurix '96*. Tilburg University Press. The Netherlands. p 59-76

37. Aleven, V. and Ashley, K.D. (1994) An instructional environment for practising argumentation skills. In Proceedings of the *Twelfth National Conference on Artificial Intelligence*, AAAI'94, Seattle, WA, July. p 485-492

38. Aleven, V. and Ashley, K. D. (1996) How different is different? Arguing about the significance of similarities and differences, In Smith, I. And Faultings, B (eds), *Advances in Case-based Reasoning*, Third European Workshop, EWCBR'96, Berlin: Springer, p 2-15.

39. Stranieri, A., Yearwood, J. and Meikle, T. (2000) The dependency of discretion and consistency on knowledge representation. (*in press*)

40. Toulmin, S. (1958) *The Uses of Arguments*. Cambridge: Cambridge University Press 41. Hutton, N. (1995) Sentencing rationality and computer technology. *Journal of Law and Society*. **22**, p 549-557

41. Hutton, N. (1995) Sentencing rationality and computer technology. *Journal of Law and Society*. **22**, p 549-557

Orthofaces for Face Recognition

Bai Li & Voon Piao Siang

School of Computer Science & Information Technology
University of Nottingham
Nottingham UK
Email: bai@cs.nott.ac.uk

Abstract: This paper describes a novel face recognition method, the orthoface method. The method is efficient and invariant to variation in lighting conditions, facial expressions and alien objects. At the centre of the orthoface method is a set of basis vectors named the orthofaces. Orthofaces are more effective basis vectors from a discrimination viewpoint because each of them accounts for the individual features of a training face. We will explain the logic behind the orthoface method. We will also justify with both mathematical reasoning and experimental results why the orthoface method is the method that leads to effective classification strategies.

1. Introduction

Face recognition [1] [3] is a difficult task with many potential commercial and industrial applications ranging from real life monitoring and security systems to videoconferencing and virtual reality systems. In the past few years many face recognition researchers have shown interests in the eigenface method developed by the MIT Media Lab [6] [7] and numerous research results have been reported based on the method [2] [5] [8]. The method applies Principle Component Analysis [4] to reduce the dimensions of the face vectors by projecting the face vectors in an image space to a low dimensional face space spanned by the eigen vectors of a correlation matrix. It is understood that those eigen vectors are in the directions that maximize the scatter of the face vectors. This property is thought to be both good and bad for classification because it scatters the face vectors regardless they are of the same person or of different. Following this argument variants of the eigenface method have been developed to maximise the interclass scatter (faces of the different people) and to minimise the intraclass scatter (faces of the same person) [2].

We now analyse the two acclaimed properties of the eigenface method stated above. Firstly it is true that the eigenface method reduces the dimensions of the face vectors to no greater than the number of training faces. This is achieved by projecting the face vectors onto the face space spanned by the eigen vectors of the matrix XX', where X is the matrix with the training faces as its columns. The matrix XX' can be huge that it is more practical to calculate the eigen vectors of $X'X$ first and then multiply the results by X to obtain the eigen vectors of XX'. The logic behind this is the fact that if x is the eigen vector of $X'X$, then $XX'Xx = \lambda Xx$, which means Xx is an eigen vector of XX'. So if Q is the eigen matrix of $X'X$ then

$P = XQ$ is the eigen matrix of XX'. P is a $m \times n, r$ matrix, where r is the number of training faces. In fact the process can be simplified by calculating the eigen vectors of $X'X$ at the outset.

Secondly, contrary to the popular misconception, the eigenface method does not physically scatter the face vectors in the face space. The transformation that the face vectors have gone through from image space to face space is $Y = PX$, where X contains the face vectors represented in the image space and Y contains the face vectors represented in the face space. As P is an orthogonal matrix so the transformation from X to Y retains the Euclidean distances between the vectors. In fact the face vectors in X and in Y are the same set of faces vectors but viewed from different spaces spanned by different sets of basis vectors. Even if we calculate the eigen vectors of $(X - U)(X - U)'$ instead rather than those of XX', where U is the average face of the training faces, it is only means shifting the coordinate system to bring the mean vector U to the origin. The covariance matrix $(X-U)(X-U)'$ indicates the dispersion of the distribution. The eigen vectors are in the directions where the density of the distribution is maximum and the eigen values are the variances of the transformed distribution. The eigen vectors are optimal coordinate axes for the face space in terms of capturing the variance of the face vectors. When the axes are ordered in decreasing order of their corresponding eigen values, the scatter of the face vectors along the axes decreases and the axes along which the scatter is reasonably small can be discarded, that is, not all the eigen vectors are needed to represent the face vectors.

In summery, after the transformation from the image space to the face space, the positions of the face vectors remain the same but the coordinate axes are re-organised (moved around and redundant ones removed) to fit into the vectors better. So either in the image space or in the face space, a classical classification method based on some distance metric should face the same difficulty in drawing the decision boundaries, which means the eigenfaces may not be the optimal basis vectors from a discrimination viewpoint. Furthermore, dimension reduction is only necessary when the 'curse of dimensionality' is a problem. All the classical classifiers suffer from this problem because the accuracy of the classifiers depends on parameters that need to be estimated with a large number of training samples. However, it is known that some classifiers such as the nearest neighbour perform very well with high dimensional data. One of the reasons is that the dimension of the data represents only an upper bound on the intrinsic dimensionality of the data. Often there is a high degree of correlation among the dimensions and the data lies in a lower dimensional manifold within the n-dimensional image space. The distance computed on the full dimensional space is roughly the same as that within the manifold. This intrinsic dimensionality is much smaller than the upper bound the curse is mitigated. Moreover, face recognition using the eigenface method may still involve correlation, calculating the distances of a test face to all the training faces to find the closest match in distance, which is computationally expensive. To improve classification rate, a classification method is often combined with variable condensing or variable subset selection to reduce the sample size and to reshape the decision boundaries so that samples of different classes stay away from one another.

We have developed the orthoface method for face recognition that allows dimension reduction, as well as boundary reshaping for efficient classification. In the following sections we will describe the method in detail and we will present experimental results obtained so far.

2. The Orthoface Method

What motivated us to develop the eigen face method was to find a new set of basis vectors that have smaller dimension than the original face vectors and onto which the projections of the face vectors discriminate the faces better. It occurred to us that for the basis vectors to represent the training faces better they have to be in some way made with the training face vectors and the results have to be orthogonal to each other. Naturally we resort to the Gram-Schimidt orthogonalization process. This allows us to create new basis vectors $\lfloor \beta_1 \quad \beta_2 \quad \beta_3 \quad \cdots \quad \beta_n \rfloor$ from vectors $\lfloor \alpha_1 \quad \alpha_2 \quad \alpha_3 \quad \cdots \quad \alpha_n \rfloor$, and under the new basis vectors $\lfloor \alpha_1 \quad \alpha_2 \quad \alpha_3 \quad \cdots \quad \alpha_n \rfloor$ is an upper triangle matrix:

$$\begin{bmatrix} k_{11} & k_{21} & k_{31} & \cdots & k_{n1} \\ 0 & k_{22} & k_{32} & & k_{n2} \\ 0 & 0 & k_{33} & & \vdots \\ 0 & 0 & 0 & \ddots & \vdots \\ \vdots & \vdots & \vdots & \cdots & knn \end{bmatrix}, \quad where \quad k_{ij} = \frac{(\alpha_i, \beta_j)}{(\beta_j, \beta_j)}$$

Applying the same reasoning to the domain of face recognition, the new basis vectors are named orthofaces, and the columns in the upper triangle matrix are the face vectors represented in the face space. The orthoface face recognition method can be stated as follows:

i) Produce a new set of basis vectors (orthofaces) $\left[f_1^t, f_2^t, \cdots, f_N^t \right]$ from $\left[f_1, f_2, \cdots, f_N \right]$, using the formula

$$f_i^{'} = \sum_{j=1}^{i-1} -\frac{(f_j, f_j^{'})}{(f_j^{'}, f_j^{'})} f_j^{'} + f_i \cdots (*)$$

ii) Represent each test face vector by the orthofaces. This is done by projecting the test face vector onto the face space spanned by the orthofaces:

$$f_i = k_{i1} f_1' + k_{i2} f_2' + \cdots + k_{iN} f_N', \text{ where } k_{ij} = (f_i, b_j),$$

$$b_j = f_j' / |f_j'|.$$

From the way that the orthoface vectors are obtained we can see that each orthoface itself is a linear combination of the training face vectors. The number of training faces involved in making an orthoface increases by one at a time, with the first orthoface being the first training face, second orthoface beiing a linear combination of the first orthoface and second training face, and so on. To be more precise, each orthoface is constructed by other orthofaces constructed already, and a new training face.

f1	f2	f3	f4	f5
Orthofaces				
1	0.0116	-0.4533	-0.1614	-0.3594
0	0.9999	-0.5172	-0.4483	-0.0163
0	0	0.726	-0.3729	-0.4558
0	0	0	0.7961	-0.8141
0	0	0	0	0
Test faces				
0.0586	-0.1733	-0.8399	-0.1314	0.0116
0.9832	0.9802	0.5097	0.9891	0.9999
-0.0543	0.053	0.1647	-0.0575	0
-0.164	-0.0802	0.087	0.0341	0
0	0	0	0	0
Euclidea Distance				
1.8829	2.3466	3.6799	2.2629	1.9769
0.0323	0.0438	1.0001	0.025	0
3.149	2.7798	1.5266	2.9874	3.0448
3.1213	2.9902	2.1701	2.7472	2.9004
1.7576	1.8252	1.7047	1.941	2.0409
Reconstruction error: 1.276749e-007				

f1	f2	f3	f4	f5
Eigenfaces				
0.415	-0.0084	0.439	-0.6285	-0.6285
-0.3962	0.5902	0.169	0.0964	-0.5157
-0.6617	0.1952	0.2397	-0.5796	0.792
0.4826	0.7833	-0.8493	-0.5097	0.162
0	0	0	0	0
Test faces				
0.0162	-0.0146	-0.2418	-0.1274	-0.0084
0.4463	0.6279	0.7527	0.6362	0.5902
0.2753	0.3744	0.6067	0.2595	0.1952
0.8513	0.6822	-0.0827	0.7153	0.7833
0	0	0	0	0
Euclidean Distance				
1.8829	2.3466	3.6799	2.2629	1.9769
0.0323	0.0438	1.0001	0.025	0
3.149	2.7798	1.5266	2.9874	3.0448
3.1213	2.9902	2.1701	2.7472	2.9004
1.7576	1.8252	1.7047	1.941	2.0409
Reconstruction error: 1.299204e-007				

Both eigenface and orthoface methods reconstruct the original faces quite accurately. This is shown in the table above. 5 training faces of different person are used to construct the orthofaces and 5 test faces are of the same person, the second training face. The Euclidean distance measured between a test face and an orthoface. Each row in the Euclidean distance section of the table stores the distances of the 5 test faces to an orthofaces. As can be seen from the table that the distances to the second orthoface are the smallest for all the test faces, indicating that the test faces belongs to the same class as the second orthoface.

3. Recognition

Like the eigen face method, the representation of the faces using the orthoface method does not change the Euclidean distances between face vector. However,
The projection coefficients of any given face onto the orthofaces can indicate its class. For example if there is a relatively large projection coefficient onto an orthoface, the face is likely to be from the same class as the training face that is last involved in constructing the orthoface (each orthoface is constructed by the existing orthofaces and a new training face). This suggests a classification method based on the projection coefficients. To see this clearly we need to have a closer look at equation with which the orthofaces are obtained. This is shown below.

$$f_i' = \sum_{j=1}^{i-1} -\frac{\left(f_j, f_j'\right)}{\left(f_j', f_j'\right)} f_j' + f_i \cdots (*) .$$

We now give an informal proof to our claim above. From (*) it is clear that the ith orthoface is a linear combination of the first i-1 orthofaces and the ith training face. When a face vector f is projected onto the orthofaces f_j', that is, when f is represented as $f = k_{i1} f_1' + k_{i2} f_2' + \cdots + k_{iN} f_N'$, the projection of f on the ith orthoface f_i' is determined by the dot product of f and f_i', which is the weighted linear sum of doc products of $f \bullet f_j'$ (j<i) and $f \bullet f_i'$. If the projection of f onto a certain f_i' stands out from the rest, because f_i' and f_j' (j<i) are orthogonal, by deduction the projection of f on other orthofaces involved in the construction of f_i' would be negligible. So the significance of the projection of f onto f_i' must be due to the significance of projection of f onto f_i , that is $f \bullet f_i$, which means f correlates particularly well with f_i , so it is reasonable to classified f as belonging to the same class as f_i . In summary, in the orthospace a test face would have a big projection on the orthoface whose last constructing vector is of the same class as the test vector and this provides a unique classification method for face recognition.

Notice that in the example orthofaces shown in Figure 1, all face vectors will have the largest projection coefficients on the first orthoface and second largest coefficient on the second orthoface. This is expected because the light intensity of each face is more similar to the first two humanlike orthofaces than to the rest of ghostly looking orthofaces. This seems to have invalidated the classification method based on projection coefficients. However, the problem can be easily solved by involving, say, the average face of the training faces in the construction of the orthofaces. The orthogonalization process may then start with the average face as the first orthoface, and the construction of each orthoface involves the previously constructed orthofaces and an extra training face. Alternatively, based on the upper triangle characteristic of the projection coefficient matrix of the training faces, classification can be done by checking, starting from the last orthoface, where the magnitude of the projections drops dramatically. The test face is most likely from the same class as the orthoface where the drop occurs.

4. Experimental results

Face recognition essentially involves the following three processes: pre-processing faces, representing faces, and classifying faces. Our experiments follow these processes. In pre-processing the background of the faces are removed as much as possible as shown in Figure 1 below.

 =>

Figure 1

The face images used in our experiments are from Yale databases. An example set of training faces and their orthofaces are shown in Figure 2 (a) and (c). It is not difficult to see the resemblance between these two sets of images, the ith orthoface resembles the ith training face, and the bigger the value of i, the more resemblance is shown between the ith orthoface and the ith training face. In Figure 2 (c) and (d) we have put side by side the orthofaces and the negative images of the training faces. The orthofaces are like some kinds of negatives of the training faces. By creating the orthofaces, the effect is that the training faces are made completely uncorrelated (orthogonal) and yet still remain their individual characteristics.

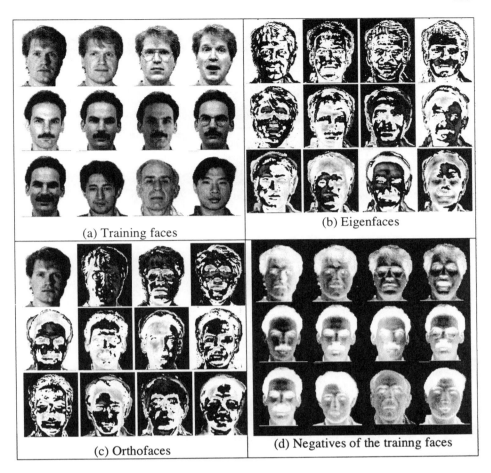

(a) Training faces

(b) Eigenfaces

(c) Orthofaces

(d) Negatives of the trainng faces

Figure 2

In our first experiment to show how the method works we use the average face of each person as a training face. 5 training faces are obtained to create the orthofaces, and 38 test faces are used, see Figure 3 and Figure 4. All the training faces are made from normal faces, no alien objects or lighting conditions are involved. Test faces are of variant facial expressions and lighting conditions to the training faces.

To see how the projection coefficients can be used to classify a test face, we have plotted the projection coefficients as shown in the Appendix. As the orthofaces are constructed with the first training face as the first orthoface, the projection coefficients of all the test faces onto the first orthofaces are quite large so we have omitted them. In the experiment the only mis-classified faces from the above experiments are the ones with heavy shadows as a result of heavy lighting conditions. This is understandable as the dark shadow obscures the outline of the face, any face recognition method, even humans would find it difficult to recognise.

264

Figure 3

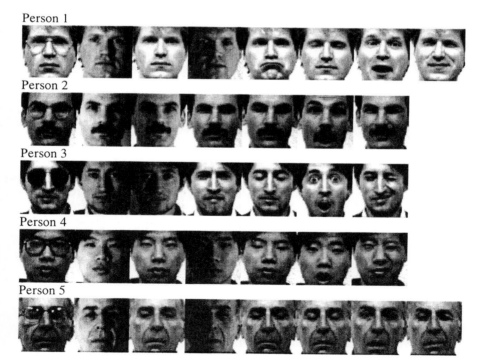

Figure 4

The orthoface method can cope with heavy lighting conditions or alien objects by having several training vectors for each person. These training vectors include faces under lighting condition, with glasses, different orientations etc. The orthofaces are then divided into groups with each group representing one class. The recognition process is to project the test face onto these basis vectors to see which group the test face correlates the best, that is, having the biggest projection coefficient.

5. Conclusion

In this paper we have described the development of a new method, the orthoface method, for face recognition. A face image can be represented as a vector in a multi-dimensional image space. Many face recognition methods use Principle Component Analysis to reduce the dimension of this image space. However, in recognition all of the components of a test face vector have to be used to compare with those of the stored face models. The advantage of the orthoface method is that it provides more effective basis vectors and that individual components of a test face can indicate the class of the test face. The new basis vectors serve as a gauge that allows face classification to be done by an one-off projection of a test face onto the basis vectors rather than by comparing it with each of the face models. The method works well with different lighting conditions and alien objects.

6. References

[1]   Anil K. Jain, Robert P.W. Duin, and Jianchang Mao, Statistical Pattern Recognition: A Review, IEEE Transactions on Pattern Analysis and Machine Intelligence, Vol. 22, No1, January 2000.

[2]   Belhumeur P., Hespanhu J. and Kriegman D., Eigen Faces vs. Fisherfaces: Recognition Using Class Specific Linear Projection, IEEE Transactions on Pattern Analysis and Machine Intelligence, Vol. 19, July 1997.

[3]   Chellappa, R, Wilson, C., and Sirohey, S., Human and Maachine Recognition of Faces: A Survey, Proceedings of IEEE, Vol 83, No. 5, 1995.

[4]   Jolliffe, I.T., Principal Component Analysis. Springer-Verlag; New York; 1986.

[5]   Pentland, A., Moghaddam, B., and Starner T.. View-Based and Modular Eigenspaces for Face Recognition. IEEE Conference on Computer Vision & Pattern Recognition, 1994

[6]   Turk, M. & Pentland, A., Eigenfaces for recognition, Journal of Cognitive Neuroscience, 3(1), 1991.

[7]   Turk, M. & Pentland, A., Face recognition using eigenfaces, Proceedings of the IEEE Computer Society Conference on Computer Vision and Pattern Recognition, June Maui, Hawaii, 1991.

[8]   Welsh, J. W., and Shah. D., Facial-Feature Image Coding Using Principal Components, Electronic Letters. Vol. 28, October, 1992.

7. Appendix

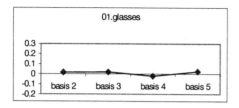

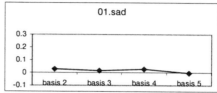

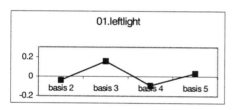

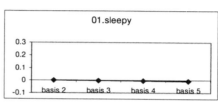

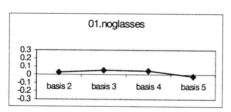

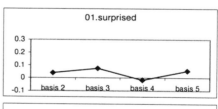

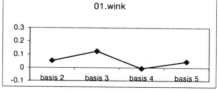

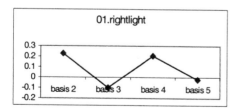

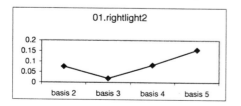

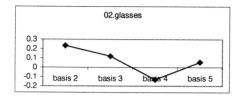

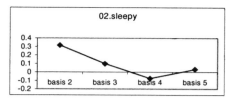

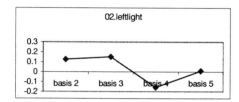

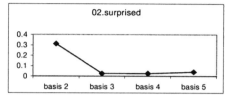

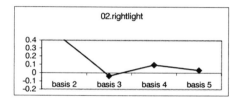

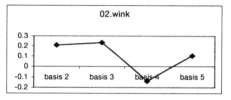

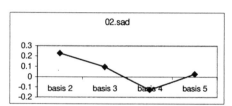

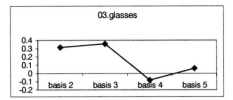

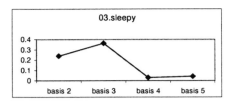

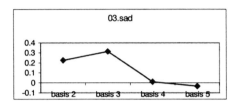

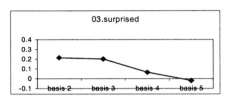

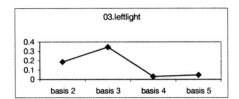

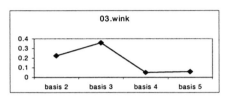

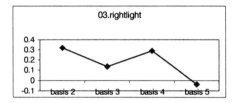

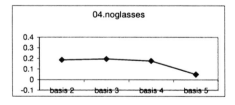

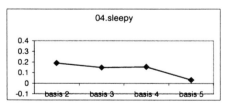

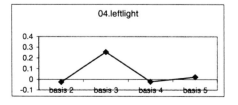

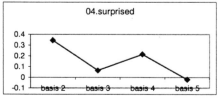

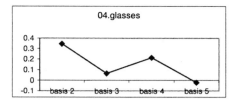

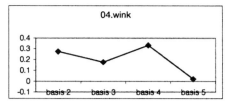

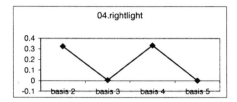

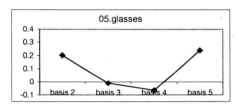

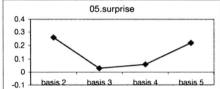

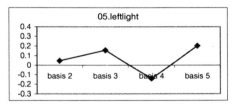

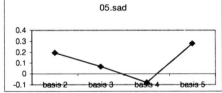

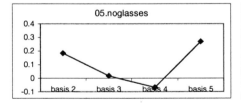

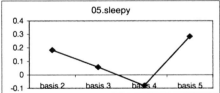

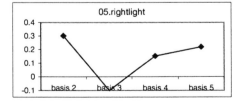

Figure 5

SESSION 5

KNOWLEDGE ENGINEERING

Supporting knowledge-driven processes in a multiagent process management system

John Debenham
University of Technology, Sydney
debenham@it.uts.edu.au

Abstract. A knowledge-driven process is guided by its 'process knowledge' and 'performance knowledge'. The goal of a knowledge-driven process may not be fixed and may mutate. Knowledge-driven processes are a characteristic of emergent processes. Emergent processes are business processes that are not predefined and are ad hoc. Process knowledge typically contains a substantial component of general knowledge and it is generally infeasible to build a system that represents it. A multiagent process management system provides substantial support for knowledge-driven processes. This system assists the users to manage these processes. The agents negotiate with each other to distribute the responsibility for managing sub-processes. Emergent processes may have goal-directed sub-processes if this is so then these sub-processes are completely managed by this system.

1. Introduction

Emergent processes are business processes that are not predefined and are ad hoc. These processes typically take place at the higher levels of organisations [1], and are distinct from production workflows [2]. Emergent processes are opportunistic in nature whereas production workflows are routine. How an emergent process will terminate may not be known until the process is well advanced. Further, the tasks involved in an emergent process are typically not predefined and emerge as the process develops. Those tasks may be carried out by collaborative groups as well as by individuals [3]. For example, in a manufacturing organisation an emergent process could be triggered by "lets consider introducing a new product line for the US market".

From a process management perspective, emergent processes may contain "knowledge-driven" sub-processes as well as conventional "goal-driven" sub-processes. A *knowledge-driven process* is guided by its 'process knowledge' and 'performance knowledge'. The goal of a knowledge-driven process may not be fixed and may mutate. On the other hand, the management of a *goal-driven process* is guided by its goal which is fixed. A multiagent system to manage the "goal-driven" processes is described in [4]. In that system each human user is assisted by an agent which is based on a generic three-layer, BDI hybrid agent architecture. The term *individual* refers to a user/agent pair. That system is extended here to support knowledge-driven processes and so to support emergent process management. The general business of managing knowledge-driven processes is illustrated in Fig. 1, and will be discussed in Sec. 2. The following sections are principally a description of how the system in [4] has been extended to support the management of knowledge-driven processes. Sec. 3 discusses the management of the process knowledge. Sec. 4 describes the performance knowledge which is communicated between agents in contract net bids for work. Sec. 5 compares various strategies for evaluating these bids.

Process management is an established application area for multi-agent systems [5]. One valuable feature of process management as an application area is that 'real' experiments may be performed with the cooperation of local administrators [4]. The system described here has been trialed on emergent process management applications within university administration.

2.   Process management

Emergent processes [1] are opportunistic in nature whereas production workflows [2] are routine. Emergent processes are inherently distributed and involve asynchronous work [6]. The tasks involved in an emergent process are typically not predefined and 'emerge' as the process develops [7].

Following [2] a *business process* is "a set of one or more linked procedures or activities which collectively realise a business objective or policy goal, normally within the context of an organisational structure defining functional roles and relationships". Implicit in this definition is the idea that a process may be repeatedly decomposed into linked sub-processes until those sub-processes are "activities" which are atomic pieces of work. [viz (op.cit) "An *activity* is a description of a piece of work that forms one logical step within a process."]. A particular process is called a (process) *instance*. An instance may require that certain things should be done; such things are called *tasks*. A *trigger* is an event that leads to the creation of an instance. The *goal* of an instance is a state that the instance is trying to achieve. The *termination condition* of an instance is a condition which if satisfied during the life of an instance causes that instance to be destroyed whether its goal has been achieved or not. The *patron* of an instance is the individual who is responsible for managing the life of that instance. At any time in a process instance's life, the *history* of that instance is the sequence of prior sub-goals and the prior sequence of knowledge inputs to the instance. The history is "knowledge of all that has happened already".

Three classes of business process are defined in terms of their management properties (ie in terms of how they may be managed).

• A *task-driven process* has a unique decomposition into a—possibly conditional— sequence of activities. Each of these activities has a goal and is associated with a task that "always" achieves this goal. Production workflows are typically task-driven processes.

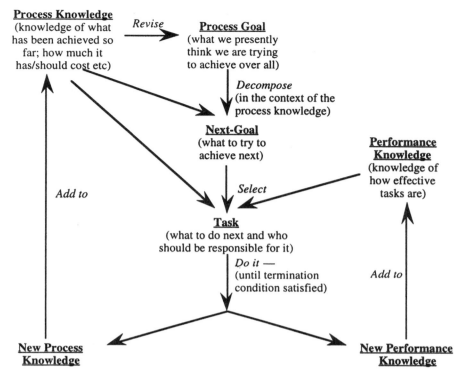

Fig. 1. Knowledge-driven process management (a simplified view)

- A *goal-driven process* has a process goal, and achievement of that goal is the termination condition for the process. The process goal may have various decompositions into sequences of sub-goals where these sub-goals are associated with (atomic) activities and so with tasks. Some of these sequences of tasks may work better than others, and there may be no way of knowing which is which [8]. A task for an activity may fail outright, or may be otherwise ineffective at achieving its goal. In other words, failure is a feature of goal-driven processes. If a task fails then another way to achieve the process goal may be sought.

- A *knowledge-driven process* may have a process goal, but the goal may be vague and may mutate [9]. Mutations are determined by the process patron, often in the light of knowledge generated during the process. At each stage in the performance of a knowledge-driven process the "next goal" is chosen by the process patron; this choice is made using general knowledge about the context of the process—called the *process knowledge*. The process patron also chooses the tasks to achieve that next goal; this choice may be made using general knowledge about the effectiveness

	Task-driven	Goal-driven	Knowledge-driven
Process goal	Determined by process patron, remains fixed	Determined by process patron, remains fixed	Determined by process patron, may mutate
Process termination condition	Process goal achieved	Process goal achieved	Determined by process patron
Next goal	Determined by instance history	Determined by instance history	Determined by process patron
Next task	Determined by instance history and next goal—should achieve next goal	Chosen (somehow) on the basis of instance history and next goal—may not achieve next goal	Chosen by process patron to generate process knowledge.
Next activity termination condition	Next goal achieved	Next goal achieved, if it fails then try another way	Determined by process patron

Fig 2. Properties of the three types of process

of tasks—called the *performance knowledge.* So in so far as the process goal gives direction to goal-driven—and task-driven—processes, the process knowledge gives direction to knowledge-driven processes. The management of knowledge-driven processes is considerably more complex than the other two classes of process. But, knowledge-driven processes are "not all bad"—they typically have goal-driven sub-processes which may be handled in conventional way. A simplified view of knowledge-driven process management is shown in Fig. 1.
Properties of the three classes of process are shown in Fig. 2.

Task-driven processes may be managed by a simple reactive agent architecture based on event-condition-action rules. Goal-driven processes may be modelled as state and activity charts [10] and managed by plans that can accommodates failure [11]. Such a planning system may provide the deliberative reasoning mechanism in a BDI agent architecture [11] and is used in a goal-driven process management system [4] where tasks are represented as plans for goal-driven processes. But the success of execution of a plan for a goal-driven process is not necessarily related to the achievement of its goal. One reason for this is that an instance may make progress outside the process management system—two players could go for lunch for example. So each plan for a goal-driven process should terminate with a check of whether its goal has been achieved.

Managing knowledge-driven processes is rather more difficult, see Fig. 1. The complete representation, never mind the maintenance, of the process knowledge would be an enormous job. But the capture of at least some of the knowledge generated during a process instance may not be difficult if the tasks chosen used virtual documents such as workspace technology, for example. The system assists with the presentation of the new process knowledge to the patron when it can. Managing the process knowledge is discussed in Sec. 4. Some performance knowledge is not difficult to capture, represent and maintain. For example, measurements of how long an individual took to complete a sub-process can be very useful. So in the system described here, the process knowledge is left in the heads of the patron or nominated delegates, and the performance knowledge is captured by the system. The initial selection, and possible subsequent mutation, of the process goal is performed by the patron using the process knowledge, and so these actions are completely unsupported by the system, see Fig. 1. Task selection is partly supported by the system which can, for example, be given authority to form a committee, capture the expertise from that committee and forward that expertise to the patron in due course. In this way the system provides considerable assistance in the management of knowledge-driven processes. Further, if a now-goal is associated with a goal-driven, or task-driven, sub-process then the management system may be given full responsibility for the management of that sub-process as long as it contains the expertise to do so.

3. Process knowledge and the goals

This section refers to the left-hand side of Fig. 1, and to the relationship between the process knowledge, the process goal and the next-goal. This is the intractable part of knowledge-driven process management.

The process knowledge in any real application includes an enormous amount of general and common sense knowledge. For example, the process trigger "the time is right to look at the US market" may be based on a large quantity of current knowledge and a fund of experiential knowledge. So the system does not attempt to represent the process knowledge in any way; it is seen to be largely in the heads of the users. The system does assist in the maintenance of the process knowledge by ensuring that any virtual documents generated during an activity in a knowledge-driven sub-process are passed to the process patron when the activity is complete. Virtual documents are either interactive web documents or workspaces in the LiveNet workspace system [6] which is used to handle virtual meetings and discussions.

The system records, but does not attempt to understand the process goal. Any possible revisions the process goal are carried out by the patron without assistance from the system. Likewise the decomposition of the process goal to decide "what to do next"—the next-goal. It may appear that the system does not do very much at all! If the next-goal is the goal of a goal-driven process—which it may well be—then the system may be left to manage it as long as it has plans in its plan library to achieve that next-goal. If the system does not have plans to achieve such a goal then the user may be able to quickly assemble such a plan from existing components in the plan library. The organisation of the plan library is a free-form, hierarchic filing system designed completely by each user. Such a plan only specifies what has to be done at the host agent. If a plan sends something to another agent with a sub-goal attached it is up to that other agent to design a plan to deal with that sub-goal. If the next-goal is the goal of a knowledge-driven process then the procedure illustrated in Fig. 1 commences at the level of that goal.

So for this part of the procedure, the agent provides assistance with updating the process knowledge, and if a next-goal is the goal of a goal-driven sub-process then the system will manage that sub-process, perhaps after being given a plan to do so.

4. Performance knowledge

This section refers to the right-hand side of Fig. 1. That is the representation and maintenance of the performance knowledge. The performance knowledge is used to support task selection—ie who does what—through inter-agent negotiation. So its role is a comparative one; it is not necessarily intended to have absolute currency. With this use in mind, the *performance knowledge* comprises performance statistics on the operation of the system down to a fine grain of detail. These performance statistics are proffered by an agent in bids for work. To evaluate a bid, the receiving agent defines payoff in terms of these statistics. In the case of a parameter, p, that can reasonably be assumed to be normally distributed, the estimate for the mean of p, μ_p, is revised on the basis of the i'th observation ob_i to $\mu_{p_{new}} = (1 - \alpha) \times ob_i + \alpha \times \mu_{p_{old}}$ which, given a starting value $\mu_{p_{initial}}$, and some constant α, $0 < \alpha < 1$, approximates the

geometric mean $\dfrac{\sum\limits_{i=1}^{n} \alpha^{i-1} \times ob_i}{\sum\limits_{i=1}^{n} \alpha^{i-1}}$ where $i = 1$ is the most recent observation. In the

same way, an estimate for $\sqrt{\frac{2}{\pi}}$ times the standard deviation of p, σ_p, is revised on the basis of the i'th observation ob_i to $\sigma_{p_{new}} = (1 - \alpha) \times |ob_i - \mu_{p_{old}}| + \alpha \times \sigma_{p_{old}}$ which, given a starting value $\sigma_{p_{initial}}$, and some constant α, $0 < \alpha < 1$, approximates

the geometric mean $\dfrac{\sum\limits_{i=1}^{n} \alpha^{i-1} \times |ob_i - \mu_p|}{\sum\limits_{i=1}^{n} \alpha^{i-1}}$. The constant α is chosen on the basis of

the stability of the observations. For example, if $\alpha = 0.85$ then "everything more than twenty trials ago" contributes less than 5% to the weighted mean; if $\alpha = 0.70$ then "everything more than ten trials ago" contributes less than 5% to the weighted mean, and if $\alpha = 0.50$ then "everything more than five trials ago" contributes less than 5% to the weighted mean.

Each individual agent/user pair maintains estimates for the three parameters: *time*, *cost* and *likelihood of success* for the execution of all of its plans, sub-plans and activities. "All things being equal" these parameters are assumed to be normally distributed—the case when "all things are *not* equal" is considered below. Time is the total time taken to termination. Cost is the actual cost of the of resources allocated. For example, if a person has a virtual document in their in-tray then the time observation will be the total time that that document spent with that person, and the cost may derived from the time that the person actually spent working on that document. The likelihood of success observations are binary—ie "success" or "fail"— and so the likelihood of success parameter is binomially distributed, which is approximately normally distributed under the standard conditions. These three parameters are useful, but the *value* parameter—that is the value added to a process by a plan or individual—is at least as important.

Unfortunately, *value* is often very difficult to measure. For example in assessing the value of an appraisal for a bank loan, if the loan is granted then when it has matured its value may be measured, but if the loan is not granted then no conclusion may be drawn. The value of sub-processes are typically "less measurable" than this bank loan example. Although some progressive organisations employ experienced staff specifically to assess the value of the work of others. The existing system does not attempt to measure *value*; each individual represents the perceived *value* of each other individual's work as a constant for that individual.

Finally, measurements of the *allocate* parameter for each individual are the amount of work w_i^j, allocated to individual j in discrete time period i. In a similar way to *time* and *cost*, the mean *allocate* estimate for individual j is made using $allocate_{new} = (1 - \alpha) \times w^j + \alpha \times allocate_{old}$, where w^j is the most recent observation for individual j. In this formula the weighting factor α is chosen on the basis of the number of individuals in the system, and the relationships between the length of the discrete time interval and the expected length of time to deal with the work. The allocate parameter does not represent workload. For example, if responsibility is delegated and then re-delegated, the *allocate* estimate of the first individual is not reduced. The *allocate* parameter is used by delegation strategies that address the density with which individuals are asked to do things. The *allocate* parameter is not normally distributed and the standard deviation is not estimated. The *allocate* and *value* estimates are associated with individuals. The *time*, *cost* and *likelihood of success* estimates are attached to plans.

The three parameters *time*, *cost* and *likelihood of success* are assumed to be normally distributed subject to "all things being equal". If working conditions are reasonably stable then this assumption is acceptable, but the presence of external environmental influences may invalidate it. One virtue of the assumption of normality is that it provides a basis on which to query unexpected observations. Having made observation ob_{i+1} for parameter p, estimates for μ_p and σ_p are calculated. Then the next observation, ob_i, should lie in the confidence interval: ($\mu_p \pm \alpha \times \sigma_p$) to some chosen degree of certainty. For example, this degree of certainty is 95% if

$\alpha = 1.645$. The set of observations $\{ob_i\}$ can progressively change without individual observations lying outside this confidence interval; for example, an individual may be gradually getting better at doing things. But if an observation lies outside this confidence interval then there is grounds, to the chosen degree of certainty, to ask why it is outside.

Inferred explanations of *why* an observation is outside expected limits may sometimes be extracted from observing the interactions with the users and other agents involved. For example, if Person X is unexpectedly slow in attending to a certain process instance then a simple interchange with X's agent may reveal that Person X will be working on the company's annual report for the next six days; this may be one reason for the unexpected observation. Inferred knowledge such as this gives *one possible cause* for the observed behaviour; so such knowledge enables us to *refine*, but *not* to *replace*, the historical estimates of parameters.

The measurement ob_i may lie outside the confidence interval for four types of reason:

1) there has been a permanent change in the environment or in the process management system—the measurement ob_i is now the expected value for μ_p —in which case the estimates $\mu_{P_{old}}$ and $\sigma_{P_{old}}$ should be re-initialised.

2) there has been a temporary change in the environment or in the process management system and the measurements $\{ob_i\}$ are expected to be perturbed in some way for some time—in which case the reason, Γ, for this expected perturbation should be sought. For example, a new member of staff may have been delegated the responsibility—temporarily—for this sub-process. Or, for example, a database component of the system may be behaving erratically.

3) there has been no change in the environment or in the process management system and the unexpected measurement ob_i is due to some feature γ that distinguishes the nature of this sub-process instance from those instances that were used to calculate $\mu_{P_{old}}$ and $\sigma_{P_{old}}$. In other words, what was thought to be a single sub-process type is really two or more different—but possibly related—process types. In which case a new process is created and the estimates $\mu_{P_{old}}$ and $\sigma_{P_{old}}$ are initialised for that process.

4) there has been no change in the environment or in the process management system and the nature of the most recent process instance is no different from previous instances—the unexpected measurement ob_i is due to—possibly combined— fluctuations in the performance of individuals or other systems.

In option 2) above the reason Γ is sometimes inferred by the system itself. This has been achieved in cases when a user appears to be preoccupied working on another task. If the reason Γ is to be taken into account then some forecast of the future effect of Γ is required. If such a forecast effect can be quantified—perhaps by simply asking a user— then the perturbed values of $\{ob_i\}$ are corrected to $\{ob_i \mid \Gamma\}$ otherwise the perturbed values are ignored.

5. Task Selection

This section concerns the selection of a task for a given now-goal as shown in the middle of Fig. 1. The selection of a plan to achieve a next goal typically involves deciding *what* to do and selecting *who* to ask to assist in doing it. The selection of what to do and who to do it can not be subdivided because one person may be good and one form of task and bad at others. So the "what" and the "who" are considered together. The system provides assistance in making this decision. Sec. 5 describes how performance knowledge is attached to each plan and sub-plan. For plans that involve one individual only this is done for instantiated plans. That is there are estimates for each individual and plan pair. In this way the system offers advice on choosing between individual A doing X and individual B doing Y. For plans that involve more than one individual this is done for abstract, uninstantiated plans only. This is something of a compromise but avoids the system attempting to do the impossible—for example, maintaining estimates on performance of every possible composition of committee. This does not weaken the system if a plan to form a committee is embedded in a plan that gives an individual the responsibility for forming that committee, because estimates are gathered for the performance of the second of these.

There are two basic modes in which the selection of "who" to ask is done. First the *authoritarian* mode in which an individual is told to do something. Second the *negotiation* mode in which individuals are asked to express an interest in doing something. This second mode is implemented using contract nets with focussed addressing [12] with inter-agent communication being performed in KQML [13]. When contact net bids are received the successful bidder has to be identified. So no matter which mode is used, a decision has to be made as to who to select. The use of a multi-agent system to manage processes expands the range of feasible strategies for delegation from the authoritarian strategies described above to strategies based on negotiation between individuals. Negotiation-based strategies that involves negotiation for each process instance are not feasible in manual systems for every day tasks due to the cost of negotiation. If the agents in an agent-based system are responsible for this negotiation then the cost of negotiation is may be negligible. A mechanism is described here to automate this negotiation.

If the agent making a bid to perform a task has a plan for achieving that task then the user may permit the agent to construct the bid automatically. As the bids consist of six meaningful quantities, the user may opt to construct the bid manually. A bid consists of the five pairs of real numbers (Constraint, Allocate, Success, Cost, Time). The pair *constraint* is an estimate of the earliest time that the individual could address the task—ie ignoring other non-urgent things to be done, and an estimate of the time that the individual would normally address the task if it "took its place in the in-tray". The pairs Allocate, Success, Cost and Time are estimates of the mean and standard deviation of the corresponding parameters as described above. The receiving agent then:

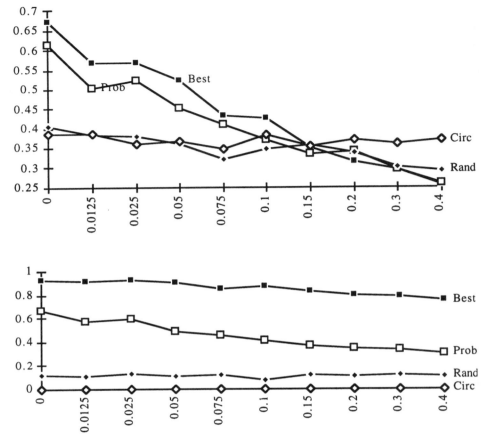

Fig 3. Payoff (top figure) and triple duplications (bottom figure) against the rebel factor
for a learning rate = 0.1, death factor = 0.05, and α = 0.6.

• attaches a subjective view of the *value* of the bidding individual;
• assesses the extent to which a bid should be downgraded—or not considered at all—
because it violates process constraints, and
• selects an acceptable bid, if any, possibly by applying its 'delegation strategy'.
If there are no acceptable bids then the receiving agent "thinks again".

5.1 The delegation strategy

A *delegation strategy* is a strategy for deciding who to give responsibility to for doing what. A user specifies the delegation strategy that is used by the user's agent to evaluate bids. In doing this the user has considerable flexibility first in defining payoff and second in specifying the strategy itself. Practical strategies in manual systems can be quite elementary; delegation is a job which some humans are not very good at. A delegation strategy may attempt to balance some of the three conflicting principles: maximising payoff, maximising opportunities for poor performers to improve and balancing workload. Payoff is defined by the user and could be some combination of the expected value added to the process, the expected time and/or cost to deal with the process, and the expected likelihood of the process leading to a satisfactory conclusion [14].

The system provides assistance to the user by suggesting how delegation could be performed using a method that the user has specified in terms of the tools described below. The user can opt to let the system delegate automatically, or can opt to delegate manually.

Given a sub-process, suppose that we have some expectation of the payoff D_i as a result of choosing the i'th individual (ie agent and user pair) from the set of candidates $\{X_1,...,X_i,...,X_n\}$ to take responsibility for it. A *delegation strategy* at time τ is specified as $S = \{P_1,...,P_i,...,P_n\}$ where P_i is the probability of delegating responsibility at time τ for a given task to individual X_i chosen from $\{X_1,...,X_i,...,X_n\}$. The system suggests an individual/task pair stochastically using the delegation strategy.

Corporate culture may determine the delegation strategy. Four delegation strategies are described. If corporate culture is to choose the individual whose expected payoff is maximal then the delegation strategy *best* is:

$$P_i = \begin{cases} \dfrac{1}{m} & \textit{if } X_i \text{ is such that } Pr(X_i \gg) \text{ is maximal} \\ \\ 0 & \textit{otherwise} \end{cases}$$

where $Pr(X_i \gg)$ means "the probability that X_i will have the highest payoff" and m is such that there are m individuals for whom $Pr(X_i \gg)$ is maximal. In the absence of any other complications, the strategy *best* attempts to maximise expected payoff. Using this strategy, an individual who performs poorly may never get work. Another strategy *prob* also favours high payoff but gives all individuals a chance, sooner or later, and is defined by $P_i = Pr(X_i \gg)$. The strategies *best* and *prob* have the feature of 'rewarding' quality work (ie. high payoff) with more work. If corporate culture dictates that individuals should be treated equally but at random then the delegation strategy *random* is $P_i = \dfrac{1}{n}$. If the corporate culture dictates that each task should be allocated to m individuals in strict rotation then the delegation strategy *circulate* is:

$$P_i = \begin{cases} 1 & \textit{if } \text{this is the i'th trial and } i \equiv 0 \text{ (modulo n)} \\ 0 & \textit{otherwise} \end{cases}$$

The strategies *random* and *circulate* attempt to balance workload and ignore expected payoff. The strategy *circulate* only has meaning in a fixed population, and so has limited use.

A practical strategy that attempts to balance maximising "expected payoff for the next delegation" with "improving available skills in the long term" could be constructed if there was a model for the expected improvement in skills—ie a model for the rate at which individuals learn. This is not considered here.

An *admissible* delegation strategy has the properties:
- *if* $\Pr(X_i \, ») > \Pr(X_j \, »)$ *then* $P_i > P_j$
- *if* $\Pr(X_i \, ») = \Pr(X_j \, »)$ *then* $P_i = P_j$
- $P_i > 0 \ (\forall i)$

So the three strategies *best*, *random* and *circulate* are *not* admissible. An admissible strategy will delegate more responsibility to individuals with a high probability of having the highest payoff than to individuals with a low probability. Also with an admissible strategy each individual considered has some chance of being given responsibility. The strategy *prob* is admissible and is used in the system described in [4]. It provides a balance between favouring individuals who perform well with giving occasional opportunities to poor performers to improve their performance. The strategy *prob* is *not* based on any model of process improvement and so it can *not* be claimed to be optimal in that sense. The user selects a strategy from the infinite variety of admissible strategies: $S = \delta \times best + \varepsilon \times prob + \phi \times random + \gamma \times circulate$ will be admissible if $\delta, \varepsilon, \phi, \gamma \in [0,1]$, $\delta + \varepsilon + \phi + \gamma = 1$ and if $\varepsilon > 0$. This leads to the question of how to select a strategy. As *circulate* is only meaningful in stable populations it is not considered here.

There are three ways that an 'optimal' strategy could be identified. First, theoretically given a specification of what strategy should achieve. Second, by trial and error in a real experiment. Third, by a laboratory simulation experiments. The value of a theoretical derivation depends on the validity of the model on which the derivation is based. In simple cases this can be done, for example to achieve uniform allocation of responsibility. Real experiments to evaluate delegation strategies are just not viable. Laboratory simulation experiments are cheap and indicate of how the strategies perform.

A world is designed in which the relative performance of the four strategies *best*, *prob*, *random* and *circulate* are simulated There are always three individuals in this world. If individuals die (ie they become unavailable) then they are replaced with new individuals. At each *cycle*—ie a discrete time unit—one delegation is made. There is a natural death rate of 5% for each individual for each cycle. The payoff of each individual commences at 0 and improves by 10% of "what there is still to learn" on each occasion that an individual is delegated responsibility. So an individual's recorded payoff is progressively: 0, 0.1, 0.19, 0.271, 0.3439, and so on, tending to 1.0 in the long term. The mean and standard deviation estimates of expected payoff are calculated as described above in Sec. 4 using a value of $\alpha = 0.6$. In addition the individuals have a strength of belief of the extent to which they are being given more work than the other two individuals in the experiment. This strength of belief is multiplied by a "rebel" factor and is added to the base death rate of 5%. So if work is repeatedly delegated to one individual then the probability

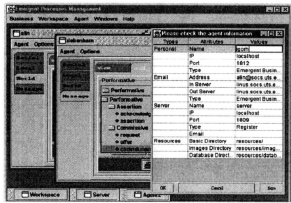

Fig 4. Setting up a task in the system

of that individual dying increases up to a limit of the rebel factor plus 5%. A *triple duplication* occurs when work is delegated to the same individual three cycles running. The proportion of triple duplications is used as a measure of the lack of perceived recent equity in the allocation of responsibility. The payoff and proportion of triple duplications for the four strategies are shown against the rebel factor on the top and bottom graphs respectively in Fig. 3. The simulation run for each value is 2 000 cycles. The lack of smoothness of the graphs is partially due to the pseudo-random number generator used. When the rebel factor is 0.15—ie three times the natural death rate—all four strategies deliver approximately the same payoff. The two graphs indicate that the *prob* strategy does a reasonable job at maximising payoff while keeping triple duplications reasonably low for a rebel factor of < 0.15. However, *prob* may only be used when the chosen definition of payoff is normally distributed. The strategy *best* also assumes normality; its definition may be changed to "such that the expected payoff is greatest" when payoff is not normal.

6. Conclusion

High-level business processes are analysed as being of three distinct types [15]. The management of knowledge-driven processes has been described. An existing multi-agent system for goal-driven process management [4] has been extended to support the management of knowledge-driven processes. The conceptual agent architecture is a three-layer BDI, hybrid architecture [16]. During a process instance the responsibility for sub-processes may be delegated. The system forms a view on who should be asked to do what at each step in a process. Each user defines payoff in some acceptable way. Payoff may be defined in terms of estimates of various parameters. These estimates are based on historic information; they are revised if they are not statistically stable. Using three basic built-in strategies, the user then specifies a delegation strategy for the chosen definition of payoff. In this way the system may be permitted to handle sub-process delegation automatically. The system has been trialed on an application in a university administrative context. Three delegation strategies $[\delta = 0.5, \varepsilon = 0.5, \phi = 0]$, *prob* and $[\delta = 0, \varepsilon = 0.5, \phi = 0.5]$ represent varying degrees of the "aggressive pursuit of payoff" and have been declared "reasonable" in very limited trials.

References

1. Dourish, P. "Using Metalevel Techniques in a Flexible Toolkit for CSCW Applications." ACM Transactions on Computer-Human Interaction, Vol. 5, No. 2, June, 1998, pp. 109—155.
2. Lawrence, P. "Workflow Handbook." Workflow Management Coalition. John Wiley & Son Ltd, 1997.
3. A. P. Sheth, D. Georgakopoulos, S. Joosten, M. Rusinkiewicz, W. Scacchi, J. C. Wileden, and A. L. Wolf. "Report from the NSF workshop on workflow and process automation in information systems." SIGMOD Record, 25(4):55—67, December 1996.
4. Debenham, J.K. "A Multi-Agent System for Emergent Process Management", in proceedings Nineteenth International Conference on Knowledge Based Systems and Applied Artificial Intelligence, ES'99: Applications and Innovations in Expert Systems VII, Cambridge UK, December 1999, pp51-62.
5. Jain, A.K., Aparicio, M. and Singh, M.P. "Agents for Process Coherence in Virtual Enterprises" in Communications of the ACM, Volume 42, No 3, March 1999, pp62—69.
6. Hawryszkiewycz, I.T. "Supporting Teams in Virtual Organisations." In Proceedings Tenth International Conference, DEXA'99, Florence, September 1999.
7. Debenham, J.K. "Supporting Strategic Process", in proceedings Fifth International Conference on The Practical Application of Intelligent Agents and Multi-Agents PAAM2000, Manchester UK, April 2000.
8. C. Bussler, S. Jablonski, and H. Schuster. "A new generation of workflow management systems: Beyond taylorism with MOBILE." SIGOIS Bulletin, 17(1):17—20, April 1996.
9. Debenham, J.K. "Knowledge Engineering: Unifying Knowledge Base and Database Design", Springer-Verlag, 1998
10. Muth, P., Wodtke, D., Weissenfels, J., Kotz D.A. and Weikum, G. "From Centralized Workflow Specification to Distributed Workflow Execution." In Journal of Intelligent Information Systems (JIIS), Kluwer Academic Publishers, Vol. 10, No. 2, 1998.
11. Rao, A.S. and Georgeff, M.P. "BDI Agents: From Theory to Practice", in proceedings First International Conference on Multi-Agent Systems (ICMAS-95), San Francisco, USA, pp 312—319.
12. Durfee, E.H.. "Distributed Problem Solving and Planning" in Weiss, G. (ed). Multi-Agent Systems. The MIT Press: Cambridge, MA.
13. Finin, F. Labrou, Y., and Mayfield, J. "KQML as an agent communication language." In Jeff Bradshaw (Ed.) Software Agents. MIT Press (1997).
14. Koriche, F. "Approximate Reasoning about Combined Knowledge" in Intelligent Agents IV, Singh M.P, Rao, A. and Wooldridge, M.J. (Eds), Springer Verlag, 1998
15. Debenham, J.K. "Three Intelligent Architectures for Business Process Management", in proceedings 12th International Conference on Software Engineering and Knowledge Engineering SEKE2000, Chicago, 6-8 July 2000.
16. Müller, J.P. "The Design of Intelligent Agents" Springer-Verlag.

The Y link oriented technique for reuse in KBS

K. Messaadia, M. Oussalah

IRIN, Université de Nantes, 2 rue de la Houssiniére,
BP 92208 - 44322, Nantes Cedex 03, France.
messaadi, oussalah@irin.univ-nantes.fr

Abstract Our study of reusability in KBS modelling methodologies leads to the description of the Y Meta modelling (Y). In the Y meta modelling, a KBS is described using the three concepts (components): task, PSM and domain plus two other components we called inter- component and intra- component links. These links describe the interdependencies of the three components keeping them really separate enhancing thus their reusability and maintenance. These components are then described in more details trough levels of description: meta ontology, ontology and application. Finally, the Y meta modelling provides a reuse methodology describing how to construct and reuse these components in order to use them for constructing specific applications.

key words : KBS, meta modelling, component reuse, semantic link, transfer link.

1 Introduction

The Meta modelling technique is a widely used technique in software engineering for integrating and defining models from different domains. It is also used for standardization purposes. Thus, it is a promising way for the definition of different models (or views) describing a system (for example the UML meta model). Reusable component libraries are proven techniques, used in software engineering, in order to reduce application development time and help maintenance and evolution.

In this paper we combine the both techniques: meta modelling and reusable component libraries for KBS reuse. In The Y meta modelling a KBS is described according to three axis (Fig. 1).

The object of reuse axis determines the minimal and sufficient components used to describe a KBS. We identify along the Y object of reuse axis three distinct and complementary components: task, PSM, and domain, plus two other components called intra- component link and inter- component link.

The levels of granularity axis determines the KBS components, at a *knowledge* level, following different layers : meta ontology, ontology and application. Thus a component can be fine grained trough these levels (layers) and users can (re)use a component at the chosen level of description.

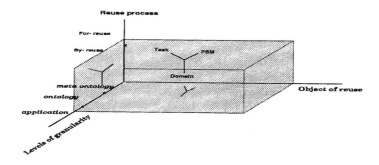

Figure1. The Y Meta Modelling

The reuse process axis determines the components with a reuse process vision. The reuse process is spliced into two stages: for-reuse engineering and by-reuse engineering. The for- reuse engineering concern is about the construction of reusable components (library construction). The by-reuse engineering concern is about how to use reusable components (library use).

The rest of the paper is organized as follow: first we introduce the object of reuse axis. Along the second axis we will introduce the different levels of granularity. Finally, along the third axis, we will see the reuse process describing how the components are constructed and (re)used.

2 Y along the object of reuse axis

According to the Y object of reuse axis, we need to identify a KBS as a set of components. To do so, we use the Multi- Abstractions Multi- Views modelling technique [Ous88].

The Multi- Abstractions Multi- Views modelling process describes a complex system (a KBS for our case) according to two decompositions: views and abstractions.

Horizontal decomposition : An horizontal decomposition allows to define different views on a given system. Having different views on a system clarifies different important aspects of it.

Vertical decomposition : A vertical decomposition defines different abstractions on a given view. Sometimes, a view is complex enough so that we need to describe it using different levels of abstractions.

2.1 Applying multi- views multi- abstraction along the Y object of reuse

The horizontal Y decomposition for KBS describes :a task view, a PSM view and a domain view á la Components of Expertise approach [Ste90]. But it differs from the components of Expertise approach (Fig.2) in the use of two decompositions with predefined inter-component links and intra-component links and an associated library.

Every view is represented in the Y model as a branch. In every view, there are

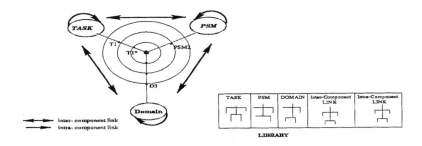

Figure2. Y and an associated library

abstractions. For example, an optimisation task T1 can be described in another abstraction T1* more in details (see Fig. 2) . For example, T1* abstraction will describe the sub- tasks decomposition of T1. We use the inter- and intra- component links to navigate from one view to another and from one abstraction to another.

2.2 inter- and intra- component links

We have identified the three components task, PSM, and domain. In order to keep every component description separate, we use inter- and intra- component links for representing their interdependencies. This representation provides a means for identifying different types of inter- and intra- component links and associating properties with them. As a consequence, the related components (in our case, task, PSM and domain) are independent from the links thus enabling a greater modularity and reusability and reinforcing their evolution.

An inter- component link links two different components: task/ PSM, PSM/ domain, Task/domain. An intra- component link is a sort of inter- component link but linking two components of the same type: task/ task, PSM/ PSM and domain/ domain. For reuse purposes, we have fine grained the description of an intra- /inter- component link. An Intra- /Inter- component link is composed of two kind of links: semantic and transfer.

Semantic Link A semantic link describes a relation between two entities(components). It has its own semantics and a clean behaviour helping the components to communicate and collaborate. Its semantics can express an association (logical, physical, etc.) a composition, an inheritance, etc. Many disciplines studied semantic

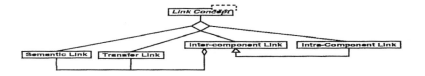

Figure3. Inter- and intra- component links [UML notation]

relations (links), such as linguistics, logic, psychology, information systems, and artificial intelligence. Based on these works, we have proposed a predefined semantic links hierarchy (meta ontology) so that users can reuse them in defining their intra- or inter- component links.

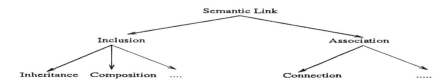

Figure4. Semantic Link Hierarchy

Transfer links A transfer link allows to transfer data flow between the related components. It expresses the transfer of information. For example, if one considers a car related to his body by a composition link, this link can convey as information that the color of the car is identical to that of its body. Thus, the mechanism of information transfer allows to define only the color of the body. The color value can be propagated to the car by using a transfer link. Moreover, instead of limiting itself to a simple transfer of values (identity function), one can apply a transfer function to the values of the source to obtain the values of the destination attributes. This function is indicated using a translator. Thus, a transfer is composed of at least one translator to establish the propagation between the dependent entities and to describe the function applied.

Each translator establishes a correspondence between the attributes of the connected components and defines the transfer function to be applied to the values of the source attributes to obtain the values of the destination attributes. Several attributes of the same component can be implied in the propagation. As for the semantic links, we have identified a transfer link hierarchy (meta ontology) helping users in describing their inter- and intra- component links.

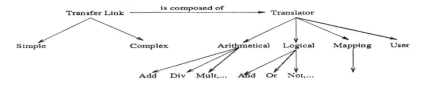

Figure5. Transfer Link Hierarchy

2.3 Domain ontologies as a multi- views multi- abstraction decomposition

Work on domain ontologies has shown that domain knowledge is described using *generic ontologies* , more *specific* ontologies , ontologies of *application* . It is significant, so, to model domain knowledge according to various abstractions. On the basis of the principle that a domain representation is a kind of knowledge representation [C.99], we apply to it the same modelling process using horizontal and vertical decomposition. Thus we can have a hierarchical description of a domain ontology using views and abstractions.

Existing ontologies such as TOVE, GUM, WordNet, consist in a concept hierarchy, often organised as a *sort of* (inheritance) hierarchy, plus a set of relationships. As far as we know, they don't use a relationship hierarchy (relationship ontology). We think that using the semantic (Fig. 4) and transfer link(Fig. 5) hierarchies can better the understanding, (re)use and evolution of these ontologies.

3 Y along the levels of granularity axis

In AI[New82] the *knowledge* level has been identified for describing a KBS independently from its implementation. This knowledge level description can be done according to different levels [Gua94]. Thus, along the Y levels of granularity axis, the five components are described throughout: meta ontology, ontology, and application.

1. Meta Ontological level : The five components of the Y model are clarified on this level. Thus, the meta ontology level provides modelling primitives [OM99] in terms of: task, PSM, domain, inter- component link and intra-component link. We will see that this level represents in fact The Y Meta model (Fig. 2).
2. Ontological level (ontology of library): at this level, various kinds of ontologies of tasks, PSM, domains and links are described. These components are described using the meta-ontology modelling primitives listed above.
3. Application level : the application level is used to describe applications [GM94]. In the reuse spirit of Y, an application is seen as an assembly of tasks, PSM, and domains components specialised using intra- component links and linked using inter- components links.

In the rest of the paper we will see more in details the components we have identified along the first axis, by describing them along the levels of granularity axis.

3.1 Meta ontology level

The meta ontological level is used in the Y model to describe the five components presented above. We will first present the task- PSM- and domain -meta

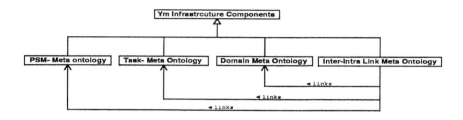

Figure6. The Meta Ontological level

ontologies. Then we will see inter- and intra- components meta ontologies more in details.

Task-, PSM-, and domain- meta ontologies A task at the meta-ontology level is specified by its name, which is a unique term designating it, its input/output, the goal it is to reach and the inter- and intra- component links attached to it.

A PSM meta-ontology level is specified by its name, its input/output, its competence to achieve tasks, and the inter- and intra- component links attached to it.

The domain meta- ontology level can be specified by giving one, two or the three views amongst: structural, behavioural and physical, plus other view types if necessary.

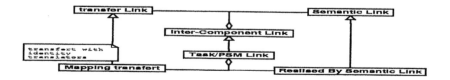

Figure7. an example of an inter-component

Inter- and intra- component meta ontologies An inter- / intra- component link meta ontology is described by its *name*, its *destination* and *source* concepts, and the *semantic* and *transfer* links attached to it. We can see the example of an inter- component link as described in (Fig.7).

		Inter- Component Link Example
Name	InterIntraComponent-name	Task/PSM
source	source-concepts	Task
destination	destination-concepts	PSM
semantics	semantic-link-names	realised by
transfers	transfer-link-names	MappingTransfer

1. A semantic link is defined by: a unique *name* specifying it, *from* and *to*, the connection attributes defining the source and destination components, the *roles* which the source and destination components play within the link, the *semantic attributes* describing the semantic properties of the modelled link. These properties enrich the representation of the semantic links and to simplify their handling [Mag94]. The *semantic attributes* can be for example the cardinality of the linked components, the functional dependence nature of a destination component with the source component.

			Semantic Link Example	
name	semantic-link-name		realised by-name	
from	from-concepts		PSM	
to	to-concepts		Task	
Roles	from-role	to-role	composite	component
Sem. attr.			dependent/ sharable	

2. A transfer link is defined by its *name*, the *source* and *destination* concepts and the *translators* attached to it.

		Transfer Link Example
Name	transfer-link-name	MappingTransfer
source	source-concepts	PSM
destination	destination-concepts	Task
translators	translator-names	Mapping-

3. A translator is defined by its *name*, the *source attributes* and *destination attributes* of its transfer connected components, plus the *transfer functions* attached to it. The translator establishes a correspondence between the attributes of the connected components and defines the transfer function to be applied to the values of the source attributes to obtain the values of the destination attributes. Several attributes of the same component can be implied in the propagation.

		Translator Link Example
Name	translator-name	Mapping-
source	source-concepts	PSM-Attributes
destination	destination-concepts	Task-Attributes
translators	transfer-function-names	Mapping

We have already introduces our pre- identified hierarchies (meta ontologies) of semantic links (Fig.4), and transfer links (Fig.5). Users can enrich these meta ontologies by adding new ones.

3.2 The ontological level

At this level we can describe different sorts of ontologies: task, PSM, domain, and links. The Y model at this level can be seen as a Y-Shape model with several branches.

Task branch describing types of tasks such as: diagnosis, configuration, modelling,

PSM branch describing types of PSM such as: classification, abduction,

Domain branch describing type of domains such as: networks and telecommunication networks.

Links are described in terms of task/PSM, PSM/domain, task /domain, task/task; PSM/PSM; and domain/domain links (Fig. 8).

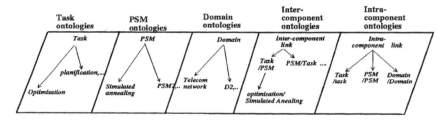

Figure8. Ontological level

3.3 The application level

An application is a composition of components described at the ontological level. For more details, readers can refer to [OM99].

4 Y along the reuse process axis

Reuse process in Information System [CR99]defines the components according to two stages : *for- reuse engineering* and *by-reuse engineering*. Thus, the Y third axis identifies the components along these two stages. Following the for-reuse engineering, the components are first identified, secondly, described using a chosen descriptive (or formal or semi formal)language and then, organized in a library using a chosen library organisation structure. Following the by-reuse engineering, the components can be found and selected using a search technique which should correspond to both the library organisation structure and the language, chosen in the first stage. Then, the components are adapted and integrated, if needed, in a user application. Before describing the different components, we will introduce the Y different users, we have identified.

4.1 The different Y users

1. The Infrastructure Builder (I.B) has to define the modelling components used to build the infrastructure. His concern is about the Meta Ontology Level.
2. The Application Builder (A.B) is the domain expert and will use the meta-ontology components for describing his/her specific components or specialise the ontological components (or applications). The A.B is concerned by the *Ontology Level and application level.*
3. The Reuse Engineer (R.E) or library manager will construct and manage the library. The library is composed of generic parts: generic meta-ontology components defined by the infrastructure builder, reusable components and reusable applications defined by the application builder. The library is spliced into different compartments:
   (a) a meta ontology library,
   (b) an ontology library and
   (c) an application library.
4. The End User (E.U) instantiates specific applications in order to solve real problems (feeding in the initial values of the problem).

The reuse process is spliced in two stages: for-reuse engineering and by- reuse engineering.

4.2 The for-reuse engineering

The for-reuse engineering concern is about how to construct reusable components. The meta ontological , ontological reusable components and reusable applications are inserted in the library respectively in the : meta ontology, ontology and application library layers. Before describing the for-reuse engineering in every layer, we will first see the identified for-reuse engineering tasks.

1. **Identify**: This task is about identifying the users needs. Often, new components emerge from Application Builders needs. The identification can concern components at the meta ontological, the ontological or the application levels.
2. **Represent**: When a needed component is identified, we need to represent using a given language. The representation language used can be formal, semi formal or descriptive. For example: CML, OCML, ML. Y uses the modelling primitives described at the meta ontology level as a representation language. As the meta ontological level can be modified, by modifying, adding or deleting meta ontology primitives, Y has a flexible modelling infrastructure.

3. **Organise:** The components are then organised in the library. Thus, the Reuse Engineer has to choose a component organisation for the different library layers : meta ontology, ontology and application.

4.3 A For- Reuse Engineering Example

In order to illustrate the for- reuse engineering, we present a matrix operations example(Fig. 9).

Meta Ontology level

1. **Identify:** The components we have identified in Y at the meta ontology level are integrated by the R.E in the meta ontology library. Thus we have the: meta-task, meta-PSM, meta -domain the inter- and intra- meta component links plus the predefined semantic, transfer and translator links. Thus the I.B identifies the task/PSM, PSM/Task, Task/domain and PSM/domain inter-component links and the Task/task, PSM/PSM and domain/domain intra-component links.

2. **Represent:** The meta ontology components are represented in Y using an object language. Thus all these components are meta-classes.

3. **Organise:** The organisation adopted *by the R.E* in Y is done according to a Multi hierarchies Multi Views description. Thus we have at the meta ontology level two abstractions.In the first abstraction we have the
   (a) meta-task description
   (b) meta PSM description
   (c) meta domain description
   (d) inter component description
   (e) intra component description
   In the second abstraction, we have the semantic and transfer links organised in a generalisation/specialisation tree.

Ontology level

1. **Identify:** The ontological components are constructed by the A.B. For example the A.B wants to describe matrix operations task:

2. **Represent:** The A.B. represents his matrix operations as a number of tasks and PSMs using the meta ontology descriptive primitives. We can give the real inversion matrix task (Fig. 9).

name	Real MatrixInversionTask
goal	inversion of a real matrix
input	a real matrix M
output	^tM
input/output constraints	the matrix should be real
inter	T/P Mat-Inv
intra	-

Name	T/P Mat-Inv
source	Real MatrixInversionTask
destination	CholeskiPSM
semantics	realised by
transfers	mapping-

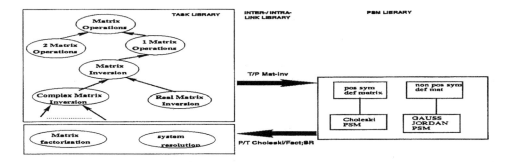

Figure9. A matrix operations example

3. **Organise:** In existing approaches, the most used organisation (for the ontological components)is the task/PSM tree structure. PSMs in such organisation are usually indexed according to their: competence, assumptions, functionalities, or as a suite of problem types. Other approaches use two separate tree structure: a task tree structure and a PSM tree structure. Then Task/PSM linking is defined dynamically according to an execution context. In the Y library, ontological components are organised in hierarchies according to the user's choice. The user can manipulate separate task trees and PSM trees or task/PSM tree structures describing the different links explicitly(Fig. 10). The organisation adopted for the matrix operations example is an organisation with separated hierarchies:
   (a) Task hierarchy
   (b) PSM hierarchy
   This organisation is described in the (Fig.9).

Application level

1. **Identify:** A final user needs to make for example an inversion of a real Matrix. The application builder will ask the R.E for the needed components. At this phase, the A.B will link the RealInversionMatrixTASK with the appropriate PSM and for our case, the appropriate PSM is the CholeskiPSM. He uses a TASK/PSM link. We have two scenarii:
   (a) Linking the task with the PSM with an existing (already identified and described)inter-component link.
   (b) if the link doesn't exist in the library, a search (Search-PSM)is done to find the best PSM among the existing PSMs for making a Real-MATRIX-inversion.
   These scenarii are described as PSMs.
2. **Represent:** The A.B. represents his application by representing the missing pieces. For example, the A.B matrix inversion operations application will be a linked TASK and corresponding PSMs with the appropriate inter- and intra- component links.

3. **Organise:** The application insertion in the library is done by the R.E. who will integrate the application, if he decides to do so. The R.E decision about integrating an application as a big piece reusable component depends for example on the frequency use of it. If matrix inversion is often used by F.U, it can be stored as a composite component (components and their links).

4.4 The by-reuse engineering

The by-reuse engineering concern is about how to reuse an exiting component in one of the library's compartment, at the meta ontological, ontological or application level. In order to reuse a component, we have identified the tasks below.

1. **Find and select:** These two tasks depend on the adopted library organisation along the first stage. For example in case of a TASK/PSM organisation, and a predefined hierarchy (fixed task-PSM associations), we can find automatically and easily the PSM associated to a given task. In the case of no predefined task/PSM associations, a search is done in the PSMs set in order to find the best PSM candidate for achieving a task according to the context. Thus, the search can be considered as a general PSM.Thus, for more flexibility and evolution, we have chosen to use a PSM to describe a search algorithm which is associated to the library organisation.
2. **Adapt:** Adapting a component to a new context is a hard task. In Y the adaptation can be done by describing a new component from an existing one by : generalisation/specialisation, by composition,...
3. **Use:** Finally the component is ready for use by integrating it to a new application.

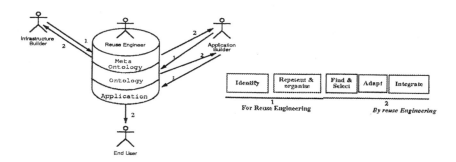

Figure10. Library description

Now we can describe an example of a component construction and component use. For this we will see the reuse engineering process in the meta ontology, ontology and application level.

4.5 By Reuse Engineering Example

We can have an example at the **Meta ontological level**:

1. **Find and Select:** If the Infrastructure Builder wants to construct a new semantic link by deriving it from an existing one. He can select an existing one from the semantic link meta ontology hierarchy.
2. **Adapt:** He can adapt an existing component by, for example, composition.
3. **Use:** The I.B can give his new component to the R.E. in order to integrate it in the meta ontology library.

At the **ontological level**, the reuse can be:

1. **Find and Select:** If the A.B needs a choleski matrix inversion PSM. He can ask the R.E in order to find and select the appropriate component.
2. **Adapt:** the A.B adapt if needed his components, by composition or inheritance.
3. **Use:** the A.B can use his components by pluging them in his application.

At the **application level**, the Application Builder can:

1. **Find and Select:** If an application exists in the application library, the R.E will find and select it for the A.B in order to solve his problem.
2. **Adapt:** the A.B can adapt the application for his needs.
3. **Use:** the End User uses the application by instantiating it and giving the initial values.

5 Discussion and Conclusion

The Y is reflexive since the three axis we have seen can be considered as task, PSM and domain axis. We can consider the task as being *Reuse*, the corresponding PSM is the *Reuse Process* and the domain is *KBS*. The table bellow can summarize this idea of applying the Y recursively.

Task axis	PSM axis	Domain axis
Reuse task	Y meta modeling process	a given domain
Objects for reuse	*Reuse process*	Levels of granularity KBS
Defining KBS- components	Multi Abs. M. Views process	Meta onto., onto., appl. levels

We use the Y for comparing existing methodologies (at the knowledge level) [Ben93], [BV94], [CJS92], [Fen97] , [GTRM94], [PGT97], [Ste90]. By projecting the methodologies following the Y three axis, we can identify the components involved in existing methodologies and the corresponding reuse and use methodology if it exists. Our future work is about comparing the existent known methodologies. bibtThis work is now applied in a telecommunication company.

References

[Ben93]   V.R. Benjamins. *Problem Solving Methods for Diagnosis*. Phd thesis, University of Amsterdam, Amsterdam, 1993.

[BV94]   J. A. Breuker and W. Van de Velde, editors. *CommonKADS Library for Expertise Modelling: Reusable problem solving components*, volume 21 of *Frontiers in Artificial Intelligence and Applications*. IOS-Press, Amsterdam, August 1994.

[C.99]   Reynaud C. technical report for hdr nř 1201. Technical report, L.R.I Paris sud university, ORSAY, 1999.

[CJS92]   B. Chandrasekaran, T. R. Johnson, and J. W. Smith. Task-structure analysis for knowledge modeling. *Comm. of the ACM*, 35(9):124, September 1992.

[CR99]   F.Barbier C. Rolland. Best of oois'98. *revue L'Objet*, Vol. 5 N 1, 1999.

[Fen97]   D. Fensel. The tower-of-adapter method for developing and reusing problem-solving methods. *Lecture Notes in Computer Science*, 1319:97–??, 1997.

[GM94]   Mauro Gaspari and Enrico Motta. Symbol-level requirements for agent-level programming. In A. G. Cohn, editor, *Proceedings of the Eleventh European Conference on Artificial Intelligence*, pages 264–268, Chichester, August 8–12 1994. John Wiley and Sons.

[GTRM94]   John H. Gennari, Samson W. Tu, Thomas E. Rothenfluh, and Mark A. Musen. Mapping domains to methods in support of reuse. *International Journal of Human-Computer Studies*, 41(3):399–424, 1994.

[Gua94]   Nicola Guarino. The ontological level. In R. Casati, B. Smith, and G. White, editors, *Philosophy and the Cognitive Sciences*. Hölder-Pichler-Tempsky, Vienna, 1994.

[Mag94]   M. Magnan. *Réutilisation de composants : les exceptions dans les objets composites*. Thèse d'Informatique, Université des Sciences et Techniques du Languedoc, Montpellier, 1994.

[New82]   A. Newell. The knowledge level. *Artificial Intelligence*, 18:87–127, 1982.

[OM99]   Mourad Oussalah and Karima Messaadia. The ontologies of semantic and transfer links. In Dieter Fensel and Rudi Studer, editors, *Proceedings of the 11th European Workshop on Knowledge Acquisition, Modeling and Management (EKAW-99)*, volume 1621 of *LNAI*, pages 225–242, Berlin, May 26–29 1999. Springer.

[Ous88]   Mourad C. Oussalah. *Modèle hierarchisés/multi-vues pour le support de raisonnement dans les domaines techniques*. Thèse, Université de Aix-Marseille, 1988.

[PGT97]   Christine Pierret-Golbreich and Xavier Talon. Specification of flexible knowledge-based systems. In Enric Plaza and Richard Benjamins, editors, *Proceedings of the 10th European Workshop on Knowledge Acquisition, Modeling and Management (EKAW-97)*, volume 1319 of *LNAI*, pages 190–204, Berlin, October 15–18 1997. Springer.

[Ste90]   Luc Steels. Components of expertise. *AI Magazine, Summer 1990*, pages 28–49, 1990.

Modelling Agents and Communication using CommonKADS

John Kingston

AIAI, Division of Informatics, University of Edinburgh

Edinburgh, Scotland.

September 22, 2000

Abstract

A number of systematic methods have been developed to formalise and direct the knowledge engineering process. One such method is the CommonKADS methodology, which consists of six models capturing knowledge at different levels of abstraction. This paper examines two of these six models: the Agent model and the Communication model. The Agent and Communication models are responsible for modelling "co-operation" within CommonKADS. The Agent model majors on *who* has the capability to carry out each task, while the Communication model highlights *where* information is needed within the process (i.e. which agent holds the information that forms the input and output of key tasks).

This paper will propose that both the Agent and Communication models can usefully be developed at two levels of detail: the level of tasks within a business process (between-tasks), and the level of subtasks (within-task). By developing both models at both levels, a comprehensive set of information is obtained. Extensions and adaptations are proposed to both models, first to ensure full and accurate knowledge representation, and then to discuss how a "shorthand" version of the models might be developed.

1   Introduction

Knowledge based systems (KBS) have been a commercially viable technology for over a decade now. As a result of their growing use, users and managers have demanded that KBS be verifiable, maintainable and repeatable. This has led to the development of a number of systematic methods which formalise and direct the knowledge engineering process. A survey of methods can be found in [5].

One such method is the CommonKADS methodology, which recommends that knowledge engineers develop a suite of models that both represent knowledge from different perspectives and gradually transform knowledge from the real world, via a conceptual representation, to a system design. Models are typically represented as one or more node-and-arc diagrams, but may also include tables or other textual representations of knowledge. This paper examines two of these six models: the Agent model and the Communication model, which focus on the capability, role, requirements and outputs of various agents in a knowledge-based process.

1.1   CommonKADS

CommonKADS is a methodology that supports knowledge management and knowledge engineering (see the comprehensive recently-published "CommonKADS book" [1]). It does this by proposing a number of knowledge models that should be drawn up, which gradually transform an identified need or opportunity for better distribution of knowledge into the design specification for a knowledge based system. CommonKADS proposes six models, which are viewed as being at successively detailed levels of abstraction (see [1]).

In addition to being at different levels of abstraction, these models also capture different perspectives on knowledge; in simple terms, this means that some represent "how" knowledge is handled, others show "what" knowledge is used or "who" uses it, and still others capture "when", "where" or "why" knowledge is used. For more details of each of these perspectives, and how they can be represented using knowledge models, see [7].

The Agent and Communication models are responsible for modelling "roles" and "co-operation" within CommonKADS. The Agent model majors on *who* has the capability to carry out each task and what role they play in the process, while the Communication model highlights *where* information is needed within the process and how information is transmitted between agents during the process. In conjunction with a third model, the Task model (which specifies *how* tasks need to be carried out in order to achieve a particular goal), these models provide a rich process description that can be used for a range of purposes, from process re-engineering to intranet development.

1.2   The Agent Model

The purpose of the CommonKADS Agent Model is to determine the roles and competences that the various actors in the organisation bring with them to perform a shared task ([1], p.48). Tasks are carried out by agents, each of whom must have authority to perform the task, may be responsible for performing that task, ought to be capable of performing that task, and should have rights to resources needed to perform that task. The degree of truth of each of these four statements will determine the competences of the agents, which in turn will help to define the roles of agents.

CommonKADS recommends that the Agent model is represented by a table defining the key features of agents ([1], p.50). CommonKADS recommends the use-case diagrams of UML [9] as a graphical representation of Agent models.

1.3   The Communication Model

A task that is carried out by one agent may produce results in the form of information objects that need to be communicated to other agents. The purpose of the Communication model is to identify the information exchange procedures that realise the knowledge transfer between agents [1]. Each knowledge transfer will have information content, a sender, one or more receivers, and an initiator;

it may also have internal structure, and/or constraints and preconditions. The Communication model is intended to capture and represent these features of transfers of information or knowledge.

In the Communication model, each information object that is communicated is described as a *transaction*. CommonKADS recommends that a communication model should include:

- A dialogue diagram: a high level description of which tasks send or receive information.

- A transaction control plan, showing ordering and dependencies of communications. This is also usually represented as a diagram.

- Specification of individual transactions: a collection of attributes of each information exchange. These attributes include the information object(s), the sending and receiving agent, and any constraints on the transaction occurring. This is represented in a table.

- A detailed description of the information exchanged, including the structure of the transaction, the role of the information object (whether it is the 'core' of the transaction or supporting information), the proposed medium of interaction, and the "illocutionary force" of the communication (e.g. 'request', 'demand' or 'warning'). These details also appear in a table.

1.4 Thesis of this paper

KADS, which was the predecessor to CommonKADS, did not separate the Agent and Communication models; both were incorporated into its "model of co-operation" [3], which could be used to identify the actors carrying out tasks as well as the inputs and outputs of those tasks. It therefore seems natural that an Agent model should be accompanied by a Communication model at the same level of abstraction i.e. containing the same tasks. Yet CommonKADS proposes that an Agent model represents agents' roles and capabilities for the various tasks in a particular business process, but the Communication model should represent communication between subtasks within a single "business process task". model. This is probably due to the clear need for communication features to form an input to the Design model; but it seems that much useful detail is lost if agents' roles are only assigned at a between-task level of abstraction, whilst communication is only detailed at a within-task level. The resulting proposed model suite is shown in Figure 1.

This paper will propose that both the Agent and Communication model can usefully be developed at both between-task and within-task levels of detail. The rest of this paper will work through an example in which both models are used to represent knowledge at both the between-task ("enterprise") level and the within-task ("system") level. The example concerns the design of small scale industrial buildings.[1]

---

[1]This example is based on a tutorial exercise originally developed with funding from

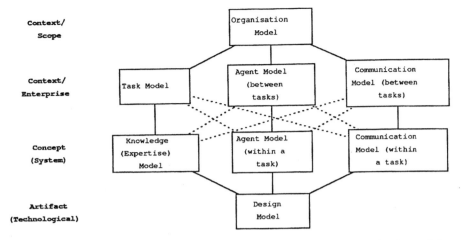

Figure 1: Revised view of levels of abstraction of CommonKADS models

2 Example: design of industrial buildings

Any task which involves designing something is a task that requires knowledge – and considerable amounts of it. It's necessary to understand how well the artifact being designed fulfils its performance requirements; which components of the design are compatible with other components; whether the final design will be robust enough to withstand the pressures it must face in normal use and in extreme circumstances; whether components are easy to manufacture; whether the design is feasible to assemble; and so on. As a result, many design companies employ strategies to reduce the difficulty of the design task. They may offer a number of "standard" designs which can be adapted to specific requirements; they may generate several design prototypes which can be critiqued and improved; or they may subdivide the different aspects of the design work so that one person or group of people is responsible for high level design, another for low level design, another for checking against requirements and constraints, and so on. They may also take different approaches to generating the design (transformational design, propose-and-revise design, etc.) – comparison of these approaches is beyond the scope of this paper, but interested readers should look at [2] among other references.

The example that will be used in this paper will be a (fictional) small company, referred to as ABC Holdings Ltd., whose task is to design small-scale industrial buildings. They specialise in a particular structural technique known as "portal frame" design, which is commonly used for buildings such as DIY stores. Their strategy is to subdivide design work between different groups of people, and it is this subdivision which is captured and represented in the

the SERC Computing Facilities Committee Support for Engineers programme. A proof-of-concept system for checking standards in portal frame designs was implemented.

Agent and Communication models below.

Before building the Agent and Communication models, however, it's necessary to determine what tasks are actually carried out in portal frame design. This is represented in the CommonKADS Task model. The Task model for designing of portal frame buildings is shown in figure 2. The upper layer represents the top level tasks, and the lower layer shows subtasks of "Design building" and "Check building meets specification".

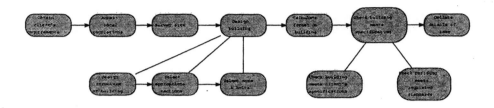

Figure 2: Task model for designing a portal frame building

The tasks identified in the Task model serve as the starting point for developing the Agent and Communication models at the enterprise level.

2.1 Agent model for portal frame design

When ABC Holdings design a portal frame building, the client's requirements are gathered by the partners, who then pass the actual design task to one of their engineers. The engineer creates a design, assisted by technicans (who do the low level design – literally, the "nuts and bolts" of the design), a CAD package that generates a numerical description of the design, and a program (written in FORTRAN) that calculates the effects of wind and snow forces on the building from that numerical description. The resulting design is then checked against legislation, company standards, and the client's requirements before being passed to the partners for approval. There are therefore at least six agents involved in the design process: the partners, the engineer, the technician, the two computer programs, and the client. Some would argue that the legislator constitutes a seventh agent; other would omit him or her because the legislator does not have any dynamic input to the design process.

CommonKADS recommends that a set of attributes are identified for each agent and presented in a table. These attributes are:

- The name of the agent.

- The agent's position in the organisation. This information should be obtainable from the Organisational model. This attribute should also define the type of the agent (typically either 'human' or "information system").

- The tasks that the agent is involved in.

- The agents that this agent communicates with.

- The knowledge items possessed by this agent.

- Other required or present competences of the agent.

- Responsibilities of the agent in task execution, and restrictions in ths respect. This item is also intended to include constraints such as limitations on authority or reponsibility to legal or professional norms.

Many values for these attributes can be derived from other CommonKADS models. The last two attributes, however, are unique to the Agent model. CommonKADS doesn't give much guidance on which "other competences" should be considered, or what "responsibilities and constraints" might arise. In order to make things a little clearer, I have drawn on the ORDIT framework for requirements engineering [4], which defines four roles for an agent with respect to a task: capability (the agent CAN do the task), authority (the agent MAY do the task), responsibility (the agent MUST do the task), and rights (the agent HAS RIGHTS TO use certain resources in order to perform the task). This definition encompasses three levels of agent-to-task mapping; CAN is the weakest, MAY is stronger because it (hopefully) implies CAN, and MUST is stronger still because it implies both CAN and MAY. It also identifies resources that are needed for a task, providing a useful link to the domain knowledge as well as the task knowledge.

Tables 1 and 2 below represent a CommonKADS Agent Model. It has been extended with the four attributes derived from ORDIT, plus a catch-all "other constraints" column.

In order to represent the agent model diagramatically, CommonKADS recommends the use of UML use case diagrams, in which each "use case" represents one task from the Task Model. While use case diagrams are well understood and widely accepted, they are intended to show which agents are involved in which use cases; there is no mechanism for representing capability, authority, roles and responsibilities of agents. As a result, an extended diagram format is proposed in which the use cases are labelled; this can be seen in Figure 3.

2.2 Communication model: Designing a Portal Frame building

Each time a new agent takes on a task where the previous task was carried out by a different agent, communication is required. The Communication model represents the communications that occur between tasks. If a Communication model is to represent the same level of abstraction as the Agent model, then it must represent the same tasks that appear in the Agent model. The reader should therefore refer back to the Task model in Figure 2 for the source of the tasks that appear in this model.

Agent	Position	Tasks	Communicates with	Knowledge items
Partner	Senior design authority	Obtain client's requirements; Collate details of case	Client, Engineer	Legislative standards; Previous designs; Best practice; Features of a good design
Engineer	Designer	Access local regulations; Survey site; Design structure of building; Select appropriate sections; Check building meets client's specifications; Check building meets regulated standards	Partner, Technician, CAD package, FORTRAN package	Location of regulations; relevance of regulations; features of good and bad sites; results of site survey; available building components; client's requirements; cost restrictions; characteristics of sections; details of final design.
CAD package	Information source/ support package	Calculate and display designs	Engineer	Client's requirements, design constraints
Technician	Detailed designer	Select nuts & bolts	Engineer	Detailed design
FORTRAN program	Support package	Calculate forces on building	Engineer	Detailed design, local wind & snow conditions
Legislator	External information source	Supply legislation	Engineer	
Client	External information source	Supply requirements	Partner	

Table 1: Agent model for designing a portal frame building (part 1 of 2)

Agent	Capability	Authority	Rights	Responsibility	Other constraints
Partner	CAN do: All tasks except those carried out by the legislator	MAY carry out all tasks except those carried out by the legislator	Has RIGHTS to view: All communication transactions; Has RIGHTS to modify: Requirements, specification, design	MUST obtain client's requirements; MUST collate details of case	Insufficient time to carry out all tasks
Engineer	CAN do: All tasks currently carried out by Engineer, technician, or (rather laboriously) CAD package or FORTRAN program	MAY do: All tasks that CAN be done	Has RIGHTS to view: Regulations, design, requirements; Has RIGHTS to modify: design	MUST produce design; MUST check design against client's specifications and regulated standards	
CAD package	CAN: calculate and display design	MAY: calculate design	Has RIGHTS to view: Design parameters	MUST calculate design	
Technician	CAN: select nuts & bolts	MAY select nuts & bolts	Has RIGHTS to view: design	Must select nuts & bolts	
FORTRAN program	CAN: calculate forces on building	MAY calculate forces on building	Has RIGHTS to view: design		
Legislator			Has RIGHTS to view: previous designs	MUST supply legislation	
Client			Has RIGHTS to view: site; Has RIGHTS to modify: client requirements	MUST supply requirements	

Table 2: Agent model for designing a portal frame building (part 2 of 2)

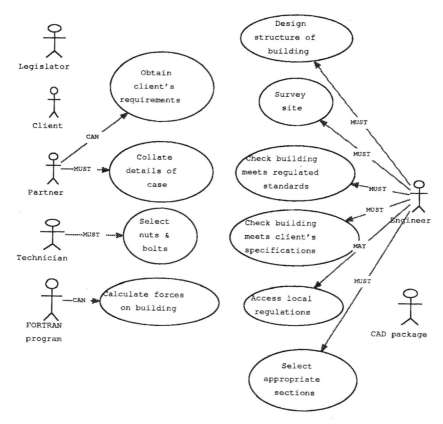

Figure 3: Agent model for designing a portal frame building: extended format

2.2.1 Dialogue diagram

The first component of a communication model is a *dialogue diagram*, which shows which tasks are carried out by which agents, and where communication is needed between agents. Figure 4 shows a dialogue diagram for portal frame design, using the format recommended by CommonKADS (p.225 of [1]). Columns headed **Dialogue** show communication transactions; each other column represents an agent, with the darker ellipses representing tasks carried out by that agent.

Note that there are links in the dialogue diagram between tasks performed by the same agent (e.g. from *Survey Site* to *Design Structure of Building*). These links do not represent communication between agents, but rather dependencies between tasks (usually inputs/outputs); this can be thought of as communication "within" an agent. These are worth describing because they may be required as input to more detailed models of individual tasks.

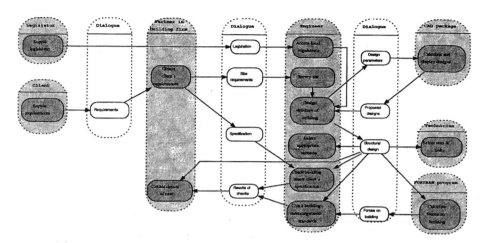

Figure 4: Dialogue diagram for designing a portal frame building

2.2.2 Control of transaction

The second component of the Communication Model is the transaction control diagram, which describes the sequence of transactions. The diagram format used for these is the state diagram notation taken from UML [9]. Transaction control diagrams may not always need to be developed, but can be very useful when flow of control is complex e.g. when external events conditionally trigger tasks or transactions. These diagrams also represent, and maybe introduce, certain design decisions regarding communication; a common design decision involves determining who takes the initiative in a transaction. Figure 5 shows the transaction control diagram associated with Figure 4.

It can be seen that the flow of control is assumed to be largely sequential, unless a design fails its checks (against legislation and user requirements), in which case looping occurs.

2.2.3 Transactions

CommonKADS proposes that a number of properties are identified for each transaction that appears in a Communication Model. These properties are identified below (from p.228 of [1]):

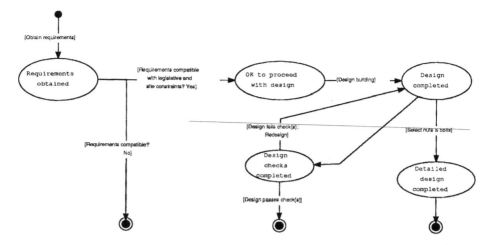

Figure 5: Transaction control diagram for designing a portal frame building

- **Transaction Identifier/Name:** A transaction is to be defined for each information object that is output from some leaf task in the Task Model or in the Knowledge/Expertise Model (i.e. a transfer function), and that must be communicated to another agent for use in its own tasks. The name must reflect, in a user-understandable way, what is done with the information object by the transaction. In addition to the name, give a brief explanation here of the purpose of the transaction.

- **Information object:** Indicate the (core) information object, and between which two tasks it is to be transmitted.

- **Agents involved:** Indicate the agent that is sender of the information object, and the agent that is receiving it

- **Communication plan:** Indicate the communication plan of which this transaction is a component

- **Constraints:** Specify the requirements and (pre)conditions that must be fulfilled so the transaction can be carried out. Sometimes, it is also useful to state postconditions that are assumed to be valid after the transaction.

- **Information Exchange Specification:** Transactions can have an internal structure, in that they consist of several messages of different types, and/or handle additional supporting information objects such as explanation or help items.

For the transactions in Figure 4, the relevant information is given in Table 3, omitting the "communication plan" attribute (which is the same for all transactions) and the "information exchange specification" (see section 2.2.4 for details).

2.2.4 Information Exchange

The information exchange specification constitutes the third layer of the CommonKADS Communication Model. It refines the description of transactions in two ways: by giving the internal message typing and structure of the transaction, and by giving information about the syntactic form and medium of the messages.

The information that could appear in an information exchange specification is shown below (taken from p. 230 of [1]). A representative example of an information exchange specification for one transaction is shown in Table 4.

- **Transaction Name:** Transaction name and identifier of which this information exchange specification is a part

- **Agents involved:** The **sender** (the agent sending the information item/items) and the **receiver** (the agent receiving the information item/items)

- **Information Items:** List all information items that are to be transmitted in this transaction. This includes the ('core') information object, the transfer of which is the purpose of this transaction. However, it may contain other, supporting information items that provide help or explanation, for example. For each information item, describe the following:

  - **Role:** whether it is a *core* object or a *support* item;
  - **Form:** the syntactic form in which it is transmitted to another agent e.g. data string, canned text, a certain type of diagram, 2D or 3D plot;
  - **Medium:** the medium through which it is handled in the agent-agent interaction e.g. a pop-up window, navigation and selection within a menu, command-line interface, human intervention

- **Message specifications:** Describe all messages that make up the transaction. For each message, describe:

  - **Communication type:** the communication type of the message, describing its intention ("illocutionary force", in speech-act terminology). Some pre-defined intentions are suggested in [1].
  - **Content:** the statement or proposition contained in the message.
  - **Reference:** in certain cases it may be useful to add a reference, for example to what domain knowledge model or agent capability is required to be able to send or process the message.

- **Control over messages:** Give, if necessary, a control specification over the messages within the transaction. This can be done in pseudocode format or in a state-transition diagram, similar to the transaction control diagram described above. I have chosen to use plain text.

Transaction name	Information object	Agents involved	Constraints	Information Exchange Specification
Requirements	Features of the building	Client & Partner	A meeting takes place; Contract agreed/signed	Requirements-IE1
Legislation	Permitted/prohibited features of the building Permitted/prohibited working practices and equipment	Legislator & Engineer	Latest version of the legislation is available; Engineer can understand legislation	
Site requirements	Load bearing potential etc.	Partner & Engineer	Site surveys have been completed in sufficient detail	
Specification	Features of the building	Partner & Engineer	Engineer must understand the specification	
Results of checks	Success/ failure/ warning	Engineer & Partner		
Design parameters	Features of design	Engineer & CAD package	Engineer must be able to use & understand results of CAD package	
Proposed designs	Design diagrams and tables	CAD package & Engineer	Engineer must be able to use CAD package & CAD libraries	
Structural design	Structural description of design	Engineer & Technician & CAD package		
Forces on building	Calculations of wind & snow forces on walls & both sides of the roof	FORTRAN program & Engineer	Engineer must input necessary information to FORTRAN program	

Table 3: Communication transactions: designing a portal frame building

Information Exchange Specification	Information items	Agents involved	Message specifications	Control over messages
Requirements-IE1	Features of the building *Role*: Core object *Form*: Requirements Specification document *Medium*: Negotiation meetings	Client & Partner	*Communication type*: Request-propose *Content*: Client's requirements on the design – as agreed by the designer *Reference*: It may be deemed necessary to refer to specific laws of contracting here	Either agent may initiate messages

Table 4: Example Information Exchange Specification

3 Concept/System level Models: Checking Design against Standards

The Concept or System level (the 3rd level identified in Figure 1) deals with the problem solving steps that comprise *one* of the tasks that were identified in the Task Model. This reflects the typical knowledge engineering process of examining tasks within a business process, and deciding which one(s) would benefit from being supported with a KBS or other automated system. In this example, the task that has been chosen for further decomposition is "Check building meets regulated standards". The knowledge that is required to perform this particular subtask – the steps involved, the resources and information required, and the order in which the steps are carried out – is expanded in detail in the Knowledge/Expertise model.

At this level of abstraction, the tasks that provide the source for the Agent and Communication models are drawn from the "task structure" component of the Knowledge/Expertise model. This component can be represented in a diagram (similar in format to Figure 2) or in a semi-formal language (CommonKADS' Conceptual Modelling Language, or CML) - see Figure 6.

task assessing-building-against-British-standards
goal check that a building design conforms to British standards
task structure
  assessing-building-against-British-standards(results of checks)
  obtain(numerical description of building)
  transform(numerical description → model of the building)
loop until all checks are completed
  select(a check to perform)
  obtain(any further information required for that check)
  match(model of building + standards relevant to the chosen check → result of check)
  report(results of check)

Figure 6: Task structure for checking a design against standards in CML

3.1 Agent Model: checking a design against standards

The Agent model for checking a design against standards, in "extended use case" format, is shown in Figure 7. It includes a number of information sources (such as manufacturer's tables) which are considered too specific to include in the higher level model. Drawing on ORDIT again, these information sources are treated as resources. Since resources are static objects, the notation used in the extended agent model diagram is the notation used for classes in the UML class diagram format.

Since a particular subtask will often be carried out by one or at the most two agents, it is understandable that CommonKADS did not consider it necessary to prepare an Agent model at this level of detail. However, when the ORDIT-based constraints of CAN, MAY, MUST and HAS RIGHTS TO are introduced, then the value of developing an Agent model at this level of detail can be seen. Tables 5 and 6 provide some further information on this Agent model.

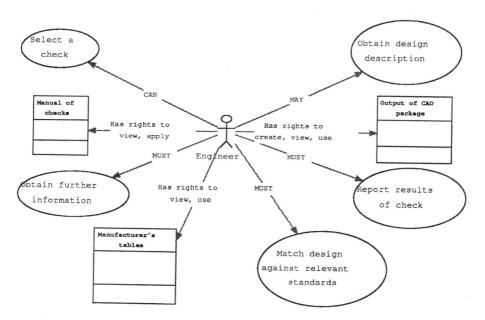

Figure 7: Agent model for checking a design against regulated standards

3.2 Communication model: Checking design against standards

3.2.1 Dialogue diagram

The dialogue diagram derived from this task structure is shown in Figure 8. In this diagram, as in the Agent model, I have chosen to represent information sources. These join with the links representing information flow between tasks and transactions to provide a reasonably good data flow diagram for the task of checking a design against standards. This is useful information when designing a system (either a technology or a technique) to support this task.

3.2.2 Transaction control diagram

Much of the transaction control at the system level is represented in the (CML) task structure, so there is little need for a transaction control diagram at the

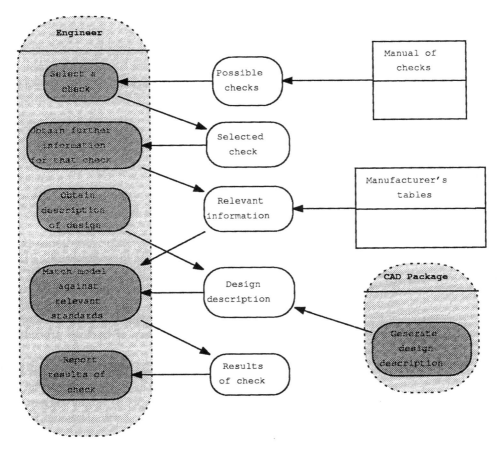

Figure 8: Dialogue diagram for checking a design against regulated standards

system level. The only remaining feature of control on transactions that needs to be noted is that the engineer takes the initiative in consulting information sources. This may seem an obvious statement, but if the reverse was true (such as might occur with an information source that supplied stock market prices, for example) then there are many important issues raised for any resulting implementation connected with asynchronous inputs and real-time processing. This information can be captured in the Information Exchange Specification tables, however.

3.2.3 Transactions

The transactions for this communication model are represented in Table 7. The most noteworthy column of this table is the Constraints column, where constraints that might otherwise be glossed over as being too obvious (e.g. that all relevant checks must actually be in the manual of checks) are identified.

3.2.4   Information exchange specification

As stated above, the information exchange specification gives details of initiative in transactions. It also plays a similar role to the Transactions table in that it makes sure that apparently obvious assumptions, such as that checks are performed one at a time, are identified. An example of a system-level information exchange specification can be seen in Table 8.

4   Discussion

4.1   Benefits

The main benefits of building these models are as follows:

- They serve as an *aide memoire*; that is, they help raise issues that may have been overlooked but which are important in understanding the business process or in system design. For example, the "Transactions" table of the system level communication model (Table 7) specifies that the CAD package must be in working order. Being forced to specify this leads to considering alternatives to the process when the CAD package is not working, as well as considering the adequacy of backup procedures for the data stored in the CAD package.

  The models are also helpful when they identify key competences that are necessary; for example, highlighting that the engineer must be able to understand the manual of design checks (Table 8) might suggest that an explanation component should be included in the final system for the use of more junior engineers who have trouble understanding the manual.

- When they are used to describe an existing system or process, they organise the knowledge well, thus both providing clear descriptions of the process and and making it easier to build complete models of all relevant knowledge – for when knowledge is laid out clearly in separate categories, it becomes easier to identify gaps in that knowledge.

- These models are arguably most beneficial when they are used to prescribe future roles and co-operation, rather than describing an existing situation. In this instance, the models can be used to analyse the situation, and to support decisions about the allocation of roles. Such decisions can have an enormous impact on the resulting business process (for enterprise level models) or system design (for system level models).

An excellent example of the last point above comes from a project carried out by AIAI for an insurance company. It was decided that a KBS was needed to assist in the identification of errors on insurance forms; it is therefore the system level of abstraction that is of concern. The task structure from the relevant Knowledge/Expertise model is shown in Figure 9.

Agent	Position	Tasks	Communicates with	Knowledge items
Engineer	Chief checker	Select a check; Obtain further information for that check; Obtain description of design; Match the design against relevant standards; Report results.	Manufacturer's tables; Manual of checks; CAD package	Which checks are relevant; Engineer can comprehend the language of the checks; Location of necessary information; Ability to derive information that isn't available (e.g. make measurements); Ability to operate CAD package and obtain information from it
CAD package	Supplier of design description		Engineer	Design description; CAD libraries

Table 5: Agent model for checking design against standards (part 1 of 2)

Agent	Capability	Author-ity	Rights	Responsibility	Other const-raints
Engineer	Derive information from design description; Operate CAD package; Locate information in manufacturer's tables; Understand checks	Carry out checks	View and use manufacturer's tables; View and apply manual of checks; Create, view and use design description;	Carry out all relevant checks	
CAD package	Represent design; Display design description; Access CAD libraries	None	None	Make accurate calculations	

Table 6: Agent model for checking design against standards (part 2 of 2)

Transact-ion name	Information object	Agents involved	Constraints	Information Exchange Specification
Possible checks	List of checks	Engineer, Legislator	All relevant checks must be listed	PossibleChecks-IE1
Selected check	Check to carry out	Engineer	One at a time? Or can multiple checks be done simultaneously?	SelectedCheck-IE1
Relevant information	Information derived from manufact-urer's tables and design description	Engineer, CAD package	Must be available where it's needed	RelevantInformation-IE1
Design Description	Description of the design, its components and capabilities	CAD package, Engineer	CAD package must be in working order	DesignDescription-IE1
Results of check	Check passed, Check failed, or Warning (borderline pass)	Engineer	Must describe results in sufficient detail so that partners are confident checks have been carried out	ResultsOfCheck-IE1

Table 7: Communication transactions: checking design against standards

Transaction Name	Agents involved	Information Items	Message Specifications	Control over messages
PossibleChecks-IE1	Engineer, Legislator	List of checks Role: Core object Form: Manual with an index. Does it have applicability constraints on checks? Medium: Paper	Communication type: TO DO Content: List of regulations Reference: British Standards BS 5750, other pieces of legislation …	The list is consulted repeatedly by the engineer, and a new relevant check is identified each time, until the end of the list is reached

Table 8: Communication model for checking design against standards: Information Exchange Specification

task identify-errors-on-forms
goal check each field on a form against its predicted value to identify errors made when filling in the form
control-terms
fields = set of all fields on the form
task structure
    identify-errors-on-forms(classified-errors)
    decompose(form → fields)
    do for each field ∈ fields
        specify(expected value)
        read(actual value)
        match(actual value + expected value → mismatches)
        classify(errors → classified-errors)

Figure 9: Task structure for checking forms for errors

Each of the five tasks identified must be carried out by either the KBS or the user. Since knowledge based systems are typically good at performing matching tasks, it would be normal for the "match expected value against actual value" task to be allocated to the system. However, this would have required the user to type in many values from many different forms, and it also required the KBS to have considerable knowledge about the nature of the data, near-matches, etc.

It was decided that the forms would not actually be input into the KBS; instead, the KBS would advise the user on fields to check, and the user would perform the actual matching. The effects of assigning the matching task to the user on the system design were immense. KBS designers often use production rules to implement matching tasks; but, with the matching task being performed by the user, it was decided that the forms processing KBS could be developed entirely using object-oriented programming.

4.2 Drawbacks

The most obvious drawback of developing all these models is the time required to produce all the tables and diagrams. In some circumstances (e.g. safety critical applications, or applications where there is a high turnover of staff), the effort of developing all these models is paid back by reduced risk or higher maintainability of the resulting system. However, many KBS developers will find the development of a full suite of agent and communication models to be more effort than it's worth.

Because of this, a shorthand version of the Agent and Communication models is suggested:

- Agent model: draw the extended use case diagram (i.e. the one with labelled arcs and "resources");

- Communication model: draw the dialogue diagram. This diagram is very similar to Role Activity Diagrams [8] which have been proposed as a shorthand format for both the Agent and Communication models in previous publications (e.g. [6]).

- Communication model: produce a table of communications that combines the Transactions table and the Information Exchange specification table.

4.3 Summary

In summary, the Agent and Communication models represent the roles and capabilities of agents and the transactions that occur during a particular process. They are a valuable component of the overall CommonKADS suite of models, and can be used to support organising acquired knowledge, re-organising a business process, or designing a knowledge based system. They organise knowledge clearly (if not concisely), and are particularly useful if used at two different levels of detail, capturing both the agents and communications at the level of tasks within a particular business process, and at the level of subtasks within a single (knowledge-based) task.

References

[1] A.Th. Schreiber, J.M. Akkermans et al. *Engineering and Managing Knowledge: The CommonKADS Methodology.* University of Amsterdam, Amsterdam, 1998.

[2] J. Breuker and W. van de Velde. *The CommonKADS Library: reusable components for artificial problem solving.* IOS Press, Amsterdam, Tokyo, 1994.

[3] H.P. de Greef and J. Breuker. Analysing system-user cooperation in KADS. *Knowledge Acquisition*, 4(1):89–108, March 1992.

[4] J. Dobson and R. Strens. Organisational Requirements Definition for Information Technology Systems. In *ACM International Conference on Requirements Engineering, Denver, USA, 1994.* ACM, 1994.

[5] R. Inder and I.M. Filby. A Survey of Knowledge Engineering Methods and Supporting Tools. In *KBS Methodologies Workshop.* BCS Specialist Group on Expert Systems, December 1992.

[6] J.K.C. Kingston, T.J. Lydiard and A. Griffith. Multi-Perspective Modelling of Air Campaign Planning. In *Proceedings of AAAI-96*, Portland, Oregon, 1996. AAAI Press.

[7] J. Kingston and A. Macintosh. Knowledge management through multi-perspective modelling: Representing and distributing organizational memory. *Knowledge Based Systems Journal*, (13):121–131, 2000.

[8] M. Ould. Process Modelling with RADs. *IOPener: the newsletter of Praxis plc*, 1-5 to 2-2, 1992-3.

[9] Rational Software. UML Resource Center. http://www.rational.com/uml/.

Designing for Scalabilty in a Knowledge Fusion System

Alun Preece, Kit Hui

Department of Computing Science, University of Aberdeen
Aberdeen, UK

Alex Gray, Philippe Marti

Department of Computer Science, Cardiff University
Cardiff, UK

Abstract

The KRAFT project has defined a generic agent-based architecture to support *knowledge fusion* — the process of locating and extracting knowledge from multiple, heterogeneous on-line sources, and transforming it so that the union of the knowledge can be applied in problem-solving. KRAFT focuses on knowledge in the form of *constraints* expressed against an object data model defined by a shared ontology. KRAFT employs three kinds of agent: *facilitators* locate appropriate on-line sources of knowledge; *wrappers* transform heterogeneous knowledge to a homogeneous constraint interchange format; *mediators* fuse the constraints together with associated data to form a dynamically-composed constraint satisfaction problem, which is then passed to an existing constraint solver engine to compute solutions.

The KRAFT architecture has been designed to be scalable to large numbers of agents; this paper describes the features of the architecture designed to support scalability. In particular, we examine static techniques that underpin the growth of large-scale KRAFT networks, and dynamic techniques that allow reorganisation of a KRAFT network as it increases in scale.

1 Introduction

The KRAFT project (Knowledge Reuse And Fusion/Transformation) aims to define a generic architecture for knowledge fusion. Knowledge fusion refers to the process of locating and extracting knowledge from multiple, heterogeneous on-line sources, and transforming it so that the union of the knowledge can be applied in problem-solving.

The KRAFT architecture was conceived to support *configuration design applications* involving multiple component vendors with heterogeneous knowledge and data models. This kind of application turns out to be very general, covering not only the obvious manufacturing-type applications (for example, configuration of personal computers or telecommunications network equipment) but also service-type applications such as travel planning (for example, composing package holidays or business trips involving flights, ground travel connections, and hotels) and knowledge management (for example, selecting and combining business rules from multiple heterogeneous knowledge and databases on a corporate intranet).

A key feature of the KRAFT project is that the form of knowledge is restricted to *constraints* expressed against an object data model defined by a shared ontology [7, 13]. This ontology specifies the knowledge available in resources external to the current KRAFT network, and allows the external resource concepts to be expressed in a common internal representation. This internal KRAFT resource is used by *facilitator* and *wrapper* agents and is managed by a special *mediator* agent.

KRAFT builds upon work done in the early 1990s on knowledge sharing and reuse, most notably the results of the Knowledge Sharing Effort (KSE) project [11]. Although it did result in a number of practical applications (for example, [5, 9]), the early work on knowledge sharing and reuse has not had the expected impact in the construction of large-scale, open, distributed knowledge systems. One area that was not addressed in the early work was that of *scalability*: few systems used more than 10 agents. However, there is now a rapidly-growing demand for "Internet scale" systems that support the exchange and processing of rich information in areas such as electronic commerce and knowledge management. Any architecture targeting these areas must be designed with scalability in mind. An important aspect of KRAFT is the use of constraints (intensional data) to reduce the quantities of extensional data being transported and so improve scalability.

This paper can be regarded as a sequel to the paper we presented on the KRAFT architecture at ES99 [13]; here, our focus is on the implementation of the architecture, and in particular on the design features that support scalability. In particular, we will examine *static* techniques that underpin the growth of large-scale KRAFT networks, and *dynamic* techniques that allow reorganisation of a KRAFT network as it increases in scale. Before we can do this, however, we need to review the KRAFT agent-based architecture and its implementation.

The paper is organised as follows. Section 2 presents an overview of the architecture, including the conceptual operations of the main types of agent, and the implementation design. Section 3 examines how scalability has been designed into the architecture as a whole, and the individual agents. Section 4 concludes.

2 The KRAFT Agent Architecture

An overview of the generic KRAFT architecture is shown in Figure 1. KRAFT agents are shown as ovals. There are three kinds of these: wrappers, mediators, and facilitators. All of these are knowledge-processing entities, and are described in sections 2.1, 2.2, and 2.3. External services are shown as boxes. There are three kinds of these: user agents, resources (typically databases or knowledge bases), and solvers. All of these external services are producers and consumers of knowledge: users supply their requirements to the network in the form of constraints via a user agent service, and receive results in the same way. Resources store, and can be queried for, knowledge and data. Solvers accept CSPs and return the results of the solving process. Within a KRAFT network, the constraints and data are expressed using the concepts defined in the shared ontology.

KRAFT agents communicate via messages using a nested protocol suite. KRAFT messages are implemented as character strings transported by a suitable carrier pro-

322

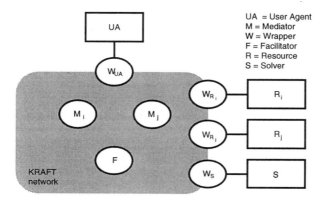

Figure 1: Overview of the generic KRAFT architecture.

tocol. A simple message protocol encapsulates each message with low-level header information, including a timestamp and network information. The body of the message consists of two nested protocols: the outer protocol is the *Constraint Command and Query Language* (CCQL) which is a specialised subset of the Knowledge Query and Manipulation Language (KQML) [10]. Nested within the CCQL message is its content, expressed in the *Constraint Interchange Format* (CIF).

In the current implementation, KRAFT messages are syntactically Prolog term structures. An example message is shown in Figure 2. The outermost `kraft_msg` structure contains a `context` clause (header information) and a `ccql` clause. The message is from an agent called `storage_inc` to an agent called `pc_configurator`. The `ccql` structure contains, within its content field, a CIF expression (in the implementation, CIF expressions are actually transmitted in a compiled internal format). CIF is described further in Section 2.1.

The following sub-sections examine the operations of each of the three kinds of KRAFT agent in more detail.

2.1 Wrapper Agents

Wrappers are agents that act as proxies for external resources — commonly, these will be "knowledge suppliers". Wrappers serve two purposes: they *advertise* the capabilites of the resource to a facilitator, when the resource comes on-line (see Section 2.3), and they *transform* knowledge between the common interchange format used within a KRAFT network, and the internal format used privately by the resource. In both these tasks they utilise the shared ontology.

2.2 Mediator Agents

KRAFT follows Wiederhold's definition of a mediator as a component that performs a specific information-processing task, often programmed by an individual domain expert [17]; every mediator "adds value" in some way to knowledge obtained from other

```
kraft_msg(
  context(1,id(19), pc_configurator, storage_inc,
    time_stamp(date(29,9,1999), time(14,45,34)))),
  ccql(tell, [
    sender : storage_inc,
    receiver : pc_configurator,
    reply_with : id(18),
    ontology : shared,
    language : cif,
    content : [
      constrain
        each d in disk_drive
          such that name(vendor(d)) = "Storage Inc"
            and type(d) = "Zip"
        at least 1 p in ports(host_pc(d))
          to have type(p) = "USB"
      ])
)
```

Figure 2: An example KRAFT CCQL message.

agents. In KRAFT, the main tasks performed by mediators are ontology management and knowledge fusion. To perform knowledge fusion, a mediator gathers constraints from other agents (typically wrappers as described in Section 2.1), and processes them to form a coherent CSP at run-time for solving. This is shown in Figure 3. As part of this task, mediators will typically pre-process the constraints in various ways; they will also need to plan and perform selective database queries as explained in [6].

There will typically be several mediators in a KRAFT network: one to perform each distinct value-adding service. For example, in a KRAFT network performing configuration of PC products, there may be a single configurator mediator, or there may be several configurators, perhaps one for each of several different kinds of PC (laptops, generic desktops, special-purpose workstations, etc) or one for each of several distinct subsystems (CPU, peripheral systems, application software bundles, etc).

2.3   Facilitator Agents

Facilitators are the "matchmaker" agents that allow agents to discover one another [9, 17]. As they come online, agents register their identities, network locations, and advertisements of their knowledge-processing capabilities with a known facilitator. When an agent needs to request a service from another agent, it asks a facilitator to *recommend* an agent that appears to provide that service.

A resource capability must be represented intentionally and generically for compactness, but in a way that minimises imprecision. The abstract characteristics of a resource are communicated by means of advertisement messages. The terms used in the body of advertisements are defined in the shared ontology. The facilitator encap-

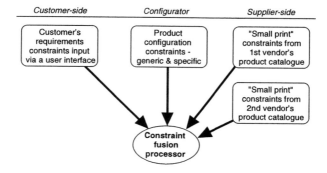

Figure 3: Fusion of constraints from multiple sources.

sulates a database of received advertisements with the above components; the CCQL facilitation operations (forwarding and brokerage) are implemented as queries on this advertisement database.

Each KRAFT network requires at least one facilitator. In a large network, there may be multiple facilitators, either for reasons of specialisation or efficiency.

2.4 Implementation of the KRAFT architecture

Inter-agent communication in KRAFT is implemented by message passing using the Linda tuple-space communication model [4]. A Linda server manages the tuple space; clients connect to the space to write or read tuples (messages). KRAFT uses a Prolog implementation of Linda, where tuples are Prolog term structures: instances of the kraft_msg term structure shown earlier. To send a message, an agent writes it to a Linda server with the name of the recipient; to receive a message, an agent reads any tuples with its own name as the value of the receiver field. An advantage of using this model is that the individual agents do not need to be multithreaded; they choose when to receive any waiting messages synchronously. KRAFT agents can be written in any language provided that they have a Linda client module. Currently, these are available for Prolog and Java agents.

The Linda model is most effective for local-area communication, so to support wide-area KRAFT networks a federated Linda space has been implemented. Each local-area (called a *hub*) has its own Linda server with which local agents interact. The agent namespace has a URL-like *hubname/agentname* syntax. Each Linda server is coupled to a *gateway* agent that relays messages between hubs in a manner similar to an internet router: if a message is posted on the local Linda server with a non-local *hubname* for the recipient, the gateway relays the message to the correct hub gateway agent, which in turn writes it to the hub's local Linda server. This architecture is shown in Figure 4. In the current implementation, the protocol used to carry messages between hubs is TCP via the socket interface; preliminary work has also been done on inter-hub communication using CORBA IIOP [12].

To support debugging, a *Monitor* user agent has been implemented to trace and

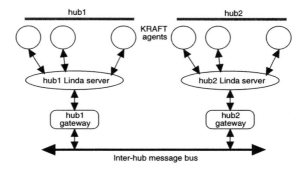

Figure 4: Implementation of the KRAFT architecture.

display the passage of messages across a KRAFT network, shown in Figure 5. Monitor agents are able to register with the gateway agents in order to display activity at non-local hubs, allowing a user to see interactions across the entire KRAFT network.

3   Designing for Scalability in KRAFT

During the design of the KRAFT architecture, scalability was borne in mind. The issue of scalability in a distributed environment is concerned with reducing the degradation in performance as the work load increases. This work load can be measured in a number of ways, such as the number of users, activities, resource providers, and sites. Inevitably as the distributed environment grows there is some degradation in performance. Broadly, there are two kinds of technique that can be used to tackle this problem: *static* and *dynamic* techniques.

- *Static techniques* are generally concerned with architectural decisions that have been taken to support the general scalability of the system and are independent of the dynamic situation.

- *Dynamic techniques* monitor the current state of the distributed system (for example, the demand on each resource, or the performance profile of each agent), and attempt to respond to fluctuating performance in different parts of the system by ameliorating the factors causing performance degradation. Hence, dynamic techniques respond to feedback from monitors which are evaluating the current performance to identify peaks and/or bottlenecks.

In KRAFT, both static and dynamic of scalability techniques have been employed. To this end, six strategies were built-into the architecture:

1. An intelligent strategy for resource querying and constraint solving aims to minimise number of messages, and volume of data transferred, conserving bandwidth.

2. The federated messaging architecture (internet-style) using Linda hubs aims to minimise network traffic, while also being easy to manage and fault-tolerant.

326

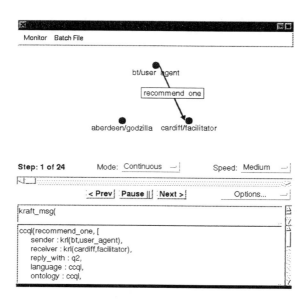

Figure 5: Screenshot of the KRAFT Monitor user agent.

3. Mediators can easily be replicated on their local hub, allowing for concurrent processing and load-balancing.

4. Use of virtual machines for agent implementations (e.g. Java and Prolog) are encouraged, to allow agent mobility in cases where processing needs to be moved local to a resource, or where it is necessary to transfer/replicate an agent on a different hub.

5. Facilitator bottlenecks are avoided by allowing for facilitator replication and specialisation (for example, having a hierarchy of facilitators, similar to DNS), and by using generic advertising to reduce the number of advertisements.

6. The shared ontology supports ontology clusters which in turn allow for evolvability (different worlds) and bottom-up integration of independently-created networks.

All of these strategies have a static aspect, in that they allow a KRAFT network designer to address the problem of scalability at design-time. However, strategies (3–5) have a significant dynamic aspect, as described below.

We will now examine each of these strategies in more detail.

3.1 Querying and Solving Strategy

As described in Section 2.2, mediators that perform constraint fusion undertake a combination of operations in constructing a CSP at run-time: gathering and pre-processing a set of constraints from contributing agents, and querying database wrappers in order to populate the domains for the CSP. The two most costly operations here are actually external to the mediator: these are:

1. the network traffic generated by the constraint and data gathering process; and

2. the constraint solving process carried out by the wrapped solver to which the mediator dispatches the CSP.

The KRAFT architecture is designed to try to minimise both these costs, as follows:

1. In terms of network traffic, constraints are a compact way of transmitting what could otherwise be substantial volumes of data. In a conventional information interchange approach, data instances would be transmitted extensionally, whereas in the constraint approach, each constraint is an intensional definition of a potentially-large amount of data [15].

   Moreover, where it *is* necessary to transfer a number of instances extensionally (for example, to populate a variable domain for a CSP), constraints can be used by the mediator as a *filter* to reduce the number of instances based on what is known about the solution space so far. For example, if it is already known that a PC customer needs at least a 17-inch monitor, there is no point in the monitor vendor shipping instances of 15-inch monitors. The "screen size $>= 17$ inches" constraint would be sent by the mediator to the monitor vendor's wrapper for it to use as part of the internal query on the monitors product catalogue.

2. In terms of constraint solving, the mediator can perform an arbitrary amount of pre-processing on the CSP before sending it to the solver. It can also select what it deems to be the optimal kind of solver for the problem-at-hand. The pre-processing can include simplifying the problem (for example, if redundant constraints are detected) or even aborting the solving process (for example, if a conflict is detected in the CSP that renders it insoluble). Also, the aforementioned process used to build the CSP in terms of gathering instances to populate the variable domains will itself tend to simplify the CSP by filtering out a significant number of "useless" values (this is similar to the forward-checking technique used in constraint solving [8], but applied in the distributed context).

These normally lead to a reduction in data being transported in the network, and so improve scalability.

3.2 Federated Messaging Architecture

Unlike some agent communication architectures (for example, JATlite[1]) KRAFT does not rely on a centralised message routing mechanism. Routing in KRAFT, like routing in the Internet, is decentralised. The Linda hub architecture shown in Figure 4 allows messages local to a hub to pass unnoticed by other hubs. When the hub is entirely local

---

[1] http://java.stanford.edu/

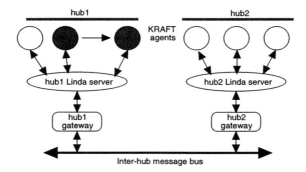

Figure 6: Cloning a mediator on a local hub in a KRAFT network.

to a single host, no network traffic at all is generated (messages are passed through the TCP/IP "loopback" interface). The only wide-area network traffic consists of inter-hub messages, which pass between widely-separated gateways. Section 3.4 explains how even this traffic can be minimised.

An important exception here is where monitor agents are configured to monitor activity at more than one hub. In this case, the hub message server is notified to "echo" messages between monitored hubs, and this can lead to substantial network traffic. Therefore, such monitoring is recommended only for testing, and never for use in an operational KRAFT network.

3.3   Mediator Replication

It is conceivable that mediators whose services are much in demand will become bottlenecks. Such bottlenecks are easily detected by the hub servers, which can see that message traffic to and from particular agents is greater than normal, or are not being processed as rapidly as would be desirable. (This is like an office manager observing the "in" and "out" trays of workers in an office: in KRAFT these "trays" are collections of messages on the Linda tuple space managed by the hub server.) Locally, it is relatively easy to clone KRAFT mediators, because these agents do not tend to have persistent storage (if they do, they will typically use a shared private database for this purpose). Therefore, a mediator can be cloned in principle by simply asking the local OS to spawn another instance of the mediator process. The mediator would be passed a unique agent name by the hub server. This is illustrated in Figure 6 — the shaded agent (a mediator) is cloned on *hub1*.

In this way, mediator services can easily be replicated locally to provide concurrent processing. This technique is equally useful for replicating ontology-management mediators as well as those performing knowledge fusion.

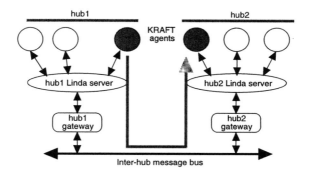

Figure 7: Replicating a mediator on a remote hub in a KRAFT network.

3.4 Agent Mobility

Section 3.3 covers the case where a mediator is replicated locally. It is also possible to replicate a mediator on a different hub. (Or indeed, to relocate the mediator, by replicating it then removing the original.) This is possible when the mediator is implemented in a language that uses a virtual machine environment. KRAFT encourages the use of such languages; currently, the trial systems have been implemented using Prolog and Java. In these cases, the code for the mediator can be encapsulated in an inter-hub message directed to a hub manager. Upon receipt, the hub can spawn an instance of the appropriate virtual machine and pre-load it with the encapsulated agent. This is illustrated in Figure 7 — the shaded agent (a mediator) is replicated on *hub2*, after being shipped over the network from *hub1*.

This kind of mobility is most advantageous when one wants to move the processing capability closer to the data. Localised communication is always far less costly than wide-area communication, so moving a mediator from a remote hub to the same hub as the data resources can improve performance significantly.

3.5 Facilitator Federations

As the scale of a KRAFT network grows, there is a danger that facilitators will become bottlenecks. A number of strategies are available to avoid this problem.

Normally, each hub will have its own local facilitator, to which requests can be directed without the cost of wide-area traffic. If each of these facilitators is to have knowledge of the entire multi-hub KRAFT network, then they obviously must exchange advertisements among one another. However, recommend requests are typically much more common than advertise requests, so most of their work then will involve local message traffic.

If the network becomes too large to allow each local facilitator to store complete advertisement information, then there are a number of possibilities to reduce the amount of information held by each facilitator. One option is to have *specialist* facilitators, each holding knowledge about a particular area of the shared ontology (for example, in a consumer electronics marketplace, there could be a facilitator that

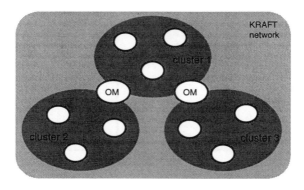

Figure 8: Three ontological clusters within the same KRAFT network.

knows about the PC sector, another that knows about the mobile phone sector, and so on). A "meta-facilitator" would be consulted first to locate the appropriate specialist facilitator for a given request. Of course, any of these facilitators could also be replicated if necessary. Another possibility is to partition the facilitation space according to location, where each facilitator would have knowledge about its local hub (or local hubs), and would direct requests that can't be answered locally to a neighbouring facilitator. This approach is essentially similar to the Internet routing scheme.

The use of generic advertisements will reduce the number of advertisements as it eliminates the need to hold specific advertisements. It also reduces the number to be examined when locating appropriate external resources, albeit at the expense of a possibly more complex matching algorithm.

3.6 Ontology Clusters

The schemes outlined in Section 3.5 cover only the cases where the entire KRAFT network uses a single shared ontology, against which all advertisements and requests are expressed. CCQL allows for mutliple ontologies to coexist within the same (using the ontology field in each message) but, more importantly, allows for agents using different ontologies to interoperate by means of *ontology clusters* and inter-ontology mappings. An ontology cluster is a community of KRAFT agents that use the same shared ontology; a cluster that uses shared ontology SO_1 can interoperate with a cluster that uses shared ontology SO_2 if and only if there is an *ontological mapping* from SO_1 to SO_2. Messages with content expressed against SO_1 would be sent to a designated *ontological mediator* (OM) that would transform the content to SO_2 before fowarding the message to the intended recipient. Figure 8 shows three ontological clusters within the same KRAFT network, bridged by ontological mediators.

This part of the design for the KRAFT architecture is elaborated in [14]. The ontological clusters allow for evolvability (different worlds which must be made to inter-operate) and bottom-up integration of independently-created KRAFT networks.

4 Conclusion

Addressing the issue of scalability in a distributed environment involves managing the potential degradation in performance as work load increases. Typically, this is done by employing a combination of static (design-time) and dynamic (run-time) strategies. In KRAFT architecture, the static techniques available to support scalability are as follows:

- the use of intensional data reduces the quantity of extensional data being transported in the network;

- the use of generic advert representation reduces the number of adverts stored and analysed;

- the use of optimal solvers and filters reduces the amount of extensional data accessed from external sources in CSP;

- the ability to clone at all KRAFT sites the facilitator, mediators and ontology mean that it is possible to design the architecture so that there is no network traffic if a CSP can be solved with local facilities only;

- the Linda hub design means that local messages are processed locally — they also support an easy implementation of monitors which trigger dynamic techniques as the tuples held in a Linda hub show the dynamic state of many of the KRAFT components; and

- the use of ontology clusters and a build-up approach to creating the local shared ontology for a cluster means they reflect their user community needs, which again restricts the number of occasions when there is a need to link to other ontologies in the cluster.

The dynamic techniques that support run-time scalability in the KRAFT architecture are founded on the use of a managed, hub-based design: the messages at the Linda hubs can be monitored to determine where the bottlenecks are occurring and which agents are involved. As a result of this monitoring, agents can be cloned at the same or another site to reduce network traffic and overall time when an agent is overloaded. Agents can migrate to new sites if the platform configuration at that site and/or the current situation is better suited to their processing needs.

We contend that these static and dynamic features mean that the degradation of performance in a KRAFT network as workload increases is graceful, and the environment is able to react to fluctuation in usage patterns if this is needed.

Acknowledgements. KRAFT is a collaborative research project between the Universities of Aberdeen, Cardiff and Liverpool, and BT. The project has received funding from the UK Engineering and Physical Sciences Research Council, and BT.

References

[1] J. Andreoli, U. Borghoff, and R. Pareschi, Constraint agents for the information age, *Journal of Universal Computer Science*, 1:762–789, 1995.

[2] N. Bassiliades and P. M. D. Gray, CoLan: A functional constraint language and its implementation, *Data and Knowledge Engineering*, 14:203–249, 1994.

[3] R. Bayardo et al, InfoSleuth: agent-based semantic integration of information in open and dynamic environments, In *Proc. SIGMOD'97*, 1997.

[4] N. Carriero and D. Gelernter, Linda in Context, *Communications of the ACM*, 32:444–458, 1989.

[5] M. Cutkosky, R. Engelmore, R. Fikes, M. Genesereth, T. Gruber, W. Mark, J. Tenenbaum, and J. Weber, PACT: an experiment in integrating concurrent engineering systems, *IEEE Computer*, 26:8–27, 1993.

[6] P. M. D. Gray, S. M. Embury, K. Y. Hui, and G. Kemp, The evolving role of constraints in the functional data model, *Journal of Intelligent Information Systems*, 1–27, 1999.

[7] P. Gray, A. Preece, N. Fiddian, W. Gray, T. Bench-Capon, M. Shave, N. Azarmi, and M. Wiegand, KRAFT: knowledge fusion from distributed databases and knowledge bases, in *Proc. 8th International Workshop on Database and Expert System Applications (DEXA-97)*, pages 682–691, IEEE Press, 1997.

[8] P. van Hentenryck, *Constraint Satisfaction in Logic Programming*, MIT Press, 1989.

[9] D. R. Kuokka, J. G. McGuire, J. C. Weber, J. M. Tenenbaum, T. R. Gruber, and G. R. Olsen, SHADE: Technology for knowledge-based collaborative engineering, *Journal of Concurrent Engineering: Applications and Research*, 1(2), 1993.

[10] Y. Labrou, *Semantics for an Agent Communication Language*, PhD Thesis, University of Maryland, Baltimore MD, USA, 1996.

[11] R. Neches, R. Fikes, T. Finin, T. Gruber, R. Patil, T. Senator, and W. Swartout, Enabling technology for knowledge sharing, *AI Magazine*, 12:36–56, 1991.

[12] A. Preece, A. Borrowman, and T. Francis, Reusable components for KB and DB integration, in *Proc. ECAI'98 Workshop on Intelligent Information Integration*, pages 157–168, 1998.

[13] A. Preece and K. Hui and W. A. Gray and P. Marti and T. Bench-Capon and D. Jones and Z. Cui, The KRAFT Architecture for Knowledge Fusion and Transformation, In *Research and Development in Intelligent Systems XVI (Proc ES99)*, Springer, pages 23–38, 1999.

[14] M. Shave, Ontological structures for knowledge sharing, *New Review of Information Networking*, 3:125–133, 1997.

[15] M. Torrens and B. Faltings, Smart clients: constraint satisfaction as a paradigm for scaleable intelligent information systems, In T Finin and B Grosof (eds) *Artificial Intelligence for Electronic Commerce: Papers from the AAAI-99 Workshop*, AAAI Press, 1999.

[16] P. R. S. Visser, D. M. Jones, T. J. M. Bench-Capon, and M. J. R. Shave, Assessing heterogeneity by classifying ontology mismatches, In *Proc. International Conference on Formal Ontology in Information Systems (FOIS'98)*, IOS Press, pages 148–162, 1998.

[17] G. Wiederhold and M. Genesereth, The basis for mediation, In *Proc. 3rd International Conference on Cooperative Information Systems (COOPIS95)*, 1995.

SESSION 6

BELIEF ACQUISITION AND PLANNING

Acquiring Information from Books

Dr Antoni Diller

School of Computer Science

University of Birmingham

Birmingham

B15 2TT

England

Abstract

People need a vast amount of knowledge in order to live in an advanced technological society. Most of this has to be obtained from others by believing what they say and what they have written. Androids and sophisticated AI systems would also have to be able to learn in this way. This obvious fact tends to be overlooked by AI researchers (such as Pollock and Brooks) involved in the design of androids. They concentrate almost exclusively on belief-formation by means of perception. However, before we can program the ability to learn from others into an android we need to have a better understanding of human belief-acquisition. Elsewhere I have proposed a two-stage model of belief-acquisition. In the first stage we do acquire beliefs by means of our senses, but also from other people. In this latter case we make use of a defeasible rule, 'Believe what you hear or read'. The second stage consists in the use of a sophisticated critical methodology in order to carefully assess a small number of our beliefs. In this paper I develop one part of this model in more detail. I look at the factors that cause us to override the defeasible rule to believe others in the situation when we are reading statements found in a book. This turns out to be far more complicated than may at first sight appear.

1 Introduction

Some people working in AI see its ultimate goal as being that of constructing an artificial person [3, p. 7]. Those working on the MIT Cog Project are more explicit: 'Building an android, an autonomous robot with humanoid form and human-like abilities, has been both a recurring theme in science fiction and a "Holy Grail" for the Artificial Intelligence community' [2]. Many of the theoretical and practical problems associated with the task of manufacturing an android are currently being tackled by a large number of researchers, both in academia and in industry, but there is one very important human ability that such an android would have to possess which has largely been overlooked. As well as having a large amount of in-built knowledge and the ability to acquire beliefs by means of observation, the android would also have to have the ability to extend its knowledge by listening to other people and by reading what they have written. Such an ability is essential if the android is going to be able to interact with human beings in any meaningful way. People acquire a large number of beliefs every day in this way and to mimic human behaviour androids would also have to be able to do this. Understanding what is involved in learning form others, so as to be able to implement it in a machine, is much more complicated than may at first sight appear and in this paper I investigate part of this human ability.

It is well known that human beings have the ability to learn from others. They have the ability to acquire knowledge and beliefs by listening to what other people say and by reading what other people have written. This ability is not optional. In order to live in a human society, especially an advanced, technological one, a person needs a vast amount of knowledge and information. The knowledge required includes what is known as *world knowledge* in AI and *stock* or *commonsense knowledge* in sociology. Although people need to know many practical things, such as how to answer a telephone or how to behave in a restaurant, in this paper I am interested in propositional knowledge. Someone living in an advanced society would need to know, for example, many things about the institution of money and how it works, how goods are bought and sold, where various goods can be bought and so on. He also needs to know some basic facts about electricity, so that he can turn lights on and off and work various electrical appliances safely. He would also need to have some knowledge about different kinds of electrical appliances such as the television, radio, dishwasher, washing-machine, microwave, telephone, computer and so on. A person would also need to know something about the legal and political system of the society in which he lives and something about its social institutions as well. In addition, he would need to know something about the transportation system of the country he lives in. There are also many further things that he would need to know, but I hope that the above gives a flavour of the knowledge required to live in a technologically advanced human society. He would, furthermore, need to have a certain amount of specialised knowledge in order to carry out his various social roles and to do his job (assuming that he has one). Thus, a medical doctor requires a huge amount of information in order to practice medicine and even a bricklayer needs a substantial amount of knowledge in order to do his job properly.

It is impossible for a person to acquire all the knowledge that he needs in order to live in a human society by himself. Most of this knowledge has to be obtained from other people. It is acquired by believing what they say and by trusting what they have written. Furthermore, it is impossible for any person to check every piece of information that he receives and that he has to make use of in his life. This is because it is usually very time-consuming to investigate the truth of an assertion that we hear or read and so a person just does not have the time available to thoroughly test every statement he needs to make use of. In addition, the critical evaluation of a statement itself involves taking for granted very many other statements which themselves have not been thoroughly checked out. It simply is a fact, that some people may regard as unfortunate, that we have to accept most things on trust.

Although most of the information that we need in order to live in a human society we obtain by trusting others, this does not mean that we have to accept an authoritarian theory of knowledge. It is a truism that even the most respected authorities can make mistakes. Although a person cannot check *every* piece of information that he accepts, he can test *some* of the assertions that he hears and reads. The way in which I accommodate these observations is by proposing a two-stage or two-phase model of belief-acquisition. This model was introduced and explained elsewhere [4] and I say more about it in the next section of this paper, but here I just want to mention that anti-authoritarianism appears in the second stage of my model. People differ in how extreme their anti-authoritarianism is. The most radical version involves the acceptance of the principle that no belief or theory is beyond criticism and may, in fact, be criticised and revised if necessary. Such a variety of anti-authoritarianism is represented by pancritical rationalism [1]. Less extreme versions may ring-fence a number of beliefs and principles as being beyond criticism. The larger the number of such things that are beyond criticism the less radical is the version of anti-authoritarianism involved. If the mass manufacture of androids ever becomes a reality, then the diversity of approaches to the extent of criticisability that exists amongst human beings would, no doubt, be mirrored in their mechanical progeny.

Most of a person's belief-system has been obtained by believing other people, but this does not mean that that person accepts absolutely everything that he hears or reads. Believing every assertion and theory that a person encounters would very quickly lead him to have a massively inconsistent belief-system. By this I mean that he would have a large number of obviously inconsistent beliefs. My proposal is that the first phase of belief-acquisition involves making use of a defeasible rule to the effect that we accept other people's assertions at face value. There are many features concerning the making of an assertion and its content that make us wary of accepting it outright. For example, a person may be very wary of accepting the assertions of a government spin-doctor when these are presented in the context of a press briefing. Any feature that we take into account in the first stage of belief-acquisition has to be, of necessity, easy to recognise. Such a factor has to be easy to recognise because we hear and read so many statements every day that we have to decide very quickly whether or not we are going to accept them. It does not, however, involve thoroughly testing an assertion before it is accepted. To use some computing metaphors, our decisions have to be made in real time and on-line. Because these features of assertions have to be straightforward to recognise, they cannot be very sophisticated. This means that people do end up having quite a few false beliefs and several incorrect pieces of information. This is another reason for holding a two-phase model of belief-acquisition. In the second stage we look more carefully at a small number of our beliefs and thoroughly check them out. In this way we can try to minimise the number of false beliefs that we have about issues that are particularly important to us.

So far in this introduction I have been writing mainly about human abilities. An android or AI system that was sufficiently advanced to be capable of interacting with human beings, talking to them, learning from them and maybe also teaching them would clearly have to have similar abilities to those described briefly above. In order to produce an android with these abilities, we first need to have a good understanding of them and that is what I am after. In this paper I make a start on the task of looking in more detail at one aspect of the first stage of belief-acquisition. I look in detail at the features of assertions found in books that make us wary of accepting them outright and I isolate many of the factors that cause us to override our default principle to accept what we read in books. My long-term goal is to formulate these things in sufficient detail so that they can be programmed into an android or AI system. People acquire knowledge from a variety of sources. For example, they get beliefs by listening to other people, by reading books and articles, from the media, from the Internet and so on. This paper is one in a series in which I look in detail at each of these sources. There are enough significant differences between how we evaluate the information coming from these sources for each to be handled separately. Looking at how we assess information given during a personal communication [5] should convince the reader of this.

2 The Two-phase Model

In this section I summarise the two-phase model of belief-acquisition that I introduced elsewhere [4] in a simpler form. Since then the model has been considerably refined, extended and improved.

In the first phase we acquire beliefs by reading what other people have written, by listening to what they say and by making judgments about our surroundings. These processes, however, do not always result in us acquiring true beliefs and so there is a second phase of belief-acquisition in which we critically examine some of our beliefs in order to weed out the false ones and replace them with better ones.

Although most of our knowledge comes from other people, this is a fact that is either ignored by epistemologists or relegated to the periphery of the subject. Centre stage is occupied with issues relating to perception. Pollock, for example, writes [10, p. 52], 'The starting point for belief formation is perception. Perception is a causal process that produces beliefs about an agent's surroundings.' I do not deny that agents do have the ability to make judgments about their surroundings and to acquire beliefs as a result of this, but this ability is much more complicated than Pollock suggests and it is not the only way in which people acquire beliefs. There are, for example, an unlimited number of judgments that an agent can make about his immediate surroundings. Using myself as an example, I can make the following judgments about my current surroundings: 'It's not raining', 'The radio is switched off', 'This room is a mess', 'There is a bookcase near to the door', 'It's peaceful in here', 'The door is open', 'Birds are singing outside' and 'There are several piles of books on the table'. The judgments an agent actually makes depend on a variety of factors in addition to the perceptual properties of his immediate surroundings. These might include his current belief-system, his goals and his values. In my case, if I was not writing this article, I would not have made any of these judgments. My purpose in making them was to make an epistemological point. Some of the factors that influenced which judgments I made originated with me, but others came from other people. We acquire some, but not all, of our beliefs through perception and those that we do are acquired against the background of a large amount of knowledge that we have not obtained through perception. Acquiring beliefs by means of perception involves not only the perceiver and his surroundings but it also involves the perceiver's beliefs, values, goals and so on and a large part of these additional things he has obtained by listening to other people, reading what they have written and by going through an extended period of enculturation.

If I was restricted to acquiring beliefs by making judgments about my immediate surroundings, I would be extremely limited in the beliefs that I could acquire. My knowledge would be very restricted and would not be sufficient for me to be able to live and function in an advanced technological society. We need to make use of beliefs that we acquire by listening to other people and by reading what they have written. Anyone who accepts this is forced to take account of the sort of issues that I am interested in, because we do not simply accept everything that we read or hear. I will illustrate the sorts of factor that we take into account in assessing what we read in books by considering a few examples.

When listening to other people or reading books, our belief-acquisition is governed by means of the defeasible rule, 'Believe what you hear or read'. Most of the time when we read a book there is no reason for us to override this rule. For example, in *The Oxford Companion to Philosophy* [7, p. 378] I read that David Hume lived for a while in Paris. Having read that I now have the belief that Hume lived for a while in Paris. There is no reason for me to doubt the veracity of this fact. For example, Oxford University Press is a well-known publishing house with a reputation for producing reliable and authoritative reference books. Furthermore, I know very little about Hume's life and this piece of information does not clash with any of my pre-existing knowledge.

There are times, however, when I do not accept what I read. For example, in *Chariots of the Gods?* [12] von Däniken writes about the Nasca lines on the plains of Peru and says that they are giant runways for space-craft. Although I have read this, I have not added the belief that the Nasca lines are the markings of giant runways to my belief-system. This is because I have overridden the rule, 'Believe what you read or hear'. I have learned from other sources that von Däniken is unreliable. Furthermore, I know that the Nasca lines are drawn on the pebbly surface of the desert and would be destroyed if an aircraft tried to land on them.

In the two examples just discussed I was dealing with a situation in which we assess the information that we receive from a single source, but it sometimes occurs that we come across several sources relating to the same event and these sources are mutually inconsistent. The sources involved do not all have to be of the same kind. Thus, what we read in a book may conflict with what we hear on the radio or what a friend tells us may conflict with something that we have read in a newspaper. In these circumstances we sometimes use rules that compare the relative merits of these different sources. Although Quine and

Ullian think that we have meta-beliefs about the relative merits of different sources of information, rather than rules, as I am suggesting, they make a similar point [11, p. 14]:

> We all hold ... that those [beliefs] gained from respected encyclopedias and almanacs are more to be relied on than those gained from television commercials.

There are additional factors involved in this example which Quine and Ullian overlook. In acquiring information when our sources conflict we may have to take other things into account in addition to the relative merits of the sources involved. There are, for example, differences between people in how they evaluate reference works. I doubt that Quine and Ullian would regard *Harper's Encyclopedia of Mystical and Paranormal Experience* [6] or *The Encyclopaedia of Occult, Paranormal and Magick Practices* [8] as respected encyclopedias, but there are people who would rate them very highly as authorities. Thus, in addition to comparing sources a person's pre-existing knowledge and general outlook on life may affect what he does with a piece of information that he comes across in a book. When Quine and Ullian write 'We all hold', they seem unaware that they are members of a particular social group with many shared attitudes and beliefs, but which may not be shared with other social groups in the larger pluralistic society that they are members of. This also shows the value of the sort of investigation that I am carrying out in looking at the various factors involved in our assessment of what we read in books.

So far I have been explaining the first phase of belief-acquisition, but I now want to say something about the second phase. We do not have the time to thoroughly check every statement that we read or hear, but we do examine critically a small number of statements that are particularly important to us. For example, earlier in this section I quoted Pollock's assertion that the starting-point for belief-formation is perception [10, p. 52]. Many people reading his statement would simply accept it and add the corresponding belief to their belief-system. However, I think that Pollock is incorrect on this point and above I presented various reasons why I think that Pollock's statement is false and why I do not believe it. In its place I have various other beliefs. For example, I believe that one of the starting-points of belief-formation is perception, but there are others as well. In particular, I believe that we often get our beliefs by accepting what others say and what they have written.

The second stage involves making use of some sort of critical methodology in order to thoroughly investigate the correctness of some of our beliefs. It involves argumentation and reasoning. If the beliefs that we are examining belong to a specialised discipline, like physics, mathematics or archaeology, then methodologies specific to those disciplines may have to be employed in order to check the truth or falsity of our beliefs belonging to those disciplines. I say more about different sorts of criticism elsewhere [4, pp. 24–26].

There is a lot of interaction between a person's belief-system, the factors that he takes into account in order to decide whether or not to override the defeasible rule 'Believe what you hear or read' and his second-stage critical methodology. The following are the three main ways in which these elements interact:

(1) Beliefs are added to a person's belief-system if they do not trigger any of the factors that cause him to override the rule 'Believe what you hear or read'.

(2) The factors that cause overriding involve various beliefs and so can change as the person's belief-system changes. For example, someone may rate a particular reference work very highly until he discovers a number of errors in it. From that time on information obtained from that source will be treated differently from the way in which it was treated before his opinion was revised. Furthermore, such a change in evaluation may entail a revision of beliefs obtained from that source in the past.

(3) Beliefs are also added and removed from a person's belief-system as a result of the operation of that person's critical faculties.

When we come to accept a new belief or reject an old one, that may have a knock-on effect on our pre-existing knowledge. We may have to engage in some form of belief-revision. This is an issue that is the subject of much interest, but I have not said much about it here, because my concerns in this paper are different.

3   Assessing Information Received from Books

Some of the information that a person has he has obtained by reading books. Human beings can be thought of as having a rule to the effect that they should believe everything that they read. This rule is, however, defeasible. If someone rigidly applied this rule and believed everything that he read in a book, then he would very quickly end up with a massively inconsistent belief-system. To see that this is so imagine someone reading Marx's *Das Kapital* followed by reading Popper's *The Open Society and its Enemies*. If such a person believed everything that he read, he would believe everything in Marx's book and everything in Popper's and, thus, he would have very many mutually inconsistent beliefs. Clearly, we do not accept everything that we read.

   Given that the rule 'Believe what you read' is defeasible, we need to enquire into the circumstances when in fact it is defeated. What factors relating to a statement that we read in a book make us wary of accepting it outright? The factors that we take into account can be grouped into four categories. The first of these comprises of a number of *external* features of the book that is being read and the others relate to the *author* or *authors* of the book, the *content* of the statement being assessed and how that content may affect the *reader* of the book. I will next look in more detail at the various factors that occur in these four categories. It should be noted that sometimes a number of factors, maybe belonging to different categories, combine together to make us wary of accepting outright an assertion that we read in a book. In other words, the reader should not assume that the factors that follow are all independent of each other.

3.1 External factors

- We take the kind of book involved into account. There are very many different kinds of book and we do not treat them all in the same way. The following is a selection of the various sorts of book that there are: novels belonging to various genres, textbooks, encyclopaedias, manuals, guide books to foreign countries, travel books, cookery books, biographies and autobiographies, various kinds of reference book, self-help books, religious books, true crime books, history books and so on. Although novels, for example, are written in a similar way to that in which factual accounts of real events are written, we do not accept what we read in novels as being factual statements to be added to our belief-system. We may, however, remember than as accounts of a fictional world.

- We may take the publisher of the book into account. There are, no doubt, differences between people concerning the status of various publishers. Many people in England, however, think highly of publishers like Oxford University Press and Cambridge University Press. There is a presumption that books, especially reference books, produced by such publishers are accurate and authoritative.

- We may take the place where the book was published into account. If we come across a book published in a country whose traditions of scholarship and publishing we are unfamiliar with, then we may be slightly more wary of accepting what we read outright. If we find that the information from such a source is generally reliable, then our confidence in similar books published in the same country may increase. Recently, for example, I came across a book published in Budapest by the Central European University Press [9]. I was slightly wary because Hungary used to be a communist state, but upon learning more about the publisher and the author I became more confident in the book's content as a source of information about Popper's thought. (The Central European University was founded by George Soros, the well-known supporter of the open society, and Notturno is a researcher in the Karl Popper Archives.)

- We may take the year of publication into account. For example, if we want to learn about recent findings in a discipline with which we are not very familiar, then we would go for a book published in the last year or so. Standards of scholarship change over the years and, thus, knowing when a history book, say, was published may help us in assessing the quality of the information that it contains.

- We may take the edition of the book into account if it has gone through several editions. For example, if a book is in its seventh edition, then that edition is likely to be more accurate than the third edition, say.

3.2 Factors relating to the author or authors

Books can be written by one or more people or they can be edited with contributions from various authors. To make the following discussion easier to follow I shall assume that we are dealing with a book written by a single author. With suitable changes, the discussion can be made to apply to other sorts of authorship as well.

- If we know something about the author, then we may take this into account when considering the quality of the information involved. For example, if he belongs to a different social, cultural or religious group, then our initial reaction may be to be more critical of what he writes, though we may, for various reasons, seek to counteract this tendency. We also take into account the author's intelligence, experience and expertise. For example, we are wary of the writings of a person about a specialist topic that he is not an expert on. Of course, on some occasions this tendency of ours might prevent us from learning something useful. If the book we are reading is a technical monograph or a textbook or something similar, then the affiliation of the author may influence our assessment of the information it contains. For example, if we regard the University of Oxford as being one of the best in the world, then a publication by a professor there would weigh heavily in our assessment of its content. If we know something of the author's goals or his agenda, this may make us wary of accepting his assertions uncritically. For example, a political or religious tract is written in order to convince the reader of the truth of some political ideology or religious doctrine. Knowing this about the tract influences the way in which we treat the information that it contains.

3.3 Factors relating to the content of the message

- The content of an assertion that we read may have characteristics that make us wary of believing it without further ado. One consideration concerns the coherence of the message and its internal consistency. Thus, we would not accept an inconsistent message or an assertion that was inconsistent with something else the author wrote in the same book. People rarely write straightforwardly inconsistent assertions, like 'It is raining and it is not raining', but may write two or more assertions that others may, being more logical and rational, see as being inconsistent.

- The content of someone's assertions may create an intense emotional reaction in the hearer and this may influence the way in which that person assesses further assertions from the same person.

- The content of an assertion may be so out of the ordinary that we are very reluctant to accept it without further ado. For example, we may read a book by someone who claims to have been abducted by aliens. There are, of course, individual differences between people and not everyone would react to an account of alien-abduction in the same way.

3.4 Factors relating to the reader

- We consider the importance of the message and its relevance to us. We tend to be less critical of assertions that are not particularly important to us than those that are really important to us. For example, if somebody has little or no interest in Egyptian history and he reads that Ramesses II reigned from 1279 BC until 1213 BC, then he is likely to simply accept this. However, if he has taken a keen interest in David Rohl's new chronology, then he is going to be wary of accepting this and will probably investigate the matter quite thoroughly using some sort of critical methodology.

- Whether or not we accept an author's assertion may be influenced by our pre-existing knowledge. For example, if the assertion is straightforwardly inconsistent with what we already know and we are confident of the truth of the statements that it is inconsistent with, then we are unlikely to accept the assertion outright. We may, though, flag it as something we should investigate more fully later. This consideration includes the case when our knowledge is that of what this author wrote elsewhere.

- We consider the obvious consequences and repercussions of accepting the message. The consequences of accepting an assertion that we read may be so significant that we insist on getting further information before accepting it. For example, if the message is such that accepting it would have a profound effect on my current plans, my life-style or my belief-system, then I am unlikely to accept it outright, even if it comes from a reliable source. In such a case I would probably flag the assertion as one that I need to consider thoroughly at some later time.

- The character of the recipient may influence his assessment of assertions that he hears. For example, a creative person may be willing to entertain wacky and unusual ideas which a less creative person would be very wary of accepting or even spend time thinking about.

- A person's maturity may influence his assessment of the assertions that he reads. Thus, an adult is likely to be far less credulous than a child. Experience would have taught him that people are not always as truthful as they should be.

4 Conclusion

There are very many problems to overcome if we are ever going to build a humanoid robot with intellectual abilities analogous to those possessed by human beings. Although it may be impossible to design and build an android whose abilities replicate those possessed by human beings, it is sensible to design androids, at least initially, whose abilities are similar to human intellectual ones. In designing an android it makes sense to design one that human beings can interact with. If the android was very different from us, then this would not be possible. In this paper I have concentrated on some of the problems that arise from the fact that human beings need a great deal of information in order to be fully-functioning members of any human society. It is impossible for them to generate all this knowledge by themselves. Most of this knowledge comes from other people. Any android that we design and build would be in the same position. Before we can even begin to design an android we have first to understand the abilities that humans have. In this paper I have made a start at investigating one aspect of how human belief-acquisition works. I have employed a two-stage model of belief-acquisition. In the first stage, as well as forming beliefs by using our senses, we also acquire beliefs by reading what other people have written and by listening to what they say. The ability to learn from others is, surprisingly, not currently being investigated very much. I am trying to rectify this curious omission from AI research. In this paper I have focused on how we acquire beliefs from books and I have identified many of the factors that may cause us to override the defeasible rule, 'Believe what you read or hear'.

A great deal of work still needs to be done before we understand human belief-acquisition sufficiently well in order to be able to implement it in an android or other AI system. Currently, I am working on identifying the factors that make us wary of accepting outright what we read or hear. In this paper I have looked at those factors that may be invoked when we are reading a book and elsewhere [5] I have identified the factors that may be invoked when we are listening to another person talk. In future papers I plan to look at those factors that are at work when we read a journal article or a newspaper, listen to the radio or watch television or find information on the Internet. After that the task still remains to further refine the two-stage model. I hope that some people reading this paper will be stimulated to join me in this exciting, but sadly neglected, field of AI research.

Acknowledgement

I am grateful to Debra Barton for reading a number of drafts of this paper and for making many helpful suggestions.

References

[1] W. W. Bartley, III, *The Retreat to Commitment*, second edn, Open Court Publishing Company, La Salle and London, 1984.

[2] R. Brooks, C. Breazeal, M. Marjanović, B. Scassellati and M. Williamson, The Cog project: Building a humanoid robot. This paper will appear in a volume of the Springer-Verlag Lecture Notes in Computer Science series of books. It is also currently available on the Internet at `http://www.ai.mit.edu/projects/cog/publications.html`.

[3] E. Charniak and D. McDermott, *An Introduction to Artificial Intelligence*, Addison-Wesley, Reading (Massachusetts), 1985.

[4] A. Diller, The belief-filter component, *Cognitive Science Research Papers CSRP-99-9*, School of Computer Science, University of Birmingham, 1999.

[5] A. Diller, Everyday belief-acquisition, *Cognitive Science Research Papers CSRP-00-7*, School of Computer Science, University of Birmingham, 2000. This paper has been accepted for presentation at the Argentine Symposium on Artificial Intelligence (ASAI 2000).

[6] R.E. Guiley, *Harper's Encyclopedia of Mystical and Paranormal Experience*, HarperCollins, New York, 1991.

[7] T. Honderich, (ed.), *The Oxford Companion to Philosophy*, Oxford University Press, Oxford, 1995.

[8] B. Lane, *The Encyclopaedia of Occult, Paranormal and Magick Practices*, Warner Books, London, 1996.

[9] M. A. Notturno, *Science and the Open Society: The Future of Karl Popper's Philosophy*, Central European University Press, Budapest (Hungary), 2000.

[10] J. L. Pollock, *Cognitive Carpentry: A Blueprint for How to Build a Person*, MIT Press, Cambridge (MA) and London (England), 1995.

[11] W. V. Quine J. S. and Ullian, *The Web of Belief*, second edn, McGraw-Hill, New York, 1978.

[12] E. von Däniken, *Chariots of the Gods? Unsolved Mysteries of the Past*, Souvenir Press, London, 1969.

Container Stowage Pre-planning: using search to generate solutions, a case study

I. D. Wilson, P. A. Roach and J. A. Ware

Department of Mathematics, University of Glamorgan,
Pontypridd, Mid Glamorgan, CF37 1DL, United Kingdom.

Abstract: Container-ships are vessels possessing an internal structure that facilitates the handling of containerised cargo. At each port along the vessel's journey, containers destined for those ports are unloaded and additional containers destined for subsequent ports are loaded. Determining a viable arrangement of containers that facilitates this process, in a cost-effective way, constitutes the deep-sea container-ship stowage problem. This paper outlines a computer system that generates good sub-optimal solutions to the stowage pre-planning problem. This is achieved through an intelligent analysis of the domain allowing the problem to be divided into sub-problems: a generalised placement strategy and a specialised placement procedure. This methodology progressively refines the arrangement of containers within the cargo-space of a container ship until each container is specifically allocated to a stowage location. Good, if not optimal, solutions for the problem are obtained in a reasonable processing time through the use of heuristics incorporated into objective functions for each stage.

1   Introduction

Containerisation (the packing of cargo into large, dedicated boxes, of different dimensions, enabling multiple units of cargo to be handled simultaneously) has increasingly facilitated the transportation of cargo since the 1970s. In order to increase the benefits of economy of scale, the size of *container ships* has increased.

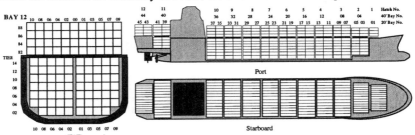

Figure 1 Stowage arrangement for a container ship

This increase in capacity has seen movement from relatively small ships with 350 Twenty Foot Equivalent Units (TEUs) to ships with capacities of more than 4500 TEUs.[1] Increasing standardisation of containers has permitted the introduction of *inter-modal* transportation systems. That is, the standard frame and dimensions of containers allows containerised cargo to be transported by rail, truck or sea.

Container ships travel on 'round-robin' routes where at each port of destination (POD) containers may be unloaded and additional containers destined for subsequent ports may be loaded. Determining a viable arrangement of containers that facilitates this process, in a cost-effective way, makes up the container stowage problem. Human stowage planners determine a stowage arrangement for a container ship. These planners work under demanding time constraints, and are limited in the number of arrangements that they can consider.

Modern container ships can require thousands of container *movements* (the loading, unloading or re-positioning of each container) at each POD to complete the discharge and load process. (Figure 1 shows such a ship from above and in transverse, longitudinal (along the length of the ship) and latitudinal (along the width of the ship) section; annotations mark positions of 'hatches' and 'bays' that are groupings of physical locations for container stowage.)

Determining the arrangement of containers is an error-prone process relying on the intuitive skills of human planners. Planners must ascertain the placement of containers so that all *constraints* (restrictions placed upon where and how containers can be stowed) are satisfied and *material handling costs* (the costs associated with loading, unloading and transporting cargo) are minimised. The most important aspect of this optimisation process is the *re-handle*. A re-handle is a container movement made in order to permit access to another, or to improve the overall stowage arrangement, and is considered a product of poor planning.

The purpose of this paper is to highlight the complexity of the deep-sea containers-ship stowage problem, and to demonstrate how suitable objective functions can be constructed to facilitate its solution.

2   Problem complexity

The container stowage problem is a combinatorial problem the size of which depends upon ship capacity and the container supply and demand at each POD. Combinatorial optimisation is made more complicated by the need to consider stowage across a number of ports. A decision made at one port will have consequences at subsequent ports. Planners will consider a fixed number of subsequent ports when planning stowage. Hence a full definition of the deep-sea container-ship stowage problem is the determination of a stowage arrangement for a container ship, on leaving a port, so that no ship stability and stress constraints are violated, and efficiency is optimised.

Even for the smallest cases, container stowage planning is a large-scale problem. The following points outline the main constraints and guidelines, common to most operators, which must be considered by planners during the stowage planning process for an individual port.[2]

The number of times a container must be re-handled before discharge is to be minimised. Reducing the number of re-handles results in large cost savings, though constraints will usually make it impossible to reduce this to zero. However, a stowage plan that minimises re-handles may itself be inefficient if the number of moves made by a crane and the distance travelled by it is excessive. Whereas it is sensible to group together cargo with the same destination in the same bay, a good disposition of this cargo between bays will permit multiple cranes to work. An optimum separation of four bays between cranes is required to facilitate simultaneous operation. This parallelisation of the loading and unloading process will permit a faster turnover of container movements to take place. Poor block stowage of cargo intended for the same destination may result in an excessive number of hatch-lid movements during unloading. Therefore, stowage should be planned so that hatch-lid movement is efficient.

Gradation in weight should be observed - that is, heavier containers should generally be placed at the bottom, and maximum allowable stack weights should not be exceeded. Stack height restrictions are to be observed and special consideration is to be given where crane height may be less than normal stack height. Vessels normally have 40' units placed on top of 20' units. Where 20' units are of a different height, 6" filler pieces can be used to bring the containers up to the required height. Stacks may not be completely filled due to stack weight limits, so stowage planning should ensure the maximum use of TEU and hence minimise the amount of lost cargo spaces. Ideally, only one discharge port's cargo should be stored under a single hatch (*e.g.* Hamburg). If this is not possible then the space should be taken up by cargo for another port with the furthest distance to travel (*e.g.* Hong Kong). 'Out of gauge' containers (of non-standard dimensions) should be placed at the top of container stacks, as this will minimise interference with adjacent slots. Empty and open top containers should usually be placed on top of stacks.

Cargo should only be placed in appropriate areas of the ship, although this is not always possible. For example, some cargo can only be placed in areas specifically allocated for its use. Each of the two types of *Reefer* unit (refrigerated container either independently powered or by the ship via a dedicated power outlet) should be stowed according to the appropriate rules and stowage requirements. On vessels that support this type of container, care must be taken to segregate the reefer commodities, so that tainting does not occur. Priority is given to placing reefers in designated reefer slots. Where possible, 40' reefer containers should be placed in stowage slots where only one reefer slot is used, rather than occupying two 20' reefer slots. Reefers should be stored away from locations that give off radiant heat, such as the Engine Room and Fuel Tanks. Empty reefers should occupy standard locations, *i.e.* not locations designated for reefer storage. *Fantainers* (containers that are ventilated by an internal fan) must be stowed near to reefer power points. Wet hides and wet salted hides tend to leak and give off a pungent odour.[2] Hides can only be stowed within cells that have been specially treated to receive them. Additionally, hides must always be at least two cells horizontally away from reefers or open topped containers, three bays away from crew accommodation, and are not allowed above or next to foodstuffs. Sometimes, so that vessel utilisation is maximised, containers may be stored in areas that are difficult to access at certain destinations (*e.g.* the berth at which the ship docks may not have cranes that can access an extreme part of a vessel).

A minimum distance must separate combinations of containers with hazardous cargo from other containers containing conflicting hazardous cargo. Stowage is planned so that hazardous cargo is separated according to the segregation rules. Where conflict with the segregation table does not occur, hazardous cargo should be stowed on deck and away from crew accommodation. The effect that loading hazardous cargo has upon TEU utilisation should be minimised. Placement of hazardous or special cargo may make some slots unacceptable stowage locations for other cargo types and care must be taken to prevent this from happening. Access to some containers (*e.g.* hazardous) may be required during a voyage and these should be stowed accordingly. (In most cases this means on deck.)

Intact stability[3] is constrained by guidelines set down by the Classification Society.[19] Placement of containers along the ship affects weight distribution and, as a consequence causes stress. To minimise torsion stresses, cargo must be stowed evenly across the vessel. The vessel must operate as close to zero trim as possible. If zero trim is unattainable, stern trim is preferred to bow trim so that propeller immersion is maintained and slamming force is reduced.[3] The cargo weight distribution should be within acceptable bounds set by metacentric height (GM) requirements, dead-weight limits, draft restrictions, and hull strength limitations. Ballast is used to correct stability problems, minimise torsion and shear forces and bending moment stress. However, ballast should be minimised since the vessel is in effect carrying dead weight, which directly affects its efficiency.

As a result of this diversity of factors influencing the stowage planning of containers the problem of determining a pattern of stowage that is close to optimal, whilst meeting all stowage constraints, is complex. Even over a few ports the determination of the optimum allocation of specific containers to stowage locations is computationally explosive and is not solvable in a realistic length of time. An alternative method for solving the container stowage problem, developed by the authors, is presented in this paper. In this approach, all characteristics of the problem are considered, but optimality is not necessarily sought.

3   Literature Survey

Researchers, drawn from academic and commercial shipping organisations, have examined the stowage-planning problem since the 1970s. Those methods developed have been grouped into the following five main classes: simulation based upon probability, heuristic driven, mathematical modelling, rule-based expert systems, and decision support systems.[4] None of these approaches have provided a solution to the complete stowage-planning problem. A brief review of relatively recent research into automating stowage planning follows.

The first class includes the work completed by Shields[1]. Here a small number of stowage plans are created, which are then evaluated and compared by simulation of the voyage across a number of legs. The order in which loading heuristics are applied is determined using a weighted random selection procedure and this generates a limited number of different solutions. The second class of automated planning processes incorporates human planners' experience encoded in the form of heuristics. This class includes the work completed by Martin[5] automating stowage planning at container-terminals. These heuristics can produce a complete, but rarely near-optimum, solution to the container-terminal stowage problem without the interaction of a user. The third class includes work carried out by Botter[4] and Cho[6] exploring the application of mathematical models and linear programming to the problem. Those practising this method of solving the stowage problem have incorporated too many simplification hypotheses, which have made their approaches unsuitable for practical applications. The fourth class explores the potential of applying the theory of artificial intelligence to cargo stowage problems.

This class includes the work of Dillingham[7], Perakis[8], Wilson[9, 10, 11] and Sato[12]. The work included within the, fifth and, last class is entirely separate to the rest. No effort is made here to automate the generation of stowage solutions. Instead, sets of tools are made available to the users that *assist* in the generation of stowage solutions. The works of Saginaw[13], Lang[14] and Sansen[15] belong to this class. The partnership of stowage planning tools and human expertise has, to date, provided the best commercial improvements.

4   Planning Methodology

This section describes the stowage planning model, overviews of the model's underlying data-structures and the planning processes, along with a summary of stowage objectives and their corresponding mathematical formulation within the planning methodology. Intact stability constraints are well documented in existing literature[2] and are omitted from the following discussion of the planning methodology. Emphasis is given to the underlying heuristics used to generate stowage solutions and their subsequent evaluation. For the voyage considered:

- At each POD, unloading and loading occurred, but the latter did not begin until the former had finished;

- Two cranes were available for loading and unloading at each POD.

Given the computational difficulties associated with producing an exact solution for the stowage problem, it was necessary to decompose the planning process into two sub-processes[7,8] that modelled the human planner's approach, namely:

1. A *strategic planning process*, where generalised containers are assigned to a blocked cargo-space in which slots corresponding to hatch-lids are grouped together (illustrated in Figure 2 and Figure 3).

2. A *tactical planning process*, where specific containers are assigned to specific slots within blocks determined during the strategic planning phase (illustrated in Figure 4).

The *strategic planning process* generates a generalised cargo stowage distribution. This models human planners' use of documents called the *General Arrangement* and the *Outline Plan*[16] to plan stowage, and reduces the combinatorial size of the problem whilst retaining its inherent characteristics.[7, 8]

Cargo can be seen as having a specific relationship to hatch-lids, which are the removable separators of above-deck and below-deck cargo, and are usually composed of a number of sections that interlock latitudinally. In particular, above deck cargo can be placed across two sections of the lid (see Figure 4). This allows the grouping of locations into blocks of cargo locations that have both the same longitudinal position (indicated in Figure 2) and a partnership relationship with these sections of hatch-lids. This has consequences for which lids and containers must be removed by cranes to allow access to other containers and locations.

Blocking the cargo-space of the container-ship enables the number of options for specifying container placements available at any stage of the planning process to be reduced from, perhaps, thousands of possibilities to within a hundred.

BAY (12)

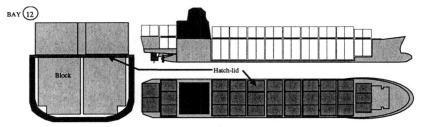

Figure 2 Blocked container ship abstraction

Now, the problem is reduced to allocating specific containers within a *part* of the container ship (a block).[7,8] In a second, tactical planning, phase, the exact slot occupied by each container at the current port-of-call is determined. The combinatorial difficulties associated with attempting to make specific placements within the entire cargo space and avoided by this two-stage process.

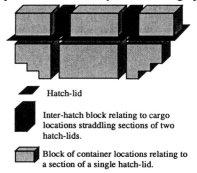

Figure 3 Example of cargo-space blocking relating to a single hatch

Each block is composed of a number of locations in the same hatch (latitudinal grouping), shown in Figure 4. This procedure models the human planner's conceptual approach and their use of documents called *Bay Plans*.[14]

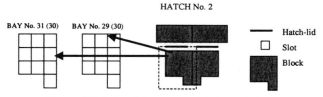

Figure 4 Relationship between blocks and slots

4.1 Strategic planning phase

Here, the underlying representation for the blocked cargo-space and the formulation of an objective function that measures how well a stowage arrangement meets these objectives, are given.

4.1.1 Strategic stowage objectives

The objectives of the strategic planning phase are to:

- Minimise the number of cargo spaces occupied by each destination;

- Maximise the number of cranes in operation at each POD.
- Minimise the number of hatch-lids moved;
- Minimise the number of re-handles;
- Minimise the number of cargo blocks occupied by containers.

4.1.2 Underlying model and definitions

The objective function used to evaluate solutions to the strategic planning problem requires a number of definitions that model the underlying structure of the problem. These are shown below, employing Z Notation[20], as sets and functions applied to sets. (In these, dom is *domain*, ran is *range*, # is set cardinality or size.)

❑ $C:\{c_1...c_{nc}\}$ is the set of all containers;

❑ nc is the number of containers;

❑ $P:\{p_1...p_{nd}\}$ is the set of all POD;

❑ nd is the number of POD;

❑ $S:\{s_1...s_{ns}\}$ is the set of all stowage locations;

❑ ns is the number of stowage locations;

❑ $D:P\rightarrow\Pi C$ is each set of containers associated with each destination;

❑ $H:N_1\rightarrow\Pi C$ is each set of containers associated with each hatch;

❑ nh: #{dom H} is the number of hatches;

❑ $B:N_1\rightarrow\Pi C$ is the set of containers associated with each block;

❑ $R:\ N_1\rightarrow\Pi S$ is the set of blocks associated with each corresponding upper-block;

❑ nr: #{dom R} is the number of upper-blocks;

❑ $L:\ N_1\rightarrow\Pi C$ is the set of containers stowed under each hatch-lid;

❑ nl: #{dom L) is the number of lids;

❑ $max:\ N_1\rightarrow N_1$ is a function that returns the capacity of a block;

❑ $vol:\ N_1\rightarrow N$ is a function that returns the volume of used space within a block;

4.2 The strategic objective function

The objective function used to evaluate solutions to the longitudinal stowage problem examines a stowage pattern in nine ways. Its general expression is:

$$f = \left(\begin{array}{c} (f_1*2)+(f_2*1)+(f_3*1)+(f_4*4)+(f_5*3) \\ +(f_6*10)+(f_7*2)+(f_8*4)+(f_9*3) \end{array} \right)$$

where f_i and its weight represent, respectively, an abstracted measure of one factor of the attractiveness of a solution and its relative importance. A low value of f indicates a good solution.

One set of terms of the objective function concerns the production of good block stowage, which in turn brings about efficient hatch-lid movement. The first of these terms, f_1, counts the number of hatches occupied by containers of each POD.

$$f_1 = \sum_{i=1}^{nd} \sum_{j=1}^{nh} \left(\begin{array}{c} 1 if\left(\exists c:C \mid c \in \left(ran(d_i) \cap ran(h_j) \right) \right) \\ else\, 0 \end{array} \right)$$

Secondly, f_4 counts the number of POD that exist within each hatch.

$$f_2 = \sum_{i=1}^{nh} \sum_{j=1}^{nd} \left(\begin{matrix} 1if \\ else0 \end{matrix} \left(\exists c : C \mid c \in \left(ran(d_i) \cap ran(h_j) \right) \right) \right)$$

Then f_6 counts the number of blocks occupied by containers of each POD. Minimising these three terms ensures good block stowage.

$$f_3 = \sum_{i=1}^{nd} \sum_{j=1}^{nb} \left(\begin{matrix} 1if \\ else0 \end{matrix} \left(\exists c : C \mid c \in \left(ran(d_i) \cap ran(b_j) \right) \right) \right)$$

A second set of terms measures whether effective crane usage is possible, with low values reflecting such good stowage. The term f_2 counts how many hatches are occupied by containers of each POD and then compares this with how many cranes there are at that POD (in this case 2). Ideally, the number of cranes at a given POD should be a factor of the number of hatches occupied by that POD.

$$f_4 = \sum_{i=1}^{nd} \left(mod \left(\sum_{j=1}^{nh} \begin{matrix} 1if \\ else0 \end{matrix} \left(\exists c : C \models \left(ran(d_i) \cap ran(h_j) \right) \right) \right) 2 \right)$$

A good spread of containers between hatches allows all cranes to be used simultaneously throughout the unloading process, as reflected by, f_3.

$$f_5 = \sum_{i=1}^{nd} ABS \left(Max \left(\begin{matrix} \forall_j : 1..\#nh \mid count = \langle \rangle \bullet \\ count = count \frown \#\{c : C \mid d_i \cap h_j\} \end{matrix} \right) \right) - \left(\sum_{j=1}^{length(count)-1} \left(\begin{matrix} \left(\forall_j : 1..\#nh \mid count = \langle \rangle \bullet \\ count = count \frown \#\{c : C \mid d_i \cap h_j\} \right) - \\ Max \left(\begin{matrix} \forall_j : 1..\#nh \mid count = \langle \rangle \bullet \\ count = count \frown \#\{c : C \mid d_i \cap h_j\} \end{matrix} \right) \end{matrix} \right) \right)$$

Next, f_5 penalises stowage patterns in which containers of a particular destination are stowed inside two hatches and those hatches are adjacent (preventing the two cranes from working simultaneously).

$$f_6 = 1if \left(\begin{matrix} \forall_i : 1..\#nd \mid \forall_j : 1..\#nh \mid \exists c : C \mid \left(\sum_{k=1}^{nh} \left(1if \exists c : C \mid c \in \left(ran(d_i) \cap ran(h_k) \right) \right) = 2 \right) \\ \wedge c \in \left(\left(ran(d_i) \cap ran(h_j) \right) \cap \left(ran(d_{i+1}) \cap ran(h_{j+1}) \right) \right) \end{matrix} \right)$$

Lastly, the spread of containers over the removable hatch-lids also provides a measure of crane efficiency, as reflected by f_8.

$$f_7 = \sum_i^{nc} \sum_j^{nd} \sum_k^{nl} \left(\begin{matrix} 1 if \ c_i \in \left(ran(d_j) \cap (ran(l_k)) \right) \\ else \ 0 \end{matrix} \right)$$

The third, and final, set of terms measures container rehandles and overstows, with low values of the terms indicating low numbers of these undesirable movements. The term f_7 counts how many containers are stowed on hatch-lids, beneath which are containers destined for an earlier POD.

$$f_8 = \sum_{i=1}^{nb} \sum_{j=1}^{nb} \sum_{k=1l}^{nc} \sum_{=1}^{nc} \begin{pmatrix} 1 if\left(c_k \in \left(ranb_i\right)\right) \wedge \left(c_l \in \left(ranb_j\right)\right) \wedge \\ \left(\left(domr_j\right) \in \left(ranr_i\right)\right) \bullet D^{\sim}[c_l] > D^{\sim}[c_k] \\ else 0 \end{pmatrix}$$

Also, f_9, counts how many empty spaces exist below a hatch-lid that supports containers. These spaces are unavailable without first removing the hatch-lid and any containers stowed on it, and therefore indicate of poor stowage.

$$f_9 = \sum_{i=1}^{nr} \sum_{j=1}^{nr} \begin{pmatrix} \left(\max(r_i) - vol(r_i)\right) \\ if \begin{pmatrix} \left(r_j \in ran(r_i)\right) \wedge \left(vol(r_j) > 0\right) \\ \wedge \left(vol(r_i) < \max(r_i)\right) \end{pmatrix} \end{pmatrix}$$

4.3   Implementation using Branch & Bound Search

The branch and bound approach to search is a very useful method for solving discrete optimisation, combinatorial optimisation and integer problems in general.[17] For the blocked stowage problem, the Branch and Bound algorithm and related sub-procedures are specialised as follows.

1.   Initialisation

The initial state is made up of the cargo-space, an ordered list of all containers to be loaded at the current port of call and a fitness value of the stowage arrangement. The cargo-space is composed of a list of areas to fill that correspond to blocks within the ship. The list of containers to be loaded has containers with the fewest available legal stowage locations first. Within the groups of different types of containers, those groups with the furthest POD are placed first in sequence. The fitness of the solution reflects an abstract measure of the cost, based upon simulation of the unloading process at PODs.

2.   Branching

New solutions are generated that reflect placements of the first container in the load-list within the cargo-space of a partial-solution. All invalid solutions are then removed from the list of new states. If after expanding a partial solution a feasible solution for the longitudinal stowage problem is found, then it is set aside.

2.   The search strategy

The candidates produced during the branching process are ordered according to the least fitness value determined by the objective function and the least number of containers remaining within its associated load-list. This new list is placed at the front of the existing list of partial-solutions. This strategy reflects a depth first approach to the search process.

3.   Pruning

When one candidate has the same, or worse, fitness value as another but has more containers to load then it can be deleted from the pool of partial solutions.

4.   Choice of new sub-problem

The partial-solution with the best fitness value is selected as the new current candidate problem and the algorithm continues in a similar manner until n solutions are found and d destinations are processed. Upon delivery of n candidates the search process for the current port of call is terminated, the problem is reinitialised, and the process repeated again for each of the n solutions at the next POD.

This process simulates a planning procedure at a given number of destination ports. Once this process has been repeated for each destination, the best solution is the one with the least summation of the fitness values accumulated at each port.

5 Tactical planning phase

In this phase, the best, generalised, long-term solution determined during the strategic planning phase is refined. Here, the stowage objectives followed when making short-term stowage decisions are presented, along with the underlying representation for the cellular cargo-space and the formulation of an objective function that measures how well a stowage arrangement meets these objectives.

5.1 Tactical stowage objectives

Planners employ a variety of generalised and specialised stowage to direct the placement of containers.[7] For the model under consideration, the following are considered salient:

- Re-handles are to be minimised;
- Container weight is to be graded upwards, heaviest to lightest;
- Stacks of containers) with mixed POD are to be minimised.

5.2 Underlying model and definitions

The objective function used to evaluate solutions to the tactical planning problem requires a number of definitions that model the problem's underlying structure, specifically:

- $I: \{c_1...c_{nc}\}$ is the set of all containers;
- D_i is the destination port of container i;
- DR_i is the set of restows related to container i;
- DW_i is the set of containers in the same stack stowed above container i with a greater weight;
- DS_i is the set of containers stacked with container i with a different POD.

5.3 The tactical objective function

The general expression for the objective function for the problem of container assignment within a block is:

$$f = (f_{10} * 3) + (f_{11} * 1) + (f_{12} * 2)$$

where f_i and its weight represent, respectively, an abstracted measure of one factor of the attractiveness of a solution and its relative importance. Better solutions will return lower objective function values.

The first term of the objective function, f_{10}, counts the number of restows.

$$f_{10} = \sum_{i=1}^{nc} \sum_{j=1}^{nc} \left(\begin{matrix} 1 \ if \ j \in DR_i \\ else \ 0 \end{matrix} \right)$$

The second term of the objective function, f_{11}, counts the number of containers with a different POD stowed in the same stack.

$$f_{11} = \sum_{i=1}^{nc} \sum_{j=1}^{nc} \left(\begin{matrix} 1 \ if \ j \in DS_i \\ else \ 0 \end{matrix} \right)$$

The third term of the objective function, f_{12}, examines weight gradation by counting the number of containers with a greater weight stowed above each other in the same stack.

$$f_{12} = \sum_{i=1}^{nc} \sum_{j=1}^{nc} \left(\begin{matrix} 1 \ if \ j \in DW_i \\ else \ 0 \end{matrix} \right)$$

5.4 Optimisation using Tabu search

Tabu search can be viewed as an iterative technique that explores a set of problem solutions by repeatedly making moves from one solution s to another solution s' located in the neighbourhood $N(s)$.[18] For the container stowage problem, s is the stowage configuration for the entire container ship and $N(s)$ is the set of all configurations obtained by making moves within a single hatch, with each hatch being optimised separately. These moves are performed with the aim of reaching a near optimal solution by the evaluation of some objective function $f(s)$ to be minimised. To prevent the search process from returning a local optimum f, a guidance procedure is incorporated that accepts a move from s to s' even when $f(s')>f(s)$. Should no improving move be found in a given number of iterations then the original, best, local solution is returned as the global solution. This in itself could lead to cycling causing the process to return repeatedly to the same local solution without moving towards a global solution. Tabu search circumvents the problem of cycling by preventing recent moves from reoccurring for a given number of iterations. For each solution s, m is a set of, legal, non-tabu moves which can be made to obtain a new solution s'. ($s' = s \pm m|\ N(s) = s' \ |\ \exists\ m \in M(s)$) For the assignment problem of container within a block, the neighbourhood $N(s)$ was determined by the blocked stowage procedure. An initial random value for s would suffice, but the application of a packing heuristic that generates a sensible value for s ultimately improves the efficiency of the search algorithm. [7] The form of the procedure used to optimise the arrangement of containers is as follows:

$s^* := f(s),\ k:=1,\ j:=1;$

While ($j<$Max (j)) and ($k<$Max (k)) and ($f(s^*)\neq 0$)

   $j:=j+1;$

   $M^* \subseteq N\ (s,k)$ (all legal, non-tabu, states);

   Choose the best s' in M^* and set $s:=s';$

   If $f(s') < f(s^*)$ then $s^* := s',\ k := 1$ else $k := k + 1.$

End of While

The form of Tabu search described is a very simple version. The pre-planning that occurs during the strategic phase prunes the search space significantly, resulting in sub-problems where optimal solutions can be found easily. Consideration given to aspiration levels, intermediate or long term memory, and other features described in the literature[18] proved unnecessary.

6 Computational experiments

Results were obtained on a 166MHz Pentium with 40 megabytes of memory using Allegro Lisp to encode the blocking and GFA (a PC-based 3GL with a high degree of functionality and graphic display features) to encode the specific placement algorithm. A generalised solution to the described problem was obtained in approximately 90 minutes whereas specialised solutions for all blocks were produced in under an hour. The state space size for the strategic planning phase will vary with vessel capacity and number of ports considered, but the blocking of cargo-space is believed to ensure that solutions of acceptable quality can always be generated in a viable time.

The application of Tabu Search during the tactical phase requires little processing time, as it involves the placement of fewer than 100 TEUs (and typically cargo blocks will hold approximately 12-60 TEUs). Below-deck blocks have restrictions on container lengths, and experimentation on typical loads generated optimum solutions in as few as 15 iterations, and a recency list of just two moves. For above-deck blocks, this number increases due partly to variations in container lengths, but mostly due to the increased likelihood of hazardous cargo segregation requirements. However, in the worst cases, no more than 200 iterations, and recency lists of up to 7 moves are required.

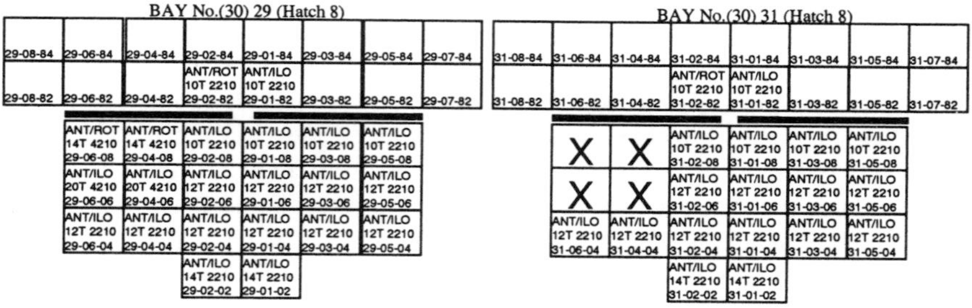

Figure 5 Bay plan giving container POD, origins, types and weights

The commercially sensitive nature of real data used, preclude further meaningful quantitative analysis of the results of this approach here. However, qualitatively, and from a knowledge-engineering perspective, the authors observe that the solutions obtained in experiments meet all constraints and reflect the stowage objectives described. The plans generated being reported by industry experts consulted as comparable with those of human planners. Further, the automated approach outlined in this paper allows consideration of more stowage plans in the time available for planning than human planners can manage.

This procedure was used to generate a complete set of Bay Plans, optimised with respect to cargo allocated in the strategic phase (an example of which is shown in Figure 5). Note that in Figure 10: X marks the tail end of a 40' container; ROT is an earlier POD than ILO; containers numbered 4210 are 40' in length and ones labelled 2210 are 20' in length – hence the four 40' containers are lighter 'per foot' than the 20' containers below them.

7 Conclusion

Through a comprehensive knowledge engineering exercise, a model has been constructed for solving the container-ship loading problem that takes advantage of how human planners solve this problem. The implementation of the model described in this paper allows sub-optimal solutions to the problem to be determined without requiring the intervention of a human planner. Moreover, the solutions are obtained in a reasonable amount of processing time using available computer software and hardware.

References

[1] Shields JJ. Container-ship Stowage: A Computer-Aided Preplanning System. Marine Technology 1984; 21, No. 4:370-383

[2] Private communication with Maritime Computer and Technical Services.

[3] Goldberg LL. Principles of Naval Architecture. J. P. Comstock, 1980

[4] Botter RC, Brinati MA. Stowage container planning: a model for getting an optimal solution. IFIP Transactions B (App. in Tech.) 1992; B-5: 217-29.

[5] Martin GL, Randhawa SU, McDowell ED. Computerised Container-ship Load Planning: A Methodology and Evaluation. Computers Ind. Engng. 1988; 14, No. 4: 429-440.

[6] Cho DW. Development of a Methodology for Containership Load Planning. PhD thesis, Oregon State University, 1984

[7] Perakis N, Dillingham JT. The Application of Artificial Intelligence Techniques in Marine Operations. In: Ship Operations, Management and Economics International Symposium U.S.M.M.A., Kings Point, New York, September 1987.

[8] Dillingham JT, Perakis AN. Application of Artificial Intelligence in the Marine Industry. In: Fleet Management Technology Conference, Boston, U.S.A. 1986.

[9] Wilson ID. The Application of Artificial Intelligence Techniques to the deep-sea container-ship cargo stowage problem. PhD thesis, University of Glamorgan, 1997

[10] Wilson ID, Roach PA. The Deep-sea Container-ship Stowage Problem: Modelling and Automating the Human Planning Process. In: Proceedings of the Second International ICSC Symposium on Intelligent Industrial Automation, 1997, pp 129-135, ICSC, Canada/Switzerland.

[11] Wilson ID, Roach PA. Principles of combinatorial optimisation applied to containership stowage planning. Journal of Heuristics 1999; 5, No. 4:403-418

[12] Sato K, Itoh H, AwashimaY. Expert System for Oil Tanker Loading/ Unloading Operation Planning. In: Barauna Vieira C (ed) Computer Applications in the Automation of Shipyard Operation and Ship Design, VII. Elsevier Science Publishers B. V. (North Holland), 1992 IFIP.

[13] Saginaw DJ, Perakis AN. A Decision Support System for Container-ship Stowage Planning. Marine Technology 1989; 26, No. 1: 47-61

[14] Lang GJP. Some Computer Aids in the Loading of Deep Sea Container Vessels, - A Personal Experience. In: Computer Applications in Operation and Management of Ships and Cargoes, London, 1985.

[15] Sansen H. Ship-Planner, A Conception Support Tool for the Bay Plans of Container Ships., Systemia, Domaine de ST Hilaire, Pichaury 13290 AIX LES MILLES, FRANCE, 1989.

[16] Roach DK, Thomas BJ. Portworker development programme Unit C.2.2, Container-ship Stowage Plans, International Labour Organisation. ISBN 92-2-109271-2, 1994.

[17] Cao Transportation Problem with Nonlinear Side Constraints a Branch and Bound Approach. ZOR – Methods and Models of Operations Research 1992; 36:185-197

[18] Glover F. A user's guide to tabu search. Annals of Operations Research 1993; 41:3-28.

[19] Stowage and Segregation Guide to IMDG- Code. Published by U.O. Storck Verlag (Stahltwrek 7, D-2000 Hamburg 50, Germany).

[20] Spivey JM. The Z Notation A Reference Manual. Prentice Hall International (UK) Ltd. ISBN 0-13-983768-X, 1989.

A Correct Algorithm for Efficient Planning with Preprocessed Domain Axioms

Massimiliano Garagnani

Department of Computing, The Open University

Milton Keynes, U.K.

Abstract

This paper describes a *polynomial* algorithm for preprocessing planning problems which contain domain axioms (DAs) in the form $p_1 \land p_2 \land \ldots \land p_n \to c$. The algorithm presented is an improved version of the (incorrect) transformation for DAs described by Gazen and Knoblock in [6].

The first result presented consists of a counter-example showing that Gazen and Knoblock's preprocessing algorithm is *incorrect*. This is demonstrated by providing a specific set of planning problems which the algorithm does not transform into *equivalent* encodings.

The following result described consists of a new algorithm that avoids the problems of the previous method by augmenting the state with additional assertions ('*deduction facts*') that keep track of any application of the DAs made during the plan.

The final part of the paper illustrates how the new method proposed leads also to notable improvements in the efficiency of the planning process.

1 Introduction

When choosing a language to represent a possible real-world situation, we are confronted with the dilemma of just *how expressive* such language should be. For example, consider a simple blocks world domain, in which four blocks (labeled A,B,C and D in Figure 1) lie on a table. In order to describe this domain it seems natural to include, in the representation language, a predicate expression like $\text{on\_top}(x, y)$, indicating that block x lies on block y. The one-predicate language

$$L = \{ \text{ on\_top}(x, y) \}$$

can actually be used to specify *any* possible state of the system considered[1].

---

[1] Properties such as $\text{clear}(x)$ or $\text{on\_table}(x)$ can be *deduced* directly from the current set of $\text{on\_top}()$ propositions.

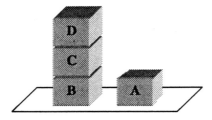

Figure 1: Blocks world domain with four blocks.

However, given an initial random disposition of the blocks, suppose our goal g to consist of building a pile of four blocks having 'A' on top. If we adopt the language L to describe this problem, we will have to express g as a six-term disjunctive expression, in which every term represents one of the possible permutations of the blocks B,C,D beneath A:

$$
\begin{aligned}
g \; = \; & (\text{on\_top}(A, B) \wedge \text{on\_top}(B, C) \wedge \text{on\_top}(C, D)) \\
& \vee (\text{on\_top}(A, B) \wedge \text{on\_top}(B, D) \wedge \text{on\_top}(D, C)) \\
& \vee (\text{on\_top}(A, C) \wedge \text{on\_top}(C, B) \wedge \text{on\_top}(B, D)) \\
& \vee (\text{on\_top}(A, C) \wedge \text{on\_top}(C, B) \wedge \text{on\_top}(B, D)) \\
& \vee (\text{on\_top}(A, D) \wedge \text{on\_top}(D, B) \wedge \text{on\_top}(B, C)) \\
& \vee (\text{on\_top}(A, D) \wedge \text{on\_top}(D, C) \wedge \text{on\_top}(C, B))
\end{aligned}
$$

To avoid this exponential growth in complexity of goals and conditions, we can *extend* the language L to include more expressive terms. For example, if we augment L with the predicate '$\text{above}(x, y)$', indicating that the block 'x' is on the same pile of 'y' but in a higher position, the goal g can be re-stated simply as

$$g = \text{above}(A, B) \wedge \text{above}(A, C) \wedge \text{above}(A, D)$$

The new predicate can be defined unequivocally through the following pair of *domain* (or *language*) *axioms* (*DAs*):

$$
\begin{aligned}
\text{on\_top}(x, y) \; &\rightarrow \; \text{above}(x, y) \\
\text{on\_top}(x, y) \wedge \text{above}(y, z) \; &\rightarrow \; \text{above}(x, z)
\end{aligned}
$$

This means that the truth of any '$\text{above}()$' expression can actually be *deduced* from the set of '$\text{on\_top}()$' expressions currently holding.

The adoption of an expressive language allows a simple, accurate and natural description of the problem considered. Nevertheless, the gain in simplicity and clarity of the problem definition language is usually counterbalanced by a loss in performance. In other words, the presence of axioms in the domain makes, in general, the automatic solution of problems more complex.

This is often the case in the field of AI Planning, where systems that support very expressive domain definition languages (such as UCPOP [8], which allows the use of DAs) are generally slower in finding a plan solution than other planners adopting more restricted languages (e.g. [1] [7]).

A possible approach to this seemingly contradictory situation consists of developing *preprocessors* that translate domains from an expressive representation language into a simpler one for which more efficient planners exist. More specifically, given a planning problem containing domain axioms, the preprocessor will transform it into a new planning problem *equivalent*[2] to the original one but containing no DAs. The new problem can then be solved by a fast planner, and the solution found re-transformed into an equivalent plan which solves the initial problem.

This is the approach that Garagnani adopted in [5] to preprocess *discourse planning* problems containing *acyclic* belief axioms (see also [4]). The same approach has been followed by Gazen and Knoblock in [6], where an algorithm for the conversion of a UCPOP domain representation into a Graphplan [1] (equivalent) encoding is presented. The algorithm described includes the transformation of domain axioms into equivalent 'deduce' operators. As the authors point out, the advantages of this approach reside in its conceptual simplicity, its modularity and the fact that it is not necessarily specific to one planner (cf. [6, p.222]).

The first part of this paper will show that Gazen and Knoblock's transformation of DAs is *incorrect*. In other words, the planning problem resulting as output of their preprocessing algorithm is *not always equivalent* to the initial problem which was given as input.

In the second part of the paper, a revised version of the algorithm for the preprocessing of DAs is presented. The new method avoids the problems of the previous solution by augmenting the state with extra assertions (called '*deduction facts*') which keep track of *any* use of the axioms made during the plan.

Finally, some preliminary results showing how the output produced by the new transformation leads also to more efficient planning are presented.

2 Gazen and Knoblock's algorithm

This section reviews the preprocessing algorithm presented by Gazen and Knoblock in [6] and demonstrates its incorrectness.

The algorithm described in [6, p.225] for the transformation of DAs in the form *premises* → *consequence*[3] into 'deduce' operators is reported below:

---

[2] Two planning problems $\mathcal{P}, \mathcal{P}'$ can be considered 'equivalent' if there exists a bijective function which associates every solution (successful plan) of $\mathcal{P}$ with one (and only one) solution of $\mathcal{P}'$, and vice versa.

[3] '*premises*' is an expression which can contain predicates and which must be true before the axiom can be applied, whereas '*consequence*' is a single predicate c with n arguments $(c\ x_1 x_2 \ldots x_n)$.

ALGORITHM α

Given: an axiom $p \to c$ and a list of operators l_o, let o be a new operator:

1) set the precondition of o to p
2) set the effect of o to c
3) for each op in l_o
        if effect(op) contains any predicate in p,
        then add $(\forall(y_1 \ldots y_n)\,(\text{not } (c\ y_1 \ldots y_n)))$ to effect(op)
4) add o to l_o

The reason for the introduction of step 3) in the above algorithm is that if a step in the plan solution modifies one of the components of the premise p of an axiom, the proposition c deduced by the operator o may lose its validity. Hence, according to Gazen and Knoblock, "it is necessary [during the preprocessing phase] to find the operators that modify the propositions from which the axiom is derived, and to add an effect which negates the deduced proposition" [*ibid.*, p.224].

However, the modification of the premises of a specific axiom does not require to *unconditionally* delete *every instance* of the axiom's consequence. This is, in fact, the origin of the algorithm's incorrectness. The following subsection describes an example in which this weakness is exploited to construct a situation in which the planning problem given as input to Algorithm α is *not equivalent* to the output produced.

2.1 Proof of *in*correctness

In order to prove that Algorithm α is not correct, it is sufficient to provide a counter-example in which the input planning problem is not transformed into an equivalent one. Consider the following problem $\mathcal{P}$, consisting of two operator schemes (represented, as in STRIPS [3], like triples (P,A,D) of preconditions, add and delete lists), initial state I, goal set G and single domain axiom A_1:

$$
\begin{aligned}
Op_1(x) &= (\,[Q],[C(x),S],[Q]\,) & x &\in \{a,b,c,\ldots,w,z\} \\
Op_2(x) &= (\,[S,P(x)],[R(x)],[S,P(x)]\,) & x &\in \{a,b,c,\ldots,w,z\}
\end{aligned}
$$

$$
\begin{aligned}
I &= \{Q,P(b)\} \\
G &= \{C(a),R(b)\}
\end{aligned}
$$

$$
A_1)\qquad P(x) \to C(x) \qquad\qquad x \in \{a,b,c,\ldots,w,z\}
$$

The given problem has one (and only one) solution, shown in Figure 2. Notice that the solution does not make use of the axiom A_1.

The planning problem $\mathcal{P}'$ produced by the preprocessing algorithm α is:

$$Op_1{}'(x) = ([Q],[C(x),S],[Q]) \qquad x \in \{a,b,c,\ldots,w,z\}$$
$$Op_2{}'(x) = ([S,P(x)],[R(x)],$$
$$[S,P(x),\forall y \overset{Del}{\Rightarrow} C(y)]) \qquad x,y \in \{a,b,c,\ldots,w,z\}$$

$$I' = I = \{Q,P(b)\}$$
$$G' = G = \{C(a),R(b)\}$$

$$O_1(x) = ([P(x)],[C(x)],[]) \qquad x \in \{a,b,c,\ldots,w,z\}$$

Due to the presence of the *unconditional* deletion in $Op_2{}'$, the plan $\langle Op_1{}'(a),$ $Op_2{}'(b)\rangle$ would now produce the state $S_2' = \{R(b)\}$, which is not a goal state. As a matter of fact, the problem $\mathcal{P}'$ produced by the algorithm α presents *no solution* at all, and therefore is not equivalent to the initial planning problem $\mathcal{P}$. Hence, the preprocessing algorithm proposed by Gazen and Knoblock is incorrect.

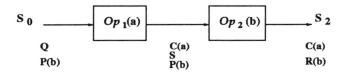

Figure 2: Correct plan solution.

3 The new algorithm

This section describes a revised version of Gazen and Knoblock's algorithm α for the transformation of domain axioms into equivalent 'deduce' operators. The new algorithm, reported below, avoids the previous problems by producing operators that effect *conditional* deletions based on '*deduction facts*' – assertions in the form $A(\vec{v})$ [4] which do not belong to the definition language L. The task of the deduction facts is to record *all instances* of application of the DAs, so that if a premise p of an axiom is deleted by an operator, *all (and only)* the consequences of p can be identified and removed from the state:

ALGORITHM β

Given: a list of domain axioms $\{A_1, A_2, \ldots, A_l\}$ in the form

$$A_i)\ p_{i,1}(\vec{x}_{i,1}) \wedge p_{i,2}(\vec{x}_{i,2}) \wedge \ldots \wedge p_{i,k_i}(\vec{x}_{i,k_i}) \to c_i(\vec{y}_i)$$
$$\vec{x}_{i,j} = (x_{i,1}, x_{i,2}, \ldots, x_{i,m_j})$$
$$\vec{y}_i = (y_{i,1}, y_{i,2}, \ldots, y_{i,n_i})$$

and a list of operators l_o in the form (P,A,D),

---

[4] $\vec{v}$ is a tuple $(r, s, \ldots, t)$ of variable length.

- for each axiom A_i, let O_i be a new deduce operator:

  1) set the preconditions P of O_i to $\{p_{i,1}(\vec{x}_{i,1}), \ldots, p_{i,k_i}(\vec{x}_{i,k_i})\}$
  2) set the add list A to $\{c_i(\vec{y}_i)\}$
  3) append the *conditional effect* $[\neg c_i(\vec{y}_i) \overset{Add}{\Rightarrow} A_i(\vec{x}_{i,1}, \vec{x}_{i,2}, \ldots, \vec{x}_{i,k_i}, \vec{y}_i)]$
  4) for each premise p_{ij} that appears also as *consequence* c_w of an axiom A_w, append to O_i the conditional effect

     $\forall r, s \ldots t \, [A_w(r, s, \ldots, t, \vec{x}_{i,j}) \overset{Add}{\Rightarrow} A_i(r, s, \ldots, t, \vec{y}_i)]$

  5) for each $Op=(P,A,D)$ in l_o,

     5.1) if D contains a premise $p_{i,j}$,
          then append to Op the conditional deletion

          $\forall r, s, \ldots t \, [A_i(r, s, \ldots, \vec{x}_{i,j}, \ldots, t, \vec{y}_i) \overset{Del}{\Rightarrow} c_i(\vec{y}_i)]$

     5.2) if A contains the consequence c_i,
          then for each axiom A_w with consequence c_i, append

          $\forall r, s, \ldots t \, [\emptyset \overset{Del}{\Rightarrow} A_w(r, s, \ldots, t, \vec{y}_i)]$

- add $\{O_1, O_2, \ldots, O_l\}$ to l_o

Perhaps the first thing to notice is that the complexity of this transformation is *polynomial* in the number 'l' of DAs and in the cardinality of the initial list l_o of operators. As in [6], for each axiom A_i — with premises p and consequence c — a new deduce operator $O_i = (P,A,D) = ([p], [c], [\,])$ is generated. However, the operator is also augmented with the (conditional) addition of a deduction fact $A_i(\,)$ (see step 3) which records unequivocally the *bound values* of the variables in A_i at the moment of its application. This will allow the identification of exactly *which premises* have led to *which consequence* at any subsequent point in the plan.

In what follows, the functioning of the Algorithm β is explained through a detailed example.

3.1 An explanatory example

Consider the blocks world definition language L of the example in Section 1 enriched with the term 'under(x, y)', indicating that the block 'x' is on the same pile of 'y' but in a lower position. The extension of the expressiveness of L requires the addition of the two following DAs:

A_1) on_top(x, y) $\qquad\qquad\quad \rightarrow$ under(y, x)
A_2) on_top$(x, y) \wedge$ under(z, y) $\rightarrow$ under(z, x)

The following subsection illustrates how steps 1)–4) of the β algorithm transform the above DAs into equivalent deduce operators.

3.1.1 Steps 1)–4)

Consider the axiom A_1 first. The steps 1)–3) of β will initially produce the following deduce operator O_1 (represented as in [7]):

$$
\begin{aligned}
\text{P} &= [\text{on\_top}(x, y)] \\
\text{A} &= [\text{under}(y, x)] \\
\text{D} &= [] \\
\textit{Effects}: \quad & [\neg\text{under}(y, x) \overset{Add}{\Rightarrow} \text{A}_1(x, y, y, x)]
\end{aligned}
$$

Notice that the addition of the deduction fact $\text{A}_1(x, y, y, x)$ is subject to the condition $\neg\text{under}(y, x)$. This guarantees that the 'tag' $\text{A}_1(x, y, y, x)$ is added to the state only when the term $\text{under}(y, x)$ is present *solely* as a consequence of the premise $\text{on\_top}(x, y)$.

Step 4) of the algorithm does not add any effect to O_1. Let us postpone, for the moment, the execution of step 5), and move on to the analysis of the transformation of axiom A_2. The operator O_2 resulting from the first 3 steps of β is shown below:

$$
\begin{aligned}
\text{P} &= [\text{on\_top}(x, y), \text{under}(z, y)] \\
\text{A} &= [\text{under}(z, x)] \\
\text{D} &= [] \\
\textit{Effects}: \quad & [\neg\text{under}(z, x) \overset{Add}{\Rightarrow} \text{A}_2(x, y, z, y, z, x)]
\end{aligned}
$$

In this case, one of the premises of the axiom — namely, $\text{under}(z, y)$ — appears as consequence in other DAs. This means that the corresponding precondition of the operator could have been *derived* from other premises through the application of deduce operators. If any of such premises is deleted, then $\text{under}(z, y)$ should be removed, and so should $\text{under}(z, x)$. Hence, the premises which led to the derivation of $\text{under}(z, y)$ should be considered also as premises of $\text{under}(z, x)$. This is the reason for the introduction of step 4), which causes the addition of the following conditional effects to the deduce operator O_2:

$$
\begin{aligned}
\forall r, s \quad & [\text{A}_1(r, s, z, y) \quad \overset{Add}{\Rightarrow} \quad \text{A}_2(r, s, z, x)] \\
\forall r, s, t, u \quad & [\text{A}_2(r, s, t, u, z, y) \quad \overset{Add}{\Rightarrow} \quad \text{A}_2(r, s, t, u, z, x)]
\end{aligned}
$$

Having analysed the output that β produces in steps 1) to 4) for the two DAs, let us now move on to step 5), which modifies the initial set l_o of operators.

3.1.2 Step 5)

Step 5.1) concerns the deletion of one of the premises $p_{i,j}$ appearing in the left-hand side of an axiom. Such deletion will cause the removal of all (and only) the consequences which have been *directly or indirectly* derived from it. These consequences can be easily identified from the set of recorded deduction facts containing $p_{i,j}$ (or, rather, its *ground instance*) as one of the premises.

In the example considered, if an operator contains the term $\text{on\_top}(x, y)$ in its delete list D, then it will be augmented with the following conditional deletions:

$$\forall t, u \qquad [\mathsf{A}_1(x, y, t, u) \quad \overset{Del}{\Rightarrow} \quad \text{under}(t, u)]$$
$$\forall r, s, t, u \quad [\mathsf{A}_2(x, y, r, s, t, u) \quad \overset{Del}{\Rightarrow} \quad \text{under}(t, u)]$$

These effects will remove all and only the consequences '$\text{under}(t, u)$' which have been derived (directly or indirectly) from the term '$\text{on\_top}(x, y)$' through the application of axioms A_1 and A_2.

Finally, step 5.2) is necessary in order to guarantee that any deduction 'tag' $\mathsf{A}_i(\vec{v})$ is present in the state *iff* the consequence it contains has been added *exclusively* because of the application of the axiom A_i. In fact, if one of the operators in the list l_o *explicitly adds* a proposition c (i.e., $c \in A$), such term should be no longer considered as 'derived' from others, and *all* of the deduction facts containing c as a consequence should be deleted.

In the example, if an operator Op contains the term $\text{under}(x, y)$ in its add list A, then Op will be augmented with the following (unconditional) deletions:

$$\forall r, s \qquad [\emptyset \quad \overset{Del}{\Rightarrow} \quad \mathsf{A}_1(r, s, x, y)]$$
$$\forall r, s, t, u \quad [\emptyset \quad \overset{Del}{\Rightarrow} \quad \mathsf{A}_2(r, s, t, u, x, y)]$$

3.2 Correctness of β

In order to show that the new algorithm does not present the same problems of Gazen and Knoblock's version, let us consider the counter-example of Section 2.1. Such example was built explicitly to prove that Algorithm α was incorrect, as not always producing a planning problem equivalent to the one given as input. The output $\mathcal{P}''$ of the transformation β applied to the planning problem $\mathcal{P}$ of the example is reported below:

$$Op_1{}''(x) = ([Q], [C(x), S], [Q, A_1(x, x)])$$

$$Op_2{}''(x) = ([S, P(x)], [R(x)], [S, P(x)])$$
$$\textit{Effects}: \qquad \forall y [A_1(x, y) \overset{Del}{\Rightarrow} C(y)])$$

$$I'' = \{Q, P(b)\}$$
$$G'' = \{C(a), R(b)\}$$

$$O_1(x) = ([P(x)], [C(x)], [\,])$$
$$\textit{Effects}: \qquad [\neg C(x) \overset{Add}{\Rightarrow} A_1(x, x)])$$

The execution of the plan $\langle Op_1{}''(a), Op_2{}''(b)\rangle$ yields now the correct goal state S_2 of Figure 2. This is because the conditional deletion in $Op_2{}''(x)$ has been *limited* to the terms $C(y)$ for which $A_1(x, y)$ holds.

Hence, the output produced by β consists of a planning problem $\mathcal{P}''$ having one and only one solution, that is, *equivalent* to the problem $\mathcal{P}$ given as input.

4 Planning performance and preliminary results

Although the algorithm α has been shown to be incorrect in a specific case, one might argue that such situation was created 'artificially', and will never occur in real-world problems. Nevertheless, not only is Gazen and Knoblock's algorithm incorrect, but it also produces problem encodings that lead to *inefficiencies* during the planning process. In fact, consider the following example, taken from the original paper [6, p.225]. Given

- Axiom is-clear: (or (eq x Table) ($\not\exists$ (obj b) (on b x))) $\rightarrow$ (clear x)

- Operator put-on(x, y, d):
  Precondition = (and (on x d) (clear x) (clear y))
  Effect = (and (on x y) (not (on x d)))

the preprocessing algorithm α would transform them into:

- Operator deduce-is-clear(x):
  Precondition = (or (eq x Table) ($\not\exists$ (obj b) (on b x)))
  Effect = (clear x)

- Operator put-on(x, y, d):
  Precondition = (and (on x d) (clear x) (clear y))
  Effect = (and (on x y) (not (on x d)) ($\forall$ (v) (not (clear v))))

The effect '$\forall(v)$ (not (clear v))' deletes every occurrence of the proposition (clear v), regardless of which instance of 'deduce-is-clear' had actually produced it. This leads to inefficiencies during the planning process, as the unconditional deletion forces *any* '(clear v)' proposition to be re-evaluated subsequently if needed by another operator.

Gazen and Knoblock are well aware of this problem: "in the worst case an axiom may need to be asserted after each step". For example, the 'put-on' operator above "does not have to assert (not (clear x)) because x is still clear after this action, but because it does, the axiom needs to be applied to re-assert (clear x) if another action requires (clear x) later" [*ibid.*,p.225].

In contrast, the new method presented is correct and avoids the above kind of inefficiencies by keeping track of each application of the deduce operators, so that when the premise of an axiom is removed, only the propositions which were actually *derived* from it are deleted.

Results showing a comparison between the performances of the UCPOP planner [8] and those obtained using the preprocessing algorithm α in conjunction with Graphplan [1] are discussed in [6]. In order to have at least a preliminary quantification of the possible gain in efficiency produced by the adoption of the new algorithm, the planning problem reported below (Figure 3) with axioms A_1, A_2 and language L — in fact, a variation of Sussman anomaly [2] — was preprocessed with both the α and β versions varying the number of blocks present in the initial pile, and the results produced were given as input to the IPP planner [7].

$$L = \{\texttt{on\_top}(x,y), \texttt{on\_table}(x), \texttt{clear}(x), \texttt{above}(x,y)\}$$

A_1) $\texttt{on\_top}(x,y)$ $\qquad\qquad\qquad \rightarrow$ $\texttt{above}(x,y)$
A_2) $\texttt{on\_top}(x,y) \wedge \texttt{above}(y,z) \rightarrow$ $\texttt{above}(x,z)$

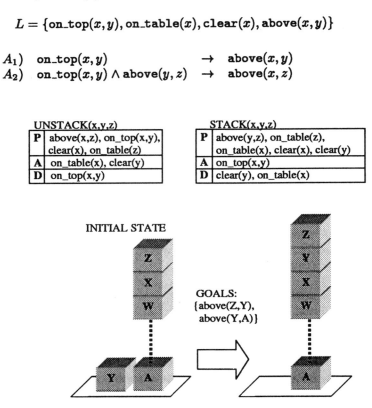

UNSTACK(x,y,z)	
P	above(x,z), on_top(x,y), clear(x), on_table(z)
A	on_table(x), clear(y)
D	on_top(x,y)

STACK(x,y,z)	
P	above(y,z), on_table(z), on_table(x), clear(x), clear(y)
A	on_top(x,y)
D	clear(y), on_table(x)

INITIAL STATE

GOALS:
{above(Z,Y),
above(Y,A)}

Figure 3: Blocks world planning problem(s) used for comparing α and β.

It should be noticed that the operator schemes Stack and Unstack were deliberately adopted instead of the more common Pick-up, Put-down and Put-on in order to obtain a situation in which their application were always preceded by a sequence of 'deduction' steps. Such behaviour, in fact, is guaranteed by the presence of the term 'above( )' in their preconditions. As a result, although the solution to the given problem(s) always required essentially the three steps Unstack(Z,X,A), Stack(Y,X,A) and Stack(Z,Y,A), the plans obtained with the output of the β algorithm were found to be roughly 75% *shorter* than those obtained with the α version. Such difference was due to the fact that both of the α versions of the operators removed *all* the 'above( )' terms from the state. This forced the plan to re-assert them all again after each step in order to re-deduce the required 'above( )' preconditions and, at the end, the final goals.

5   Discussion and Future work

The advantages of adopting a preprocessing approach to the problem of planning with DAs lie in its modularity and in its wide range of applicability. More specifically, the solution proposed is correct, more efficient than the existing version and not tied to any particular planner.

A possible extension of the algorithm presented consists of modifying it in order to deal with DAs containing *existentially* and **universally** quantified variables. This would be required to transform the example reported in Section 4. An extended version of β able to deal with axioms containing negated existentials has been already developed and is currently under testing.

Another direction in which work is in progress consists of using the deduction facts added to the state to automatically *learn new* operators and axioms. This can be done during the planning process through '*constant-variable*' substitution[5] or, in alternative, by exploiting the set of deduction facts $A(\ldots, c)$ present in the state. In fact, at any point in the plan, the set of deduction facts containing a consequence 'c' identifies unequivocally the set of premises which have been used to conclude c. Hence, for each axiom it is possible to introduce in the problem a new operator that *learns* from past 'chunks' of the plan and improves the efficiency of the subsequent planning process. A possible version of such a learning operator for an axiom A_x with premises $p_1, p_2, \ldots, p_n$ and consequence c is proposed below:

$$
\begin{aligned}
P &= [\forall \vec{r}, \vec{s}, \ldots, \vec{t} \cdot A_x(\vec{r}, \vec{s}, \ldots, \vec{t}, \vec{y}),\ p_1(\vec{r}) \wedge p_2(\vec{s}) \wedge \ldots \wedge p_n(\vec{t})] \\
A &= [c(\vec{y})] \\
D &= []
\end{aligned}
$$

In brief, regardless of the *intermediate steps* which led to the deduction of the consequence c (and which may be 'forgotten'), the list of deduction facts $A_x()$ identifies unequivocally the collection of premises that have been progressively used to derive 'c'. Hence, if all of them hold again, then c can be added to the state.

In summary, the automated translation from a high-level domain definition language into a simpler one makes it possible to use simple but fast planners in complicated domains. The gain in planning performance is achieved by making the information initially encoded within the DAs and the operators more *explicit* in the problem description. Having axioms in a domain definition language allows the domain engineer to represent problems easily, accurately and naturally, and leads to 'cleaner' and less error-prone problem definitions. In a way, preprocessing undoes that, and although the resulting problem is not as compact, its correctness is preserved (work is in currently progress to produce a formal proof of the soundness of the preprocessing algorithm β).

---

[5] A collection of axioms is generalised and grouped into a single deduce operator by substituting identical constants with identical variables.

In conclusion, the preprocessing of problems containing domain axioms and, more in general, of complex real-world situations defined using expressive languages seems to represent a valid method for the construction of efficient AI systems, able to learn and support high-level, natural domain-definition languages.

References

[1] Blum, A. L., Furst, M. L. (1997) "Fast Planning Through Planning Graph Analysis", *Artificial Intelligence*, 90:281–300.

[2] Chapman, D. (1987) "Planning for Conjunctive Goals", *Artificial Intelligence*, 32(3):333–377.

[3] Fikes, R.E., Nilsson, N.J. (1971) "STRIPS: A New Approach to the Application of Theorem Proving to Problem Solving", *Artificial Intelligence*, 2:189–208.

[4] Garagnani, M. (2000) "Speaker-hearer beliefs for discourse planning", *Proceedings of the 17th International Conference on Artificial Intelligence (IC-AI'00)*, Las Vegas, Nevada, June 2000.

[5] Garagnani, M. (1999) "A sound Linear Algorithm for Pre-processing planning problems with Language Axioms", *Proceedings of PLANSIG-99*, Manchester, England.

[6] Gazen, B.C., Knoblock, C.A. (1997) "Combining the Expressivity of UCPOP with the Efficiency of Graphplan", *Proceedings ECP-97*, Toulouse, France.

[7] Koehler, J., Nebel, B., Hoffmann, J., Dimopoulos, Y. (1997) "Extending Planning Graphs to an ADL Subset", *Proceedings ECP-97*, Toulouse, France.

[8] Penberthy, J. S., Weld, D. (1992) "UCPOP: A Sound, Complete, Partial-order Planner for ADL", *Proceedings of the International Workshop on Knowledge Representation (KR-92)*, pp.103–114.

Multi-layered PSMs for Planning

Francisco Teruel-Alberich, Marcos Romero-Castro, Abraham Rodríguez-Rodríguez
The University of Las Palmas de Gran Canaria,
Canary Islands, Spain
{fteruel,mromero}@gisc.dis.ulpgc.es, arodriguez@dis.ulpgc.es

Abstract: PSM are essential components in any modern knowledge methodology because they provide us with some guidelines that facilitate the building of knowledge-based system and promote the reusability of development efforts. However, it is recognised that the reusability of any PSM will decrease as the complexity of the task to be modelled increase. If we consider that actual tasks are complex enough, we may conclude that the effective reusability of a PSM is very limited. In order to minimise this inconvenience, we propose to use two layers of PSM. One layer will model the primitive tasks the system is composed of. The other layer will control the execution order of these tasks in order to reach to a global solution. This paper describes how we have applied this schema over a planning task on the Search and Rescue domain.

1. Introduction

Problem Solving Methods (PSM) are high-level structures that indicate us how to solve a generic task such as diagnosis, assessment, planning, etc. They provide us with a set of inferences and knowledge descriptions that allow us to build a solution without any reference to specific domain elements. Thus, PSMs work at the knowledge-level as was defined by Newell in 1982 [1]. Clancey validated some of the Newell's ideas in 1985 with his work on *Heuristic Classification* [2]. He analysed a set of well-known first generation expert systems and induced a shared behaviour for solving classification problems. McDermott [3] with his work on *Role-Limiting Methods* and Chandrasekaran's *Generic Tasks* [4] enriched and evolved the notion of PSM. Methodologies such as CommonKADS [5][6], MIKE [7], or PROTÉGÉ [8] consider the PSMs as essential structures useful for controlling the methodological activities that must be carried out to build the expertise model. PSMs claim to be useful pieces to build KBS because they enforce the reutilization of proven problem solving strategies, and also facilitate organising and structuring a knowledge base through the use of knowledge structures (sometimes referred as knowledge-roles).

In spite of the optimism that can be deduced from some conclusions appearing in [9], reusing PSM has face some difficulties in the last years. First, it is a complex issue to select the most suitable PSM from a PSM catalogue. In this direction, we can find the works such as [10], [6] or [11]. The other issue is related to the reusability-usability trade-off for the PSM. It is said, *the more components become reusable, the less usable they become* [12]. This is because there are some gaps between the PSM and the task it realises on one side, and between the PSM and the knowledge it applies [13].

Our experience with the planning PSM limits the utility of PSM, at least at the abstract specification of the generic task because of its inherent complexity. We propose to first analyse the application domain and to identify a set of primitive domain tasks. Then, we will model the system with two layers of PSMs. The highest layer will work over the primitive tasks *names*, while the other layer will model them. Only these intensive-knowledge tasks will be modelled using PSMs. The high level layer will decide upon the execution of specific primitive tasks; it will detect inconsistencies with the outputs from other tasks; and it will control the overall execution of the System. The domain task layer will model each primitive task using the traditional approach in which a PSM is recursively decomposed until basic inferences are identified [14].

Splitting the Domain in a set of simpler tasks facilitates the selection of a generic PSM from the PSM Catalogue, and the possibility of re-using a PSM without further adaptation is increased. This approach allows us to make a better domain analysis, enabling a smooth transition to the design model.

We have applied these ideas on the SARPA system, a planner assistant for the Search and Rescue (SAR) domain. Next sections will describe the SAR domain and its architecture in detail.

2. SAR Domain

The Search and Rescue Service (SAR) is an important element of the Spanish Air Force. Its main function is to participate in any emergency situation in which it could be required. Although SAR is essentially a military organism and it was founded to rescue crashed military aircrafts. Actually, SAR has collaboration agreements with different Spanish local governments to perform rescue missions, so most of the missions in which it participates are civilians.

The Canary Islands are situated on the Atlantic Ocean, in the North-West African Coast, with a distance of less than 100 Kms. to morocco coast. The Canarian archipelago has a rough and varied orography. The oriental islands are mountainous and with deep precipices, while the occidental islands are mostly deserted and flat. Besides, the distance from the Canary Island to the Iberian Peninsula is about 2000 Kms. and the distance to the Saharian Fishing shoal is very short.

The 802 SAR Squadron is the responsible to cope with the emergencies, which could occur in our Islands. The Squadron operates over a 1.500.000 Kms. zone (SAR Influence Zone), where the 80% is sea (see Figure 1). This influence area is very important because it is a transit zone for most of the maritime routes (fishing and cargo vessels, sailing vessels) between Europe, America and Africa. Due to the particular characteristics of our Archipelago, Air Search and Rescue is the only feasible solution in most of the emergencies.

There exist a great range of emergency types in which SAR participates. These types vary from rescue of a lost person in a mountain to cope with search and rescue vessels or a large air-crash. Obviously, It is essential the participation of a great number of material and human assets as well as the co-ordination with other military and civilian organisms which collaborate in rescue missions.

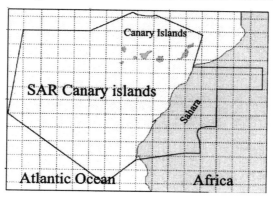

Figure 1. SAR 802 influence area

SAR units are constituted by two main parts: The Rescue Co-ordination Centre (RCC) and the Squadron itself. The RCC is in charge of the decision making about the missions planning, involved resources, search procedures to execute, co-ordination with other organism, etc. It is responsible for generating and controlling search and rescue plans. The success of the mission depends on the right decisions made by RCC. However, the decision-making is a dynamic task and the building of a SAR plan results a complex and difficult task. The RCC works with imprecise information like the local current information; incomplete information as could be initial data about a particular accident in which the number of injured persons is unknown; erroneous information which could be that the number of persons to rescue is different to the number which initially supposed; fast changing data like the weather information of the zone which could easily change. Besides there exist inherent limitations with the airplanes (i.e. helicopters have less autonomy than planes, or it is difficult to operate with planes in mountainous areas in land search missions); the vessels and persons searches are very difficult because of the situation and geographic characteristics of the Canary Islands.

The staffs who constitutes the RCC are:

1. The Search and Rescue Co-ordinator: This person is the maximum responsible of the mission. He is in charge of planning the different tasks for a particular mission, building the operation plan, validating and controlling it during the mission development. He is responsible for controlling the work made by the Co-ordinators.

2. Co-ordinators: This member is responsible of executing all the planned tasks by the Search and Rescue Co-ordinator. He has to make the co-ordination of the mission assigned assets. They also control the tasks made by Radius-Operators. Co-ordinator must carry out the same functions of

the Search and Rescue Co-ordinator, although his responsibility is not the same. There are usually one or two Co-ordinators per SAR units.

3. Radius Operators: His main function is to compile and confirm all the information needed to perform the mission. He is in charge of generating documentation for each incident that may happen during the mission, and performing all the communications with the assigned mediums to supply and request information. There are usually two operators per mission; one who performs the documentation activities and the other who compiles and carry out the communications.

RCC members have a great experience in rescue missions. This experience has allowed them to develop an Operation Guidelines, which they work with. All the procedures to follow for every mission types in which RCC can operate, are described in this Guidelines (what air mediums to use, rescue material to carry, etc). They have made a missions repository with all the information related to each mission. They use it to resolve other similar emergency situations.

The Squadron is responsible for carrying out the search and rescue mission. They have a set of airplanes (planes and helicopters), experienced crews in search and rescue missions and qualified land staff in the maintenance and repair of aircrafts. The Canary Island 802 Squadron has three Fokker planes and four French Helicopters Superpuma. If they needed more airplanes in any emergency, they could use other aircrafts assigned to Spanish Air Forces like Light Transport CASA-Aviocar C-212.

3. SAR Tasks

Figure 2 shows some complex tasks that we have identified in the SAR domain.

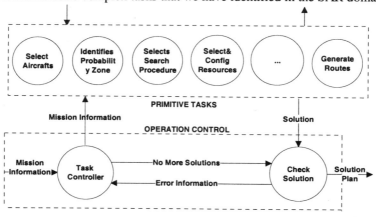

Figure 2. SAR Tasks

These tasks are carried out by RCC members, who perform the control and validation of a search and rescue plan. We have identified two SAR tasks categories (see Figure 2):

Control Tasks: These are carried out by the Search and Rescue Co-ordinator or the Co-ordinators when the main responsible is not present. There are two types of control tasks:

- *Tasks Controller:* This task is responsible for evaluating all the information obtained during the mission to use it in performing different primitive tasks. It uses all the compiled and confirmed information to decide what tasks and in which order these have to be executed. It also controls the execution state for each primitive task.

- *Check Solution:* It checks the partial solutions obtained by different tasks and it also validates the whole plan. At the same time as the subtasks are being executed, the obtained results are evaluated to confirm whether there are errors or inconsistencies with other already finished tasks. If any kind of problem is detected, the culprit tasks can be re-evaluated. This may lead to the re-execution of any other already finished task.

Primitive Tasks: They allow the RCC to build the search and rescue plan. Some of these primitive tasks are quite complex and knowledge-intensive. However, there are other sets of tasks which are very simple. These are the information related Tasks, as for example informing to different organisms or requesting target data. The order in which they are executed is not always the same, because it depends on the availability and precision of the information. There can be tasks which have not needed data to execute itself and other which could have it. We want to point those that are complex and knowledge-intensive because they are very problematic when a plan is built:

- *Select Aircrafts:* It selects the needed air resources to accomplish a particular mission with success. There are many factors that affect this task as the type of the mission to perform, the distance to the target area, the target type to search and rescue, the air mediums availability (if they are operative or not at the beginning of the mission), the available autonomy for each aircraft.

- *Determine the Maximum Probability Zone:* This task calculates the area where the target could be found with the maximum probability. It also restricts the search zone of the airplanes. This work is carried out using the acquired experience by the RCC members in the performed missions. There are numeric methods available to determine the search zone which are used by RCC. These calculate an estimation of the influence zone with mathematical estimations that are later modified with the expertise of the RCC members. This tasks is can benefit by the existing missions database. Among the factors which influence the calculus of the search are: the reliability and precision of the information about the accident, because if data are not reliable enough the search zone will be too big; the knowledge about the area currents to calculate which is the drift followed by the target, for the case of sea search missions; the weather information of the zone; the elapsed time from the emergency is notified which affects to the area dimension, the higher the elapsed time the higher the area dimension will be and vice versa. All these factors make this tasks one of the most complex one.

- *Select and Configure Search Procedure:* A search procedure is the route that must be flown by the planes to track all the search area. The selection of the search method affects to the mission success. This task selects which is the most appropriated search procedure depending on the available information of the mission, for example the weather information; the dimension of the search area; whether the target is located or not; if the search is over the sea or land. All these factors are very important because they allow the RCC to select between one procedure or another. If the available information is not precise, all the procedures that guaranty a larger area to be swept at a minimum time will be used (e.g. Ladder method); these types of procedures are better and they will assure a minimum of success in the case in which there exists too much unknown information. However, if the available data is precise, the RCC will use all the procedures which try to find the lost object/person sooner (e.g. Sector method).

- *Select and Configure Resources:* This task is the responsible for selecting and configuring all the assets of each selected air medium to accomplish a mission. Among the resources to be selected and configured, we find the plane crews, the auxiliary fuel tanks for helicopters and SAR material. There exist many dependencies between these three resources types because there are crews and configurations that are not compatibles with certain types of fuel tanks and SAR material configurations; and, in the same way, it happens with the other two elements. In the crews selection and configuration the RCC members decide which is the most appropriate crew depending on the aircraft type and the mission own characteristics. The same is for the SAR material and auxiliary fuel tanks configurations. To solve the dependencies that could exist between the configurations of the different resources, there should exist a commitment among those configurations to accomplish with success the mission development.

- *Generate The Route:* It builds the routes that each selected aircraft must follow to accomplish its goal in the mission. There are some factors to take into account in the route generation as the geographic coordinates of the search area, the target type to be searched, knowledge about the injured people number, the selected aircrafts and their autonomy, the available airports, heliports and hospitals, etc. When the route has been calculated it is possible to optimise the fuel tank configuration assigned to a selected aircraft which will use the route.

The primitive tasks identified facilitate the development works, allowing us to make a domain-structured analysis. We do not have to cope with the problem as a whole, but just to work with each of the identified tasks in independently. This enhances the system modularity, because each knowledge intensive task has been modelled in a specific different. Non-knowledge intensive tasks can be solved with numeric methods, while each knowledge-intensive one can be solved using independent PSMs. In this way, PSMs can be simples and reused in multiple tasks, obtaining, in this way, a significant save of the development efforts.

We selected this point of view because we were not interested in using a global PSM to cope with the entire problem since all the modularity should be lost and the development efforts should be very high. The design model would also not reflect the structure derived in the analysis (the structure preserving design as defined in [14]).

4. System Architecture

The software orientation we adopted to cope with the problem of the SAR domain was to design an assistant to help the user in the decision-making and the planning of the search and rescue missions. We also designed a complete Information System constituted by tool kits which are used by the Assistant as well as the user in the planning task. Usually, the Operator is the user who interacts with these tools to accomplish the compilation and documentation tasks in a SAR mission.

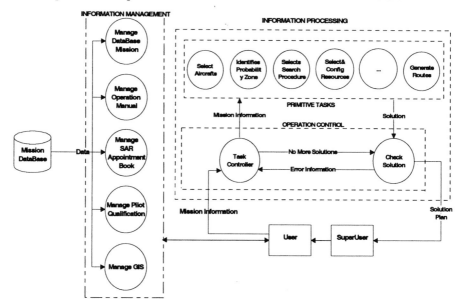

Figure 3: SARPA software architecture

We have to point out the figure of the supervisor user (the Search and Rescue Co-ordinator is usually this user type) who checks and accepts the proposed solutions by the software that assists in the planning works. Figure 3 shows the SARPA Software Architecture. We will explain it in the next paragraphs:

The derived architecture is composed of two modules:

Information Processing Module: It is the module responsible for accomplishing decisions making and planning. This module is divided in two sub-modules:

Operation Control: It is in charge of setting up the execution precedence of the tasks and validating the consistence and correction of the solutions proposed by primitive tasks and final plans. We used a hierarchical decomposition model to be able to perform the operation control. This model is shown in Figure 4:

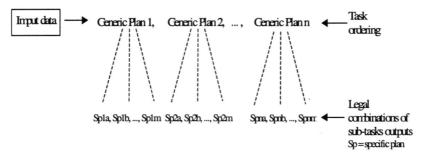

Figure 4.Hierarchical Descomposition Model

In Figure 4 we see the two planning levels that correspond to the high layer described in a previous section:

- *Generic Level:* This level sets up which primitive tasks have to be performed and which is the execution order of them. All valid task orders are generated. We created a new task responsible of generating all possible skeletal plans for a particular mission (*Generate Skeletal Plans*). These skeletal were constituted by an order sequence of primitive tasks names. We used a Planning PSM because it was the most appropriated for modelling this task.

- *Specific Level:* It sets up the outputs for the primitive tasks. Outputs of these tasks are fixed in this level because there are strong dependencies between them, and they cannot be fixed independently and without taking into account the other ones. Resources Configuration and Selection task is an example of this type because there are dependencies when crews, SAR material and fuel tanks for helicopters are selected and configured. Some task may have an unlimited number outputs; so a partial specification of the tasks outputs must be performed in this level. Outputs of some tasks are elaborated to restrict the set of possible solutions. For example, some data are abstracted like the search area size (i.e. instead of using a quantitative parameter we use a qualitative one), or they are grouped by linguistic labels like in the standard crews configuration. To model this level, we created a new task to generate the entire specific skeletal (*Generate Specific Plans:* skeletal plans partially described). In addition, in the specific level we used the same PSM that the one used by Generic Level, with the resulting saving in the development efforts.

Primitive Task: In this module we modelled instances of primitive subtasks. We have designed all those tasks which are used to accomplish the SAR plan building. All tasks have been modelled in an independent way and different resolutions methods have been applied. In some situations we have used a planning or assessment PSM because of different tasks types, for example *Generate Route Task* or *Select and Configure Search Procedure*. We have also used numeric methods to solve some tasks because of their simplicity and precision as in the case of *Optimise fuel* task. Table 1 shows some primitive tasks:

Task Name	Knowledge Intensive	Resolution Method
Select Aircrafts	Yes	Assessment PSM adapted from [14]
Determine the Maximum Probability Zone	Yes	Mixed
Select and Configure the Search Procedure	Yes	Assessment PSM
Select and Configure Resources	Yes	Design PSM
Generate the Route	Yes	Planning PSM
Optimise fuel	No	Numeric

Table 1. Primitive Tasks

- *Select Aircraft:* We used an adapted Assessment PSM because the other PSM which we worked with, did not arrange good enough to this selection task.

- *Determine the Maximum Probability Zone:* To design this task we decided to use a numeric method which allows us to estimate mathematically the search area where a target would be found with the maximum probability. This procedure is based on an estimation mathematical model of drifts that a target experiments on the sea or in the air. Also we worked in the development of Case-Base Reasoning (CBR) to calculate the search zone using a repository of missions.

- *Select and Configure the Search Procedure:* We used a standard Assessment PSM because this task can be consider as a classification sub-type task.

- *Select and Configure Resources:* We applied a Design PSM. We selected a generic PSM for Synthesis Tasks, which was modified to perform the task [14]. With this PSM, we could solve the crews, materials and fuel tanks selection and configuration.

- *Generate the Route:* We selected a Planning PSM to resolve it, because it is a planning task itself. To calculate a particular route we have to planning all the points where the selected aircrafts would have to go through.

- *Optimise Fuel:* We applied a numeric method to model it which allow optimising the auxiliary fuel tanks for helicopters which were assigned to be able to perform the mission.

Figure 5 is a snapshot of the SARPA GUI showing the primitive tasks for the active mission.

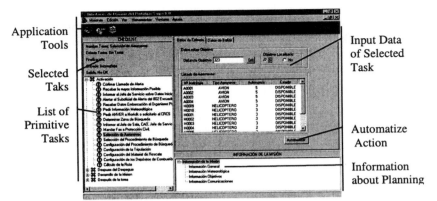

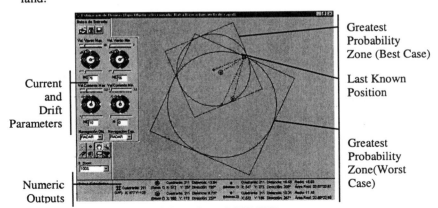

Figure 5. Snapshot of the Planning Assistant GUI

Information Management Module: This module is the Information System of our software architecture. The functions allowed by this system are:

- *Manage Mission database:* This system can manage a Missions database, where all the missions information is stored. These data has been compiled and stored by the SAR operators.

- *Manage the Operation Manual:* It is responsible of managing the SAR operation Manual that is stored in the database. In this manual, all the procedures to follow for each type of mission are specified.

- *Manage SAR Appointment Book (Chronologies):* In the chronologies it is specified the times for each mission event. These chronologies are stored also in the database, so SAR personnel can consult the events of any finished mission.

- *Manage Pilot Qualifications:* Pilots have a qualification level which allow them or not to accomplish certain missions types, as night and reduced visibility search and rescue missions, or search and rescue missions in land.

Figure 6. Snapshot of GIS GUI

- Manage GIS: The system has a completed geographic information system where it is showed in visual manner mission information as search zones, aircrafts routes, islands maps and other information types. Figure 6 shows a snapshot of this tool with the output from the *Determine the Maximum Probability Zone* task:

5. Planning Template

Figure 7 shows the PSM used to model the two planning tasks from high layer (*Generate Skeletal Plans and Generate Specific Plans*. This PSM is based on the *forward checking* algorithm as defined by [15]. Both tasks were modelled using the same algorithm because they share most domain characteristics. This algorithm provides us with good response times for relatively simple domain, allowing us to clearly analyse and differentiate the various knowledge types that are present at each level.

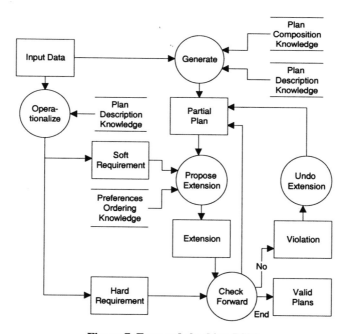

Figure 7. Forward checking PSM

The PSM is composed of a set of static roles, dynamic roles and inferences [14] that we detail in the next paragraphs:

Static Roles: They represent the domain knowledge used to solve the task. They are applied in inferences to perform them. They are static information. The static roles used in this PSM are:

- *Plan Composition Knowledge:* Knowledge that will be useful to generate skeletal plans which are consistent with the input information.

- *Plan Description Knowledge:* It is the Domain Specific Knowledge which it is used to generate partial plans, preferences and restrictions.

- *Preferences Ordering Knowledge:* this knowledge sets the context for ranking the actual relevant preferences.

Dynamic Roles: They represent the dynamic information (input & output data from the inferences). This information is used in the task resolution. Dynamic Roles used in this PSM are:

- Input Data: They are input data of the mission.

- Soft Requirement: They are preferences which have been obtained after that the mission information has been analysed.

- Extension: It is a new element to include in the partial plan specification.

- Hard Requirement: Any partial plan must comply with all the hard requirements (restrictions).

- Partial Plan: It is the partial specification of the plan.

- Valid Plans: It constitutes the set of valid and checked plans.

- Violation: The Error Output from the CheckForward Inference.

Inferences: Inferences are like black boxes. They have the dynamic roles as input data. These roles are used by the inferences in a particular way, generating outputs that are represented by dynamic roles too. Inferences use domain knowledge in the form of static roles. Each inference is implemented using a resolution method, although there can be many resolution methods for implementing the same inference. It depends on the design and computational restrictions imposed over the inference. For example in a *sorting* inference, we can use different sorting methods to perform it. Inferences constituting this PSM are:

- *Generate:* It is responsible of generating partial plans using the mission information, where *mission information* is mapped to the dynamic role *input data* (i.e. injured people number, critical injured people number, mission type). This inference also uses the *plan composition knowledge* and *plan description knowledge* (static roles) to generate consistent partial plans (for example which low-level task can not be situated before other). The output of this inference is a partial plan (dynamic role).

- *Operationalize:* It is in charge of transforming the mission input data in soft and hard requirements (static roles), which will be applied later in the PSM to make an extension plan and validate the obtained plan. With these two roles it is possible to restrict the set of valid plans. The inference uses as static knowledge *the plan description knowledge* to perform this change. Inference Outputs are hard and soft requirements.

- *Propose Extension:* an extension to the current partial plan is proposed. A new primitive task is added to the plan depending on a soft requirement (preference). The inference uses knowledge about sorting preferences to select the soft requirement to apply. The static knowledge indicates us what preference to use first.

- *CheckForward:* This inference checks whether the partial plan is consistent or not with generated hard requirements (restrictions). It generates three possibilities: (a) the proposed extension constitutes a complete plan; this plan is very consistent and it is added to the set of found valid plans. (b) It is a consistent partial plan and it is necessary to propose other extension plan until a complete valid plan has been found. (c) The proposed extension is not consistent with requirements, so an error output is generated and the proposed extension is undo because it is not valid.

- *UndoExtension:* Inference which undoes the proposed change by the *Propose Extension Inference,* after a violation of restrictions has been produced.

6. Conclusions

Problem Solving Methods are structures aimed to facilitate the development of KBS providing us with a generic method for solving certain types of task. In spite of their unquestionable utility, there are some problems associated with the PSM. Actual tasks are too complex to take advantage of the use of an existing PSM. Therefore, it is difficult to select the appropriate one and deep rearrangements must be done over the PSM to adjust it to the actual task.

Our experience with the planning PSM limits the utility of PSM, at least at the abstract specification of the generic task because of its inherent complexity, and recommends decomposing the system analysis into two layers of PSM. The highest layer will work over the primitive tasks names, while the other layer will model them. The high level layer will decide upon the execution of specific primitive tasks; it will detect inconsistencies with the outputs from other tasks; and it will control the overall execution of the System. The domain task layer will model each primitive task using the traditional approach in which a PSM is recursively decomposed until basic inferences are identified.

We have applied these ideas on the SARPA system, a planner assistant for the Search And Rescue (SAR) domain. We have implemented the high layer using the same PSM for its two levels:

1. Generic level: actions are primitive tasks names. The goal is to select the appropriate ones and to sort them. This level generates all valid sub-task orderings.

2. Specific level: actions are compatible sub-tasks outputs. The input to this level is the generic level output (an ordered list of tasks). Not all the tasks will have a limited number of outputs, so this level must cope with a partial specification of the tasks outputs (e.g. a solution abstraction)

The layer composed of primitive task have been implemented using multiple PSM (one for each knowledge intensive task)

388

This high level structure reduces the development efforts and allows us to focus on specific aspects of the application domain, instead of considering the planning tasks as a whole. It also allows us maintain the smooth transition principle to the design model as defined in [14].

7. References

1. Newell, A. The Knowledge Level. Artif Intell 1982; 18: 27-127.

2. Clancey, WJ. Heuristic Classification. Artif Intell 1985; 27: 289-350

3. McDermott, J.: Preliminary Steps towards a taxonomy of problem-solving methods. In S. Marcus (ed.). Automating Knowledge Acquisition for Expert Systems. 1988; 225-256

4. Chandrasekaran, B. Generic Tasks in Knowledge-based reasoning: High level building blocks for system design. IEEE expert 1986; 1(3): 23-30.

5. Wielinga, B.J., A.Th. Schreiber, J.A. Breuker; KADS: A Modelling Approach to Knowledge Engineering. Knowledge Acquisition, Special issue "The KADS Approach to Knowledge Engineering", 4, 1, 1992.

6. Breuker, J., Van de Velde, W. CommonKADS Library for Expertise Modelling. IOS Press, Amsterdam, 1994.

7. Angele, J.; Fensel, D.; Studer, R. Domain and Task Modelling in MIKE. In Suthliffe, A et al. (eds). Domain Knowledge for interactive system design. Chapman & Hall. 1996

8. Eriksson, H, Shahar, Y; Tu, S.; Puerta, A.; Musen, M. Task Modelling with reusable problem-solving methods. In Artificial Intelligence 1995; 79 (2): 293-326.

9. Benjamins, V.R., Fensel, D., Chandrasekaran, B., PSMs do IT!. In International Journal of Human-Computer Studies, 1997; 47(4).

10. Benjamins, R. Problem-Solving Methods for Diagnosis and their Role in Knowledge Acquisition. International Journal of Expert Systems: Research & Applications, 1995; vol. 8, no. 2, pages 93-120

11. Motta, E., Fensel, D., Gaspari, M., and Benjamins, V.R., Specifications of Knowledge Components for Reuse. Eleventh International Conference on Software Engineering and Knowledge Engineering (SEKE'99). 1999.

12. Beys, P., Benjamins, V.R., van Heijst, G., Remedying the Reusability -- Usability Trade-off for Problem-Solving Methods. In proceedings of KAW'96 (Banff), 1996; 2.1-2.20.

13. Benjamins, V.R., Fensel, D., Editorial: Problem-Solving Methods. International Journal of Human-Computer Studies (IJHCS), 1998; 49 (4): 305-313.

14. Schreiber (Editor). Knowledge Engineering and Management: The CommonKADS Methodology MIT Press; 1999.

15. Shanahan, M. Search, inference and dependencies in Artificial Intelligence. Ed. Ellis Horwood. 1989.

AUTHOR INDEX

Albrecht, A.	199	Meikle, T.	243
Anderson, T.	157	Messaadia, K.	287
Bi, Y.	157	Mullins, M.	129
Borisov, A.	185	Neal, M.	19
Cleary, J.	35	O'Dell, T.	102
Debenham, J.	273	Oussalah, M.	287
Díaz-Agudo, B.	115	Preece, A.	320
Diller, A.	337	Raileanu, L.	62
González-Calero, P.A.	115	Roach, P.A.	349
Gragnani, M.	363	Rodríguez-Rodríguez, A.	375
Gray, A.	320	Romero-Castro, M.	375
Hall, M.	35	Saward, G.	102
Hamilton, H.J.	73	Siang, V.P.	257
Hickey, R.	145	Smyth, B.	89, 129
Holmes, G.	35	Steinhöfel, K.	199
Hui, K.	320	Stoffel, K.	62
Karimi, K.	73	Swift, S.	171
Kingston, J.	301	Takahashi, A.	185
Lalmas, M.	215	Tate, A.	3
Li, B.	257	Taupitz, M.	199
Liu, X.	171	Teruel-Alberich, F.	375
Loomes, M.	199	Timmis, J.	19
Marti, P.	320	Trigg, L.	35
Martin, N.	171	Tucker, A.	171
Martin, R.	145	Ware, J.A.	349
McClean, S.	157	Wilson, I.D.	349
McKenna, E.	89, 129	Yearwood, J.	243
McSherry, D.	48	Zarri, G.P.	229